Running for Office

CHATHAM HOUSE SERIES ON CHANGE IN AMERICAN POLITICS

edited by Aaron Wildavsky
University of California, Berkeley

Running for Office
The Political Education
of Campaigners

MARJORIE RANDON HERSHEY
Indiana University

CHATHAM HOUSE PUBLISHERS, INC.
Chatham, New Jersey

RUNNING FOR OFFICE
The Political Education of Campaigners

CHATHAM HOUSE PUBLISHERS, INC.
Box One, Chatham, New Jersey 07928

Copyright © 1984 by Chatham House Publishers, Inc.

All rights reserved. No part of this publication may be reproduced, stored in a retrieval system, or transmitted in any form or by any means, electronic, mechanical, photocopying, recording, or otherwise, without the prior permission of the publisher.

PUBLISHER: Edward Artinian
COVER DESIGN: Lawrence Ratzkin
COMPOSITION: Chatham Composer
PRINTING AND BINDING: Hamilton Printing Company

LIBRARY OF CONGRESS CATALOGING IN PUBLICATION DATA

Hershey, Marjorie Randon.
 Running for Office

 (Chatham House series on change in American politics)
 Bibliography: p.
 Includes index.
 1. Electioneering—United States. 2. Political parties—United States. I. Title. II. Series.
JK2281.H47 1984   324.7'0973   84-17609
ISBN 0-934540-22-5

Manufactured in the United States of America
10 9 8 7 6 5 4 3 2 1

To *Katie and Lissa*

Contents

1 **The Environment of Political Campaigns**   1
Campaign Finance Reform: Campaigning Becomes a Regulated Industry. PACs: The New American Fat Cats. The Independent Spenders. Single-Issue Politics. Preacher-Politicians and the New Christian Right. New Campaign Technologies: The Computerized Constituency. The Era of the Media Campaign. The Parties: When the Landmarks Shift. The Learning Experience of a Campaign. Social-Learning Theory as a Useful Guide.

2 **Social-Learning Theory as a Guide**   36
Learning from Response Consequences. Observational Learning. What Observational Learning Teaches. Abstract Modeling: Learning the Rules of Behavior. Modeling, Innovation, and Invention. Contingency-Learning. Symbols and Generalization. Self-Regulation. Interdependence: "Person Variables" and Environmental Variables.

3 **Preparing for the Race**   60
The Beginnings of a Campaign. The Campaigner's First Moves: Generalization of Earlier Learning. What's Needed: An Arsenal of Strategies. Generalizing from Earlier Campaign Experiences. Learning from Noncampaign Experiences. Learning from Models. The Widespread Use of Models by New Candidates. Modeling: Who Does It and When? Who Will the Models Be? The Channels of Campaign Learning. What They Learn. Modeling: Summary and Implications.

4 **The Campaign as a Learning Experience**   86
Campaign Events and Reactions: Where Do They Come From? The Impact of the Election Result. Constructing Explanations for Election Results. Incumbency: The Advantages and Drawbacks of Winning. Interactions: Candidates and Situations. Campaign Learning: Summary.

5 **Do Political Parties Matter in Campaigns?**   113
The Thesis of Party Decline—And Its Critics. Party Influence on Voters. Party Organizations. Party in Government. A Social-Learning Approach to Party Influence. Resources: To What Extent Do Parties Affect Campaigners' Outcomes? Resources: Money. Party Money: The National

Republicans. Party Poverty: The National Democrats. Selective Influence: State Party Money. Selective Existence: Local and Congressional District Parties. Party Money in Context. Influence Through the Provision of Resources: Party Services. State and Local Party Services to Candidates. Party Resources: The Rich Get Richer. The Impact of Party Reform: Two Contrasting Directions. The Effects of Campaign Finance Reform. Party Influence Through Modeling. Party-Based Learning Without the Party Organization's Help. The Parties' Rivals for Influence on Campaigns. PAC Power. Political Consultants and Other Hired Guns. Conclusion: The Conditions of Party Influence.

6 A Tale of Six Races: The Abortion Issue
   Enters Campaign Environments   152
   The Special Nature of Single-Issue Politics. How Abortion Came to Be a Political Issue. Abortion as a "Single Issue." The Pro-Life Movement's Legislative Action. The Movement into Campaigns. The Potential Clout of the Pro-Life Challenge. The Campaign Settings. The Learning Environment of Senate Campaigns. The Bayh Race in Indiana. The Church Race in Idaho. The Culver Race in Iowa. The Leahy Race in Vermont. The McGovern Race in South Dakota. The Packwood Race in Oregon. The Research Hypotheses.

7 Pro-Life Groups Act in 1980: The Importance of
   Observational Learning   186
   The Iowa Model. The Learning Spreads. Observational Learning: Idaho, Oregon, and Vermont. Modeling Plus Previous Experience: South Dakota and Indiana. Pro-Life Campaigning: How Helpful Was the Learning Approach?

8 The Senate Campaigns Respond   213
   The Senate Campaigners: Early Days. What Was Learned in the "Hill Meetings"? The Disadvantages of "Negative Models." Learning About the Pro-Lifers. Trying to Learn from a Negative Model: The Case of John Culver. Learning from Other 1980 Targets. Professional Consultants: Other Sources of Models. Other Limits on the Use of Modeled Behaviors. The Big Strategic Decision: What to Do About the Church Leafletting. Conclusion.

9 Campaigning and Representation: Learning to Run,
   Learning to Represent   246
   Learning from 1980: Candidates and the New Right. Learning from 1980: Pro-Lifers. A Lesson in Humility. The Quality of Campaign Learning. Party and Single-Issue Influence. Candidates as Learners. Learning to Represent.

Bibliography   277

Index   297

Tables

1.1	PAC Contributions to House and Senate Candidates, 1981-82	8
1.2	Strength of Party Identification and Political Independence, 1960-82	25
1.3	Two Measures of the Decline in Straight-Ticket Voting, 1960-82	26
5.1	National Party Committees' Fund Raising and Spending, 1981-82	122
5.2	Average Contributions and Spending by National Party Committees in House and Senate Races, 1981-82	123
5.3	Average Party and PAC Money in the Campaigns of House and Senate General Election Candidates, 1981-82	131
6.1	The Cast of Characters	172
8.1	Behaviors Learned from Models: A Comparison of Pro-Life Groups and Targeted Senate Campaigns	236
8.2	Election Results in the Six Targeted Senate Races, 1980	241

Figures

1.1	Growing Numbers of Political Action Committees, 1974-82	6
5.1	Party Fund Raising, 1977-82	128

Preface

Campaigns are learning experiences—for social scientists as well as people more central to American elections. They have been so for me during the past 12 years. The ideas expressed in this book began developing out of field research conducted in the early 1970s. They came together with the help of social-learning theory during a year's leave in Heidelberg, West Germany, in the mid-1970s. Then, when a major pro-life group targeted six well-known members of the Senate for defeat in the 1980 elections, I was intrigued by the chance to find out how experienced campaigners would respond to a threatening new stimulus—to confront all my cogitating with a bit of the real world. At the time, I was interested in the pro-life challenge simply as a handy new stimulus in campaigners' environments, not as a source of fascination in itself. I soon saw things differently, for the conflict between these two forces—each driven by principles almost completely irreconcilable with those of the other—remains one of the richest and most remarkable stories I have ever encountered.

It is a pleasure to thank the people who played major roles in the development of the book. Albert Bandura, Murray Edelman, Richard Fenno, John Kessel, John Kingdon, Jim Kuklinski, Tom Mann, and Paul Sniderman read parts of earlier versions, Larry Dodd read chapters of the manuscript, and Sandy Maisel read all of it. I would love to be able to blame them for all its faults, but I know I'd never get away with it.

I am grateful to Tony Broh, Ted Carmines, Burdett Loomis, and Leroy Rieselbach for much-valued discussions; to Lin Ostrom and Doris-Jean Burton for their support; to the Indiana University Dean of Faculties for funding; to Fern Bennett, Helen Harrell, Jeralee May, Marcie Pickett, and most of all Helene Sackmann for their skill on the word processor and their patience with me; and to Steve Flinn for helping our word processor talk directly with the Chatham House Composer, thus limiting the interference of error-prone humans.

My former student and now colleague Darrell West contributed greatly by joining me in the empirical work reported in chapters 7 and 8. Many other Indiana University graduate students have given me the benefit of their reactions. Ed Artinian has been a genuinely delightful publisher. I owe a special debt to the many campaign and Senate staffers, pro-life leaders, and journalists who took time from pressure-ridden schedules to talk with Darrell and me.

Very special thanks are due to the most important people in the world: my husband Howard, our daughters, Katherine and Elizabeth, my parents and grandmother, and the other members of our families. Katie, who was born at about the same time as was my research on the 1980 Senate races, has tolerated it all with wonderful good grace. Lissa was thoughtful enough to postpone her birth until the manuscript was in the mail. And Howard, with a scientist's precision, continued his long-standing efforts to tame my garrulous prose; quite simply, he made it all possible.

RUNNING FOR OFFICE

1. The Environment of Political Campaigns

"It is a grueling, debilitating, and often dehumanizing ordeal that exacts an extravagant price not only for winning but also for the mere running and losing . . . lofty purpose, private fortunes and personal dreams all are bumped and jostled in the process, and as often as not, bruised or even crippled."[1] Reporter Jules Witcover was describing the process of campaigning for President, but thousands of candidates for other levels of public office might see themselves in his words.

The political campaign is a special kind of ordeal. It is a proving ground in which candidates' endurance, if not their leadership, is tested. The presidential campaign, in particular, is a season when politics becomes a major spectator sport — until the coverage of three dozen presidential primaries leaves many voters begging for release. A campaign for any office can be a crucible for new directions in public policy, when new ideas for programs catch fire or fail. It is rich human drama. It can shock, as in the unforgettable election years when television cameras recorded the murder of one presidential candidate and the attempted murder of another.

But perhaps most important, campaigning for any office is a time of learning — a time when candidates, members of their staffs, other activists, and voters come into contact with their political environments, when they can test their beliefs and respond to their experiences. The effects of this learning process are reciprocal: campaigners are influenced by their environment and in turn help to create and change it. The learning that campaigners do can make a big difference in politics; it can affect candidates' awareness of people's needs and interests, influence the stands candidates take, and determine the issues that make their way onto the political agenda.

This is a book about campaigns as learning processes. To begin, this chapter explores the environment in which political campaigners learn, an environment that the candidates of the early part of this century would barely recognize. In fact, people who ran for office during the 1960s might find current electioneering practices to be almost as unfamiliar, for the environment of political campaigns has changed in a number of important ways during the 1970s and 1980s. Many of these changes have already left their mark on the representative process.

The influence of political parties on campaigns, for instance, is in flux; the parties' hold on voters has clearly weakened in recent years, yet there are signs of revival in some party organizations. New political forces offer channels of influence that are independent of party: the big increase in Political Action Committees and "independent spenders," the vital role of mass media, the targeting of candidates by single-issue groups, the mobilization of "born-again" Christians into a potentially powerful political movement. Developing in tandem with these forces are several particularly effective tools for creating new, tailor-made constituencies: computerized direct mail, voter identification programs, the use of religious broadcasting networks to transmit political messages. Changes in the election and campaign finance laws have encouraged these trends and at the same time have made the job of campaigner more complicated and more difficult.

Each of these developments is an intriguing story in itself. So let us take a closer look at these changes in the campaign environment, to see what they mean for people who run for office. To start, let us explore one of the most dramatic changes: the results, many of which were unexpected, of a decade of efforts to reform the role of money in political campaigns.

CAMPAIGN FINANCE REFORM: CAMPAIGNING BECOMES
A REGULATED INDUSTRY

It takes money—and in contests for major offices, lots of money—for candidates to explain their views to the voters. House Speaker Thomas ("Tip") O'Neill has said, "As it is now, there are four parts to any campaign. The candidate, the issues of the candidate, the campaign organization, and the money to run the campaign with. Without money you can forget the other three."[2] The issue of campaign money—where it comes from, what the givers want and get in return, how it affects a candidate's chances and a democracy's functioning—gave rise to one of the most sweeping changes in campaign environments in modern political history.

Who should pay for political campaigns? Each of the possible answers has some troublesome implications. Expecting candidates to finance their campaigns out of their own or their families' pockets would allow only the wealthy to run for office. Asking political parties to pay for campaigns has not been very productive; many party organizations do not have the money. Proposing that government provide the funds has not met with great enthusiasm in these times of awesome federal budget deficits.[3] Typically, then, campaigns have been financed mainly by private interests: labor unions acting through their Political

Action Committees (PACs), executives of corporations (frequently at the urging of corporate management), other interest groups, and individual citizens.

Until the early 1970s, the most prominent source was the fabled "fat cats"— very wealthy people who invested in a candidate as they would in the stock market, in the expectation of a good return. They were not alone in that expectation, of course; union groups, corporate executives, and other interests frequently had more in mind than civic virtue when they contributed to a political campaign. Very likely, they hoped for a more specific benefit: the chance to plead for something they wanted from government, and the assurance that they would have the candidate's attention when they did so.

Not all of the "fat cats" and other contributors were trying to buy favors with their contributions. But enough were, and in fact enough succeeded in the attempt, to make private financing of campaigns a recurring sore point with journalists, public interest groups, and candidates themselves.

Pressure mounted during the 1960s to do something about the influence of big contributors. The main federal law that governed campaign finance, the Federal Corrupt Practices Act of 1925, was full of loopholes. The provisions it did have—limits on the amounts that individuals could give to campaigns, for instance—were hardly ever enforced. At the same time, new and expensive campaign technologies were developing and driving the cost of campaigning sky high. To afford those technologies, candidates had to raise much more money than ever before. Their need—and the golden opportunity—for big givers was increasingly obvious.

Perhaps inevitably, the scramble to attract big contributions broke through the thin wall of propriety that the old law provided. Blatant cases of money-for-favors reached their peak in the 1972 reelection campaign of President Richard Nixon when, to cite two well-known instances, dairy industry groups' promises of $2 million in campaign contributions were followed by a presidential decision to raise price supports for milk (an action worth many times that amount to the milk producers), and the Justice Department was directed by the President to settle (rather than press) an antitrust suit against International Telephone and Telegraph Corporation (ITT) after an ITT subsidiary pledged to help pay the expenses of the 1972 Republican National Convention.[4]

By this time, campaign finance abuses were no longer the equivalent of the dead mouse in the corner—an unpleasant reality that was ignored by polite observers. With the reporting of example after pungent example of such abuses, the dead mouse was now on the congressional table. What followed was a set of stronger regulations on presidential and congressional campaign funding, through passage of the Federal Election Campaign Act of 1971 and amendments to the act in 1974 and after. The shape of the law changed somewhat in 1976, when the Supreme Court ruled on a challenge to several provisions. But in brief, the new regulations made the following changes in order to limit private influence on campaigning, at least at the federal level:[5]

Public funding. Presidential candidates could get public funding (i.e., federal tax revenue) for their campaigns under certain conditions. In the primaries, if candidates met several fund-raising requirements to show that they had broadly based support, then the government would match a portion of the private contributions they received. Candidates who accepted these matching funds were limited to a spending ceiling in each primary and in the entire prenomination race. Once a candidate became a party's presidential nominee, he or she could elect to receive a flat sum of government money for the fall campaign. In return, the nominee could accept no additional campaign money from private sources.

Limits on campaign contributions. Contributors to federal campaigns also had spending ceilings. An individual could give no more than $1000 to any candidate in a federal primary or general election (up to a total of $25,000 in one year), and a Political Action Committee could give no more than $5000 per candidate in each election. This was a direct attempt to limit the impact of big givers.

Public disclosure. Campaigns had to disclose the name and address of each contributor of more than $200, and had to list their own expenditures bigger than that amount.

Regulation. A Federal Election Commission (FEC) was set up to administer and enforce these laws. Campaigning, on the federal level at least, became a regulated industry.

The new regulations have changed campaign environments in important ways. The availability of public funding in presidential campaigns, for example, limits some well-heeled candidates and encourages some long-shots to run. The federal money—President Jimmy Carter and challenger Ronald Reagan each received $29.4 million in the 1980 general election—is actually a much smaller sum than some presidential candidates had raised in the years before the law went into effect. Even though the law provides cost-of-living increases in the amount of public funding, federally funded presidential campaigns have to watch their budgets and pace their spending carefully if they are to make those dollars last until election day.[6] The era of the free-spending presidential campaign may now be history.

In the primaries, the chance to qualify for federal matching funds allows a little-known candidate to double his or her fund-raising capability. That helps reduce the challenger's traditional disadvantage in raising money. In consequence, more people are running for presidential nomination than ever before;

even challenges to an incumbent President have become commonplace. The cost to these "dark horses" is an early start; to be sure of qualifying for matching funds, a candidate must often begin serious fund raising at least a year before the first primary.

Limits on the size of campaign contributions have affected congressional as well as presidential races.[7] Individual donors can give no more than $2000 apiece to a candidate ($1000 in the primary and $1000 in the general election) — a far cry from the glory days of the "fat cats." To raise a respectable campaign budget, then, candidates need to attract more contributors than ever before; it takes a lot of small contributions to replace one fat cat. One of the most effective ways to raise large amounts of money in small chunks is computerized direct mail — a fascinating phenomenon about which more is said later. Campaign finance reforms have raised direct-mail experts to the status of indispensable consultants.

The new regulations also opened up a potentially more lucrative source of campaign money than individual donors. The 1971 law specifically allowed corporations and trade and professional associations to form Political Action Committees (PACs), groups that funnel contributions into the treasuries of favored candidates, just as labor unions had done for years. In the 1974 amendments, this privilege was extended to businesses, unions, and other groups that held government contracts. Compared with the ambiguity of previous regulations, these reforms offered a clear invitation for corporate and other PACs to participate in campaigns. Corporations, of course, have a powerful motive for doing so; candidates elected to Congress or the Presidency often make decisions on legislation that affect corporate profits and business conditions. The result is another demonstration of the remarkable ability of reforms to confound the intent of their designers. In limiting the influence of individual fat cats on campaigns, the reformers in fact created a new breed of cat: PACs, whose goals are even more frankly directed toward influencing public policy than the old fat cats had been.

PACS: THE NEW AMERICAN FAT CATS

In response to the campaign reforms, Political Action Committees grew like mushrooms after a rain. Their numbers more than quintupled between 1974 and 1982. The phenomenal increase largely reflected the growth in corporate PACs; only 89 existed at the end of 1974, but during the next eight years almost 1400 new corporate committees were formed, or an average of one every two days. They outstripped labor unions' PACs by a country mile (see figure 1.1).

The movement of thousands of new actors onto the campaign stage would be enough in itself to attract candidates' attention. But the real appeal of the

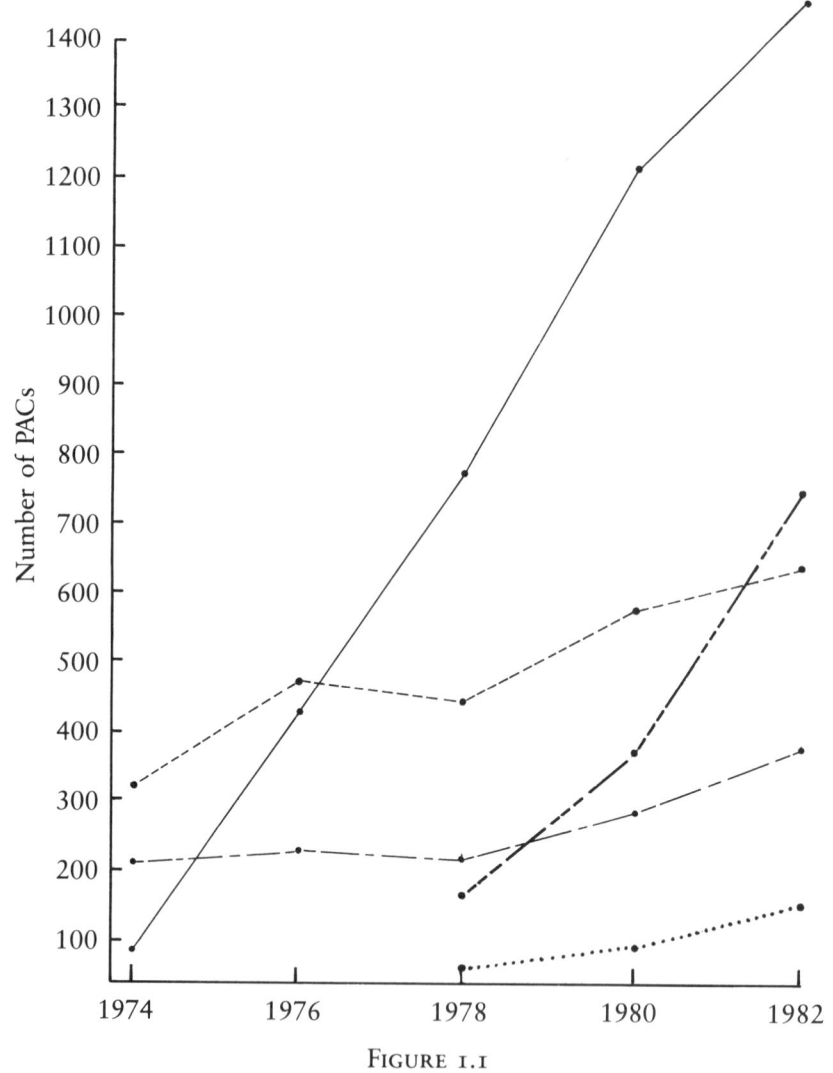

FIGURE 1.1
GROWING NUMBERS OF POLITICAL ACTION COMMITTEES, 1974-82

Type of PAC	1974	1976	1978	1980	1982
Corporate ———————	89	433	784	1204	1467
Labor — — — — — — —	201	224	217	297	380
Trade/membership/ health ------------	318	489	451	574	628
Nonconnected —— --- —— ----	—	—	165	378	746
Other ················	—	—	36	98	150
TOTAL	608	1146	1653	2551	3371

Figure 1.1 data from Federal Election Commission; cell entries are the numbers of PACs registered with the FEC on 31 December of each year listed.

PACs is their money. The biggest recipients of PAC dollars have been congressional campaigns.[8] In the 1979-80 election cycle, House and Senate candidates got no less than $55.3 million of the $60.4 million given by PACs to federal-level campaigns.[9] In 1981-82, PACs gave $83.1 million to House and Senate races, out of a total of $87.3 million in contributions at the federal level.[10] In that election, 169 House races each picked up more than $100,000 from PACs, and ten Senate candidates received over $600,000 apiece.[11]

In short, this rapid growth in PACs is a potential gold mine to many congressional campaigners (and increasingly to state-level candidates as well). And many have developed systematic methods of tapping that gold. While campaigns of the past often assigned a staff member to keep in touch with wealthy individuals who might be courted and coaxed into making a substantial donation, campaigns in the 1980s hire PAC liaisons. Take the 1980 Senate campaign of Iowa Republican Charles E. Grassley. Among Grassley's lieutenants was a man with the title of Political Action Committee Director, one Dragutin Stamenkovich, who spent the campaign on the telephone convincing corporate and conservative PAC managers to give to Grassley's campaign. Just as canvassers might keep a card file on undecided voters, listing their concerns and requests, Mr. Stamenkovich kept a card file on PACs for use in his phone solicitation. "In the early morning, we start calling the East Coast PACs," he said, "and we work across the country with the sun."[12]

The result of these ardent efforts was almost three-quarters of a million dollars in PAC contributions to the Grassley campaign. Just four years earlier, most of these PACs did not exist. But by 1980, Mr. Stamenkovich's activities were "one fruit of the quiet revolution in American politics being fomented by the groups."[13]

Like any other political force, the proliferation of PACs has helped some kinds of candidates more than others. Incumbents have profited most, especially in House and Senate races (see table 1.1); the goal of PAC giving, after all, is to promote the groups' interests by gaining access to people in power, and there is no percentage in having good access to a likely loser. The understandable desire to be friendly with incumbents also helped Democratic congressional candidates during the 1970s, when Democrats held a majority of seats in both houses of Congress. In 1976, for example, Democratic congressional candidates got almost as much money from business and professional PACs as Republicans did.[14] Together with the contributions from labor union committees, which have gone almost exclusively to Democrats, Democratic campaigns had the edge in PAC funding in the 1970s.

Since 1980, that has begun to change. Perhaps because 1980 looked like a Republican year, corporate PACs paid more attention than before to conser-

TABLE 1.1
PAC CONTRIBUTIONS TO HOUSE AND SENATE CANDIDATES, 1981-82
(in millions of dollars)

Type of PAC	Total Contributions	Party Democrats	Republicans
Corporate	$27.4	$9.4	$18.0
Labor	20.2	19.1	1.1
Trade/membership/health	21.7	9.3	12.4
Nonconnected	10.7	5.4	5.2
Other	3.2	1.9	1.2
TOTAL	83.1	45.1	38.0
(Number of candidates)	(2239)	(1024)	(846)

Type of PAC	Incumbents	Type of Candidate Challengers	Open Seats
Corporate	$19.8	$3.6	$3.9
Labor	11.5	5.6	3.1
Trade/membership/health	16.0	2.8	2.8
Nonconnected	4.9	3.7	2.1
Other	2.6	.2	.3
TOTAL	54.8	16.0	12.3
(Number of candidates)	(432)	(1281)	(526)

NOTE: Figures do not always equal total contributions because of rounding.
SOURCE: Federal Election Commission data.

vative Republican challengers. So did many "nonconnected" PACs, including several conservative committees that led all PACs in spending in 1980.[15] By 1982, PACs were stepping away from their increased investment in challengers; PAC money in the 1982 congressional races flowed largely to incumbents, as table 1.1 shows. But since the number of corporate PACs is continuing to grow rapidly while the number of labor union committees is not—and since New Right PACs have proven much more successful than liberal groups at raising money—Republican campaigns can probably look forward to an increasing share of PAC dollars.[16]

Other big spenders among the PACs have been corporations and labor unions whose work is most directly under the government's thumb: public utilities and military contractors, for example, whose profits are highly sensitive to government priorities and actions.[17] And therein lies the irony of the campaign finance reforms. Rather than limit the power of private interests, the reforms institutionalized a means by which private money might play an increasing role in the financing of congressional races: the thousands of newly formed PACs.

THE INDEPENDENT SPENDERS

Private money was not even to be confined to campaign contributions. Ruling on a challenge to the 1974 reforms,[18] the U.S. Supreme Court declared that the act's limitations on campaign contributions were constitutional. But, the Court added, if individuals or groups chose to run ads or any other communication *on their own,* without coordinating their efforts with a campaign, then Congress could *not* limit their spending. These "independent expenditures" by people or PACs, the justices ruled, were forms of political expression protected by the First Amendment.

Many analysts see these independent expenditures as a loophole in the 1974 law, as a way for private interests to get around the limits on their contributions to campaigns.[19] Many candidates, even those supported by independent spenders, see them as a nuisance; even by comparison with a strong opponent, few things are more fearsome than an overzealous supporter whose public messages are entirely beyond the candidate's control.

Beloved or not, independent expenditures have cut a wide swath in several recent campaigns. Most of the independent spenders are PACs: pro-gun groups, pro-life organizations, and a variety of other familiar faces in campaigns. In 1980, however, when the PAC use of independent spending really came of age, most of the attention went to a relatively new group. The National Conservative PAC (NCPAC, or "nickpack" to the campaign afficionado) quickly became known for a take-no-prisoners approach to electioneering that came to tar other independent spenders as well.

NCPAC started early to defeat six liberal Democrats who were seeking reelection to the U.S. Senate in 1980. Its plan was to broadcast a series of highly critical ads in the senators' home states well before any potential senatorial opponents began their campaigns. The aim was to define the Senate races to voters as a kind of referendum on the Democratic incumbent. Any opponents, NCPAC figured, would have their own liabilities and weak points; thus once an opponent began to be featured in the media, voters would see a fallible incumbent facing an also-fallible challenger. But in early 1979, when NCPAC's independent expenditures started, there was only the fallible incumbent. NCPAC ads were designed to turn the spotlight on *his* political liabilities: in the words of NCPAC chairman Terry Dolan, to "destroy the popularity ratings of many of these incumbent liberals."[20]

NCPAC spent $1.4 million on its campaign activities in 1980. In the process, its efforts—what one writer called Dolan's "instinct for politics as demolition derby"[21] — linked independent spending with negative campaigning in many people's minds. It is not hard to see why. Here is a sample NCPAC ad, used in several of its target races, through the eyes of a reporter:

> The 30-second television commercial opens with a picture of a large baloney surrounded on a cutting board by other meats. Suddenly a cleaver slices through the baloney and a voice says, "One very big piece of baloney is Birch Bayh telling us he's fighting inflation."
> The price tag appears on the sliced baloney, reading $46 billion and the voice says, "That's how much deficit spending Bayh voted for last year alone." Pause. "So, to stop inflation, you'll have to stop Bayh first." And then the kicker: "Because if Bayh wins, you lose."[22]
> [And in California]: "Because if Cranston wins, you lose."
> [And in Iowa]: "Because if Culver wins, you lose."

Did these negative campaigns make a difference in 1980? Many Republican party officials and candidates argued that the independent expenditures had no impact or even hurt the (Republican) candidates they were intended to help. The attacks, they felt, were so savage as to create sympathy, or at the least an issue, for the targeted incumbent. Those attacked felt differently: "We really haven't seen these kinds of tactics and this negative approach to this degree in a long time. We take them very seriously. We have to. They're well-financed and they're making their money felt," said Tom Baker, executive director of the Democratic Senatorial Campaign Committee.[23] Indeed, whether because of NCPAC's independent spending or in spite of it, four of the six NCPAC targets lost their races for reelection in 1980.

But one thing was clear. While it was not always used that way, the independent expenditure was very well suited to doing a challenger's dirty work. An independent spender could come into a state early, bloody the incumbent with negative ads, and then step back. Some time later, the challenger would be able to enter the race on a positive tone and remain on the high road — knowing that the mud has already been slung by a group that, because it is formally independent of the challenger's campaign, can always be disavowed.

The strategy was painfully clever. Thus it was soon imitated. When NCPAC plunged eagerly into the reelection race of liberal Democratic Senator Paul Sarbanes in 1981 — a tempting target because Sarbanes was from Maryland, so every member of Congress and the entire national press corps were within television and radio range of the NCPAC blasts — it no longer had the field to itself. The new PROPAC (Progressive Political Action Committee), Democrats for the 80's, and other liberal PACs tried their hand at independent expenditures.[24] Sarbanes must surely have wished that this battle of the titans were taking place in somebody else's Senate race.

And soon it was; independent spending begat more independent spending, at ever-increasing rates. According to the FEC, $5.6 million was spent independently on the 1982 House and Senate campaigns (an increase of 143 percent over 1980), of which $4.4 million was used to fund negative campaigning (an increase of 238 percent). That prompted many candidates to try to raise more campaign money than ever before, and to raise it earlier, against the chance that they would face an independent spending drive in their district. As one writer reported, "Every senator wants to be sure he has money to compete with negative campaigns that may be waged against him by independent pressure groups."[25]

SINGLE-ISSUE POLITICS
Also prominent among the independent spenders are single-issue groups: organizations believing that one particular policy issue has such overriding importance that it justifies political action strictly on its own terms, without compromise or equivocation. Single-issue politics is no newcomer to the campaign environment, of course; American elections have been witness to the power of "single issues" from slavery to prohibition, from the peace marches of the 1960s to the nuclear freeze movement of the 1980s.

But a singleminded approach to politics seems to have taken root and flowered in the fertile soil of the 1970s and 1980s. Dozens of groups have come into political campaigns to insist on the primacy of their cause: banning abortions, bringing prayer back into the public schools, taking sex education out of the public schools, banning handguns, preventing a ban on handguns. Their numbers pose a great challenge to the victory-minded candidate: how to deal with groups demanding that the candidate take uncompromising stands on a number of controversial issues and yet build a coalition capable of attracting majority support.

Many observers see single-issue politics as a response of frustration, as a reaction against the complexity of society's problems and government's seeming inability to cut through that complexity and put things right. Listen, for example, to a Senate press secretary try to put his finger on the cause:

> You have a situation where people find it very difficult to get their hands on the overriding issues of the day. I think people feel impotent politically in the face of the problems that we face. No one seems able to get their hands on inflation. No one seems to be able to get their hands on an economy that keeps going downhill. People seem frustrated by what they regard as overburdensome levels of taxation. Foreign policy seems so far away that it cannot be touched. I'm not saying this is *true;* I'm just saying that the complexity of it is such that people feel left out of the process. And so I think you find that people tend to look for things

that they can have impact on politically.... "I can't get my hands on inflation and I'm against abortion; I know that if I get involved in the anti-abortion fight, for example, I might be able to do something that has tangible results."[26]

Increasingly, as the scope of government power has grown, government programs and regulations have come to touch more aspects of people's lives than ever before.[27] Groups have become accustomed to asking government for solutions to problems once defined as private. But the solutions do not always work; in fact, sometimes they create new problems and add to individuals' sense of frustration.

Other political forces also contribute to the feeling that society's problems are immediate, compelling, and yet somehow impenetrable. In the years before television, citizens may have suspected that their elected leaders did not know all the answers to complex economic and social problems. Now, through the magic of the evening news, their suspicions can be confirmed. At the same time, political parties, which once may have offered people a means of simplifying the alternatives as well as an avenue of attack on these problems, have lost their hold on many voters' political thinking. It is no wonder that a growing number of citizens react with frustration, turn away from the complexity and the ambiguity, and look for more satisfying ways of understanding politics.

But it is not simply the frustration and the complexity that have produced an increase in single-issue politics. In the course of the creeping expansion of government power, legislation and regulation have touched a number of nerves. When the Supreme Court in 1973 overturned state laws banning or severely restricting abortions, some groups were outraged; the pro-life movement mushroomed and took its intense opposition to abortion into political campaigns.[28] When legislators considered some mild limitations on the availability of handguns, spurred by the assassinations of numerous public figures from John F. Kennedy to John Lennon, gun-owners rose up in horror; groups such as the National Rifle Association and the Gun Owners of America, among others, swung into action in campaigns.

What happened in these cases was the politicization of a special kind of issue. A "single issue" is one defined by its proponents as so basic to their value system, so deeply rooted and compelling, that it cries out for priority in politics. To its partisans, the issue is too fundamental to permit halfhearted commitment or brook any negotiation. It justifies, they believe, singleminded political action.[29] At another time, by a different group of proponents, the same issue might have been defined in a more limited, less emotional manner. But in the hands of a group whose concern about the issue is intense, a question such as abortion or gun control or nuclear power takes on single-issue character.

Abortion is a good example. To committed members of the National Right to Life Committee, the Life Amendment PAC, and other organizations, abortion is murder. When government sanctions the right of choice on abortion, these groups argue, it cuts the very heart out of society's moral code. In an election, then, a candidate's position on abortion is not one among many big issues, or even one of the more important issues. It is *the* issue. To pro-life activists, abortion is a moral litmus test. If a candidate fails that test, his or her electoral fate is sealed. All other issues, in this view, must take a back seat until abortion has been banned.

The support of a single-issue group can be very attractive to a candidate. Such a group can provide dedicated campaign volunteers as well as voters who are highly motivated to go to the polls. These are big assets in American elections, where turnout is typically low and enthusiasm even lower. But the price of that tempting support is the candidate's freedom on the issue. To a single-issue activist, the issue is much too important to allow politicians any maneuvering room. A candidate who tries to develop a more moderate position — a compromise, for example, between those who want all abortions banned and those who believe that some abortions should be allowed for health reasons — fails the group's litmus test. For candidates who believe that the job of an elected representative is to build coalitions, to find positions on which majorities can agree, the increasing presence of single-issue groups makes life difficult. A senatorial aide comments on the implications:

> I think single-issue organizations and campaigns are the biggest threat right now to our whole system, to representative democracy. If and when the Congress is ever full of people who have been sent there on a single issue, whether it's the Panama Canal or abortion or gun control or anti-food stamps or whatever — if the balance of Congress is ever made up of people like that, you'll have no measure of what they stand for as an individual and as a member of their political party. And it will be a very volatile group; it'll be a very regressive group, and, I think, a very dangerous group of people in the Congress.

In the short run, however, many campaigners would rather have zealous activists in their camp than in their opponent's. Such candidates, says former Senator John Culver (who, a year after these remarks, was himself beaten in a race where single issues took a prominent role), may well try to "form a necklace of all these single-issue constituencies devoid of common purpose or values," simply for reasons of self-protection: "When you have these rifle-shot constituencies, with their money and discipline, their influence on the outcome of elections is obviously disproportionate to their numbers."[30]

Once a campaign has attracted the notice of single-issue groups, the candidate must consider whether a stance that fails a group's litmus test is important enough to justify the risk—the loss of a group of voters whose numbers may mean the difference between victory and defeat. Taking that risk, after all, jeopardizes the candidate's opportunity to have a say in other areas of public policy. The pressure on campaigners is intense, even if the single-issue support is beyond their grasp. Consider this example:

> In South Dakota, a group of 25 young college kids turned up at the state fair and stridently demanded that Sen. George McGovern vote for the Hyde anti-abortion amendment. He declined. "They left without a good word for anything I had ever done in twenty years in public life," he said.[31]

The speaker is now ex-Senator McGovern, and the story of his struggle with single-issue politics is told later in this book.

Unlike the rain, the hail of single-issue pressure has not fallen on conservatives and liberals alike. From the New Deal to the early 1970s, many of the major single-issue movements gave their support primarily to Democrats and liberals. The union movement, the civil rights movement, the crusade against American participation in the Vietnam war—all had single-issue qualities, and all helped elect many liberals to office.

The "newer" single issues have a decidedly more conservative tilt. Many of the most active single-issue groups in the 1980s speak for some aspect of social conservatism, particularly for a traditional, religious-based morality that they fear is threatened by forces such as women's rights, homosexual rights, abortion, and the absence of prayer in the public schools. Together, these single-issue groups have given new life to the conservative movement in the United States, as a leader of this "New Right" explains:

> . . . when political conservative leaders began to reach out and strike an alliance with social conservatives—the pro-life people, the anti-E.R.A. people, the evangelical and born-again Christians, the people concerned about gay rights, prayer in the schools, sex in the movies or whatever—that's when this whole movement began to come alive.[32]

But if single issues have been the New Right's life force in the 1980s, its muscle has come from the political reawakening of "born-again" Christian leaders.

PREACHER-POLITICIANS AND THE NEW CHRISTIAN RIGHT

Like single-issue politics, the mixing of politics and religion is not new in American life. The line between "moral issues" and political issues has always been elusive, as church involvement in the efforts to abolish slavery, promote civil rights, and get U.S. troops out of Vietnam would suggest. In fact, mainline churches and synagogues have maintained Washington lobbies for decades, usually in behalf of liberal and humanitarian causes. But by the late 1970s, a conservative counterforce was mobilizing within a variety of churches under the banner of the evangelical or New Christian Right. From there it moved with fervor into political campaigns.

This counterforce of fundamentalists and evangelicals has potentially massive proportions. A 1979 Gallup poll found that 20 percent of its respondents (which would generalize roughly to 30 million voting-age Americans) considered themselves strict Bible believers—those who believe in biblical inerrancy—of the kind that many evangelical leaders regard as their natural constituency. Nearly as many more, representing another 21 million, called themselves "born-again Christians" who have experienced a personal conversion, or "rebirth," in Christ. Add to this the many individuals in other faiths—Mormons, Catholics, Jews—who are conservatives on theological matters, and the numbers of potential sympathizers with the New Christian Right may reach as high as 80 million.[33]

It used to be easy for campaigners to overlook these groups. Fundamentalist Christians, for example, traditionally registered and voted less often than nonfundamentalists. Their preachers had taught that politics is irrelevant to the most important problem, people's innate sinfulness, which can be cleansed only by the individual's personal conversion and commitment to live in accord with biblical principles. Thus fundamentalist preacher Jerry Falwell, whose "Old Time Gospel Hour" reaches millions of television viewers, used his influential pulpit during the 1960s to decry the mixing of religion with politics. By 1980, however, the Reverend Mr. Falwell, now president of Moral Majority, Inc., had quite a different message: "During the 1980s, preachers, we have a threefold primary responsibility. Number one, get people saved; number two, get them baptized; number three, get them registered to vote."[34]

What had awakened (or, more accurately, reawakened) the sleeping giant to politics? To some extent, government had. The Internal Revenue Service and other federal agencies had begun investigating the curricula and admissions standards of the growing number of Christian schools. The Federal Communications Commission briefly cast a regulatory eye at religious broadcasting on FM radio—and evangelical and fundamentalist leaders prompted more than 12 million letters of protest, most of which were written long after the agency had decided not to regulate. Other government actions, especially the Supreme Court's decisions to ban prayer in public schools and legalize abortion, convinced many preachers that the government was taking the side of sin.

But equally important in this reawakening were several New Right political organizers, including Paul Weyrich of the Committee for the Survival of a Free Congress and Howard Phillips of the Conservative Caucus. They saw the potential power of this huge, socially conservative group. They saw a number of highly successful evangelists who had made television and radio their pulpits, who had a collective audience of millions, and who raised enormous sums in donations every year. Their followers attended church frequently. Those fundamentalist and evangelical churches were like new political precincts waiting to be organized. As one analyst writes:

> Politicians less astute than the late Mayor Daley could recognize a powerful political machine when they saw one: a large clientele identifying with several charismatic leaders, well-developed lines of two-way communications, large organizational bureaucracies and a host of volunteer activists, and, above all, demonstrated fund-raising capabilities.[35]

They saw a new constituency for the New Right.

To touch that constituency, Weyrich and others encouraged several evangelical leaders to form political groups. One result was the founding in 1979 of Falwell's Moral Majority, soon followed by The Christian Voice, the Religious Roundtable, and the National Christian Action Coalition. Several groups launched drives to register millions of new voters in time for the 1980 elections.

But that wasn't all. According to Weyrich:

> It is not going to do any good to register millions of voters and then not tell them who the good guys are and who the bad guys are. [Instead, he urged preachers in 1980 to] frame [issues] in such a way that there is no mistaking who is on the right side and who is on the wrong side. Ultimately, everything can be reduced to right and wrong. Everything.[36]

To tell the new voters which candidates were on the "wrong" side, several groups issued "moral report cards" on incumbents. Hundreds of thousands of these ratings were distributed in congressional districts beginning in 1980. Perhaps the best-known is the Moral Issues Index developed by Christian Voice. Created in part to attract media coverage (which it did), the index judged the morality of members of Congress on the basis of their votes on several "single issues." In 1980, for example, an incumbent's morality rating increased if he or she had voted against school busing for racial balance, against penalties for racially segregated private schools, against government funding of abortions and sex education, and against an extension of time for ratifying the Equal Rights Amendment.

Other issues have been included in the index, even though, according to its author, their correct "moral" stance may have been "a little obscure."[37] To be rated as "moral" in 1981, for instance, an incumbent would have to have opposed a measure requiring the United States to abide by the Strategic Arms

Limitation agreements with the Soviet Union. A strong national defense is a Christian position, according to Falwell, because "Jesus was not a sissy. He was not a pacifist."[38] And morality (as defined by Christian Voice) required a vote for a balanced federal budget; its connection with biblical principles, one evangelical leader explained, was that "when people's life savings are deteriorating at 15 to 20 percent a year, that is *evil*."[39]

But a senator or House member could score no points on these "moral report cards" for favoring arms control, feeding the poor, or sheltering the homeless, though these are biblical concerns too. Perhaps that is why five of the six clergymen in Congress scored lower than 50 percent on Christian Voice's 1980 moral index. In the words of one, Republican John Buchanan, a Baptist minister who lost his 1980 primary when his support of school prayer was not precisely the type that Moral Majority activists required, "I'd say they did a rather thorough job of beating my brains out with Christian love."[40]

Beginning in 1980 the New Christian Right and its conservative agenda were difficult for candidates to ignore. To many bemused reporters and editors, the sight of preachers classifying members of Congress as 50 percent moral, or 17 percent moral, was exotic enough to warrant a lot of coverage. The Moral Majority and its leaders became a hot news story. In that way, media reports amplified the impact (and the reputation for electoral power) of the evangelical Right.

But even without the press attention, this new political force expected to make its influence felt in campaigns. Just as the urban political machines built their power on a geographical constituency, the New Christian Right pinned its hopes on a social constituency: a group of people in many different places who shared certain religious and moral beliefs. The movement had both organizational and substantive reasons to believe that it could appeal successfully to that social constituency. Substantively, the New Christian Right had seized the offensive on many of the most affecting issues of the times: from protection of the family to abortion to busing. As Paul Weyrich readily acknowledged, "in sheer numbers, the potential outreach of [the "pro-family" organizations in Washington] is greater than the whole range of [traditional] conservative groups."[41] Organizationally, the movement could draw on the resources and authority of thousands of evangelical churches and the audiences of several "electronic preachers"— a ready-made communication link with millions of potentially receptive voters.

Those voters are not blank slates, of course, ready to be filled by their preachers, by Jerry Falwell, or his New Right allies. In fact, in the 1980 presidential election voters who called themselves "born-again" Protestants did not vote differently, as a group, from other Protestants.[42] The result is that the real electoral impact of the evangelical Right fell far short of its leaders' hopes, at least at the national level. But as the Reverend Mr. Buchanan would testify, evangelical leaders made a difference in some campaigns and cast a long shadow over others. Their influence was strengthened by sophisticated new campaign techniques by which evangelical and New Right leaders could add to the social constituency they had developed. Chief among these techniques is computerized direct mail.

NEW CAMPAIGN TECHNOLOGIES:
THE COMPUTERIZED CONSTITUENCY

Most candidates love to get exposure on the evening news and in paid television ads. Nevertheless, the main virtue of these techniques—that they attract big audiences—is also one of their biggest drawbacks. A mass audience contains many different kinds of people and interests. As one media expert explains it, "When you advertise [on television] at seven in the evening, you are talking to the president of the local bank as well as the person on welfare."[43] It is not easy for a candidate to construct a message that will sound attractive to both groups.

There are real advantages to tailoring an appeal to its audience; a candidate who makes a moving appeal for compassionate treatment of the poor, when speaking to a group of social workers, may prefer to emphasize other parts of his or her platform when addressing the Chamber of Commerce. The approach is not necessarily dishonest; the candidate may favor social welfare programs *and* a strong economy. And it is very practical; people cannot be persuaded unless they are listening, and they will listen more attentively when the topic interests them.

An answer to the dilemma has been provided by computerized direct mail, a technique raised to the status of an art form in recent campaigns. Its logic is simple and compelling.

With computerized direct mail, the candidate designs his or her own audience—one whose characteristics will make it receptive to the candidate's appeals. Consider a campaigner who favors a freeze on nuclear weapons. His or her logical supporters and contributors include people who strongly support a nuclear freeze. But how to find them? More important, how to appeal to them without alarming and activating people who want more nuclear weapons built? One way is to get lists of voters who have declared their support for a freeze: people who have signed petitions, given money to nuclear freeze groups, or contributed to other pro-freeze candidates. Another way is to learn what kinds of people are likely to favor a nuclear freeze: upper-income people, for instance, or members of certain churches. Then the campaigner requests mailing lists from groups that contain a lot of these people: environmental groups, perhaps, or humanitarian groups, or even lists of subscribers to the magazines they are likely to read. Or the campaigner learns where—in which census districts or precincts or zip codes—these kinds of people are concentrated.

The names on these lists, then, are a specially designed audience that should be much more sympathetic to an appeal stressing the candidate's nuclear freeze stance than should the public at large. All that remains is to compose a powerful letter emphasizing the candidate's position and to send a copy to each person on those lists. That can be done fastest and most accurately by computer.

Computers can do much more. Different mailing lists can be cross-classified, for example, to identify people who want a nuclear freeze *and* a ban on abortions; to this audience, the candidate can send a special letter appealing for support on both grounds. Computers can store huge quantities of information, including each recipient's response, the amount of his or her donation, the kind of letter that stimulated the donation. And computers can produce millions of letters in a few days—a handy skill, since only two or three "prospecting" letters in every hundred are likely to bring a contribution.

Direct mail is not new. It was first used by the Republican National Committee on an experimental basis in 1962,[44] and later by such presidential candidates as Barry Goldwater, George Wallace, and George McGovern. But it was New Right leader Richard Viguerie who nurtured and fine-tuned the technique. He started with a list having a lot of potential for conservative groups: the names of people who had contributed at least $50 to the Goldwater presidential campaign in 1964. Since then, he has bought and borrowed enough lists to build a Fort Knox of names: an estimated 16 to 20 million people who contribute to his clients, which are primarily New Right groups. His firm raised more than $40 million in 1980 alone; it mails over 70 million letters each year.[45]

According to Viguerie, direct mail was perfectly suited to build the New Right. Because he believes that the print and broadcast media are controlled by liberals, "the New Right really didn't have access to the microphones of this country until we discovered direct mail. And now we can go directly to our people,"[46] in the privacy of their homes, hitting them with the kinds of issues that provoke a response, all without having to alert the liberal opposition. In Viguerie's memorable phrase, direct mail is "like using a water moccasin for a watchdog—it's very quiet."[47]

A technique with such promise could not remain the exclusive preserve of the New Right. Liberals found that they too could create constituencies and raise money with direct mail. The use of the technique got a tremendous boost from the campaign finance reforms of 1974; limits on the size of individuals' campaign donations forced candidates to look for a much larger number of contributors. The most efficient way to find lots of small donors was through computerized direct mail. So in the 1980s the technique has been adopted by candidates of all political stripes, party organizations, PACs, and other groups.

Other sophisticated technologies have been adapted to campaign use. Staffs can choreograph a set of simultaneous "meetings" between the candidate and groups of potential contributors, with the candidate present at each by means of a broadcast transmitted by satellite. Computers can be used for precinct targeting: processing large amounts of voting and census data to determine where the campaign should concentrate its efforts. Simulated campaigns can be run on computers, to let campaigners "see" the results of different strategies. Public opinion data can be tabulated so quickly by computer that reactions to an opponent's charge or a televised debate can be measured within hours of the event.

These new tools demand special skills. Increasingly, there is little room for amateurs in campaigns for major offices. Presidential and senatorial campaigns, and many for House seats and governorships, subcontract parts of their electioneering. They hire specialists in a wide variety of fields, from pollsters to media advisers, from direct-mail experts to delegate hunters, precinct targeters, professional managers, attorneys and accountants who specialize in the new campaign finance rules, and many others who promise to unlock the secrets of these powerful techniques.

And candidates usually find these specialists outside the political parties. When campaigning was a simpler process and candidates concentrated on walking the precincts, meeting with group leaders, and speaking at rallies, they could learn these skills from party leaders. As campaigning changed, the parties and their skills were left behind. Experts in direct mail and other new techniques are not party functionaries but independent entrepreneurs like Richard Viguerie. In turn, these independent specialists give candidates the tools to reach voters outside party channels. Viguerie says,

> I just talked to a congressman today who's got 27,000 contributors to his campaign . . . and by the time the campaign's over, there'll be 40,000 contributors to his campaign. What influence does the Republican National Committee have on this man? Can Bill Brock [former RNC chairman] call him up and say, "Hey, you're stepping out of line on this issue or that, and I want you to know that we are going to withhold contributions"? I mean, this man raised a million dollars, and Bill Brock can give him a handful of dollars.[48]

In the same way, direct mail and other techniques help single-issue and other interest groups to flourish in the 1980s. As long as these groups can get

The Environment of Political Campaigns

access to people like Viguerie, they do not need to fold into a party coalition in order to make their mark. They can enter campaign environments on their own terms.

THE ERA OF THE MEDIA CAMPAIGN

Television and radio are both the ancestors and the contemporaries of these new campaign technologies. Together with newspapers, they form the eyes through which most people see political campaigns. Especially since the 1960s, it can fairly be claimed that the great majority of Americans either experience political campaigning through the mass media or not at all. The alternative — seeing a candidate in person — has gone the way of the corner grocery store, except perhaps in local elections.

The mass media are not neutral transmitters of all the political sights within view, nor can they be. News editors have a limited space or time to fill; inevitably they must choose which campaign "stories" will be covered that day. Reporters and broadcast correspondents must decide which details of those stories are important and interesting, and which will be ignored. None of these decisions can be made on totally objective grounds; they are made, after all, by people — people with a sense of what makes an event "news," with the need to attract and hold an audience, people with political beliefs of their own.

Each of those decisions affects the environment of political campaigns.[49] For example, campaigners soon learn that to get much-needed media exposure, they must generate the kinds of activities that reporters and editors define as newsworthy. If the prevailing definition of "news" among media people refers to a timely and discrete event that is controversial or dramatic in tone,[50] then candidates who want media coverage must supply those qualities.

In this process by which campaigners adapt to the media's needs, the pure case is the "media event" — the campaign activity created primarily for the purpose of enticing media coverage. Candidates can express their feelings about the state of the economy in many different ways, but some of those ways are more "newsworthy" — more dramatic, more immediate — than others. Film footage of the candidate shopping for food with the family of an unemployed auto worker (with a few choice words of empathy and indignation, normally expressed in front of the meat section) may not be as weighty as a long position paper on economic policy, but is certainly more likely to make the evening news.

Some media events have become minor classics. Take, for example, the effort by George Bush to remind voters in 1980 of a delicate point: Mr. Bush's chief rival for the Republican presidential nomination, Ronald Reagan, would be seventy years old the following year, while Bush was a vigorous fifty-five.

Reagan had scheduled a meeting one morning at a Florida hotel. As he arrived on the hotel's patio, looking rather tired in the bright sunlight, suddenly Bush appeared. Jogging. The energetic candidate sprinted through the waiting media people to shake hands with his very exasperated-looking rival. Reagan, appearing older and weaker in the context that Bush had so carefully created, smiled through clenched teeth. The cameras rolled. It was "newsworthy."

Media coverage affects campaigners' choices in many other ways. The competition for audiences, for instance, leads broadcasters and reporters to stress the colorful "horse-race" aspects of campaigns—who's running ahead, who's closing the gap, how fast the finish line is approaching—rather than analyses of policy issues, which are more important to the nation's future, but also more complicated. The result is that events indicating the standings of the various horses—in a presidential race, for example, state primaries, new public opinion polls, and other "hard" indicators of the race's progress—dominate campaign coverage.[51] Because these events get such prominent play, a serious candidate cannot afford to do poorly in the early soundings. The media focus on likely winners; a candidate who is reported to be trailing will rapidly lose the spotlight.

Even in the horse-race style of reporting, some interpretation of "hard facts" is necessary. Again, presidential elections offer a useful example. To make sense out of the four-month blizzard of state primary and caucus results, reporters try to judge which events are the ones to watch, how a candidate's performance in a given event should be interpreted, what are the signs that a candidate is building momentum. In 1980, for instance, Ronald Reagan and George Bush won almost equal support in the Iowa Republican precinct caucuses; Bush edged Reagan, 33 to 30 percent. But Reagan had the misfortune to have come into Iowa as the front-runner. Because of the expectations that produced among reporters—even though the caucuses themselves elected no delegates to the national nominating convention—"the story" of the Iowa results was that of a major setback for Reagan and of momentum (though it proved to be short-lived) for Bush.

And what media people declare to be "the story" in a particular campaign thus *becomes* the story for much of the public. For that reason, campaigners often work very hard to affect reporters' expectations about a race in order to influence the coverage they get. In the early months of an election, before there are many events to report, the impressions of media people as to which candidates are serious contenders may mean life or death for a candidate's fund raising and recruitment of staff and volunteers. During the race, every candidate has a big stake in convincing reporters that the most recent poll or primary has strengthened the candidate's position.

The way media people define "news" even affects the structure of campaigns. Most candidates focus on a small number of themes—ideas they stress again and again in order to cement a particular image of themselves in voters' minds ("It's time for a change"; "I'll never tell you a lie"). But such repetition quickly becomes old news, because news, to reporters and editors, is what's different, what's out of the ordinary. The new wrinkles in the candidate's speech, the off-the-cuff deviations from a prepared text draw the media attention. If those deviations are embarrassing, they may well overshadow the rest of the speech in the media's portrayal. A candidate who is a "textual deviate,"[52] then, can get into big trouble. Candidate Ronald Reagan did just that in the early weeks of the 1980 general election campaign. His apparently unrehearsed answers to reporters' questions, characterizing the Vietnam war as a "noble cause," admitting his doubts about the theory of evolution, suggesting that trees were the major cause of air pollution, got more coverage than the substance of his speeches. The result is candidates and their staffs learn the dangers of spontaneity. They learn the need to gain some control over the coverage they get, by creating media events and carefully limiting reporters' access to the candidate.

In short, media people and campaigners need one another; theirs is a symbiotic relationship. Television, radio, and newspapers have become increasingly interested in covering political campaigns because the drama and excitement of campaigning draw audiences. Those aspects of campaigns that seem to hold audiences—horse-race reporting, an emphasis on slip-ups, photogenic situations, conflict and change—get the lion's share of media attention. The nature of that attention affects campaigners' decisions and prospects. If media coverage can help create the environment of a campaign, then candidates and their staffs will try to influence what media people see, how they interpret what they see, and what they define as worth covering.

The increasing importance of media in campaigns has affected other political forces as well. Decades ago, candidates spoke to voters primarily through a party's canvassers and brochures. The expansion of media markets changed all that; through news coverage and paid media advertising, candidates can talk to voters with or without a party's help. The growing use of these media both reflects and intensifies some weaknesses in American parties.

THE PARTIES: WHEN THE LANDMARKS SHIFT
In sheer scope and intricacy, changes in the two major parties can easily match any of the other dramatic alterations in campaign environments. For the past two decades, observers have witnessed the most extensive party reforms in 150 years, and some fascinating shifts in the parties' organizations and appeals— but also a steady erosion in their hold on voters.

As recently as the early 1960s it was possible to argue that party identification—a psychological attachment to one of the political parties—was the key to election results. Most people maintained a "standing decision" to vote for a particular party's candidates, and voted consistent with that decision in most races.[53] Campaigns did not, perhaps could not, do much to convert voters from the ranks of the opponent's party. In that context, wise campaigners concentrated their efforts on their own partisans plus those voters unattached to either party. When party labels made so much difference in elections, there was some incentive for candidates (particularly those of the majority party in their area) to campaign as party loyalists and coordinate their electioneering with the party organization.

But the situation in the 1980s is quite different. Although most voting-age Americans still express a psychological attachment to one of the major parties, that attachment has weakened and means less and less in elections. The proportion of *strong* party identifiers slipped to a low in 1976 from which it has only partly recovered (see table 1.2). And party has less influence on people's voting choices than it once did; fewer people vote a straight party ticket than did in the 1960s (see table 1.3). The parties, quite simply, are becoming irrelevant to large numbers of Americans.[54]

Not only do people depend less on party labels in deciding how to vote, but the party labels call forth changed meanings. Issues that gave rise to the modern party alignment—economic differences arising from the Great Depression and the Roosevelt New Deal—are part of the personal experience of only the oldest fraction of current voters; those who cast their first ballots for Franklin Roosevelt in 1932 are now in their seventies. The youngest voters in 1984 were only two years old when the author of what might be called the final flowering of the New Deal, President Lyndon Johnson and his Great Society program, left office. The New Deal, 30 years older still, is a history lesson.

Within the parties, there is a keen sense that the engine that powered the New Deal Democratic coalition has been running well past warranty and began making ominous noises years ago. One reason is the changing relationship between groups in the Democratic coalition and the party's leadership. Before the New Deal, the chance for some small measure of economic security—a safety net against personal economic disaster—was no more than a dream for most elderly people, the poor and unemployed, and even many working people. Democratic leaders articulated these dreams. Beginning with Roosevelt's Presidency and the New Deal, Democratic officeholders established government programs to fulfill them: social security, medicare, minimum wage laws, unemployment compensation, public housing. Then, as the economy expanded, more and more working people moved from have-nots to haves, joined the

TABLE 1.2
STRENGTH OF PARTY IDENTIFICATION AND POLITICAL
INDEPENDENCE, 1960-82
(in percent)

Partisanship	1960	1964	1968	1972	1976	1980	1982	Percent Change 1960-82
Strong party identification (Democrats + Republicans)	35	37	30	25	24	26	30	−5
Weak party identification (Democrats + Republicans)	38	38	39	38	39	37	38	—
All independents	23	23	30	35	36	35	30	+7
Independents leaning toward one party	15	15	19	22	22	22	19	+4
"Pure" independents	8	8	11	13	14	13	11	+3
Apoliticals; don't know	4	2	1	2	1	2	2	−2

SOURCE: American National Election Studies, 1960-82, University of Michigan Center for Political Studies.

ranks of the lower middle class, and understandably wanted to protect their newly won economic stake.[55]

But later, Democratic leaders of the 1960s and 1970s, rather than speak for the formerly poor and formerly unemployed, often continued to advance the hopes of the more disadvantaged in society. Some of these were groups whose disadvantages had not been widely acknowledged in earlier times: women, the physically handicapped, those accused of crimes, those whose sexual preference and living habits differed from the norm. The concerns of these groups went beyond economic advancement to questions of social justice, to the achievement of "rights" that did not sit well with the more culturally traditional groups in the coalition.

To complicate matters, the economy slowed down. As one writer put it, "giving people a larger slice of the economic pie now increasingly means tak-

TABLE 1.3
TWO MEASURES OF THE DECLINE IN STRAIGHT-TICKET VOTING, 1960-82

	1960	1962	1964	1966	1968	1970	1972	1974	1976	1978	1980	1982	Percent Change Since 1960
1. Gallup poll data: "For the various political offices, did you vote for all the candidates of one party—that is, straight ticket—or did you vote for the candidates of different parties?" Percent straight ticket:	66	*	59	*	44	*	38	*	42	*	38	*	−28
2. National Election Study data: "How about the elections for other (than governor) state and local offices—did you vote a straight ticket, or did you vote for candidates from different parties?" Percent straight ticket:	73	58	60	50	52	48	42	40	*	*	41	45	−28

SOURCES: For 1960-72, both measures: Everett Carll Ladd, Jr., with Charles D. Hadley, *Transformations of the American Party System*, 2nd ed. (New York: Norton, 1978), 325. For 1976 and 1980 Gallup data: *Gallup Opinion Index* no. 137 (December 1976) and no. 183 (December 1980). For 1974-82 National Election Study data: NES codebooks, University of Michigan Center for Political Studies.

* Question not asked.

ing it from somebody else."[56] Without the flexibility provided by a fast-growing economy, it was painfully clear that aid to the currently deprived would have to come, at least in part, from taxes paid by the formerly deprived: the newly *embourgeoised* workers. Not surprisingly, many New Deal Democrats became suspicious of a Democratic leadership that supported expensive government programs designed to benefit other people.

As if this were not enough, a spate of reforms deepened the fractures within the Democratic party and affected campaigns all over the nation. Since 1968, Democratic reform commissions have made several fundamental changes in the way the party chooses its presidential candidates.[57] They mandated broader citizen participation in the selection of delegates to the party's presidential conventions. They urged (and at times required) that more women, young people, and blacks be selected as convention delegates. In 1980 they ruled that (with few exceptions) each state's delegate votes be distributed among presidential candidates to reflect the candidates' share of the primary or caucus vote.[58]

The purpose of these reforms was to make the Democratic party more democratic internally, to give minority views greater representation within the party. The minority views in question were those of the so-called new liberalism—women's rights, busing to achieve school integration, the rights of the accused, affirmative action. In that sense, the reforms succeeded. Presidential conventions run under the reform rules have in fact paid greater attention to these issues. But these are the very questions on which the new Democratic constituents differ sharply with the pre-reform party leaders and their labor and "old liberal" supporters. As a disgruntled member of the older Democratic coalition, AFL-CIO President Lane Kirkland, commented ruefully, "Someone once remarked that the man who said patriotism is the last refuge of the scoundrel overlooked reform."[59]

Throughout the 1970s the national Democratic party was rent by these antagonisms. Primary fights between "old liberal" and "new liberal" Democrats could be seen in campaigns at all levels. The election of Ronald Reagan in 1980 produced a temporary truce. The loss of both the White House and the Senate to the Republicans in 1980, the rapid rise in unemployment, and the administration's efforts to dismantle a decade of environmental legislation gave Democrats some reasons to lay aside their differences and stress matters of shared concern. But the differences remain, potent and treacherous, just beneath the surface.

In sharp contrast, the Republicans during the 1970s placed less emphasis on a reform of rules than on the provision of sophisticated new services. The national party has built a substantial fund-raising operation using direct mail. It has incorporated new technologies—computer analysis of precinct-level data, campaign simulations, professional management techniques — into its services to state and local parties and candidates. It has concentrated on the development of a stronger, richer, and more effective party structure at all levels.

Still, Republican efforts to reinvigorate their party organizations were bucking a powerful trend. As an indirect result of the Democratic reform rules, dozens of states moved during the 1970s to elect their presidential convention delegates by direct primaries rather than state conventions or other systems. In 1968, the last presidential race prior to the party reforms, only 17 states held presidential primaries, electing (or binding) about one-third of the votes in each party's convention. By 1980, primaries for President were held in 37 states and territories, determining about three-quarters of the delegate votes, more than at any other time in American history.[60]

The primary system effectively cuts most party organizations out of the nomination campaigns. Many candidates like it that way. They do not have to ask permission from party slatemakers to run for the office they want. They are not constrained by their party's platform and are free to criticize party leaders. They can hire consultants, buy television time, use direct mail, and attract volunteers independent of the party organization. They can raise money from single-issue groups and other PACs for their own use, not for the party's treasury. They can become, in David Broder's apt phrase, "a political party of one."[61]

But the weakening of parties, and the freedom that gives candidates, has its costs. It enhances the power of single-issue groups, of one-issue people putting pressure on one-candidate campaigns. It forces candidates to develop a substitute for the party's organization and outreach, perhaps by heavy use of the media. It stimulates the need for ever-larger campaign budgets. It leads candidates and PACs alike to rely on direct mail and other costly techniques to develop constituencies and raise money.

So we come full circle. The dramatic recent changes in campaign environments reinforce one another in many ways. They also provide a marvelous opportunity for students of politics. The process of change often calls attention to the assumptions that underlie a behavior. To study campaigning in an era of change, then, can pay special dividends in insight.

But to understand campaigning fully, it is not enough to look at these environmental changes alone, nor is it enough to look at the campaigners' actions alone. Rather, we can benefit from examining the relationships between the two: the ways that campaigners respond to their environment, and the ways they help form and change that environment. These relationships — the interactions of individual attitudes or behavior and environmental conditions, the acquisition of attitudes and behaviors as a result of experience — are the central concern of people who study human learning. This book contends that it is particularly informative (and intriguing as well) to view political campaigning as a learning process.

Individual campaigns differ from one another in many ways. They vary according to the office being sought; the circumstances and "rules" of presidential races differ systematically from those of Senate campaigns, which differ in turn from races for the House of Representatives, the statehouse, state legislatures, and local offices (variations we explore in later chapters). Campaigns differ depending on their location, their attractiveness to the media, the presence or absence of an incumbent.

But campaigns share many important features. By viewing campaigns as learning experiences, these shared characteristics (as well as variations) and their impact become more clear.

THE LEARNING EXPERIENCE OF A CAMPAIGN

Interaction is central to the purpose of campaigning. Campaign organizations are set up for the purpose of influencing voters (no matter how imperfectly they may succeed) and learning from voters as well. Campaigners interact with one another, with reporters and other media people, with strong supporters and contributors, with political party activists, and with other group leaders.

These interactions are not limited to the few months before an election. It is common to think of "the campaign" as the period of time that begins with an individual's formal declaration of candidacy and ends with election day—the time when a headquarters can be seen, and when the evening news is heavy with campaign promises.

But this intense period—the "active phase" of a campaign—is only a part of the longer-range process of political campaigning. As Richard Fenno so clearly shows,[62] the activities of an officeholder who intends to run again really form a continuing campaign, interrupted at intervals by elections. The incumbent's contact with voters and groups, position taking, and presentation of self, from the day after the election until the opening gun of the next one, is in large part a way of setting the stage for the active phase of the campaign to come. Listen to the comments of administrative assistants to two members of the House:

> I think it's a mistake to think of the campaign as a specified period of four or five or however many months or weeks. To a real political animal, he's campaigning all the time. Every letter that we write to every individual, every appearance the congressman makes, every newsletter and a whole variety of contacts of that form, are a campaign effort—not in a crass sense, but in the sense that they reflect the man, and generate an impression in the recipient or the one who hears him speak.

Well, of course we have, as every congressman does, carried on a continuous campaign, whether we admit it or not. We have put out newsletters on a once-every-two-months basis to postal patrons, and I don't care what anybody says, that's campaigning. . . . This year we also put out a questionnaire to all the constituents, and we've also offered agricultural bulletins to all the constituents—all as the duty of a member of Congress and not as a candidate, but nevertheless it's a little difficult to separate one from the other.

It is indeed—fortunately for the incumbent who can use the resources of office, the newsletters and constituent service, to build up a base of support in preparation for the next election.[63] In fact, if a challenger's efforts are confined to the active phase of a race, as is usually the case, then the real campaign may be over before he or she has held the first briefing.

As the longer-range process of campaigning leaves its mark on the active phase of a race, the reverse is also true. The heightened contact of the active phase can teach candidates about new political forces that may affect their futures: new groups forming in the district, changes in the loyalties and influence of older groups, attractive candidates for lesser office who in time might become potent rivals, changes in the importance of various issues. In short, what campaigners learn during this active phase affects, and is affected by, their actions and policy stances between elections.

The active phase affects citizens' relationships with politics as well. Drawing upon the drama of conflict and the manipulation of powerful symbols, this intense season of campaigning can heighten public attention to politics for a time. During that time, leaders can influence the personal political agendas of citizens as well as respond to them. The active campaign focuses the media spotlight on some issues and lets other fade; in that way, it affects the nation's policy agenda.

In all these interactions we can see development and change: change in candidates' expectations, evolution of their behavior as they experience and think about events in their environment. In other words, we can see learning. Books about campaigning are filled with vignettes of candidates learning about their constituencies in the course of a campaign, about public needs and private pain, and carrying that learning with them into office. Jules Witcover, for example, describes how then-Senator John F. Kennedy "first came upon the full meaning of the toll taken on human beings in coal-mining when visiting mines in West Virginia as he campaigned there in 1960," and how the "searing experience colored not only his candidacy but later his presidency," as he dealt with matters of poverty and public health.[64] Other campaign participants learn as much. Here is Witcover himself, coming to grips with the world beyond the press bus:

One night I went knocking on doors in a low-income neighborhood of Pittsburgh and came upon a middle-aged woman, her hair in curlers, looking at television. "Have you been watching the presidential debates?" I asked her.

"Oh, I watched a few minutes of the first one and then I turned it off," she said. "I don't want either of them influencing my vote. I want to make up my own mind.". . . It was frustrating to anyone who earned his livelihood following candidates around and trying to convey the substance of what they had to say to the electorate. So many Americans were not listening, and so many were listening but not believing.[65]

Campaigns do not always produce a change in the personnel of political institutions. In elections for the House of Representatives, for example, voters boot out fewer than one in ten incumbents after each campaign. But while the newspapers, radio, and television concentrate on who wins and who loses, political campaigns may leave their mark on American politics less by changing the officeholder's face than by influencing the officeholder's thinking—and the perceptions and behavior of challengers, activists, reporters, and others as well. In this important way, campaigning is a vital component of the linkage between political leaders and the public. By looking at campaigns as learning experiences, it is possible to observe that linkage from both sides: to see how the attitudes of constituents and other political actors affect elected officials, but also to see how the actions of those officials affect citizens' and groups' response to politics. Thus the political campaign, and the learning about policies and constituencies that occurs in campaigning, is central to, and in many ways inseparable from, the representative relationship.

SOCIAL-LEARNING THEORY AS A USEFUL GUIDE

To best understand this important learning process—the interaction of campaigners and their environments that we call the political campaign—we need a framework to guide us to the major questions. Because campaigning is an interactive process, we need an approach that permits us to examine those interactions systematically and productively. Many different frameworks have been used to gain insight into campaign behavior; some of them are considered in chapter 2.

This book argues that to examine the campaign as an interactive process, we can learn a great deal from a social-learning approach. Social-learning theory is capable of explaining not only campaigners' behavior, nor only the effects of the environmental changes discussed above, but the relationships among them. The theory is systematic; it is based on experimentation and clear reasoning. It deals with human learning and social behavior more generally, so it provides a set of ideas that can link the study of campaign behavior to that of other political processes. Learning frameworks have been used to illuminate the development of political attitudes and behavior in other settings.[66] Thus, in the chapters that follow, this book tries to show how the application of social-learning theory can give new insight into political campaigning.

The second chapter introduces the theory itself, with the help of political illustrations. Chapters 3 and 4 apply the theory to campaigners' behavior, specifying how campaign interactions would be expected to look, based on social-learning principles. The impact of party on campaigning is explored in chapter 5—why parties are variously seen as declining in influence, gaining strength, or simply irrelevant to campaigns, and how parties can have continuing impact.

Chapters 6 through 8 put the theory to work in a particularly interesting and informative context: the targeting of six senatorial campaigns by pro-life groups in 1980. Chapter 6 sets the stage, tracing the development of the abortion issue and presenting the cast of characters. Chapter 7 measures the behavior of the six pro-life groups against the social-learning predictions. In chapter 8 the analysis shifts to their senatorial quarry and examines the special character (and the impressive difficulties) of political learning in campaigns. And chapter 9 considers the implications of this view of campaigning as a learning process, for the nature of campaigns and the quality of representation in American politics. But let us begin by getting to know the guide.

NOTES

1. Jules Witcover, *Marathon* (New York: Viking, 1977), xi.
2. Quoted by Jimmy Breslin in *How the Good Guys Finally Won* (New York: Ballantine, 1975), 14.
3. For a discussion of public funding of campaigns, see Gary C. Jacobson's *Money in Congressional Elections* (New Haven: Yale University Press, 1980), chap. 7. Public funding does exist now for presidential campaigns as a result of the 1974 Federal Election Campaign Act Amendments, which are discussed below.
4. See Congressional Quarterly, *Watergate: Chronology of a Crisis* (Washington, D.C.: Congressional Quarterly, 1974), 2: 191-200.
5. See Jacobson, *Money in Congressional Elections,* chap. 6. Several states have also reformed their campaign finance laws.
6. See John H. Kessel, *Presidential Campaign Politics* (Homewood, Ill.: Dorsey, 1980), 116-17.
7. See Gerald Pomper et al., *The Election of 1980: Reports and Interpretations* (Chatham, N.J.: Chatham House, 1981), 5-6.
8. A major reason is that presidential candidates who accept federal funding in the general election are barred from receiving any other funds.
9. See Larry Light, "The Game of PAC Targeting: Friends, Foes and Guesswork," *Congressional Quarterly Weekly Report* 39 (21 November 1981): 2267-68.

10. Federal Election Commission data.
11. Ibid.
12. Quoted in E.J. Dionne, Jr., "On the Trail of Corporation Donations," *New York Times,* 6 October 1980.
13. Ibid.
14. See Jacobson, *Money in Congressional Elections,* 82.
15. "Political Groups Raised $131 Million in 1980," *Bloomington Herald Times,* Sunday, 21 February 1982, A6.
16. See Jeremy Gaunt, "Money Flows to the Right in 1982 Campaign," *Congressional Quarterly Weekly Report* 40 (27 February 1982): 482. Note, however, that corporate PACs in 1980 and 1982 continued to give one-third of their dollars to Democrats.
17. See Jacobson, *Money in Congressional Elections,* 77-83.
18. In *Buckley* v. *Valeo,* 424 U.S. 1 (1976).
19. An example is the analysis by Larry Light, "Surge in Independent Campaign Spending," *Congressional Quarterly Weekly Report* 38 (14 June 1980): 1635-39.
20. Undated fund-raising letter, National Conservative Political Action Committee.
21. Peter Goldman with Howard Fineman, "The War of the Wolf PACs," *Newsweek,* 1 June 1981, 38.
22. James M. Perry, "Liberal Incumbents Are Main Targets of TV Ads as Political-Action Groups Exploit Court Ruling," *Wall Street Journal,* 25 January 1980.
23. Quoted in Bernard Weinraub, "Million-Dollar Drive Aims to Oust Five Liberal Senators," *New York Times,* 24 March 1980, B5.
24. Some of this money was earmarked for negative campaigning too, often with NCPAC as the featured villain. The response by NCPAC's Dolan must have made many NCPAC targets smile; the liberal groups' ads, he protested, were "the most vitriolic, vicious, mean, untrue stuff I've ever seen." Goldman, "The War of the Wolf PACs," 38.
25. Jeremy Gaunt, "Senators' Fund Raising: Millions for Self-Defense," *Congressional Quarterly Weekly Report* 40 (13 February 1982): 278.
26. All quotations in this chapter that are not otherwise attributed come from personal interviews by the author.
27. For a provocative explanation, see Theodore J. Lowi, *The End of Liberalism,* 2nd ed. (New York: Norton, 1979).
28. As we see in chapters 6 and 7.
29. This argument is elaborated in Marjorie Randon Hershey and Darrell M. West, "Single-Issue Politics: Prolife Groups and the 1980 Senate Campaign," in *Interest Group Politics,* ed. Allan J. Cigler and Burdett A. Loomis (Washington, D.C.: Congressional Quarterly, 1983), 31-59.
30. Quoted in Elizabeth Drew, *Senator* (New York: Simon & Schuster, 1979), 113.
31. In Tom Mathews et al., "Single-Issue Politics," *Newsweek,* 6 November 1978, 54.
32. Richard Viguerie, quoted in Leslie Bennetts, "Conservatives Join on Social Concerns," *New York Times,* 31 July 1980, A1ff.
33. See Bill Keller, "Evangelical Conservatives Move from Pews to Polls, But Can They Sway Congress?" *Congressional Quarterly Weekly Report* 38 (6 September 1980): 2627-34.
34. Quoted in Bill Moyers' Journal, "Campaign Report no. 3," transcript, 26 September 1980, 10.

35. James L. Guth, "The Politics of the 'Evangelical Right': An Interpretive Essay" (paper presented at the annual meeting of the American Political Science Association, New York, 1981), 6.
36. Quoted in Keller, "Evangelical Conservatives," 2631 and 2630.
37. Ibid., 2631.
38. Quoted in Lisa Myers, "Falwell a Political Kingmaker," *Bloomington Herald-Telephone,* 11 July 1980, 4.
39. Keller, "Evangelical Conservatives," 2630. The New Christian Right has no monopoly on the political uses of morality, of course; many other groups, including liberal groups, have been defining their political preferences as "morally correct" for years.
40. Ibid., 2627.
41. Richard Viguerie, *The New Right: We're Ready to Lead,* rev. ed. (Falls Church, Va.: Viguerie Company, 1981), 154.
42. See Everett Carll Ladd, *Where Have All the Voters Gone?* 2nd ed. (New York: Norton, 1982), 99-100.
43. Richard Viguerie, in an interview with Darrell West, 9 September 1980.
44. See Kessel, *Presidential Campaign Politics,* 115.
45. Moyers, "Campaign Report no. 3," 3.
46. Ibid.
47. Background memorandum prepared by the McGovern Campaign Committee, July 1980, 3.
48. West, interview with Viguerie.
49. See especially David L. Paletz and Robert M. Entman, *Media—Power—Politics* (New York: Free Press, 1981).
50. Ibid., chap. 3.
51. See Thomas E. Patterson, *The Mass Media Election* (New York: Praeger, 1980), chap. 3.
52. The term is Joel Swerdlow's in "The Decline of the Boys on the Bus," *Washington Journalism Review* 3 (January/February 1981): 14-19.
53. Norman H. Nie et al., *The Changing American Voter,* enlarged ed. (Cambridge, Mass.: Harvard University Press, 1979), chap. 4.
54. See Martin P. Wattenberg, "The Decline of Political Partisanship in the United States: Negativity or Neutrality?" *American Political Science Review* 75 (December 1981): 941-50. In the words of one reporter, "It's not that people have become less political. Possibly, they have become more political. But their political energies increasingly do not find expression inside the parties." Robert J. Samuelson, "Fragmentation and Uncertainty Litter the Political Landscape," *National Journal,* 20 October 1979, 1731.
55. This position is developed by Everett Ladd in "The New Lines Are Drawn," *Public Opinion* 1 (July/August 1978): 48-53.
56. Allan J. Mayer et al., "End of the Democratic Era?" *Newsweek,* 18 August 1980, 22.
57. See Austin Ranney, "The Political Parties: Reform and Decline," in *The New American Political System,* ed. Anthony King (Washington, D.C.: American Enterprise Institute, 1978); and Ranney, *Curing the Mischiefs of Faction* (Berkeley: University of California Press, 1975).
58. This latter rule was substantially relaxed in time for the 1984 Democratic conven-

tion. See Rhodes Cook, "Democrats' Rules Weaken Representation," *Congressional Quarterly Weekly Report* 40 (3 April 1982): 749.
59. Quoted in Mayer et al., "End of the Democratic Era?" 22.
60. See Ranney, "Political Parties," 218 (for 1968), and Pomper et al., *The Election of 1980*, 2 (for 1980). In 1984 the Republicans scheduled 35 primaries but the Democrats scaled back to 26 (which still elected about two-thirds of the Democratic delegates).
61. David S. Broder, "Parties in Trouble," *Today*, 11 May 1979, 10-11.
62. See, for example, his *Home Style* (Boston: Little, Brown, 1978), chaps. 3-5.
63. For the advantage this gives House members, see Jacobson, *Money in Congressional Elections*, 145-46.
64. In *Marathon*, 209.
65. Ibid., 609.
66. An especially good example is Paul M. Sniderman, *Personality and Democratic Politics* (Berkeley: University of California Press, 1975).

2. Social-Learning Theory as a Guide

Our aim is to understand campaigners' behavior. But campaigns are rich in variety and detail; observers of a single election year might meet with thousands of interesting events, anecdotes, election results, bits of information about the personal lives of candidates, and life histories of political issues. Some of these pieces of information can illuminate the campaign process; others only clutter the observer's path without teaching anything of real value. Anyone who enters this morass of fascinating events without a guide—a means of concentrating attention on the most relevant information—will leave it in confusion.

That guide is a theory. Theories help expand our understanding by telling us where to look and what to look for.[1] A theory should provide three things. First, it makes certain assumptions about the area under study, assumptions about the way people behave in campaigns, for example. Second, it specifies how the assumptions and elements of the theory—its concepts, or terms—relate to one another. Third, a theory tells how it can be tested: how the important concepts and variables can be measured in the real world. Those measures enable us to compare what the theory *says* should happen with what *does* happen. Armed with these tools, we should be able to make sense out of what we already know about campaigning. And we should be able to go beyond what we now know to gain new insight into the nature of the beast.

Any theory directs our attention to some ideas and events and away from others; that is its job. The result is that the choice of a theory is important, since it will have a major effect on what we find. That choice is not dictated by the data—the facts we have about campaigning. The same data—that House incumbents tend to stress their experience and seniority when campaigning, rather than their stands on particular issues, for example—can be explained by any of several different theories. So in choosing a theoretical approach, a researcher is "exercising a free creative choice that is different from the artist's only in the kinds of evidence upon which it focuses and the grounds upon which its fruitfulness will be judged."[2]

Because theories are designed to narrow and define the focus of an investigation, the choice of theory can be made by asking some important questions.

What does a given theory lead us to focus upon? What kinds of questions about political campaigns does it prompt us to ask, and which would we be led to ignore? If we ask those particular questions, in what ways will our understanding of campaigners' behavior be enhanced? Let us look briefly at some options.

Several kinds of theories would encourage us to explain campaign behavior by looking inside the minds of candidates and other activists: to examine their motivations and ways of looking at the world. Take, for example, psychoanalytic theories.[3] With their guidance, we would be led to assume that people's behavior is driven by the mechanisms of their unconscious mind: the needs, conflicts, and impulses that operate beneath the surface of their awareness. These drives and motivations are assumed to derive from an individual's earliest experiences and relationships, and so we would focus our attention on the candidate's childhood and try to unlock the secrets of his or her personality. Alternatively, one of the many kinds of cognitive theories might be our guide; in that case, we would focus on the mental or psychological structures that affect people's views of their world. Depending on the particular theory selected, we might be drawn to investigate the ways candidates selectively perceive reality in order to satisfy their needs, or the accuracy of their beliefs about voters, or the level of consistency in their beliefs.

With these theories as guides, and especially in the case of psychoanalytic theories, we would not be led to examine the realities of the campaign environment in much detail. The rules under which primaries are held, the effects of single-issue group targeting or campaign finance reforms — these political realities would not take a very prominent place on the research agenda, except as they are perceived by people in campaigns.

On the other hand, some theoretical approaches would fix our attention on the campaign environment much more than on the individual campaigner. By using role theory we would expect to see candidates' behavior as reflections of one or more roles, or sets of expectations attached to a given social position.[4] Relevant questions would be these: What role(s) is the candidate playing (party loyalist, "delegate" or "trustee," issue advocate)? How clear are the expectations attached to the roles? Are they in conflict? Does he or she have the skills that are demanded by each role? Or we could eliminate the trouble of dealing with candidates' attitudes and beliefs altogether by using a behaviorist approach.[5] In that case we would explore the contingencies of the environment and the candidate's internal physiological states, on the assumption that the two together accounted for his or her behavior.

Each of these theories could provide some intriguing explanations of campaigners' behavior. But none of them really meets the need discussed in chapter 1: to focus on the interaction between the candidate's beliefs, experiences, and behavior, on the one hand, and the nature of the situation (or environment) on the other. We need a theory that allows for reciprocal influence—one through whose lenses we can see how single-issue politics affects candidates' behavior, for example, and also how candidates' behavior influences the action of single-issue groups.

Rational-choice theories could serve our purpose in some ways; this set of approaches has given rise to many fruitful analyses of politics.[6] Rational-choice models apply economic reasoning to situations such as those in campaigns; they assume that people's behavior is based on a rational calculation of self-interest in which individuals will normally try to maximize their expected gain. In the world of rational choice, people must be capable of calculating which of the possible courses of action will enable them to reach their goal. And it is assumed that they act so as to maximize their chance of achieving that goal—to increase their expected benefits and minimize their costs.

These theories do focus on the interaction between candidates' choices and the alternatives provided by their environment. But the theories' assumptions about people's knowledge—about levels of information—put us in a predicament. Information is often a scarce commodity in campaigns. Early in a race, for example, a candidate may not even know the identity of the opponent-to-be, much less the circumstances in which the campaign will be run. And there are internal limitations on information gathering. As one theorist puts it,[7] people's capacity for formulating and solving problems is much smaller than the problems that need to be solved. There are limits on the amount of information most people can get and retain. When making choices, people usually consider only a subset of all the possible alternatives that are open to them. The situation at the time will probably call attention to some alternatives and obscure others.

These limitations on rationality are often more interesting, in terms of what they tell us about campaigners' behavior and the nature of campaigns and elections, than the processes that many rational-choice theorists would have us examine. Some derivations of rational-choice theories—called theories of "bounded rationality"—address these limits on individual choice. In the ways they do so, the most effective of these could more appropriately be called learning theories.[8]

There are many different strands of learning theories, each focusing on the way behavior develops and changes. The efforts of theorists such as Albert Bandura to account for the richness and complexities of human behavior have produced *social*-learning theory.[9] Like the recent trend toward "contextual analysis" in the study of politics,[10] social-learning theory directs our attention to the fact that individual actions take place within a setting. That setting, or environment, includes the many things that impinge on the individual's actions and thoughts: in a campaign, for example, the health of the economy, the local media and interest groups, the opponent's campaign, and so on. Very often, some event in that environment impinges directly on a campaigner. Perhaps the other candidate announces, "My opponent in this election has accepted contributions from dozens of self-serving, vote-buying private interests." And the campaigner responds. The response may be only a thought—or an epithet. It may be a plan, a strategy designed to refute the charge at a later time. It may be an action: a verbal rebuttal or a change in a television ad about to be put on the air.

That response has consequences; newspaper editorials may react to it, political activists will probably express their opinions about it. From those consequences, the candidate draws some ideas: expectations about the effectiveness of his or her response, about the relationship between action and outcome in that situation. The development of those ideas, as a result of the interaction of candidate and environment, is an instance of learning.

This brings us to the basic assumption of social-learning theory: people's behavior is acquired largely through such interaction—in short, behavior is learned. People's strategies of dealing with events are not innate or determined only by forces within themselves. Nor is their behavior completely at the mercy of environmental controls. Rather, people's behavior is the result of a continuous interaction, in which events in the environment, the individual's understanding and expectations about those events, and his or her previous experiences and current behavior all act as interlocking determinants of one another.

Keep in mind that this is a somewhat different picture of "learning" than the word itself may often convey. We frequently think of "learning" as a fairly specialized process that takes place in a school or some other formal setting, in which the result is to become more skilled in meeting certain technical or social demands. But in the sense that behavior occurs in interaction with other personal and environmental factors, learning is a continuous process that is basic to people's very survival. The development of skills through learning, while a happy prospect, is not inevitable; people's strategies interact with environmental forces, but there is no guarantee that those strategies become more and more appropriate over time.

People's behavior can be acquired through their direct experience. In addition, a great deal of people's behavior is learned vicariously through observing the experiences of others and the results that their actions and strategies produce. But the process is much richer and more elaborate than these simple statements suggest. Any new environmental event takes its place in the long line of the individual's past experiences; its impact will depend in part on his or her earlier learning. Further, environmental events rarely make solo appearances; people's behavior is affected by, and affects, many different kinds of events at the same time. And through processes of learning, people acquire their own internal standards of behavior, which can then become prompts for their thoughts and actions. So the theory sees campaigners (and other people) as influenced by environmental events and contingencies, but also capable of self-regulation and actions that can change their environments.[11]

With these assumptions in hand, let us explore the processes by which learning occurs, with special attention to that group of learners called campaigners. These processes of learning differ from one another in several ways: in terms of the type of event involved, the nature of the component processes, and the role of "response consequences."

LEARNING FROM RESPONSE CONSEQUENCES

In the more rudimentary process of learning, people adapt their behavior by learning from the results—the response consequences, or reinforcements—that their actions produce. As Bandura writes, "behavior is, in fact, extensively regulated by its consequences."[12] When people act, some of their actions bring positive results for them, other actions have no impact, and still others lead to unpleasant or unwanted consequences. As a result of this experience with actions and results, people come to anticipate which strategies are likely to work in a given situation and which are likely to fail.

Response consequences play two main roles in this learning process. First, they provide information. When people see the results of an action, they know more about what to anticipate: which actions are most likely to be appropriate and effective in which settings.

Second, response consequences are motivators. People's experiences with rewarding and unpleasant outcomes lead them to envision certain benefits (or troubles) in return for certain actions. Those expectations—that a campaign fund raiser featuring a well-known rock group will bring in a lot of money, for example—provide the inducement to act in that particular way and sustain the incentive for that action.

In these ways, learning from response consequences allows—even encourages—people to anticipate the results of their future actions and behave accordingly. If a presidential candidate grants an interview with *Playboy*, makes some offhand remarks about lust and politics, and finds himself roundly criticized in pulpits and editorial pages throughout the country, he has an opportunity for learning. The response consequence has information value: it teaches that many people demand more discretion in a political candidate (especially with regard to sex and marriage) than they might ask of themselves. And it has motivating value: it stimulates the candidate to avoid a repetition by staying away from similar opportunities in the future.

The essential mediator in this process is the individual's awareness and understanding. People are not "controlled" in some mechanical way by the consequences of their actions. Instead, people's awareness of the effects of their behavior makes several things possible. They can develop ideas about how to get the results they want, test those ideas with further action, and use the acquired information to guide their future behavior in similar situations.[13]

In fact, the vital role of beliefs and expectations in this kind of learning can be shown convincingly in cases where expectations differ from results, where people are misinformed about the effects of their actions. Experiments have been performed in which people were told they would receive rewards on a given schedule (a unit of reward for every three items they produced, for instance) but actually were rewarded on a different schedule (say, a reward every five minutes, regardless of how much they produced). The results were instructive: people responded according to the way they had been *told* they would be rewarded, not according to their actual experience with the rate of reward.[14] Over time, of course, most people in this kind of situation come to realize that their expectations about response consequences are not coming true. But there are other circumstances in which people's beliefs do not necessarily become more accurate. Sometimes people hold unrealistic expectations because they have been given false information; consider the case of citizens who have been misled by their government into believing that another nation's activities are threatening world peace.[15] Sometimes people develop inaccurate expectations simply because they have paid only partial attention to events. In any case, in the process of learning from response consequences, the beliefs people derive from their experiences—even when those beliefs are wrong—are the mediators.

OBSERVATIONAL LEARNING

Learning would be a very long, error-ridden, even life-threatening process if we had only the results of our own experiences to rely on. Imagine the consequences if people could become brain surgeons (or, perhaps more important, auto mechanics) only by taking an action and then seeing what happened. Social-learning theory posits a second learning process: people can learn behaviors simply by watching others perform them, or by reading or hearing about them, independent of the results those behaviors may produce.

In observational learning (or vicarious learning, or modeling), people watch, read, or hear about the behavior of others—their actions, their words, their feelings and strategies—and form an image in their minds of how that behavior is performed. On later occasions, those images can guide the observer's own actions. As Bandura points out, almost anything that can be learned from direct experience can also be learned by observing other people's behavior.[16]

Modeling (and note that this includes much direct teaching, or instruction) is a very economical means of learning, especially in the case of complex behaviors. It allows people to acquire whole patterns of behavior quickly and effectively, rather than have to develop them gradually through trial and error. It opens people's minds to many more alternatives than they would find in their personal experiences; television alone, for example, is a gargantuan storehouse of models, a massive opportunity for observational learning.

Modeling is vitally important to campaigners. Candidates learn what issue appeals are effective by watching other candidates experiment with them. Consultants sell themselves as transmitters of models of winning campaign strategies. Political parties set up "schools" for campaigners, teaching everything from precinct targeting to recommendations on the color and length of the candidate's sox.

Four processes constitute observational learning: attention, retention, motor reproduction, and motivation. Response consequences play a role in each of them, but observational learning (in contrast to the process of learning from response consequences) can take place without any reinforcement to either the observer or the model. Here are the steps:

Attention. First, the observer's (let's say a candidate's) attention must be drawn to the model's behavior. A number of factors make this more likely. Some behaviors capture people's attention simply because they are distinctive, or because friends and associates call attention to an action or idea. Some get people's attention because they are so prevalent; a number of advertising or campaign slogans and comedians' catch phrases, no matter how inane ("Excu*uuuu*se me!"), are learned because it is so hard to escape noticing them.

There are other ways in which our environment draws our attention to certain behaviors and thus makes them "available" as models. The actions and expressions of the people we spend the most time with—friends, family members, co-workers—are particularly available to us. We have more chances to observe these behaviors, to see how their component parts fit together, to form a detailed representation of them in our minds. It would be easier for a candidate to learn the fine points of responding to a labor union's demands if he or she had grown up in a neighborhood of steelworkers, where union activists gathered every Sunday in the family's kitchen to talk shop, than if the candidate had never known any union members nor ever been inside an industrial plant.

People's attention is drawn to behaviors that seem to produce effective results; here is the first way in which response consequences can affect observational learning. But in a number of social situations, particularly that of a political campaign (as I argue later), the consequences of a model's behavior may not be visible for some time, or the nature of the relationship between an action and a later result may be open to question. In those cases, observers will look for cues, for characteristics of a model that may predict whether his or her behavior will be effective, or for evidence that the model's actions have brought good results in the past. A reputation for effectiveness, personal prestige, political power, signs of expertise, past successes—all these can act as indicators that a model's current behavior will prove to be effective as well. Models who are attractive or engaging will capture more attention, partly because of the suspicion that attractive people are more successful, and partly because they are easier to watch. Characteristics of the observer matter too; people's levels of interest, emotion, self-esteem, and even their visual skills affect their ability to pay attention to events around them.

Retention. Creating an image of a behavior in our mind, which allows us to "see" that behavior even after it is no longer present, is the heart of observational learning. It is a vital ability; it permits us to expand our environment within our minds, through the use of symbols, and to "try out" a new plan or strategy without yet taking any real risk.

People mentally retain the behaviors of models in coded form. Some of these behaviors are filed away as visual images (as when a campaign manager can "see in his mind" another candidate showing a particularly dramatic photo of a dangerous chemical dump site to bring home a point in a speech). More often, people code the behaviors of models in verbal form—remember the instructions for carrying out a particular behavior. A candidate might recall, for example, the way that challenger Ronald Reagan gained what was widely acknowledged to be the upper hand in the second 1980 presidential debate with this powerful closing statement:

> I think when you make that [voting] decision, it might be well if you would ask yourself, are you better off than you were four years ago? Is it easier for you to go and buy things in the stores than it was four years ago? Is there more or less unemployment in the country than there was four years ago? Is America as respected throughout the world as it was? . . . And if you answer all of those questions yes, why then, I think your choice is very obvious as to whom you will vote for. If you don't agree, if you don't think that this course that we've been on for the last four years is what you would like to see us follow for the next four, then I could suggest another choice that you have.[17]

Understandably, people are more likely to code and remember an *effective* behavior; all other things equal, a winning strategy is more memorable than one whose impact is unclear. But the results of a model's behavior are not the only important factor. People are more likely to retain a behavior if they can rehearse it mentally or actually practice it (as they might, for example, in a party's "campaign school"). Retention increases if the model's actions are likened to behaviors that are already familiar and meaningful to the observer. A candidate who has often done door-to-door campaigning is more likely to retain an image of a new twist on that practice than is a candidate who prefers to talk to television cameras.

Motor reproduction. In this third step, the individual converts those images of a model's behavior into his or her own actions. Some circumstances make this process easier than others. Imitating another candidate's behavior is more likely, and probably more effective, if the observer has already mastered its component skills. It would be hard to model President Reagan's effective manner of speech making, for instance, if a candidate had not already learned how to appear in front of the cameras without going into a panic. In turn, learning is enhanced if the candidate has had the chance to see and code each component part of the model's strategy. If some parts of that strategy are not visible or "available," such as the way President Reagan prepares mentally for a speech, then it will be harder for the candidate to learn and use that strategy effectively.

This process of converting a model's behavior into action normally requires some refining. A new candidate rarely transforms into a polished "communicator" overnight. This step in modeling, if it is to be successful, needs feedback: information about the strengths and weaknesses of the performance, attempts to improve it, and often a bit of remedial looking at the model.

Motivation. By now we have crossed an important conceptual line. There is a difference between the *learning* of a strategy and its *performance*. Attention and retention are part of the learning process; they give us a mental image of the strategy. But whether or not we perform, or act on, that strategy is a separate step, governed mainly by the strategy's expected results.

People *learn* a lot of what they see; campaigners watch other candidates' ads, listen to campaign consultants' ideas, and code much of that information in their minds. People *learn* behaviors and strategies whether or not they are rewarded for doing so, and whether or not they believe the model's behaviors would work for them. The result is that people learn many more strategies than they actually use.[18] Some of those learned strategies may be too difficult for the learner to perform, or too risky. Other learned behaviors may go unused simply because the learners never find themselves in a situation to which the behavior seems to apply. A lot of candidates who are football fans have watched and coded the action of a defensive back tackling a ball carrier, and some may even be physically capable of translating the image into a performance. But very few candidates ever find themselves in circumstances where such action is tolerated, much less encouraged.

Of the many things a candidate learns from models, then, which will he or she actually use? We have seen that the expected results of a strategy affect people's learning; the better the expected results, the more likely people are to pay attention to that strategy and retain it in their memories. The expected results play an even more important role in the *performance* of a strategy: they regulate the use of learned behaviors. People are more inclined to use a model's behavior if they believe it will bring them good results (especially in money or votes) or if it meets their standards for "self-reward" (more on this later).

WHAT OBSERVATIONAL LEARNING TEACHES

The modeling process has a profound influence on all sorts of political behavior. A particular approach to a tricky problem (say, a nuclear freeze as an answer to the perilous arms race) is tested in speeches by one or more public officials and then spreads rapidly among certain candidates and consultants. A leader of a pro-life group, frustrated with the Democratic party's pro-choice stance on abortion, changes her registration to Republican; soon many of her friends in that group follow suit. Unemployment among the inner-city poor has been threateningly high for years; early one summer the central core of one large city explodes in riots, and within days several similar cities are on fire. All these events are examples of the spread of observationally learned behaviors.

Above all, observational learning provides information on how behaviors can be used, and how they can be combined and tailored to produce new strategies. It does so in several ways. The observation of models can strengthen or weaken inhibitions on behavior that the observer has already learned. Consider a hypothetical member of Congress who has been caught accepting bribe money from an FBI agent disguised as an Arab sheik. At best, the congressman is in an awkward position; his enthusiastic receipt of the money has been captured on color film (without his knowledge, of course), and he is up for re-election in two months. Denial does not look like a promising strategy.

Instead, he buys television time for a kind of confessional. He was ill with alcoholism, he says, and sincerely believed at the time that he was helping U.S. foreign policy. He takes full responsibility for his crime, he says, though it was actually due to his illness. He has been humbled, he says; rather than take the easy way out and resign, he will lay his soul and his long record of pork-barrel projects before the ultimate judge: the voters. Public opinion polls taken after this performance show that the congressman's steady drop in voter approval has been halted. His poll ratings begin to rise, especially after some newspaper editorials applaud either his frankness or his chutzpah.

Two of his congressional colleagues, similarly nailed by the FBI, are watching carefully. They *learned* his strategy immediately; his televised confessional was compelling. At the time, neither would have dreamed of making such a confession; their experience had impelled against it. But seeing the positive media and poll responses to his performance, they reconsidered. The model's behavior, and the results it produced, weakened his colleagues' inhibitions against confessing their own guilt. (If the model had been condemned by the media and ridiculed by voters, however, observational learning would have strengthened his colleagues' inhibitions against confessing.[19])

Modeling can also trigger the use of a socially accepted response that the observer has already learned. Most candidates, for example, are familiar with the use of billboard advertising in campaigns; the technique has its partisans and its doubters. When one candidate sees the opposition investing heavily in billboards, very often he or she will be prompted to do the same. This process of copycat strategizing is common to campaigns because it is so hard to be sure which campaign techniques are effective and which are not; the opponent's use of a given technique can make campaigners wonder whether it might not be more effective in swaying voters than they had thought.

Two other kinds of modeling influences are at least as important in campaigns. One, abstract modeling, gives the campaigner a basis for applying modeled ideas to new situations. The other, innovation and invention through modeling, lets us see how the collection of political campaigns in many different areas, and through time, becomes a system through which strategies and issue appeals travel.

ABSTRACT MODELING: LEARNING THE RULES OF BEHAVIOR

Observational learning is much more than the simple imitation of someone else's behavior. People can also learn the "rules" that underlie certain responses made by other people. For example, an ambitious young lawyer observes several press conferences given by a popular state legislator. What, the lawyer wonders, makes that legislator such a successful candidate? The lawyer finds that the legislator's responses to questions have certain features in common: the use of self-deprecating humor, direct answers that are easily quotable, and a solicitous concern for deadlines and the comfort of the reporters present. Having come to understand these "rules" that structure the legislator's performance, the lawyer can then apply this learning to her own aspirations. If she later runs for city council, she has the model of a successful style to guide her. In this very important way, people's observational learning can be utilized in new situations—circumstances different from the model's. The learning, then, can be generalized.[20]

MODELING, INNOVATION, AND INVENTION

Through observational learning, people can expand their range of responses, ideas, and strategies. Interestingly, people can also devise entirely new strategies from watching models.

An innovation, according to a massive body of research, is something that the individual has not done before, though other people may have done it; in short, innovation is "an idea, practice, or object perceived as new *by an individual.*"[21] Observational learning can be seen, then, as the learning of innovation. One candidate sees another using a strategy that seems effective, and tries it. A consultant notices both candidates using the strategy to their advantage and starts recommending it to other campaigners who face similar problems. As a succession of campaigners learn and use that strategy—from observing one another, from reading about it in a party's campaign manual, from seeing it on television—the process called "diffusion of innovation" takes place.

A great deal of theorizing and research has been done on the diffusion of innovations and on an analogous process in which legislators take their cues from trusted legislative colleagues on policy matters.[22] The findings of both sets of literature parallel those of social-learning researchers on modeling; the commonalities suggest that observational learning is a "core" behavior not only in campaigning but in other political and social activities as well. Thus in the coming chapters we can bring this long investigative tradition to bear on the study of campaigns.

By examining observational learning in campaigns, we can see how a new issue catches fire in national politics. We can see, for example, how the call for a "school prayer" amendment—a constitutional amendment to allow voluntary prayer in the public schools—moves from church group meetings to the campaigns of sympathetic candidates to a spot on the nightly news. We can find out what happens to that issue when its proponents win elections, and what happens to the issue when they lose. Most important, we can see how this process of diffusion affects the making of policy, how it puts some issues on Congress's and the President's agendas and lets others fade.

Modeling can account not only for the adoption of strategies that are new to the individual but strategies that are new altogether—for the invention of new directions in campaigning or policy. In campaign environments, as well as in families and other settings, people usually have many potential models. Each model has a repertoire of behaviors and strategies. The usual tendency is for an observer to watch and learn from several of those models: to learn some features of one person's behavior, others of a second model, and so on. In acting, the individual can put together combinations of those features, and the resulting pattern is likely to be different from that of any of its sources.

This can often be seen in families, when two children have developed very different styles of behavior as the result of observing and modeling different combinations of features of their parents' and close relatives' actions and attitudes.[23]

For that reason, the amount of variety present among the available models can make a difference in the amount of inventive behavior to be seen in a community or set of campaigns. If the established candidates in an area all follow the same standard approaches to electioneering, then observational learning by new candidates might produce an impressive amount of continuity in political campaigning in that area over time. But when the potential models are a very diverse group, the campaigners-in-training will have more opportunities to develop inventive combinations of strategies. Similarly, the more heterogeneous big cities tend to serve as incubators for more new directions in political activity, art and architecture, and even styles of clothing and personal behavior than do smaller, more homogeneous areas where the available models are more alike. Yet even in those smaller areas, the possibilities for invention have been greatly increased by the reach of mass media. Symbolic models such as television and films offer a tremendous variety of models to people and attract people's attention very effectively; even in remote, culturally homogeneous communities, candidates (and other people) have had their opportunities to learn innovative ideas greatly expanded by television.

In sum, people acquire new behaviors and strategies through two processes: learning from response consequences and observational learning. One process rests on direct personal experience, the other on vicarious experience. The results of an action are clearly the regulators of behavior in the first process; they must share the spotlight in the second. The two processes have different components. But whether people learn from the results of their actions or from the behavior of models, that learning provides information, generates expectations, and produces motivations that serve as the basis for future behavior. From these learning principles, several other important concepts of social-learning theory are derived. One of these is the learning of relationships—the concept of contingency-learning.

CONTINGENCY-LEARNING

In campaigning as in other kinds of behavior, it is enormously helpful to be able to anticipate what's coming—to be able to predict that a particular action will be followed by a particular result, or that when event *A* occurs, event *B* cannot be far behind. For instance, if a presidential challenger understands that an incumbent President almost always rises in public support after a crisis in foreign policy erupts,[24] then he or she has a better chance of dealing effectively with that event.

This contingency-learning can take place through either of the two learning processes discussed above. As a result of their experiences with actions and results, people can come to predict what will happen if they behave a certain way. A Senate candidate who consistently draws more applause for her stands on social issues than for her economic or defense proposals will come to expect those differential results, and will plan accordingly. But people can also become aware of these patterns through vicarious learning. A consultant observes the effectiveness of social issues in the Senate campaign and recommends that strategy to other candidate-clients in similar circumstances.[25] Or campaign staffers notice that whenever a particular *Washington Post* reporter leads with new details about a race, those details are picked up and repeated quickly by other press and television news people; but when a story breaks first in any of several other newspapers, it may get no wider notice. The political value of this learning is tremendous; when the campaign has information that it wants distributed to the largest possible audience, it knows which journalist holds the key to those hopes.

The learning begins with regularities in the occurrence of environmental events; the regularities allow people to predict what will happen under given circumstances. But the regularities or paired experiences do not automatically become teachers; people are not likely to learn from paired events, and act on that knowledge, without first recognizing that the events are related. If someone gets information that those two events are *not* related—that they took place in sequence for a while, by chance, but will not do so anymore—then the link between them will probably be *un*learned. In other words, it is not merely the joint appearance of environmental events that accounts for the learning of these expectations, nor simply the individual's perceptions, but rather the interaction of the two.

A number of personal attributes can influence the meanings that people give to a set of events. People's past experiences, for example, can make them more attentive to certain cues and predispose them to certain explanations. Several people, all watching a campaign commercial that associates President Reagan's policies with an improving economy, may yet come away with very different beliefs about the nature of that link. Their partisanship and their economic experiences, among others, will surely affect their feelings as to whether any economic improvement is due to, or is taking place in spite of, Reagan's policies. Differences in people's levels of attention, retention of information, and even reasoning skills can lead them to develop different expectations from the same events.

Sometimes, people's attributes lead them to develop some very mistaken expectations. Think of the well-publicized occasions when some small religious cult has concluded that the world will end on a given date, a few months or years away. Frequently, the prediction has been based on the occurrence of several events that they interpret as biblical signs of the coming of Judgment Day. Their religious training motivated them to look for such signs and predisposed them to jump to an apocalyptic conclusion. Happily for the rest of us, the track record of such predictions has been very poor. But even if people have misperceived the relationships among events, we can still expect that they will act according to their perceptions; some cults have sold all their belongings and moved to some special spot to wait for the big day.

In the same sense, people may develop mistaken expectations about the relationship between their political behavior and its impact, and be guided by those expectations. Since most campaigns are times when information is scarce and emotional arousal is high—a situation not conducive to careful reasoning—campaigners are vulnerable to misperceptions, too. The kind of superstitious learning in which an incumbent continues to use the same campaign headquarters year after year, on the assumption that the building is somehow associated with winning elections, is not uncommon. So while contingency-learning is a vital guide to behavior, it is heavily affected by the individual's past experience, and by the quality and quantity of information available.

SYMBOLS AND GENERALIZATION

Clearly, none of these learning processes could take place without people's capacity for representing events in their minds, as symbols. Observational learning rests on the individual's ability to form mental representations of other people's actions and experiences, to retain those images for long periods of time, and to infuse them with the power to guide behavior at some later time when the events that prompted the learning are long past. Learning from response consequences would be an extremely limiting process if people could not conjure up images of the outcomes they expect and those they hope for, and explore the possible results of different strategies, all within their minds. Their ability to symbolize frees them from having to learn by bouncing off the immediate effects of their actions.

Further, the use of symbols lets people "generalize" their learning—apply it to situations they have not yet experienced, or even been told about. Recall that both learning processes described by the theory work mainly by providing information about the likely effects of different strategies used in various settings. By doing so, they enable people to develop expectations about the relationships between actions and results. These expectations can be applied to new situations. A good example of such generalization is the process of abstract modeling, discussed above; people extract the "rules" underlying a model's behavior in a particular situation and can then use those rules to act as the model would in a similar setting, even without having seen the model in that setting. Other kinds of learning can generalize to new situations too, once they have been given symbolic form in the learner's mind.

People's learning will generalize most readily to new situations that resemble those of the initial learning experience; the more similar the circumstances, the more readily the expectations apply. For example, imagine a Democratic activist in 1980 who has been thinking about running for senator at some later time. He sees several incumbent Democrats, most of them liberals like himself, go down to defeat in the 1980 campaigns; the prevailing explanation by reporters and consultants is that Democratic Senate candidates were swamped by the bad economy, the Reagan tide, and a set of election issues that cut heavily in favor of conservatives. In early 1981, it looks as though the 1982 elections will produce more of the same; President Reagan is doing well in the polls, and those conservative issues have not lost their hold. The activist generalizes what he had learned in 1980 — that those are not conditions in which a Democratic Senate candidate can expect to be rewarded at the polls — and decides against making the race in 1982.

But new information about the links between actions and results — or information suggesting that previously learned expectations will not apply to an upcoming situation — can quickly outweigh this generalized learning. Say, for instance, that the national political climate changes in late 1981 and early 1982. President Reagan's standing in the polls has taken a real dive. The Reagan cuts in social and environmental programs have begun to take effect, and their impact is resented by many traditional Democrats who cast Republican votes in 1980. Even interpretations of why Republicans won in 1980 have shifted; many analysts point out that several liberal Democratic senators held their seats despite the Reagan victory and that it was the more senior members of the Senate, regardless of party, who took the worst beating in that election.[26] Conditions have changed; indications are that the activist's learning in 1980 may not be applicable to 1982. Though the hour for beginning a candidacy is late, he takes the plunge and enters the 1982 primary for his state's Senate seat.[27]

With this new information, people can learn how to adapt their previous learning to changing situations. The results of their early efforts at adaptation tell them still more. The fact that conditions change does not necessarily mean that people will realize and respond to those changes. But with attentiveness to new information and with experience, people can become skilled at discriminating — at learning more and more subtle distinctions among settings and events, and at relating these distinctions to the results of various strategies. Thus, when we examine people's expectations and their behavior, we can expect to see an interplay between the results of their prior learning (the generalization of expectations) and the effects of new settings and new information, which provide the opportunity for discriminative learning.

SELF-REGULATION
People's ability to symbolize makes possible another learning process, one that is a vital part of social-learning theory. While response consequences are central to the theory, the consequences of people's actions do not come only from other people or influences. A given action will probably have internally produced consequences as well; people evaluate their *own* behavior, feel pleased with themselves when they live up to their own standards of conduct, and respond self-critically when they do not act as they think they should.[28]

Where do these personal standards come from? Like other aspects of behavior, standards of conduct are not born with the individual, nor are they entirely the product of his or her own mind, acting in isolation from others. A person's values and standards are learned, through the same principles that guide other behavior. Children learn standards for evaluating their actions in part through direct instruction; parents, teachers, and even many television programs spend a great deal of time telling their young charges which kinds of behavior are appropriate, in their view, and which are not. The first two of these sources can offer a lot of inducements to encourage conformity with their standards.[29] And children come to judge their actions in ways that echo this hail of instruction.

They also notice what the instructors do, as well as what they say. They notice the standards that other people use to reward themselves. If a model's own standards are praised by others and are applied consistently, if the model's abilities are not too different from the observer's (so the standards are not "out of reach"), then they are more likely to be adopted by an observer. Through abstract modeling, people learn these standards as "rules" that can be applied to behavior in other settings and at other times.

These rules affect people's behavior mainly as motivators. Once people have learned to set standards for their conduct, their success in meeting those standards makes a difference in their self-perception. That is a powerful inducement—so powerful that people often create more tangible incentives or set intermediate goals to spur themselves along. As Bandura points out, "there is no more devastating punishment than self-contempt."[30]

But if people's actions have self-generated as well as external consequences, which ones have more impact on their behavior? In many cases, the two sets of consequences point in the same direction; since people's standards for self-evaluation are learned, and since the models often are people close to the learner, the individual's personal standards and those of "significant others" will probably be very similar in many areas.

But upon becoming a political campaigner, an individual encounters people and groups that may apply different standards: editorial writers, interest groups, an opponent. Some, especially the opponent, may see benefits to themselves in making those differences public. Perhaps a candidate accepts a lot of money in campaign contributions from oil companies' Political Action Committees (PACs). The candidate believes those contributions to be perfectly proper; the oil industry, he argues, is entitled to take part in politics and to support qualified candidates, and his oil company contributors have all adhered to the letter of the campaign finance law. The opponent and several newspaper editorials disagree, charging that the candidate has become PACman, the willing captive of Big Oil. What does the candidate do?

The answer depends in large part on the relative strength of the two sets of response consequences in the individual's experience. If the candidate has long held the belief that private industries have a rightful role in campaigns, and especially if that belief has been rewarded by others, then the chances are that it will outweigh the opponent's criticisms. But if the candidate values winning above all else, and gets convincing information that those criticisms are costing him necessary votes, then his actions will probably be guided by the responses of the opposition and the editorial writers.[31]

Keep in mind, however, that people's personal standards, once developed, are not set in concrete; people can change their environment and be changed by it. A candidate who risks defeat in order to stand up for a principle, for example, affects other people's evaluations of themselves—perhaps even the opponent's.[32] Further, just as people can learn how to avoid harsh treatment from others, they can also learn how to avoid harsh treatment by their own conscience: how to duck their own censure.

Candidates might justify violating their standards by looking for evidence that someone else's violation was worse ("My opponent took twice as much money from Consumers' Union"), that the responsibility lies elsewhere ("My finance chairman took the money without my knowledge"), that the situation is ambiguous ("The Federal Election Commission doesn't regard that as a violation"), or that the behavior was in the service of a higher cause (as in the case of liberation groups that blow up inhabited buildings in the name of human rights).[33]

So the power of people's personal standards over their conduct is not unlimited. Bandura concludes, "a society cannot rely on control by conscience [alone] to ensure moral and ethical conduct."[34] Nevertheless, people's capacity to set standards for themselves—standards that may, in many situations, have even greater power over their behavior than external consequences can — plays a primary role in the direction of their actions.

INTERDEPENDENCE: "PERSON VARIABLES" AND
ENVIRONMENTAL VARIABLES

What social-learning theorists have built, then, is an intricate and dynamic structure. It is dynamic in the sense that it shows us a set of interdependent variables affecting one another over time: people's expectations, their behavior, and environmental forces.

And the key word is "interdependent." An environmental event is not an independent entity like a rock or a stone, which, if it becomes airborne in the direction of some unfortunate person, affects that person without being itself affected. For an event to influence people, they must first notice it; thus it is partly through "person variables" such as attention levels and learned patterns of interpreting events that portions of the environment come to affect people's behavior. For instance, on a given day in the 1984 campaigns, several events will occur: unemployment may fall a little, a new toxic waste emergency may arise, President Reagan may sign a bill in the Rose Garden. One candidate, who has gotten a lot of mileage out of economic issues before, will be watching for those new unemployment statistics and will lead off the evening's press conference with them. Another candidate, whose personal commitment to environmental protection is strong, is absorbed by the toxic waste story and devotes several hours to learning more about it; later she plans to call for a congressional hearing on the subject. A third candidate, preoccupied with finding out which staff member is leaking confidential campaign memos to the press, is completely unaware of all three events. Each of those events *might* potentially have affected all three campaigns; the campaigners' expectations and past experiences help to determine which environmental forces are *actually* activated, and what sorts of influences they can be. So the actual environment of a campaign — the influences affecting its actions — is to some extent created by the characteristics and behavior of the campaign itself.

In the same way, those "person variables" can be called into action by features of the situation. Consider an incumbent member of Congress who has won elections year after year with overwhelming margins, taking 70 percent of the vote or more. That margin becomes a reference standard, the result that he or she comes to expect. The current race again produces a victory, but this time by 51 percent; other party colleagues in similar districts have done much better. The newly humbled incumbent, though a winner, looks at the election result as a painful experience; his or her interest in effective campaign practices and expectations about future elections are profoundly affected.

While expectations, behavior, and events are interdependent, they do not necessarily have equal weight in a given instance. Some events have so powerful an impact that they leave little room for variation in people's expectations and behavior. Other situations are much more ambiguous; they put fewer limits on individual behavior, or they give the impression that any of several different strategies could bring acceptable results. In these less structured situations—deciding which issues to emphasize in a campaign, for example—"person variables" can play a greater role.[35]

Social-learning theory does not demand that every researcher study all the reciprocal influences at once. Asking how the Evangelical Right's "moral report cards" are affecting candidates' strategies is a fascinating question in itself, even without going on to ask how candidates' approaches to the situation are in turn affecting the political behavior of evangelical groups. But the theory does require us to acknowledge, in any study, that people's expectations, their behavior, and environmental events are interdependent. Each can influence the others.

Such a perspective gives us a valuable tool for understanding politics. For instance, consider the more complete view it provides of the representative process. Too often, researchers have looked at representation as a one-way avenue of influence; constituents have attitudes, and representatives respond to them. But the causal arrow points both ways. Just as constituents' attitudes are part of the representative's environment, so the actions of the representative are part of the constituents' environment; each can impinge upon the other. It is important to keep that reciprocal influence in mind, even if a researcher is interested only in the impact of public opinion on elected officials, because those officials' actions—the stands a senator takes on major issues, the casework done by a congressional office—can influence the kinds of cues that constituents direct at them.[36]

We have examined the main assumptions of social-learning theory, its concepts, and the relationships among them. The theory differs in several ways from others we might have used. It does not require us to assume that all behavior is goal-directed, nor that people necessarily act as utility maximizers. It is not a deterministic view of people, in the sense that deep-seated psychological needs *or* external forces have human behavior under their collective thumb. Central to social-learning theory is people's capacity for self-direction, for selecting and organizing information about events that affect them, for altering their environments. Yet the vital role ascribed to environmental events gives us the opportunity for a *political* theory of campaigners' behavior, rather than a psychological or cognitive theory—an approach in which political institutions and forces share center stage with people's expectations and behavior.

The theory directs our attention to the interaction between candidate and situation, rather than just the candidate alone. It leads us to ask questions like these: Where do new campaigners learn the strategies they will use in their first try for public office? What kinds of models do candidates study, and what determines the patterns by which issues and strategies move from campaign to campaign? Once the active phase of the race begins, what kinds of events affect those strategies? What response consequences does the race have to offer? How powerful is the election result—and campaigners' anticipation of it—in influencing their strategies? In short, what kind of learning situation is a campaign, and how does the nature and adequacy of that learning situation affect the central concerns of a democracy: representation, the making of public policy, the selection of good leaders? These are the concerns of the next two chapters.

NOTES

1. See Carl G. Hempel, "The Theoretician's Dilemma: A Study in the Logic of Theory Construction," in *Aspects of Scientific Explanation,* ed. Carl G. Hempel (New York: Free Press, 1965), 173-226.
2. Calvin S. Hall and Gardner Lindzey, *Theories of Personality,* 3rd ed. (New York: Wiley, 1978), 10.
3. For an application, see Harold D. Lasswell, *Psychopathology and Politics* (New York: Viking, 1960).
4. See Theodore R. Sarbin and Vernon L. Allen, "Role Theory," in *The Handbook of Social Psychology,* vol. 1, ed. Gardner Lindzey and Elliot Aronson, 2nd ed. (Reading, Mass: Addison-Wesley, 1968).
5. See B.F. Skinner, *About Behaviorism* (New York: Vintage, 1976).
6. A fine example is John F. Aldrich's *Before the Convention* (Chicago: University of Chicago Press, 1980).
7. Herbert A. Simon, *Models of Man* (New York: Wiley, 1957), 198.
8. "Bounded rationality" is the assumption that an individual's information-processing and decision-making capabilities are limited. People deal with complicated situations, then, by using "decision rules" or cognitive predispositions to simplify the range of possible choices to a manageable number. An example is Simon's "satisficing" model, which posits that people search only long enough to find a course of action that is "good enough," rather than the course of action that provides the maximum possible utility. See Simon, *Models of Man.*

    Simon's work leads researchers to ask about the premises people use to simplify and choose among the range of alternatives. These premises, he feels, derive from the individual's environment and training (ibid., 201). In other words, models of bounded rationality are centrally concerned with people's learning, as this chapter defines it. In fact, Simon's dynamic representation of his "satisficing" model (ibid., 255)—its concern with the payoffs for each trial in a sequence and the effects of earlier trials on later trials—looks very much like a learning model. As a result,

the predictions of these models have come increasingly to resemble those of social-learning theory, even though their intellectual origins are very different.
9. The most complete statement of Bandura's work is his *Social Learning Theory* (Englewood Cliffs, N.J.: Prentice-Hall, 1977). See also Bandura's "Behavior Theory and the Models of Man," *American Psychologist* 29 (December 1974): 859-69, in which he discusses the philosophical underpinnings of the theory, and "Analysis of Modeling Processes," in *Psychological Modeling: Conflicting Theories,* ed. Albert Bandura (Chicago: Aldine-Atherton, 1971), 1-62. Another helpful source is Walter Mischel, "Toward a Cognitive Social Learning Reconceptualization of Personality," *Psychological Review* 80, no. 4 (1973): 252-83, which emphasizes the role of cognitive processes in social learning.
10. "Contextual analysis" argues that researchers have too often analyzed people's attitudes in grand isolation from the influences of their environment: the attitudes of people's family members, neighbors and colleagues at work. See Adam Przeworski, "Contextual Models of Political Behavior," *Political Methodology* 1 (Winter 1974): 27-61. Recent studies of voting behavior such as Norman H. Nie et al., *The Changing American Voter,* enlarged ed. (Cambridge, Mass.: Harvard University Press, 1979), have also begun to take contextual variables more seriously, treating the vote as responsive (at least in part) to the stimuli (the clarity of candidates' policy stances, for instance) that campaigns offer.
11. For a fuller explanation of the theory's assumptions, see Bandura, *Social Learning Theory,* chaps. 1 and 2.
12. Ibid., 96.
13. Some researchers still argue that response consequences affect the behavior of people *directly:* in short, that people's actions will be influenced even if they are not aware of what is being rewarded or disapproved. But in most cases, especially in the case of complex behaviors like those found in political campaigns, it is not the simple existence of a rewarding or an unpleasant result that regulates behavior, but the information that the result brings: the circumstances in which an action brought benefits, the extent of the benefits, the likely conditions under which the same action will be rewarded again. See ibid., 19-21; and W.K. Estes, "Reinforcement in Human Behavior," *American Scientist* 60 (November-December 1972): 723-29.
14. See Bandura, *Social Learning Theory,* 165-67.
15. The writings of Murray Edelman (see especially *Political Language: Words That Succeed and Policies That Fail* [New York: Academic Press, 1977]) show the extent to which political authority depends on the manipulation of expectations.
16. On observational learning, see Bandura, *Social Learning Theory,* 22-29.
17. See *Congressional Quarterly Weekly Report* 38 (1 November 1980): 3289.
18. See Bandura, *Social Learning Theory,* 36-39. He notes: "After the capacity for observational learning has fully developed, one cannot keep people from learning what they have seen" (38).
19. Other factors would also bear on the impact of observational learning in this case, such as the congressional colleagues' standards of behavior and the value they place on newspaper editorials and public opinion polls as measures of their reelection chances. See ibid., 49-50 and 118-21.
20. See Barry J. Zimmerman and Ted L. Rosenthal, "Observational Learning of Rule-

Governed Behavior by Children," *Psychological Bulletin* 81 (1974): 29-42; and Bandura, *Social Learning Theory,* 40-42.
21. Everett M. Rogers with F. Floyd Shoemaker, *Communication of Innovations: A Cross-Cultural Approach,* 2nd ed. (New York: Free Press, 1971), 19. Italics added.
22. Perhaps the best summary of the diffusion of innovations literature is Rogers with Shoemaker, *Communication of Innovations.* On cue taking, see John W. Kingdon, *Congressmen's Voting Decisions,* 2nd ed. (New York: Harper & Row, 1981); and Donald R. Matthews and James A. Stimson, *Yeas and Nays* (New York: Wiley, 1975).
23. See Bandura, *Social Learning Theory,* 48-49.
24. An example was the Iranian crisis of 1979-81. In late October 1979, Senator Ted Kennedy was leading President Jimmy Carter in the polls for the Democratic presidential nomination. A week later, a group of American diplomats, soldiers, and others was taken hostage in the U.S. embassy in Teheran by supporters of the Ayatollah Khomeini. The President chose to treat the hostage taking as a major crisis. Within a month, his approval rating in the polls had jumped from about 30 percent to 61 percent. See Nelson W. Polsby, "The Democratic Nomination," in *The American Elections of 1980,* ed. Austin Ranney (Washington, D.C.: American Enterprise Institute, 1981), 44-45.
25. The important role of similarity in the learning of a model's behavior is discussed in the next section.
26. Thomas E. Mann and Norman J. Ornstein make this point in "The Republican Surge in Congress," in Ranney, *The American Elections of 1980,* 294-96.
27. This example is a social-learning interpretation of a rather ingenious argument by Gary C. Jacobson and Samuel Kernell (though they couch it in rational-choice terms) in *Strategy and Choice in Congressional Elections* (New Haven: Yale University Press, 1981). Note, however, that the individual's attention must be engaged if the new information is to have an impact. And many factors can affect an individual's attention to events. Among them is prior experience; if an expectation has been very firmly established in the individual's mind by repeated or dramatic experience, its strength may lead him or her to overlook subtle (or even not so subtle) evidence that it no longer holds in a particular setting.
28. Thus there are three types of response consequences in social-learning theory: external (i.e., directly experienced), vicarious, and self-produced. On the latter, see Bandura, *Social Learning Theory,* 128-58.
29. The initial result is probably best portrayed by the anonymous seer who defined "conscience" as the little voice deep in our minds that warns, "You're going to get caught!"
30. *Social Learning Theory,* 154.
31. For a fuller discussion, see ibid., 153-55.
32. See, for example, ibid., 126-27 and 133-36.
33. In a classic example of people's ability to justify violating their own standards, many people administered what they believed to be strong and painful electric shocks to others in an experiment, despite their own personal distress, simply because an experimenter—an authoritative figure in a seemingly legitimate scientific enterprise—ordered them to do so. See Stanley Milgram, *Obedience to Authority: An Experimental View* (New York: Harper & Row, 1974).

34. "Behavior Theory and the Models of Man," 862.
35. Fred I. Greenstein reaches a similar conclusion in his important work on personality and politics, though his theoretical perspective makes different assumptions about the nature of "person variables." See his *Personality and Politics* (New York: Norton, 1975).
36. This view of representation as a process of mutual influence is used to special advantage in the work of Richard F. Fenno, Jr., *Home Style* (Boston: Little, Brown, 1978); Donald J. McCrone and James H. Kuklinski, "The Delegate Theory of Representation," *American Journal of Political Science* 23 (May 1979): 278-300; and Heinz Eulau and Paul D. Karps, "The Puzzle of Representation: Specifying Components of Responsiveness," *Legislative Studies Quarterly* 2 (August 1977): 53-85.

3. Preparing for the Race

We have seen the principles on which the theory is built; now it is time to put them to work. Let us begin with a new campaigner, someone who is becoming a candidate for office for the first time. How does the newcomer know what to do? What are the forces that act on his or her learning, and with what result?

The Beginnings of a Campaign

Running for office for the first time is a riveting experience. It may be gratifying or terrifying (more likely, it will be both), but it is seldom boring. And unhappily for the candidate, it is seldom obvious what to do. When someone decides to run for office, he or she enters an environment that is to some extent new. There is great pressure to do *something,* but equally great uncertainty as to what will work. Should the new candidate start by hiring a campaign consultant, or is that a waste of precious money? Out of the broad sweep of public policy questions, what are the best issues to emphasize in the race? What must a new candidate do to attract press coverage? The reaction of one congressional candidate would probably bring sympathetic groans from first-time candidates everywhere: "I don't have any organization, I don't have any plan, I don't have any money. How can I do anything?"[1]

The theory suggests that the campaigner's first responses to these questions are guided by two processes: generalization of earlier learning and current observational learning. Then the results of those first moves (and the campaigner's interpretation of those results) should guide the learning that follows. First in the time sequence comes generalization of earlier learning.

THE CAMPAIGNER'S FIRST MOVES:
GENERALIZATION OF EARLIER LEARNING

While the campaign situation may be new, the campaigner is not. To borrow James David Barber's apt phrase, a candidate is "a man [or woman] with a memory in a system with a history."[2] In social-learning terms, that campaigner's "memory" consists of the situations he or she has faced (or learned about) in the past, the individual's responses to those situations, their results, and the expectations derived from them. A new campaigner, then, will reach back into past experiences in (or knowledge of) similar situations and draw on the expectations formed in those situations to guide current action. As Barber goes on to say regarding successful candidates for the nation's highest office, "like all of us, he draws on his past to shape his future."[3] The campaigner will probably do some improvising in response to the nuances of the present environment. But the more the situation of this infant campaign resembles past learning experiences, the more likely the candidate is to act on the expectations developed in earlier times.

To predict which expectations will shape the beginnings of a candidate's first race, we need to know more about his or her learning history. We need to search the candidate's experiences, both direct and vicarious, for learning that is relevant to the current situation. Here the theory leads us to ask two broad questions. First, what kinds of responses are likely to be necessary at the beginning of a campaign? Second, in what situations can these responses have been learned? In what ways is the campaign situation unique so that only the learning in earlier *campaigns* is likely to be relevant to one's first race as a candidate? And to what extent can campaigners draw on what they have learned in noncampaign experiences as well: in party organizations or other political groups, at work, or even in the family?

WHAT'S NEEDED: AN ARSENAL OF STRATEGIES
A new candidate is likely to need three kinds of responses, or "behavioral strategies."[4] First, there are organizational strategies: those used in setting up the organizational structure of the campaign. New candidates will usually find it necessary to recruit a campaign manager and other important staffers and advisers, set up (or help set up) an initial division of labor among them, and help motivate these key people—not an easy task, given the likely prospects of most first-time candidates.

Second, there are information-gathering strategies: approaches to learning more about the election district, its prominent groups and leaders, its media and their reporters and editors, its voting patterns. The candidate will need to become better acquainted with various political issues and their impact on the district and to learn the strengths and weaknesses of likely opponents.

The third class of responses involves the "presentation of self"—the strategies, verbal and nonverbal, that an individual uses to affect other people's impressions of him or her. Above all, candidates need to attract other people's support, to win the trust of various constituencies, to be seen as a "good person." To do this, according to Richard Fenno's perceptive analysis, a campaigner must do three things: give the impression of being qualified for the job, seem to identify with the constituents (to be *like* them), and show empathy and understanding of their needs.[5]

Candidates might use verbal cues to create these desired impressions—for example, referring in speeches to the values they share with their audience, stressing their qualifications, attacking the opponent's understanding of the district and its people. They can use nonverbal behaviors: making public appearances with people valued by groups in the district, campaigning in some settings (churches, union halls) rather than others. And they can avoid bloopers that call these impressions into question; perhaps the classic example is that of Sargent Shriver, a Kennedy brother-in-law who, in his 1972 primary campaign for President, is reported to have scheduled a campaign stop at a working-class bar in order to show how well he identified with people less wealthy than he was, genially ordered beers for the entire clientele—and then, absent-mindedly, requested a glass of cognac for himself.

This is the "general mode" of presentation of self. It is a delicate enterprise, made even more difficult by the time pressures of a campaign. The shortage of available time puts a premium on communicating those impressions to each member of each audience as quickly as possible, on forming an intense acquaintanceship with each available constituent. Then there are subclasses of presentation of self, aimed at more specific target groups: getting money from potential contributors, endorsements from interest groups and other important organizations, volunteer help and other resources from party organizations. These specialized presentations often require more plain-spoken commitments on particular issues and more concrete evidence that the candidacy is both viable and valuable in relation to the group's goals.

These are the kinds of strategies a new candidate will need. Where are they most likely to have been learned?

GENERALIZING FROM EARLIER CAMPAIGN EXPERIENCES

One can make a good argument—Barber, in fact, has—that campaigning is markedly different from other kinds of experiences.[6] To the extent that this is true, a new candidate in search of strategies should be most likely to draw them from his or her previous experience in (or knowledge of) other campaigns. That learning should generalize to the current race to the degree that the circumstances of the two races are comparable.

The process could happen this way. Many Democratic and antiwar activists, who were later to become candidates themselves, got their introduction to big-league politics as staff members in the 1972 presidential campaign of Senator George McGovern (D-S.D.). As active participants in that race, they learned how the McGovern campaign was organized, what kinds of information were gathered, how money was raised, and how the campaign dealt with the media and other groups. Then they observed the results of these strategies—some encouraging and some devastating.

Staff members saw the success with which McGovern raised money through direct mail and television; mailings and televised speeches sometimes produced such a flood of contributions that staffers had to work through the night just to process the checks.[7] They also saw the results of the campaign's strategy for dealing with the press. They heard the frequent charge that key campaign workers were too open with reporters, too prone to leak the details of decisions (and indecisions) in progress, internal squabbles, and other matters a campaign would rather keep to itself. In consequence, McGovern's organization was portrayed by the media as disorganized and incompetent—a sharp contrast with the image of incumbent President Richard Nixon's campaign as a well-oiled machine.[8] The expectations that each staffer developed about the effectiveness of these strategies then became part of his or her learning history.

When one of these McGovern alumni decides to run for office, this learning is available for generalization to his or her own race. Whether or not the learning *will* apply depends upon the degree of similarity between those earlier circumstances and the new candidate's own campaign. The more similar the situation, the more likely the new candidate is to draw on those McGovern strategies that seemed effective and avoid those that were recognized as duds.

So some of McGovern's more successful strategies *were* applied again in the next presidential race—by former staff members facing similar enough situations that they could generalize their earlier learning. An example is McGovern's approach to the New Hampshire primary in 1972. Before New Hampshire, McGovern was stuck in the "pack"—the many Democratic candidates given little chance of winning their party's nomination. But he and his staff went into the state early, put an extensive campaign organization in the field, canvassed large numbers of Democratic voters, and kept up that pace for months. When the primary votes were counted, McGovern ran much better than political analysts had expected; overnight, he won the national prominence he had sought for so long.

Four years later, many McGovern alumni were back in New Hampshire—as strategists for other presidential candidates. Most of those candidates were longshots for the nomination, as McGovern had been in 1972. Their races were similar to McGovern's in many other ways. And the former McGovernites did bring their earlier learning with them into the campaigns they joined in 1976. There was a diffusion of those techniques believed to be responsible for McGovern's impressive New Hampshire showing: the early forays into the state, the extensive field organization, the canvassing. As an instruction sheet for 1976 Democratic presidential candidate Birch Bayh's canvassers put it, "we must tell you that the techniques we are using are also being used by other campaigns as well. This is natural, as many of us had the same training ground—the [1972] McGovern campaign."[9]

If the circumstances remain fairly similar and the strategy continues to seem effective, a campaigner may well rely on that strategy through several elections, resulting in what often comes to be called his or her "characteristic style" of campaigning. Take John Sears, for example, a Republican strategist whose imprint appears on virtually all recent presidential races. From Richard Nixon's campaign in 1968 through Ronald Reagan's bids for the Republican nomination in 1976 and 1980, there have been several recurring themes in Sears's strategizing. One is the careful effort to control the candidate's accessibility to the press and public by scheduling a very limited number of personal appearances and avoiding campaign events (candidate debates, for instance) that are hard to orchestrate in advance.[10]

Some might call those approaches "characteristic" of Sears's campaigning. One could even argue that Sears has an inborn "drive" to control his candidates' appearances, and that if he had been advising George McGovern in 1972, he would have used the same strategy. But there is a more apt explanation. Recall that the strategy seemed to get good results for the Nixon campaign; Nixon won. Moreover, the 1976 and 1980 Reagan campaigns began with many important similarities to Nixon's 1968 race: a conservative Republican challenger with a long political history, given a good chance to capitalize on public discontent with the incumbent administration. Sears's learning in 1968, then, could be relevant to the Reagan campaigns.

But only up to a point—an important point in understanding the sources of a candidate's learning. When this Imperial Candidate approach was widely blamed for Reagan's defeat in the 1980 Iowa caucuses, Sears's advice changed. In the next electoral test, the New Hampshire primary of that year, Sears not only sent his candidate into an intensive round of personal campaigning but even made arrangements for Reagan to take on his opponents in two rather free-wheeling debates.[11] The "characteristic style" disappeared in a flash after it was linked with unpleasant results and changed circumstances.

In short, the learning a new candidate draws from prior campaign experiences can be an important source of his or her first moves in the current race. That learning may even continue to guide the candidate for some time, as long as the situation remains similar and the results are good. In fact, candidates may try to structure their environment so that their earlier learning continues to be relevant; Sears, of course, did *not* volunteer to advise Democrat McGovern

Preparing for the Race 65

in 1972, and did choose to work in the next two elections for a candidate whose situation was similar to Nixon's in 1968. But when the circumstances change, the earlier learning becomes much less useful.

Differences among campaigns, then, may limit a new candidate's ability to rely on strategies learned in previous races. Districts may change, the national political climate may change in ways that cause campaigners to doubt the relevance of their prior learning. Imagine, for instance, the prototypical midwestern congressional district where a long-time incumbent retires, his administrative assistant runs to replace him (perhaps even running against his mentor's last opponent), and wraps himself in the presentational style that he learned in his boss's campaigns—as a kind of "Son of the Watchdog of the Treasury." The race is a replay of the last one, with Watchdog running against a liberal Democrat in a blue-collar conservative area. Suddenly, the district's biggest employer, an industrial plant, closes down indefinitely; unemployment in the area zooms to 20 percent. The Watchdog's popular speech on the virtue of cutting federal assistance programs and tracking down "welfare cheats" is not so popular anymore. New circumstances have undermined the candidate's ability to draw on earlier campaign learning.

Another limiting factor is that the simple fact of becoming a candidate, instead of remaining a staff member or volunteer, changes the individual's environment. A staff member who does canvassing is acting in a different environment, even a different physical setting, from the campaign people who run the headquarters and from those who deal with the press. The biggest gap lies between any of these campaign roles and that of the candidate. Candidates do different things, meet different people, and face different pressures than their campaign workers do. This separability of tasks limits the flow of information from one part of the campaign to another, and so limits the ability of canvassers to learn about media relations, and media advisers to learn about being a candidate.[12] Thus, even if the race is very similar to earlier ones, the first-time candidate will probably face an environment that differs from his or her previous experience as a staff member.

The office being sought matters too. Presidential races are run under different "rules" than Senate races are: different campaign finance systems, different constituencies, different media coverage. Each type of contest has some unique features; chapter 6 has more to say on this point. A successful Senate candidate, then, cannot expect to apply his or her prior campaign learning to an upcoming race for the Presidency without making allowances for the differences between the two contests.

Finally, some types of campaign learning may apply more readily than others to later campaign experiences. Information-gathering strategies do not depend as much on the characteristics of a given race as many other strategies do, so a new candidate may bring with her some patterns of reconnoitering the district and studying the local issues that were learned in her experience as campaign manager for another candidate. Some elements of presentation of self may transfer well too. Consider Gary Hart, McGovern's campaign manager in 1972. Hart then became a candidate for the first time in 1974, seeking (and winning) a Senate seat from Colorado. Shortly after his reelection to the Senate in 1980, he began running for President himself. Hart had learned a great deal about grass-roots campaigning in his experience with McGovern, and that learning could transcend the change from manager to candidate. As a Hart press aide said in 1983, "the grass-roots strategy we're focusing on in this campaign is the same basic strategy Hart developed during the McGovern race."[13]

Other elements of self-presentation were not as transferable; most important, the "self" to be presented was quite different. Hart had a different learning history from McGovern — a different set of experiences in trying to affect other people's impressions of him. His ability to learn from the McGovern campaign when developing his own style of self-presentation would certainly be limited by the differences between the two men's learning histories, as well as by differences in the political climate at the time of the race.

So people's experience in other campaigns, as a staff member or volunteer, can be an important source of strategies and expectations when they begin their own first race as a candidate. Situational differences between those earlier campaigns and the present one can limit the use of this learning. But some of the responses needed by a candidate are not as specialized as, say, grass-roots organizing or targeting precincts; new candidates, then, can also draw on some noncampaign experiences as sources of campaign behavior.

LEARNING FROM NONCAMPAIGN EXPERIENCES

The belief that people's nonpolitical learning has an important impact on their political behavior is long-standing. In particular, there is a tradition of interest in politicians' occupations and socioeconomic backgrounds, presumably on the assumption that the views and strategies politicians learn in their "real" jobs and in certain social environments can carry over into their political activity.[14] For example, observing that there are much larger proportions of lawyers among elected officials than in the public at large, researchers have asked whether training in law, and lawyers' experience in taking various perspectives on questions, provide them with unique campaigning skills or with approaches to political issues and legislative service that differ from those of nonlawyer candidates.[15]

These broad questions raise some intriguing possibilities. But their very breadth covers up a lot of diversity. "Being a lawyer," for example, could describe a wide range of experiences. We would not expect a young public defender working with indigent people to take the same learning experiences into his or her first try for public office as would a Harvard-trained corporate lawyer, nearing retirement after years of prosperous work. The social-learning approach would suggest that we set aside the broader categories of occupation and education in favor of the individual candidate's own learning history. What we need to know, then, is the interaction between the individual's own learning in previous similar situations and the circumstances of the current campaign.

Consider the corporate lawyer mentioned above. Suppose that he left Harvard at age twenty-five with a law degree, but with little else that would make him feel confident of success. He set up his own law practice in an urban area, and he struggled. The fees from his few clients barely paid the rent. But he held on, hoping for a break, built a reputation, and finally caught the attention of a major oil company looking for an addition to its legal staff. His work environment now is as comfortable and controlled as his earlier environment was insecure and risky.

After many years' experience with the law, he decides he would like a hand in writing it. He runs for Congress. He has no prior campaign work to draw upon. Looking only at his own experiences (we explore the use of models later), where should we expect him to derive his expectations about the race?

If he is running in a wealthy suburban district dominated by his party, and his opponent is unknown and inexperienced, then the more recent phase of his legal career may yield some comparable situations: circumstances where he has had to organize a staff, supervise research, and make his case to a client, where his position is secure and his ties with the business community are strong. But if his district is varied, his party is weak and disorganized, and the opponent is a very popular incumbent, then he will be less likely to apply the strategies learned late in his career; the circumstances differ too much. In fact, the coming campaign may recall for him the early years of his law practice and the more risk-acceptant strategies that were effective for him at that time.

Many campaign behaviors can be drawn from the learning people do in their careers. Consider the story of one Ronald Reagan, an actor whose film career was on the wane in the early 1950s.[16] He was hired by General Electric as a spokesman for its products and its aims. For years he traveled the "rubber chicken" circuit, giving speeches to business and community groups and filing away vivid examples of cumbersome government regulations affecting his company. With this extensive experience and the many opportunities it provided to learn from audiences' reactions, he developed an unusually effective speaking style: an ability to condense widely held beliefs into memorable one-liners that touched his listeners. Later, this presentational skill came to the attention of Republican leaders seeking a candidate for the governorship of California. Ronald Reagan's work experiences were a good match with the circumstances of his first campaign, and he drew heavily on them, particularly for strategies involving presentation of self.

Other kinds of noncampaign learning can transfer to a candidate's first race. Approaches to organizing a campaign may be drawn from experience in coordinating political party activities or establishing field offices for an insurance agency. The more similar a situation, the more easily a new candidate can apply what he or she learned from it.

Earlier learning also affects the candidate's first moves by affecting his or her standards of conduct. As the last chapter suggested, people learn rules of behavior, which they apply to themselves. These rules are enforced by their self-evaluations: by feelings of self-pride when they live up to their own standards, and by self-criticism when they do not. People *can* become skilled, as the last chapter indicated, at sidestepping their own censure. But there are many ways in which those personal standards can affect a candidate's behavior: when he or she is deciding whether to put in long hours campaigning or to relax on the golf course, when thinking about whether and on what grounds to attack the opponent.

So a new candidate's prior learning—through personal or vicarious experiences with situations, actions, and their consequences—is one major source of his or her strategies early in the race. That learning, from campaign or noncampaign experiences, creates expectations about the likely results of different strategies. These expectations can be applied to similar situations in the future. They can motivate a candidate to aim for the desired results.

But these expectations, and strategies based on them, can be modified when new information or events affect the candidate. For example, when Jimmy Carter won the White House after an earlier term as governor of Georgia, he first approached the Congress as he had learned to treat the Georgia state legislature — not surprisingly, since that had been his most comparable learning experience. When his first steps in Washington produced harsh criticism from Congress and media people, he gained new information about the results of his behavior:

> The authority of the Congress [Carter explains to an interviewer] in helping to shape foreign decisions is greater than I had anticipated. . . . My dealing with the Georgia legislature, although it taught me a great deal about the personal interrelationships with members of Congress, didn't prepare me well for the profound influence that Congress both warrants and asserts in defense and foreign matters. . . . In some ways, I have to share more authority than I had anticipated.[17]

Thus the future of a candidate's early strategies depends on their results; they will remain in place if they bring good results (or predictions of good results) and will be modified or dropped if, like Carter's early approach toward Congress, they do not. But what about a new candidate facing a decision for which he or she has had no relevant experience? Or a situation that the new candidate has handled before, but unsuccessfully?

Learning from Models

THE WIDESPREAD USE OF MODELS BY NEW CANDIDATES

Not all candidates have the advantage of prior experience to guide them. Many, especially in state and local races, but even in campaigns for Congress, have never run for office before.[18] And even the most experienced campaigner may find the current election to be a whole new ballgame. A long-time incumbent might find his past learning to be of little help if the state legislature redraws his congressional district, adding a few hundred thousand supporters of the other party. A state legislator accustomed to easy races could find it hard to apply past experience if she enters a congressional race against a very well financed and attractive opponent.

If the campaign situation looks new, then the campaigner has two choices: devise an entirely new set of approaches to begin the race, or borrow one. Inventing a set of strategies can take a lot of time. It is also risky; there is no way to tell whether the new approaches will work. So candidates (and legislators and organizations when they find themselves in the same predicament) are much more likely to borrow some strategies.

Fortunately, the opportunities for borrowing are almost everywhere. There are about half a million elected officials in the United States—one candidate for every 440 (other) people. Any new campaigner, then, has many potential models. There are professional "lenders" as well: campaign consulting firms and advertising agencies who will provide strategies to a candidate in need. This borrowing—called observational learning, or modeling—is the new candidate's other primary source of strategies early in the race.

The study of modeling offers an important perspective on campaigners' behavior. It helps us see that people running for office do not act in splendid isolation from one another; rather, there are interrelationships among campaigns. Various political issues, methods of organization, and other strategies are communicated from one campaign to another and modified in transit. By looking at modeling, we can discover how campaigners and consultants behave in response to one another as well as to voters and interest groups. And we can lay bare some of the important features of political campaigning: how various campaign behaviors evolve, and how responsive the campaign process is to changing conditions.[19]

MODELING: WHO DOES IT AND WHEN?

Imagine two candidates making their first moves in an election year. One is a first-timer; she recently moved into the congressional district, impressed the local party leaders as a committed and enthusiastic worker, and got drafted to run—largely because more experienced party prospects had no desire to take on an apparently hopeless race against a popular incumbent. It is a situation for which she had no previous experience. There is not enough time to sit back and evaluate all the possible alternatives; besides, she wants to start with an approach that will impress people, not an experiment that may prove embarrassing.

The second is a seasoned campaigner. He thought he was a shoo-in this year, just as he has been for the past 20 years. After announcing his intention to seek reelection, he always simply scheduled a few speeches at Rotary clubs, accepted the flood of contributions that poured in, and planned his victory party. But there is something ominous about this race. First, his new opponent seems much more capable than earlier opponents were. Next, some of the interest groups that had lined up to give money in the past have stopped returning his calls. Now he finds that he is slipping in the polls.

These are classic circumstances in which modeling takes place: situations that are new enough, different enough from the campaigner's previous experience, that he or she lacks a strategy that is expected to work.[20] New and inexperienced candidates often fit this picture. So do political veterans who foresee unpleasant changes in their campaign environment or who are not willing to take chances when that environment changes, even though there is no evidence that they will be in trouble if they do. In addition, candidates who have been rewarded in the past for relying heavily on the advice of other people—for following the lead of models—will be especially likely to learn by observation in their current race; the principle of learning from response consequences would predict that.

WHO WILL THE MODELS BE?

Of the many factors that guide people in their choice of models, two matter most: success and similarity. A campaigner will choose models who are successful (competent, expert, or at least reputed to get good results for their efforts) and similar to the campaigner in important respects.

Preparing for the Race 71

People's attention is drawn to successful models. People learn, from a model's success, what sorts of strategies are likely to be rewarded in particular circumstances. They are motivated to remember and use approaches that have been well received. In a campaign, the universal currency of success is a majority of the votes on election day. Candidates who win their races consistently and by comfortable margins would be logical models for a newcomer. So would those who carve out victories in races they were expected to lose. Candidates might develop reputations for effectiveness if they regularly lead their ticket, or even if they do better than observers expected. Because reporters and campaign consultants are interested in winners, they tend to repeat the stories of successful races; in doing so, they enhance the reputations of winning candidates and make those candidates' strategies more "available" for observational learning.

In the 1976 campaign, for example, most of the Democratic presidential candidates chose to run in only a few carefully selected state primaries. Jimmy Carter was the one Democrat who entered every state primary, beginning his drive for the nomination with an early victory in the Iowa caucuses. Months later, he won the Democratic nomination. Whether or not his run-everywhere strategy was the reason for his success, his campaign promptly gained a reputation for great expertise. The long planning memos of his chief strategist, Hamilton Jordan, were cited respectfully, and Carter's preconvention moves studied. After the election, Jules Witcover wrote that "in 1980 it seems likely that Carter's run-everywhere strategy will be emulated if there is a large field in either party, if only because it worked in 1976."[21]

In fact, it was. Four years later, Witcover and Jack Germond were explaining the race for the 1980 nomination in these terms:

> Politicians always fight the last war, and the lesson of Jimmy Carter's unprecedented success in 1976 had been that the way to succeed was to start early and build a following brick by brick.[22]

Who learned that lesson? Several new and long-shot candidates for their party's 1980 nomination. One was Republican George Bush, who began working Iowa in the spring of 1979, drawing on the widely held belief that it was Jimmy Carter's victory in the Iowa caucuses that gave him credibility as a serious presidential candidate. Another was Republican Congressman Phil Crane, who did Bush one better; all but invisible in the polls, Crane announced his candidacy for President in August of 1978, fully a year and a half before the first primary of 1980. For these and other new presidential campaigners, Jimmy Carter's 1976 successes — and the reputation for expertise they engendered — made his prenomination strategy an obvious model.[23] Thus the run-early-and-often strategy was established in presidential campaigning. The ink on the 1980 election analyses was barely dry when, in early 1982, the next batch of presidential hopefuls began visiting Iowa to drum up support for the 1984 campaign. Through this process, a model's success changes the expectations that observers hold.

The second major factor is similarity. People borrow the strategies of successful campaigners *who are like them in important respects.* Similarity is important because it allows people to expect that the model's behavior will work for them as well; by learning from a successful candidate who is *like* us in important ways, we increase our confidence that if we act like the model, we will win like the model.[24] What are those "important ways," those similarities that will make a difference in the choice of models?

Clearly there is reason to expect that a shared party affiliation is one such similarity. Even though party identification continues to lose its grip on *citizens'* political behavior, it remains an important symbol to candidates and other activists (as we see later). Its importance is reinforced among many incumbent campaigners; for example, the main networks of formal and informal communication in the House and Senate tend to stay within party lines.[25] And national trends that affect the parties' fortunes—for instance, the Democratic gains in the 1982 elections—give many candidates the feeling that a party colleague will be a more relevant model than a candidate of the opposition party.

If someone is running mainly to call public attention to a particular issue, then he or she will probably draw on models with a similar issue orientation. Other important sources of similarity between model and learner have to do with the nature of their constituency: its racial, ethnic, and economic characteristics; its geographic location and industrial or agricultural base; its partisan composition. Party colleagues running in a similar district in the same state are a very likely set of models for a candidate.

Interestingly, gender will probably affect the selection of models. Because many citizens still regard certain activities and qualities as more "appropriate" for a man than for a woman, a female candidate may have reason to wonder whether she can successfully adopt all the campaign activities used by male candidates for the same office. Further, a woman candidate may face some situations that male candidate-models do not—for example, needing to convince some voters that running and winning will not lead her to neglect her family (especially if holding office requires a move to a new location, such as the state capital or Washington, D.C.).[26] Even her husband's finances may receive closer scrutiny than if the candidate's spouse were a wife; consider the case of Congresswoman Geraldine Ferraro, the first woman nominated for vice-president, whose husband's real estate development business attracted such avid media attention in the 1984 presidential campaign.

Preparing for the Race

To deal with these situations, women running their first campaigns might hope to learn the approaches tried by more experienced women candidates; the use of models, after all, is a vital source of campaign learning. But the number of successful female models is limited; most candidates, and thus most potential models, are men. An even smaller number of women candidate-models will resemble the newcomer in other important ways: party affiliation, kind of district, issue orientation. This limited availability of successful, similar models may well discourage more women from running, and make the learning situation more difficult for those who do run.

Note that it is possible to learn from losing candidates too. Someone running for an office for the first time will probably have more information about the actions of his or her predecessor—the last candidate of the same party in that district—than about any other potential model. Because that information is handy, the new candidate is likely to have in mind the problems faced by that earlier campaign and the actions thought to have been its "mistakes." If the predecessor lost, then he or she might be viewed as a perfect example of what *not* to do: a "negative model." The new candidate's aim, then, will be to avoid repeating the predecessor's mistakes; the similarities in the two situations—same party, same district—will encourage observational learning.

A good example of this kind of campaign learning involved the selection of a vice-presidential nominee a decade ago. In the summer of 1972, Democratic presidential nominee George McGovern invited Senator Thomas Eagleton to become his running mate. Not long afterward, the news leaked that Eagleton had been under treatment for emotional problems in the past, a fact unknown to McGovern when he chose Eagleton. After a messy and embarrassing delay, Eagleton was dumped from the ticket—and treated by many reporters as a martyr. The incident cut the heart out of McGovern's image as a caring, consistent, and candid man. As he later admitted, "the vice-presidential selection fiasco was, after all, the most painfully obvious mistake of 1972."[27]

It was a mistake not to be repeated by his successor. Well aware of the damage caused by McGovern's hasty selection of Eagleton, 1976 Democratic nominee Jimmy Carter established unusually elaborate procedures for screening vice-presidential prospects. Each was asked to fill out a questionnaire covering possible marital, economic, and medical problems. Each was then rated on ability, integrity, and acceptability. The finalists were summoned to Carter's home in Georgia, replete with sheepish grins, for personal interviews. There are many possible approaches to the choice of a running mate. Jimmy Carter's approach inevitably reflected the lessons he and his advisers drew from the negative model of his predecessor, on one of the well-publicized disasters of the McGovern campaign.

THE CHANNELS OF CAMPAIGN LEARNING

For needy campaigners to borrow the strategies of successful, similar models, those models must become "available" to the campaigner. How do candidates find out about the actions of prospective models?

Incumbents often have an easier job of learning than challengers do, because those elected to office are in frequent contact with other incumbents. They have institutionalized arrangements for getting together—among legislators, for example, in committees, in legislative session, in party caucuses, in cloakrooms, at parties. They have occasion as well as motivation to exchange ideas on many subjects. And they share the intense experience of having been through at least one campaign. With these common bonds and well-established communication channels, incumbents can learn from one another about new issues, campaign strategies, and changes in the political environment.

Challengers have to find other means. Some are provided by party organizations in the form of campaign "schools." The schools are designed to direct their "students' " attention to successful, similar models—for example, by bringing new and promising campaigners together with successful consultants and incumbents of the same party. The "curriculum" may include approaches to organizing a campaign, fund raising, media use, and pointers about the presentation of self (although as one analyst put it, "most challengers would simply have preferred more cash . . ."[28]).

The logic of encouraging campaigners to learn observationally has been adopted by nonparty groups as well. Conservative groups such as the Committee for the Survival of a Free Congress and liberal groups such as the National Committee for an Effective Congress have both offered instruction to likeminded campaigners. Some labor unions and trade associations run campaign schools for prospective campaigners among their membership.

In addition, professional consultants are natural "carriers" of innovations from one campaign to another. In fact, that is what they are hired to do: provide models of effective campaigning to their clients. To maintain their reputations as professionals, and to generate more business for themselves, they try to match needy campaigns with appropriate strategies in the consultant's area of expertise. Since they often work on several campaigns in a given election year, consulting firms are in a position to draw conclusions about the effects of different strategies under various circumstances, and bring their learning to the next batch of campaigns.[29]

Many consulting firms work only one side of the fence; they accept clients only from one party (and sometimes, only from one ideological strand of that party). That is to be expected. A Republican candidate might worry justifiably that his or her campaign plans, entrusted to a bipartisan consulting firm, might leak to the consultant's Democratic clients and then to the Democratic opponent in the candidate's own race. Besides, consultants often have principles; it is difficult to work effectively for someone with whom you disagree, who carries the other party's banner. The result is to reinforce the importance of party as an influence on the choice of models.

Among the examples of observational learning "carried" by professional consultants are endless variations on that eternal theme, the fund-raising letter. A direct-mail specialist who hits on an effective way of phrasing such a letter—effective in that the letter brings in a lot of money—will surely bring that learning to similar campaigns in which there is reason to expect the approach to work again. During the 1970s, for instance, experience showed that liberal candidates could raise more money from liberal donors by sending a lengthy, issue-oriented letter than a short one. Since then, direct-mail consultants have recommended long fund-raising letters for use by other liberal campaigns; we see an interesting example later in this book.

Many consultants also instruct candidates on stylistic matters. A candidate who rambles might be taught how to answer questions in a more precise way; one who looks too stiff and formal could be advised how to appear more casual and folksy. He or she might be directed to observe other candidate-models, or be given lessons by a drama coach, or simply told how to behave. Listen to one consultant who advised George Bush in 1980:

> I told George to perform, use his skills, get emotionally psyched up [Bush's consultant for television and radio said]. Show your feelings. Show your vulnerable side. Look at Hubert Humphrey. He cared. He was loving. That's what people want.[30]

Increasingly, the lure of successful models does not end at the water's edge; more and more American consultants are plying their trade in other nations' elections. A graphic example was the Venezuelan presidential campaign of 1978. Not only the incumbent president but three of his opponents each imported consultants from the United States. One candidate hired David Garth, who was then also working for the reelection campaign of New York Governor Hugh Carey. Another hired John Deardourff, who was at the same time advising Carey's Republican opponent. A third candidate apparently wanted to cover all bets: he brought in both Joseph Napolitan, a veteran Democratic consultant, and Clifton White, who works for conservative Republicans.[31] The result was an electronic campaign quite different from the style to which Venezuela had grown accustomed—and a spread of models to which Americans have grown accustomed.

The same thing happens on a more limited scale when campaign staff members and volunteers move from one race to another, in successive election years or even within a given year, and bring their earlier learning with them. Some political enthusiasts make campaigning virtually their life's work, practicing law or otherwise biding time between elections, but looking forward with relish to the next race. In the process, they act as traveling agents of observational learning; they can bring new models to a campaign by describing the strategies and experiences of the other candidates for whom they worked. Like professional consultants, these "amateur" campaigners generally work only for their own party's candidates, and often for only one *wing* of that party's candidates; thus they add to the tendency for campaigners to draw on models within their own party.

As these amateurs and professionals move from one campaign to another, they come into close contact with other consultants. They share information about other races in which they are involved. One nationally known Washington pollster explains, "I've always said there's a network of 100 people in this town [Washington] through which you can find out about any race you're interested in; just name a campaign, and at least one of those hundred people will be working as a consultant on it or will know about it in some other way." Through that network, candidates get access to a wider range of models.

Finally, campaigners can learn from symbolic models that are also readily available: books. There are "how to win" books. There are "how they won" books. They are used as models. When James A. Baker III was asked to head the 1980 presidential campaign of George Bush, Baker's first move was to give his candidate a copy of Jules Witcover's *Marathon*. The book, about the 1976 race, included the now-famous memorandum by Hamilton Jordan outlining how Jimmy Carter could (and did) win the Democratic nomination. Baker's gift, in effect, was to introduce Bush to the model for his prenomination race. As Baker said, "We made no bones about the fact—and still don't—that we were pursuing the Carter strategy as far as the early start and organization were concerned."[32]

WHAT THEY LEARN

Campaigners, then, have a lot of potential models. But what do they learn, and which models do they actually use? What campaign strategies are most and least contagious?

There are many reasons why a new candidate might *not* use an attractive strategy that he or she learned from a model. For instance, it might cost too much. Some recent presidential candidates have run very engaging half-hour ads on prime-time television—engaging enough to draw the attention of other candidates. But there is a clear limit on the numbers of campaigners for other offices who are likely to borrow the strategy because the cost of producing and broadcasting such ads—often several hundreds of thousands of dollars—is larger than the entire campaign budgets of many congressional and state and local candidates.

Other strategies cost much less to borrow. The use of particular issue appeals is a case in point. Trying a new campaign "theme" costs only the time needed to become informed about the issue (and sometimes less). The spread of new issue appeals is hastened by the fact that the short-term results are so prompt; when a candidate-model uses a new appeal in a speech, reactions from audiences and media people can be determined quickly by other campaigners. When presidential candidate Ronald Reagan in mid-1980 announced his commitment to a massive tax cut, the so-called Reagan-Kemp-Roth proposal, the plan was immediately applauded by many Republican constituencies. Seeing that initial positive response, many Republican candidates followed Reagan's lead. The Reagan-Kemp-Roth appeal was very contagious among Republicans.

This suggests the most important factor in the spread of a campaign strategy: its functional value. Strategies that bring clear, visible, and rewarding results are most likely to be modeled by other campaigners. In contrast, the effectiveness of a candidate's presentation of self, as well as many other aspects of campaign behavior, may not be readily apparent until election day; in fact, the evidence might not be clear even then. But the results of a particular fund-raising letter are easy to see: how much money did it bring in? The answer will be fairly prompt. Contributors are likely to respond to the letter within a few weeks, often early enough for other candidates to hear about the size of the "take" and borrow the approach before the campaign ends.

Consider a fund-raising letter sent by former President Gerald Ford in 1979, requesting contributions to Republican state legislative races. "I am writing you today," Ford began, "on a vital life-and-death subject that could shape American politics and your future for years to come." State legislators elected in 1980, Ford wrote, would be redrawing congressional district lines for the 1980s; the more state legislatures a party could control, the better would be its chances in getting district lines drawn to the advantage of that party.

The letter produced a good monetary return. Twice. The second time, a virtually identical version was mailed over the signature of Democratic Speaker of the House Thomas P. O'Neill in behalf of Democratic state legislative candidates. The Democrats' direct-mail consultant had access to Ford's letter and knew how much money it had raised. The response was sufficiently positive and clear-cut that the model crossed party lines.[33]

Strategies are more likely to spread widely if they are seen to be effective for other candidates and if they do not put much strain on a campaign's resources (especially money, but also staff time, the candidate's reputation, volunteer help). It helps, too, if the strategy can be easily demonstrated, if it is compatible with the prospective user's values and experiences, and if it is not too radical a change from accepted campaign practices.[34]

In addition, predictions can be made as to *where* a strategy will spread.[35] Some campaign ideas will move mainly to other campaigns in the same geographical area or the same media market. Where the strategy is designed to meet the needs of a particular district—for example, a proposal offered by a Detroit labor leader for keeping the auto industry afloat—it will be of greatest interest and greatest potential benefit to other campaigners in the same district. An innovation in television advertising will probably be learned first by other candidates within reach of the television station, and then spread to similar areas on the recommendation of consultants. A strategy best learned through personal contact—ways of dealing with hostile questions at a coffee, relationships with local business and civic leaders—will be learned most easily by candidates who see the model regularly, because they campaign in the same geographical area, for example.[36]

Earlier in the chapter I suggested that candidates pay special attention to candidate-models who resemble them in important ways. Many campaign innovations, then, will spread first to campaigners who share the model's party affiliation and ideological bent. These patterns of contagion will dissolve and re-form as changes in the nation's political climate call attention to different characteristics of campaigners. When the public mood turns sour on incumbents, for example, then incumbency will become an important basis for the spread of responses to that mood, and for other strategies as well. Recall the rapid spread of "I am not a politician" campaigns among scores of politicians in the late 1970s and 1980s—including the remarkable efforts of several governors and at least one President to campaign against the very governments they presumably had been running in the meantime.[37]

The results of this use of models, interestingly, can produce not just substantial continuity in campaign behavior over time but also adaptation and even the invention of new strategies. We can easily see evidence of continuity in campaign practices. A presentational style that seems to work in an area, such as the effort to show empathy with ethnic voters by being photographed in the act of eating Polish sausage while wearing a Mexican hat, is learned by so many generations of new candidates in that area that it seems to be obligatory in any campaign. These continuities can be the result of modeling—a series of new campaigners borrowing an idea long associated with successful races by similar candidates. The effect is what we call tradition.

Or the candidate may adapt a borrowed strategy to his or her own race through the process of "abstract modeling"—applying the rule that underlies the model's behaviors. Door-to-door canvassing, a traditional campaign device whose meaning has been modified by observational learning, is a case in point. Canvassing was a major activity of the great urban political machines earlier in this century—a means of informing voters about the party's slate of candidates and gathering voters' requests for party services.

By the late 1960s, most of the once-great machines had fallen into disrepair. But as machine canvassing dwindled, a very different group claimed the strategy as its own. Antiwar students provided a willing source of workers, moving out into neighborhoods and talking to voters about the Vietnam war. Eugene McCarthy, an antiwar candidate for President in 1968, drew on this pool of available talent. McCarthy and his staffers adapted the principles of canvassing to the aims of his Democratic insurgency. In the process, the meaning of the technique was measurably changed; once an intraparty channel by which favors were exchanged for votes, it became a means of getting information about a foreign policy issue, and a candidate running against his own party's establishment, to citizens regardless of party. A traditional party activity was modified for use in challenging that party's hold.

The use of models can also produce novel campaign strategies. That happens when a campaigner draws some ideas from one model's behavior, other ideas from additional models, and combines those elements in a new way. Early in Jimmy Carter's Presidency, for example, he made news with a radio program; citizens were invited to call the President with questions or problems, and a small number of those calls were aired live, followed by Carter's live response. CBS anchorman Walter Cronkite served as moderator. Quickly dubbed "Dial-A-President," the program was hailed as an innovation. More accurately, it was an interesting amalgam of several well-established campaign and media techniques: campaign "town meetings," radio call-in shows, constituent service, and the use of media stars to attract voters' attention.

It is intriguing, then, that people can develop very traditional styles of campaigning by learning from models, or can derive something entirely new. A campaigner who has access to diverse models—who has taken part in the campaigns of different candidates, and worked with several consultants, attended campaign schools run by interest groups or a political party—can learn a wide variety of strategies relevant to the current race and can use some creative combinations of those strategies.

A campaign environment in which potential models are limited in number and diversity—a small town, say, in which candidates are expected to do no more than work the county fair and distribute brochures door-to-door—discourages innovation as long as those traditional campaign practices continue to appear effective.

MODELING: SUMMARY AND IMPLICATIONS

Campaigners learn a great deal from one another. They watch and remember other candidates' media ads, approaches to issues, fund-raising techniques, general styles of self-presentation. New candidates with little relevant experience, and campaigners whose environment has changed enough to cast doubt on the relevance of their earlier learning, will be especially attentive to the strategies used by candidate-models.

In this learning situation, some models are "more equal" than others—more likely to leave their imprint on political campaigning by affecting the behavior of large numbers of campaigners. Needy candidates will pay special attention to the strategies of campaigners and consultants with winning reputations, known for raising big money, overcoming big odds, and most important, winning. They will be guided by the similarities between their situation and that of a potential model. In this cafeteria of learned strategies, they will be most likely to use those that have been shown to work, that do not strain their resources too much, or challenge their personal standards, or are too remote from their own experience.

Needy candidates differ too in the number and kinds of models available to them. Incumbents are likely to have the advantage over challengers on this point; the established channels of information exchange in Congress, state legislatures, and other official settings can be used to convey ideas about campaigning as well as about legislation. Easier access to models, especially to winning models, gives these incumbents a big edge.

The vital role of modeling has some interesting implications for the political process. First, it shows that there is reason to look at campaigning as a series of networks, of relationships among campaigners that go beyond the current election year, extending back into previous elections and ahead to coming ones. Central to those relationships is learning: the communication of information, ideas, and strategies that bear on campaigners' interaction with their environment.

Candidates and staffers are part of many other learning networks in their own activities as lawyers or family members or residents of a neighborhood; occasionally they may draw on models within those networks when they face decisions in a campaign. But as campaigners, their most useful models will be other candidates and staff members; those are the people whose situations are most similar to theirs. Through their attention to one another and their experience with shared problems (such as fund raising, organizing, meeting the press), campaigners, like other specialists, tend to develop a rather specialized "language"—a set of terms and shared symbols referring to their important tasks.

Preparing for the Race

A small example can be seen in the spread of voter identification systems. In the Voter ID, staffers draw on voter registration lists, other lists of residents of an area, and telephone books in order to learn the addresses and phone numbers of all potential voters. The list is broken down into precincts or other small chunks so that door-to-door or phone canvassers can contact each person on their list and ask his or her preferences in the race. Voters are then classified into categories according to their level of support for the candidate. The system was used effectively in the 1968 presidential campaign of Eugene McCarthy. As McCarthy's staffers moved into later campaigns, they took the Voter ID with them. George McGovern's campaign refined its use in 1972, and it has since spread to other presidential campaigns, to congressional and state races, and to the campaign efforts of parties and single-issue groups—all through modeling. In the process, its specialized language spread also:

> In a system that now has become standard in most campaigns, voters are given a rating of one through five: (1) Positive commitment to your candidate; (2) Leaning to your candidate; (3) Undecided; (4) Hostile to your candidate or committed to some other; (5) Not home, recently moved or otherwise not classifiable 1 through 4.
> This canvassing code, once insider's stuff, has become so well known in the political community and among the press that long conversations are held wherever those interested in campaigns gather, using only the numbers: "Things look better. Our ones and twos are up forty percent over last week," or: "We're recanvassing our threes and getting considerable movement to twos and some to ones."[38]

It is not a very complicated language compared, for example, to the jargon of tax lawyers or solid-state physicists. But it suggests that to some extent, campaigning becomes a world of its own in which candidates, staffers, consultants, and the reporters who cover them can talk about their activities in a language outsiders may not understand.

Like other specialized language, one of its uses is to convey specialized knowledge that transcends the individual campaign as to what works in certain campaign situations and what does not. That knowledge, as the next chapter shows, is very limited and is vulnerable to rapidly changing conditions: a paper-thin protection against the strong winds of change. And even with the ease of observational learning, campaigners do not all have equal access to the channels of information exchange. The use of consultants costs money. Nonincumbents will have to spend their time and other resources to match an officeholding opponent's access to successful models. Incumbents and candidates with ample resources, in short, will have a much greater opportunity to learn from models than will newcomers or challengers without a lot of resources—who, of course, need it most. But as this knowledge develops and spreads through observational learning, the campaign process becomes even more professionalized.

Campaign tactics are not the only subjects that move through these networks of campaigners. Candidates and staffers learn about issues—not only from newspapers and research reports but also from one another's speeches, campaign literature, and direct conversation. They learn not only about the substance of political issues but about aspects that are more immediately vital to a campaign: the importance of particular issues to various groups and audiences, the appeal of different approaches to an issue in the eyes of these groups.

Beginning with the 1978 campaigns, for instance, several New Right candidates and consultants found that the abortion issue troubled certain groups of normally Democratic voters. They found that many fundamentalist and Catholic Democrats could be encouraged to vote against a Democratic incumbent when his or her challenger stressed pro-life themes. Several 1978 New Right campaigns were widely modeled by conservative candidates in 1980 and 1982. Candidates who learned the impact of the abortion issue from these models— who learned that an antiabortion stance could sway a certain proportion of voters, while a pro-choice stance seemed to have less electoral power—could certainly use that information in their own races.

There is no reason to expect that they forgot that learning once they took office; information of that kind is no less helpful to elected officials in dealing with their constituency than it is to candidates trying to win. Networks of campaign learning convey information that affects the treatment of issues *between* elections as well as during them by those candidates who win seats in state legislatures and statehouses, Congress, and the White House. Other forces also affect the agendas of legislatures and executives: the working environment of the legislature itself, the political skills of its members, the press of major events competing for attention. But clearly, what campaigners learn about issues during the race from other campaigners, consultants, and other sources carries over into their behavior as officeholders and representatives and influences the political agenda.

Finally, this discussion of modeling suggests that the influence of political parties on public life may not be nearly as frail as it is often pictured to be. Recall that campaigners will be especially attentive to models who are *like* them in important respects; the similarities help assure that the model's behavior will work for the observer too. To many campaigners, party affiliation will probably be an important kind of similarity. The periodic sweeps of one party at the polls remind candidates that at times, members of the same party are treated alike by many voters. Candidates whose political roots are in party activities are likely to place special importance on a shared party tie. Many political consultants and campaign activists direct candidates' attention to models of the same party. Party organizations do too, as chapter 5 shows.

To the extent that party is an important construct in campaigners' minds, then party affiliation will be an important determinant of their choice of models. That, in turn, reinforces the importance of party among elected officials; the links established for campaign purposes are very likely to continue once the winning candidates take office. We look more closely at parties in chapter 5; it may be, with apologies to Mark Twain, that the reports of their death are greatly exaggerated. But, first, let us get the active phase of the campaign in motion.

NOTES

1. Quoted in Alan L. Clem, *The Making of Congressmen: Seven Campaigns of 1974* (North Scituate, Mass.: Duxbury, 1976), 137.
2. James David Barber, *The Presidential Character,* 2nd ed. (Englewood Cliffs, N.J.: Prentice-Hall, 1977), 14.
3. Ibid.
4. As a means of simplifying the analysis, in this chapter I am assuming the candidate to be the primary strategist in the campaign. That is not always true; in fact, in campaigns for higher office the big decisions are often made by the campaign manager in consultation with pollsters, media advisers, and others. In those cases, of course, it is the experience of the manager, and his or her observational learning (including the instruction received from those consultants), that produces the strategies and responses. But no matter whose behavior is being predicted, the rules of learning are the same.
5. The concept of "presentation of self," derived from Erving Goffman's *The Presentation of Self in Everyday Life* (Garden City, N.Y.: Doubleday, 1959), has been applied with great insight by Richard Fenno in *Home Style* (Boston: Little, Brown, 1978), esp. chaps. 3 and 4.
6. In *The Lawmakers* (New Haven: Yale University Press, 1965), Barber writes: "Initial political candidacy represents a marked shift in the continuity of the person's regular life at work, in the home and community, a shift not clearly evaluated by general cultural norms nor clearly guided by special norms" (225).
7. See George McGovern, *Grassroots: The Autobiography of George McGovern* (New York: Random House, 1977), 177-78 and 242. Consistent with McGovern's support in the November election, the checks were generally for small sums. But they were viewed by the campaign as powerful rewards; listen to McGovern's account of one televised appeal, following an October speech on the war in Vietnam: "It raised one and a half million desperately needed dollars, the largest amount of money contributed in response to a political speech in American history. . . . An elderly couple sent $2; it was all they could afford from their social-security check. One family sent $100 of the money they had saved for a vacation they would postpone. Messages like that reconfirmed my conviction that I owed it to such people to continue to make the case for peace" (242).

8. As an indication of the differences between the two campaigns' strategies for handling the press, Jules Witcover writes that "an inquiring reporter was for Nixon a loaded bomb." See Witcover, *Marathon* (New York: Viking, 1977), 93.
9. Ibid., 231.
10. Witcover describes these Sears touches in the 1976 Reagan campaign for the Republican presidential nomination (ibid., 93). On 1980, see Jack W. Germond and Jules Witcover, *Blue Smoke and Mirrors* (New York: Viking, 1981), 109-15.
11. Well-described in Germond and Witcover, *Blue Smoke and Mirrors,* 120-30.
12. On the separability of tasks in a campaign, see Xandra Kayden's *Campaign Organization* (Lexington, Mass.: Heath, 1978), 53. On the differences between candidates' environments and those of their staff members, see Marjorie Randon Hershey, *The Making of Campaign Strategy* (Lexington, Mass.: Lexington, 1974), 99-104.
13. Tom Watson, "Hart Pushes 'Third Options' in Long-Shot Presidential Bid," *Congressional Quarterly Weekly Report* 41 (3 December 1983): 2539.
14. See Donald R. Matthews, *U.S. Senators and Their World* (New York: Vintage, 1960); and Sidney Verba and Norman H. Nie, *Participation in America* (New York: Harper & Row, 1972), chap. 8.
15. For an interesting argument on the relationships between occupational skills and politics, see Herbert Jacob, "Initial Recruitment of Elected Officials in the U.S.—A Model," *Journal of Politics* 24 (November 1962): 703-16.
16. Film director Otto Preminger, when told that Reagan had just been elected governor of California, is reputed to have mused, "I should have given him more work."
17. Quoted in Saul Pett, "President Carter: 'I am at ease' But Lack of Time, Experience Trouble Him," *Louisville Courier-Journal,* 23 October 1977, D-E3.
18. See Barbara Hinckley, *Congressional Elections* (Washington, D.C.: Congressional Quarterly, 1981), 26.
19. As Theodore Lowi has argued, "a theory of political innovation is virtually a theory of politics, and a theory of party innovation virtually a theory of party." See his "Toward Functionalism in Political Science," *American Political Science Review* 57 (September 1963): 571.
20. This is what organization theorists call "problem innovation": seeking new ideas because the existing behavior patterns are unsatisfactory or the environment has changed. See James G. March and Herbert A. Simon, *Organizations* (New York: Wiley, 1967), chap. 7. Note, however, that social-learning theory sees people as *learning* by observation—though not necessarily acting on that learning—constantly, whether or not they are in the market for new strategies.
21. In *Marathon,* 648.
22. In *Blue Smoke and Mirrors,* 98.
23. The same process seems to be at work when members of Congress decide how to vote on various issues. The major studies of "cue giving" find that expertise is a primary determinant; members of Congress are most likely to take their cues on issues from a colleague whose judgment is regarded as well informed and credible, and often one whose committee or leadership position gives him or her special access to information. See John W. Kingdon, *Congressmen's Voting Decisions,* 2nd ed. (New York: Harper & Row, 1981), 82-88, 105.
24. Other research traditions also conclude that people will learn observationally from

others who are similar to them in important ways. To someone interested in the diffusion of innovations, similarities between two sources allow them to communicate more effectively (and share a common "language") and thus make it more likely that they *will* communicate. See March and Simon, *Organizations*. In the cue-giving studies, similarities make the legislator more confident that he or she would agree with the cue giver, if there had been time and information to reach an independent judgment. See Kingdon, *Congressmen's Voting Decisions,* 75-82, 88-91, 105.

25. Ibid., 75-82.
26. See Jeane J. Kirkpatrick's *Political Woman* (New York: Basic Books, 1974), esp. chap. 5.
27. McGovern, *Grassroots,* 263.
28. Jeff Fishel, *Party and Opposition* (New York: McKay, 1973), 104.
29. This is probably as close as campaigns come to what organization theorists call "slack innovation" (March and Simon, *Organizations,* chap. 7)—innovation prompted by the existence of unused resources and a willingness to use them for change. Most campaigns are normally in such a bind for funds that their resources are hardly ever regarded as "unused"; in fact, resources are often committed to a use even before they are known to exist. But consultants do have slack periods between campaigns, and an incentive to use those periods to expand their information about workable strategies. That is the means by which they attract new clients.
30. Robert Goodman, quoted by Bernard Weinraub, "Bush Gets Lessons in Performing on TV," *New York Times,* 13 January 1980, 23.
31. See David Vidal, "U.S. Image-Makers Put Stamp on Venezuelan Campaign," *New York Times,* 2 August 1978, 2.
32. Douglas E. Kneeland, "A Casual Comment Led to George Bush's Candidacy," *Bloomington Herald-Telephone,* 27 January 1980, 15.
33. See "Gerrymandering: Matter of Life and Death?" *Common Cause* 6 (October 1980): 9.
34. For similar ideas in the literature on diffusion of innovations, see Everett M. Rogers with F. Floyd Shoemaker, *Communication of Innovations,* 2nd ed. (New York: Free Press, 1971), chap. 4.
35. The discussion here is necessarily general. As innovation research has found, different strategies will have different patterns of diffusion, depending on the nature of the strategy (how much it costs, how complicated it is, etc.) in relation to the nature of the individual campaign (its budget, type of district, the campaigners' learning histories, and other factors).
36. On the role of personal contact in diffusion, see Rogers with Shoemaker, *Communication of Innovations,* 164. In relation to geographical diffusion, see Elihu Katz et al., "Traditions of Research on the Diffusion of Innovation," *American Sociological Review* 28 (April 1963): 243.
37. See Richard Fenno's *Home Style* (Boston: Little, Brown, 1978), 164-68.
38. Witcover, *Marathon,* 230.

4. The Campaign as a Learning Experience

The candidate's first steps have been taken, and the race is on. Campaigners are no longer limited to speculating about the effects of their opening strategies; reactions are beginning to come in. Events of the current campaign start to loom larger as influences on campaigners' behavior. A congressional challenger takes a walking tour of an unemployment office, gives a short speech on the need for change, and gets good press; she issues an elaborate position paper on damage done by high interest rates and finds that nobody reads it. Day by day, event by event, new campaigners build up experience with various strategies and the reactions those strategies evoke. They learn more about the actions and track records of available models. They may revise their expectations about the likely results of certain strategies and relationships among events.

As in the case of the candidate's first moves, as the campaign unfolds social-learning theory leads us to look for interactions among the candidate's personal characteristics and prior learning, his or her behavior, and environmental forces. To understand those interactions, this chapter explores the nature of campaigns as learning situations. What kinds of environmental forces affect campaigners while the race is on? Where do these events or reactions come from, and what are the response consequences for candidates and staff members? How do the characteristics of individual campaigners affect the reactions they are likely to receive, and in what ways do certain situations "trigger" particular qualities and actions in campaigners? Let us begin with the impact of events.

Campaign Events and Reactions: Where Do They Come From?

People's behavior is responsive to environmental forces. But which ones? Candidates do not react to *everything* around them. Environmental events must be thought of as *potential* influences; some will attract the campaign's notice, and some will not. The relationships depend in part on the characteristics of the individual campaign; a labor-oriented Democrat, for example, will be more likely to pay attention to labor groups' concerns, and to get input from labor leaders, than will a conservative Republican. But some regular, systematic skews or distortions in the learning environment affect virtually all campaigners and help define the nature of the learning situation in campaigns.

One of the most interesting of these distortions involves the flow of "stimuli"—information, reactions, evaluations—into campaigns. Scholars differ in their views about the relationship between public opinion and political leaders, and about the role of elections in shaping that relationship.[1] But in the popular mythology about elections, the campaign is a time when candidates try to find out what voters want, when prospective leaders listen to stimuli from "the public." In that comforting mythology, we see candidates talking with senior citizens, listening to workers at a construction site, meeting farmers in their fields, and then citing in their speeches the little girl who asked about nuclear war or the unemployed auto worker who said the government should (or should not) be doing more about the economy.

That vision of campaigns leads, once the election is over, to the myth of the "mandate": that the winning candidate came closest to expressing the views of most voters and, unless the election was a real squeaker, should be given a chance to translate those views into public policy. Thus the Reagan victory in 1980, it was often argued, was not just a reflection of former President Carter's unpopularity or challenger Reagan's engaging personality, but was a "mandate" for lower taxes and less government. If Reagan articulated those ideas and won, the argument goes, then he must have been saying what most voters wanted to hear. These claims are common not only in presidential races but in elections for offices from county commission to Congress.

If a candidate's job is to find out what voters want—at least in the mythology of campaigning—then it is especially interesting to find that so few of the stimuli into a campaign actually come directly from voters. In fact, that is one of the most regular, systematic biases in the flow of stimuli into campaigns. Why, in an activity where candidates and voters are thought to be exchanging ideas and preferences, does so little of that occur?

Let us ask the same question a different way. If a candidate wants to find out what most voters think, how can he or she do so? Polls and canvassing are obvious answers. They can convey information about large numbers of people, including the politically inactive citizens who would not otherwise be known to a campaign. They can offer vitally important data: the candidate's name recognition, his or her image among voters, the opponent's strong and weak points, voters' responses to issue questions, their comparative judgment of candidates with respect to these issues, the questions that matter most to particular groups.

But these magical tools have their limits. Although the clean precision of numbers can leave the impression that public opinion is a quantity like an individual's height and weight, which the pollster can measure but does not influence, in fact public opinion is a slippery and sensitive thing. Such apparently simple choices as the phrasing of survey questions and the order in which those questions are asked can profoundly affect the results of a poll. Even the most highly respected polling firms have had to relearn that painful lesson on occasion—and most campaigns, at least below the presidential and senatorial levels, get their poll data from sources less expert than the most highly respected firms.

Further, the "voice of the people" does not speak for itself, even through polls; the data require some interpretation. And they always get it; very few polling specialists see themselves as nothing more than the voices of their numbers. As Larry Sabato points out, "most polling consultants will frankly admit that the line between the roles of data interpreter and political strategist is very thin, and that it is crossed frequently without any warning to a client."[2] In short, when contracting with a polling firm, a candidate is not buying a pound or two of raw public opinion but a pollster's interpretation of a set of survey data—and hoping that as little as possible will be lost in the translation. Voters' views, then, reach the campaign through a filter consisting of the choices, the experience, and even the personal beliefs of these political professionals.

Canvassing is even more vulnerable to the danger of distorting voters' views. Canvassers are usually volunteers—and usually avid supporters of the candidate. In their zeal they may interpret undecided voters as potential supporters and negative-leaning voters as undecideds.

Moreover, polls and canvassing cost a lot. Public opinion surveys are expensive; good ones are extremely expensive. Many state and local candidates will not be able to afford a good professional poll, much less a series of such polls, and an inexpensive survey conducted by volunteers may generate some painfully misleading results. Canvassing is costly in time and effort. A thorough canvass is a major campaign investment; it requires a lot of bodies to go door-to-door and a lot of staff time spent in supervising them. Given the size of that investment, most campaigns, especially those for local and state offices, will not be able to canvass more than once. They get a picture of voters' preferences that has more of the characteristics of a snapshot (and often one that is out of focus) than the unfolding detail of a moving picture.

A one-shot canvass, or one or two polls, can be less effective as learning devices than a candidate may hope. One obvious reason is that many voters' reactions change during a campaign. In the 1980 presidential race, for example, then-President Carter's poll ratings dropped about 10 percent during the weekend before the election; voters' feelings about the Carter-Reagan debate

The Campaign as a Learning Experience

of the previous week or late reminders of the presence of American hostages in Iran could have been responsible. Other Democratic candidates who had seen Carter's approval ratings rise during October, and who were depending upon a strong Carter showing to help their own chances, would have found it hard to predict the impact of those events on the basis of polls taken in October.

Besides, other information, which may conflict with messages provided by polls or canvassing, are coming into the campaign on a much more regular basis. A classic example is the 1964 presidential campaign of Republican Barry Goldwater. The candidate had poll data showing that his stands on some big issues were unappealing to most voters—that the "conservative majority" he claimed to see just was not there (or was there and simply did not like him). But the polls were intermittent. Day after day, on the other hand, the Goldwater campaign was showered with mail from strong supporters praising his stands on those very issues. The poll data turned out to be better predictors of the election result; Goldwater lost handsomely. But supportive letters, though coming from a minority, were continuously present in the campaign environment, and their message resonated with the long-held beliefs of the candidate and his staff. The result was that stimuli from the mass of voters—the ostensible focus of the campaign—played second fiddle to reactions coming from a much smaller group of devoted supporters, whose preferences differed greatly from those of the majority.[3]

Other campaign tools tell even less about what voters want. Television, radio, and newspapers are very effective means of reaching large numbers of voters, but the audiences of these media rarely get to talk back. Even the campaigners' own contact with voters does not convey much information. Most of these contacts—when the candidate shakes hands with workers at a plant gate or a staffer hands out literature at a shopping center—carry about as much substantive detail as does the conversation between two strangers who find themselves face to face in a receiving line.

The only other chance most voters have to provide stimuli to a campaign is when they enter a polling booth on election day. While the election result is a very powerful piece of information to a campaign, it has several drawbacks as a teacher. First, it does not come until the campaign is over—far too late to prompt any change in strategy. Second, it does not explain itself; the voting machine registers an individual's choice of candidates, not the reasons for that choice.

Thus elections have an ironic quality as learning situations for campaigners. The people who, in campaign mythology, are thought to be the "teachers" —the mass of voters—have very few opportunities to provide input into campaigns. While voters are *potential* influences in the campaign environment, they do not often get to speak for themselves as sources of stimuli. Richard Fenno writes about the incumbents he has studied:

> The more one observes members of Congress at work in their districts, the more impressed one is by the simple fact that people are hard to find. Members (and their staffs) expend incredible amounts of time and energy just trying to locate people to present themselves to.

He quotes one of those incumbents, talking about a party dinner the night before:

> I hope we won't see the same people today that we saw last night. I'm afraid we will. If you subtracted all the candidates, their wives, and their managers, there wasn't a "people" at the dinner. . . .[4]

But other kinds of people are not so hard to find: leaders of organizations, active citizens, and members of groups that want something from government. Campaigners spend much or most of their time in contact with these political activists. The result is that group leaders, local elites, and organized interests populate most of the *actual* environment of a political campaign. Moreover, the stimuli that these activists provide will probably be more frequent, more intense, and more explicit than those coming from most other voters — involving attempts to persuade the candidate on particular issues, information about the campaign's effectiveness in certain areas, and suggestions about strategy and tactics.

Among the most frequent and intense providers of stimuli are the candidate's strongest supporters — the people Fenno calls the "primary" and "personal" constituencies consisting of friends, close advisers, campaign staff members, and others whose support for the candidate is fervent and reliable.[5] When a campaigner considers how to approach a new issue or tries out an innovation, not many voters will be present to respond, or interested enough to respond. Some party activists may be, and some group leaders may be. But other members of the campaign organization and the candidate's closest advisers will probably be there, and will surely care enough to respond. As another campaign analyst explains:

> By spending so much time together, the campaign eliminates much of an individual's private life, causing him or her to rely more heavily on the organization for the kinds of supports and rewards normally found elsewhere. . . . Looking to each other for both professional and personal satisfactions may have added to their sense of being a group apart from others, a group engaged in a struggle.[6]

When these co-workers are a continuing, much-valued source of reactions, and not many other such sources are available, their influence on one another's behavior increases.

The campaign's behavior often depends upon *which* of these confidants, activists, or staffers are present *at the time a problem arises*. Far from considering the whole range of potential choices, campaigners normally deal with the stimuli available to them at the time. For example, during the second presidential debate in 1976, President Gerald Ford made the curious statement that Eastern Europe was not dominated by the Soviet Union. Reporters immediately called that a "gaffe"; Eastern Europe is, after all, very plainly dominated by the Soviets. Challenged, Ford compounded his problem by refusing to admit that, as they say in politics, he had "misspoken himself."

In the meantime, Ford's opponent, Jimmy Carter, was having problems of his own. Instead of capitalizing on the chance to demonstrate generosity and understanding, qualities he was often accused of lacking, Carter blasted away with both barrels; he charged shrilly that Ford's remark was "a disgrace to the country."[7] Both candidates' home staffs tried to convince them to take a different course. Neither staff succeeded. The reason was that both Carter and Ford were getting strong backing from the people traveling with them and strong positive crowd response; they did not take their home staffs' recommendations seriously. As one former press secretary stated: "It often happens in campaigns that the people who might have some impact or input just don't happen to be in the right place at the right time to give counsel."[8]

Because campaigners tend to hear mainly from other political activists—the candidate's closest supporters, his or her most vocal critics, and other elite voices—campaigning is a much better way to learn the views of these activists, and *their* interpretation of what voters want, than to learn the views of the rest of the constituents. That would be no problem, of course, if political activists could accurately represent the interests and concerns of most voters. But that is not likely. Activists and devoted partisans, by virtue of their very involvement in politics, have experiences different from those of most other citizens. Studies show that they differ in terms of personal characteristics (socioeconomic level, for example), the distribution of views on issues, and the importance attached to various issues.[9]

The ever-present danger is that because of this systematic bias in the stimuli available, a campaigner's learning will lead him or her to focus on issues and concerns that matter greatly to portions of the political elite but that do not touch the core of many or most voters' lives. For example, in his 1980 presidential campaign Ronald Reagan could not avoid raising a series of emotional issues such as school prayer and the teaching of evolution, not because these were burning issues to most citizens, but because they were vitally important to key activists in his supporting coalition. This is not uncommon; many candidates take stands on issues (or avoid taking stands) mainly in response to the reactions (or expected reactions) of their closest supporters or other very vocal groups in the constituency. For that reason, these activists' concerns take on an importance in the political agenda that may be far out of proportion to the interest they generate in the voting public. One prominent media adviser recalls:

> I don't think a day went by in the [1972] McGovern campaign when someone didn't get absolutely livid about what somebody was saying in a column that was read by only 1.5 percent of the people in this country, and this influenced the election because it influenced us to go out and do something or react to something or get upset with something.[10]

Some might call it "rational" for campaigners to pay greatest attention to their most vocal constituents.[11] The learning approach suggests that it is also almost inevitable; in many cases, campaigners have no alternative sources of stimuli to respond to. Their learning environment is full of ideas about what voters want and need. But those are *activists'* ideas about what voters want and need. And that activist filter colors and distorts what it transmits.

It is worth emphasizing that activists close to a campaign are likely to reinforce the candidate's own views. Men and women running for office tend to attract staff members and close supporters who share their perspectives on politics, who value their beliefs and personalities. Because they work so closely together and become major sources of stimuli for one another, they often develop shared beliefs about the meanings of particular events and the importance of various issues. Tim Crouse, writing about a similar tendency among national political reporters, called it "pack journalism"—reporters come to draw their cues largely from one another and thus develop shared interpretations of the meanings of a given set of events.[12]

Some campaigners may think, as they listen to their closest supporters and other activists, that they are hearing the voters' voices. Barry Goldwater's close advisers apparently believed that their enthusiastic mail and volunteers reflected the feelings of the American public, even in the face of polls (and election results) to the contrary. Perhaps this explains why so many challengers are more optimistic about their chances of winning than the realities of the race warrant; often ignored by almost everyone else, they are too easily influenced by the reactions of their closest supporters.[13] Consultants often complain that their candidates spend too much time with the already committed, and staff members use more effort trying to impress the candidate than the voters.

Understandably so; in the pressure-filled uncertainty of a campaign it is not surprising that many candidates spend more time in the company of friends and supporters than in seeking the company of those who do not know them or know but do not value them.

More experienced campaigners are often aware that the voices they hear are not necessarily typical of the distribution of views in their district. As one House member put it:

> Inevitably, you tend to spend most of your time with the people you are most compatible with, the people you identify with. That colors your perception of your district. These people, though, are only a part of your district. So it's a very imperfect mechanism.[14]

But because it is so hard to find out what the true distribution is, they cannot be sure how to "correct for" these biases in campaign stimuli—how to know, for example, whether a pro-Israel stance among fundamentalist leaders is typical of, different from, or simply irrelevant to the majority of fundamentalists in the constituency as a whole.

This characteristic of campaign environments, then, means that campaigners have to fight the ease with which they can become insulated from the concerns of the public they hope to serve. If all we require of a democracy is that we have a choice of more than one candidate per office, then this insulation will not be a real problem. But if we hope for more, if we ask that political leaders have a real understanding of ordinary people's needs and fears, then the extent to which campaign learning takes place in an activist environment must be a cause for concern. When citizens tell pollsters that they stay home on election day because politics just is not relevant to them, perhaps the message deserves more attention than it has received.

THE IMPACT OF THE ELECTION RESULT

The broader public does have one guaranteed means of providing input to campaigns. And that means is potentially very powerful. Remember that the use of various strategies is regulated by their consequences—by experience with the results of an action, by expectations of those results. Many kinds of response consequences guide a campaigner's behavior: approval given by people he or she values, favorable mentions in the media, financial support, self-respect. But perhaps the most interesting and powerful form of reinforcement is the one that is unique to campaigns: the vote on election day.

As a stimulus, the vote on election day should easily be able to grab campaigners' attention. It is, after all, the culmination and the ultimate goal of a campaign. The "horse-race" nature of media coverage keeps it ever in view.

It alone controls the candidate's chance to move into the limelight by taking office. For all these reasons, anticipation of the election result should have a potent impact on behavior during the campaign.

But there is a catch. Ideally, the process of learning from response consequences is like a social contract: an expectation that if I do X, I can be reasonably sure that Y will follow. But when a candidate decides to take a stand on a particular issue or accept one speaking engagement rather than another, the consequences are rarely so clear. The fate of a campaigner is to take several hundreds or thousands of actions during a race—positions on various issues, choices of staff members, decisions on media—and then receive the simple verdict of victory or defeat later, on election day. Which of those many actions were responsible for the election result, and to what degree? Did the candidate win because of his television ads, or would he have done better without them? Did she lose because she spent too little time with blue-collar voters or because of national trends over which she had no control?

The election result won't tell. To paraphrase V.O. Key, voters on election day can say only "yes" or "no" to a candidate, and observers are never really sure what was the stimulus for that response. So the election result is a very powerful teacher but not a very informative one. It is a generalized form of reinforcement whose relationship to any individual campaign decision is likely to be unclear. A winning candidate can be sure that *something* worked, but the specifics are open to conjecture. Because of that, campaigners often interpret a victory as a generalized reward for the whole package of strategies they used in the campaign. What follows? Unless there is reason to believe that the next campaign will be clearly different, a winning candidate will not be under any pressure to consider changes in preparation for the next race.[15]

In fact, without specific information as to which campaign behaviors were effective and which were not, it is risky to consider changes. Suppose the behaviors the candidate decides to change were the very behaviors that produced the victory? As one reporter writes, "no one has measured the political benefits of attending patriotic parades, but most politicians are afraid to find out by not showing up."[16] A member of Congress reaches a similar conclusion:

> I'm using the same approaches [as in the last election]. They've been tested and tried, and I think the prize is too valuable—when you've been successful at it—to deviate from the idea and the principle of getting it. So since it's been tested and tried, and worked in the past, I choose to do it until I find that the vote is slipping, and then I'll look to other means.[17]

Winning elections, then, has a fairly blunt, conservatizing effect on campaigners. As long as there are not many clues to the relationship between particular strategies and the election result, winning will encourage a candidate to keep the set of strategies used in the victorious race. If the environment remains similar, those strategies should generalize to the opening moves of the candidate's next campaign. In that way, "habits" or characteristic patterns are formed. Consider the congressman who has used the same design on his campaign matchbooks since he was first elected in the 1930s. When asked about it, he says with a smile, "Well, those matchbooks probably aren't the reason I keep getting re-elected, but who wants to drop them and take a chance?"[18] New tactics may be layered on the old in later races. But a behavior long associated with a generalized reward is a hard behavior to drop. It is superstitious learning, the product of an uncertain learning situation.

As a learning experience, the election result leaves a lot to be desired in the case of losers, too. The loser's dilemma is that the election outcome brings pressure to make changes, but does not say *which* behaviors should be changed and what new ones should be used instead. The situation is especially trying in campaigns that lose by a mile. Often treated like dead fish by other activists, these campaigners are not likely to get much constructive advice as to how their strategies could be modified effectively in order to win next time. In most cases, there will not be a next time; candidates who lose badly often respond to the frustration of their learning situation by not running again (nor is there normally any great demand for their reappearance). Those who do run again will be open to substantial changes in their strategies. Candidates who lose "respectably" will probably get more suggestions about the reasons for their loss. The changes that these losing campaigners make will depend largely on the nature of those suggestions—again, stimuli from close advisers and other activists.

But even though the election result has many of the qualities of a blunt instrument, it remains the focal point of the race, and so campaigners try to learn more specific answers from it. Most commonly, they do so by constructing their own explanations of what the voters were trying to say with their ballots—just as the specific impact of other response consequences depends upon the learners' interpretations of their meaning. Campaigners have good reason to look for likely interpretations of the election results; if they can derive the most plausible explanation for why they won or lost, and why other candidates similarly situated won or lost, they can better understand how to increase their support with an eye toward the next election.

Other political actors are also motivated to construct explanations of election results. Reporters and other media people want to get or keep a reputation for political insight, and to have something more than vote totals to report in their stories. Political consultants want to enhance their reputations by demonstrating their expertise at analyzing election results, and to put their campaign performance in the best possible light ("We lost the X and Y races because party registrations were so heavily against us; we won the Z race because of my brilliant media strategy"). Interest-group and party leaders also hope to puff up their reputations for political clout, as well as to gather information on the apparent effectiveness of various strategies or on changes in the political climate that can help them to be more effective next time.

There are some interesting discontinuities in this process. First, what the voters are saying is not necessarily what the candidates, reporters, and other active participants are hearing. While these activists want to learn the reasons for the voters' behavior, their own preconceptions will affect their ability to do so accurately. Second, the people directly involved in campaigning usually have a "public" explanation for election results—the explanation they offer to reporters and other groups—that differs to some degree from their "private" explanation—the one they truly believe. The two explanations stem from their two motives: on the one hand, to put the best possible face on the current election results so as to make themselves seem more able and influential; on the other hand, to learn how they might compete more successfully (or hold on to their current success) in the next race.

Sometimes a campaigner's two explanations merge; people do, after all, often come to believe what they say. But in the critical hours and days after the election, the public explanations take center stage. Campaigners, consultants, and party and group leaders engage in quick and intense competition to get their public explanations of the race reported as fact. Media people are the objects of this competition, for they have the means of spreading and giving credibility to the contending interpretations. The results of this process in turn have a big impact on campaigners' learning.

CONSTRUCTING EXPLANATIONS FOR ELECTION RESULTS
Even before the election results are known, people connected with a candidate's organization begin to offer—sometimes to promote—their own views about the likely causes of the upcoming vote. Their judgment often reflects their expectations as to what was likely to be important in the race, arising out of their experience with actions and outcomes. Once the vote takes place, many will try to find connections between the election outcome and particular strategic choices in a campaign. Some will examine the vote totals precinct by precinct to see where their supporters came from. In prominent races, network news teams and newspapers will take "exit polls," asking people leaving the polling place why they voted the way they did. Campaigners will ask other activists for ideas about what worked, what went wrong, and why. Sometimes their

explanation will focus on an event that received particular attention during the race: for example, a slip of the tongue that reporters dubbed a "gaffe," or a scandal with obvious bearing on the campaign.

One or more such explanations then spread from one campaign insider to others. Typically, one especially plausible and attractive explanation of the meaning of the election results tends to dominate. This explanation is picked up and repeated by activists close to the race: party leaders, interest-group activists. It is spread further by reporters covering the campaign, and that repetition makes the explanation sound even more believable. If it is not soon challenged by an alternative interpretation, it begins to take on the dignity of "established fact," no matter how factual it is.

The constructed explanation *may* have a great deal of empirical support, reflecting the findings of careful polling and precinct analysis. To qualify as the dominant explanation, it will have to mesh with what are generally accepted as the "facts" of the race. But it will by no means be the only *possible* explanation of the results. Electioneering is far from being an exact science. Even with the most careful exit polls, presidential campaigners will probably be left wondering about the impact of some of their actions ("If I had spent less time in Chicago and more in Detroit, would I have won?").[19] Candidates for other offices, with less money for polls and expert advice, will have more to wonder about.

Since the voters cannot explain themselves through their ballots, and since the polls, even when present, leave room for interpretation, the accepted explanation will almost always be *constructed,* not just out of voting results and poll data, but out of the experience and the prior learning of political elites. Very often, in fact, the dominant explanation for a particular election result is nothing more than the intuitive judgment of a trusted insider, diffusing among other activists until it becomes "common knowledge."

Consider the congressional elections of 1982. The results seemed to have a clear meaning on the surface. The Democrats gained 26 House seats, seven governorships, and control of several state legislatures. Compared with other midterm elections in a President's first term of office, this was the largest gain for an opposition party in 60 years. Turnout was up. The cause seemed to be the declining economy and the failure of President Reagan's economic policies to reverse that decline; economic issues had dominated the campaign, the media coverage, and the polls.

Wasn't this a case in which the vote totals spoke for themselves? The congressional elections were a referendum on Reaganomics, they seemed to say, and the nation voted no. Yet look again. If that explanation is accurate, then why was there no net party change in the Senate? Why, of the 29 House incumbents defeated in 1982, were so many moderate eastern Republicans—some of whom had questioned Reagan's economic policies—on the losing side rather than conservative Republicans more closely identified with the President? Even more puzzling, if the elections were a referendum on Reaganomics, then why did a postelection poll taken by CBS and the *New York Times* find that although 41 percent of the respondents blamed Reagan and the Republicans for the nation's economic troubles, fully 44 percent blamed the *Democrats*?[20]

Evidently, even though many voters seemed disappointed in a number of Republican officeholders, there was room for more than one explanation of the meaning of the election results. As early as election night, groups of leaders began competing to get their interpretations accepted by members of the national press corps and other political actors. House Speaker Tip O'Neill called the results a "disastrous defeat" for the Republicans, caused by the failure of Reagan's economic initiatives. Representative Tony Coelho, head of the Democratic Congressional Campaign Committee, told reporters that "Reagan and the Republicans blew it" by following economic policies that increased unemployment among the very groups—blue-collar workers in particular—that had forsaken the Democrats in 1980 to give Reagan his victory.[21] Soon after, a group of Republican governors laid their party's losses at Reagan's doorstep too, calling the election a "cry for help" and warning that the President and his administration had two short years to respond by adjusting its economic game plan.[22]

The Reagan administration had reason to promote a different interpretation of the vote. On election night, Reagan's Chief of Staff James A. Baker III pointed out that the Democratic House gains were balanced by the lack of Democratic gains in the Senate, and called the results "a wash"—a phrase that came readily to the lips of Reagan aides for several weeks thereafter. Don't blame Reaganomics, they suggested; that isn't what the voters meant. If it had been, Republicans would have lost seats in the Senate too.

New Right leaders pressed for yet another explanation. They called attention to what Evans and Novak described as "the two most fascinating campaigns of the mid-term election: Republican losses for governor of New York and Michigan."[23] These campaigns were so fascinating, they argued, because these two Republican candidates had sounded more like the Reagan of 1980 than did Reagan himself in 1982; cut taxes, the candidates insisted, and hew to the Right in social policy. In races they had been expected to lose badly, both candidates came within five or six points of winning. So the real meaning of the 1982 elections, New Righters contended, was that Republicans had lost ground because the administration had watered down its 1980 campaign promises. The answer, then, was to return to pure Reaganomics and quit compromising.

Thus even in an election year where the trends seemed self-evident, there was still enough uncertainty about voters' behavior and poll results to invite efforts to "clarify" their meaning. The voters had not had the opportunity to speak directly on policy issues, nor to give reasons for their choices. The voters hardly ever do. Instead, political elites fought to win the battle of the constructed explanations, to get their interpretation of the vote accepted as the definitive explanation.

Following the 1982 election, media people rapidly began to converge on a modified O'Neill-Coelho explanation: the vote had been a Democratic success, though not of heroic proportions, for which the Reagan economic program and its lack of "fairness" bore the major responsibility. The growing acceptance of that explanation affected many campaigners' thinking about their futures. Not all, of course; not everyone believed it. For those whose private explanations of the vote differed from the dominant public account, the explanations they derived differed too. But many others were likely to draw conclusions relevant to their own future campaigning: for instance, that Mr. Reagan's great personal charm and speaking ability were not sufficient to protect candidates who espoused Reagan's policies and shared his party label; that as long as the current economic conditions prevailed, Democrats could touch a chord in important portions of their constituencies by questioning the fairness of the President's economic policies.

Whether the O'Neill-Coelho explanation was "correct" in any objective sense is largely beside the point. It will be remembered by attentive candidates when they make their next race, by political activists and other campaigners in search of models. In this way, the explanations that campaigners construct can modify the blunt impact of the election result and can give it more explicit meaning as a learning device — meaning supplied largely by political elites.

Presidential primaries offer another intriguing setting for examining features of election results as learning devices. In many ways, the race for a presidential nomination is like a series of learning trials. About three dozen states hold primary elections during a four-month period; each presidential campaigner, then, experiences about three dozen election results during that time. Because these events occur in a sequence, rather than all on the same day, campaigners have the opportunity to adapt their strategies in later primaries based on what they have learned from earlier primaries.

Take Ronald Reagan's 1976 presidential campaign, for instance. Though Reagan had to wait four more years before winning the Presidency, his campaign for the Republican nomination in 1976 was notable in many respects. Not least was its effect on the national political agenda; one of its most prominent accomplishments was that (in the words of one political writer) "strange as it may seem, the Panama Canal is one of the major issues of current American politics."[24] By tracing how this issue made a splash (if a short-lived one) in American political history, we find that the culprit was the effort to learn from a primary election defeat.

Ronald Reagan had gone into the 1976 Republican primaries expecting to do very well. His opponent, Republican President Gerald Ford, was the man on whose mishaps comedian Chevy Chase had built his career, imitating Ford's frequent struggles with desks, microphones, and airplane doors. There were other reasons for Reagan to be confident. Ford had the liabilities of an incumbent—he had been in office long enough to make a number of unpopular decisions—without all of the advantages. In particular he did not have an incumbent's vital advantage of having already run a successful campaign for that office; Ford had been appointed vice-president by Richard Nixon after the elected holder of that office resigned in disgrace, and became President when Nixon followed suit. By the time of the first primary in New Hampshire, many observers were predicting that the "accidental President" would fall victim to Reagan's challenge.

But a funny thing happened on the way to victory. Some of Reagan's proposals came under heavy attack during the New Hampshire campaign, from both Ford and the media. In particular, Reagan's plan to transfer a number of federal social programs to state or local control—a plan he argued would save the government $90 billion—"looked screwy and was worrisome to social security beneficiaries," as one analyst put it.[25] When election day came, Reagan narrowly lost in New Hampshire. Because he had been portrayed as the likely winner, even the credit for having *almost* beaten an incumbent President in his own party was denied him.

As we would expect, losing was a generalized negative result; Reagan's people were motivated to change their strategy, but the election outcome was mum, as usual, as to what particular changes would have given them a win. The next primary, in Florida, was fast approaching. The direction of any actual change, we have said, will reflect the conclusions drawn by the candidate's closest advisers and other activists about the reasons for the loss. In this case, the conclusions all pointed to a need for new issues. Reagan had been heavily criticized, even ridiculed, for several of his domestic policy proposals. But he had made only one speech on foreign policy during the New Hampshire campaign. Understandably, Reagan's advisers linked those domestic initiatives with the primary defeat; foreign policy, on the other hand, had not been tainted. The use of foreign policy issues had other advantages. The Reaganites knew from poll data that their man scored higher than the President on certain specific foreign policy issues. And they knew that one of Ford's weak points was

The Campaign as a Learning Experience

a public perception that he was not a strong, decisive leader. Foreign policy, they felt, could best showcase Reagan's leadership style compared to Ford's. On the day after the New Hampshire primary, by one account, Reagan's chief strategist John Sears made a decision. "We didn't quite make it last night," he told his disappointed candidate. "We're going to have to start talking about foreign policy."[26]

But which aspects of foreign policy? Reagan's polls showed Ford at a disadvantage, especially among Republican activists, on détente with the Soviet Union, Ford's support of Secretary of State Henry Kissinger, and the proposal to give Panama control over the American-built Panama Canal. The Canal issue, though it was by no means a central concern of most Americans in 1976,

> ... was a kind of litmus test for patriotism among conservatives, as Reagan knew, and certainly it was when it was discussed—as Reagan invariably did—in terms of America's inalienable rights. He had begun to weave into his speech a report from Latin America contending that the Ford administration had secretly accepted a compromise formula that would give Panama sovereignty over the canal. . . . For a while, the Panama Canal pitch was not much of an applause-getter. But then one day, before a retirement community in Sun City, near Tampa, Reagan cranked it out, and out of the blue, bedlam broke loose. "Reagan, who knows his audience very well, was so taken aback that he lost his place," [aide David] Keene said. After that, references to the Canal were sure-fire cheer lines.[27]

The tumultuous response was particularly welcome after the unexpected and painful loss in New Hampshire. Reagan did not win in Florida; the primary vote broke for Ford, 53 to 47 percent. Reagan's advisers saw Florida as a reward nevertheless, because they had expected to run much more poorly. Campaign pollster Richard Wirthlin explains:

> The press—either NBC or CBS—indicated that Reagan's foreign policy thrust [begun after the New Hampshire loss] had failed because we lost Florida. The thing they didn't know was that right after the New Hampshire primary, we were down eighteen percentage points [in Florida], and that we made up about fourteen of those percentage points in ten days using the foreign policy issues as the vehicle to contrast leadership style.[28]

And so Reagan's position on the Panama Canal ("We built it, we paid for it, it's ours, and we're going to keep it!") won an honored place in his speeches from that point on.

It is a classic case of campaign learning. A presidential candidate had come into a primary as the front-runner and came out as the also-ran. The voters' rejection was diffuse; the campaigners were hungry for more specific clues. Those available to provide stimuli were those closest to the candidate: his pollster, his chief strategist. The campaign changed emphasis in response to those stimuli. Soon, the uproarious audience approval gave Reagan's people the expectation that they were on the right track. They focused on the issue that had brought the reward. It carried their hopes. When what was expected to be a big Reagan loss in Florida turned out to be a close race, the change in emphasis was confirmed.

The change had a broader impact as well. Reagan's success with the Panama Canal issue quickly drew the notice of other candidates. Conservative Republicans, in particular, had reason to expect that the appeal might work for them too. The process of observational learning, guided by the criteria of success and similarity, was well under way. Increasing numbers of campaigners began to stress their criticisms of the proposed U.S. treaties with Panama. Other candidates in those races had to respond. The Panama Canal had moved onto the campaign agenda of 1976.

Having reached prominence in the campaign, the Panama Canal treaties remained in the public eye after Jimmy Carter was elected President. When Carter sent the completed treaties to the Senate for action, senators' statements and votes on the issue were watched much more closely than they might have been otherwise. The new President found it necessary, as a result, to use many more of his scarce resources to win those votes than he might have needed otherwise. Even House members took public positions on the agreement, though the House has no constitutional role to play in the approval of treaties.

In this way, a policy question that might have been expected to burn only in conservative circles took center stage in American politics. Other foreign policy concerns would seem to have deserved at least as much attention: the nuclear arms race, for example, where the stakes are much higher than the fate of the Panama Canal. Many other issues could have been made symbolic, as Panama was, of people's fears about America's vulnerability in an increasingly threatening world. But it was the fate of the American-built canal in Panama to become one of the relatively few issues to receive substantial attention during that time from candidates, officeholders, other activists, and the media.

The reason had to do with the learning environment of political campaigns. To summarize, the diffuse reinforcement that election results provide—the lack of a clear relationship between the vote on election day and the various issue appeals and other strategies a candidate has used to influence that vote—leaves a lot of room for interpretation. When votes add up to a victory, the temptation will be to cast a blanket of reward, of presumed effectiveness, over everything the winning campaign did (though for purposes of building a governing coalition, a winning campaigner may choose to supply meaning to the election result by calling it a "mandate" for one of the issue positions he or she stressed). When the candidate loses, the election result does not explain why.

Nor do voters normally have any other opportunity to explain why; in the absence of well-designed and very sophisticated polling operations, which many candidates cannot afford, there are simply no channels through which the majority of voters can tell a congressional candidate whether they voted no on her views about property taxes, her qualifications for the job, or her personal style. So the learning that campaigners derive from the election result—the primary response consequence in a campaign—depends heavily on the process by which they construct explanations for the meaning of the vote and work to get their explanation accepted by other actors in the race.

Other campaign reinforcements can be a lot more informative than the vote on election day. Consider fund-raising appeals. Different kinds of broadcast or mailed appeals for money can be compared in terms of their immediate, tangible results: the amount of hard cash they bring in. Fund-raising mailings ask the donor to send back a special card or envelope for that very purpose, so each donation can be traced back to the appeal that prompted it. That gives fund-raising specialists some relief from the uncertainty that plagues most other campaign behaviors. It lets them experiment, try new methods, and draw some confident conclusions as to which appeals work effectively for which candidates.

In contrast, it is ironic that while the election result plays such a prominent role in the life of a representative democracy, campaigners' ability to interpret and learn from that election result is so limited. The meaning that the vote totals take on—the information that guides campaigners and elected officials in deciding how to approach their constituencies—is provided mainly by the judgment of political activists and reporters. That voters can "speak" on election day is obviously important. But if campaigners listen for more than yes or no, what they hear is heavily filtered—and those filters bear the marks of activists' experiences and understanding. Even more, they often bear the marks of the candidate's own closest supporters.

Incumbency: The Advantages and Drawbacks of Winning

We have seen, then, that the nature of the election result as a response consequence affects campaigners' learning as they look ahead to the next race. It is especially interesting to trace the effects of the election result on incumbents' behavior, since the experience of winning an election—and other aspects of campaigning as a learning experience—gives incumbents several learning advantages. In fact, those advantages may help explain why incumbents of many offices are so likely to win reelection.

Perhaps the biggest advantage is the most obvious one: incumbents have already developed a set of strategies that seemed to work at least once, in the sense of having ended in victory. They may not know exactly why; indeed, they may have won *in spite of* some of the choices they made. But they do know that the whole package of strategies apparently brought voter approval. In the next campaign, when they must decide which of several speaking invitations to accept or which of two competing events to attend, tradition can serve as their guide. Their previous experience (and the advice of activists) has probably given them some indication as to which event is more important to attend. These simple but vital decisions are much harder for newcomers to make effectively.[29]

Incumbents also have the great advantage of more time to learn, since they receive campaign-related stimuli between elections as well as during campaigns. While potential challengers are at work in their law offices or places of business, incumbents are hearing from voters, speaking to groups, contacting reporters, and communicating with one another in the legislature or city council or Congress. The more contacts they have, the more opportunities for learning are available to them.

Incumbents receive more stimuli from a greater variety of sources than challengers do; after all, an incumbent is expected to stay in touch with his or her district between elections, while a challenger has the status of "candidate," and receives stimuli as a candidate, mainly during the briefer "active phase" of the campaign. Powerful groups in the district are likely to contact an incumbent even if they had opposed him or her because the incumbent, not the losing candidate they preferred, has a say in the policy matters that concern them.

Incumbents have a variety of means to contact constituents at less cost than challengers can. Among members of Congress, for example, free mailing and phone privileges, paid staff members, and free trips to the district can all be used to get more information about constituents and inform them of the incumbent's good qualities, all at the taxpayer's expense. The increasing importance of casework—helping to solve constituents' problems with government agencies—means that incumbents are contacted by people who might not otherwise communicate with political leaders and may not yet be part of the incumbent's supporting coalition.

An incumbent may muff the opportunity, of course. Not all incumbents handle casework well; some may find that their more extensive contacts simply give them more chances to make enemies. And some challengers—those in races for higher office, those tagged as potential winners—might be visible enough during the campaign to increase the amounts of stimuli they receive, especially from groups and individuals not represented in their supporting coalition, almost to an incumbent's customary level. Incumbency, then, "is not an automatic advantage . . . ; rather it is a *resource* that members [of Congress] are more or less successful in exploiting."[30]

In particular, in all these ways, it is a resource for learning—for gaining information, for developing more finely tuned expectations about the links between actions and their consequences. Thus it is not only the lack of money or name recognition that puts so many challengers at a disadvantage in campaigns; it is their relative inexperience with the difficult learning situation that campaigns provide. Without an already successful strategy, and with fewer opportunities to learn from experience and assess the usefulness of possible models, challengers start out with a learning deficit compared with most incumbents. It is a deficit from which most challengers never recover.

Incumbency also has disadvantages for effective learning. As the years of incumbency increase, election victories build up layers of reward, layers of incentive to repeat the rewarded strategies. The officeholder's behavior and perceptions will have been reinforced more and more as he or she attracts supporters who appreciate the incumbent's voting record and personal style. Those long-standing beliefs and strategies can easily take on the force of habit; with such regular reward, there is little reason to think about acting or believing differently. Since the learning situation is always at least somewhat uncertain, why risk change?

The building of habits can make for efficient responses—as long as the environment stays the same. But environments rarely stay the same. When change does occur, a bigger, more dramatic change may be necessary to alter the incumbent's behavior than that of a candidate whose habits are not so firmly set. If the district is changing a little at a time—different kinds of people moving in, a potential challenger gaining support, a party organization atrophying, a staff becoming more complacent—a well-ensconced incumbent may miss the signs of change, may overlook the need for new responses until the situation has become critical. The long history of reward, the cocoon of support, can buffer a long-time incumbent from an environment that is becoming, a bit at a time, more hostile to his or her habitual approach.[31]

If the incumbent is oblivious to the little alarm bells that keep ringing in the district and in the campaign, then his or her learning advantages may finally become hazards; the incumbent may no longer be able to make use of the more abundant information that comes to those with experience. Incumbents, in short, can become victims of victory. They can become better and better adapted to circumstances that are less and less prevalent.

Perhaps the best conclusion is that incumbency is a learning advantage for a limited time. Incumbents who have run two or three successful races, or more, can attract more useful information than their challengers can, and draw upon a campaign formula that has worked before. But there comes a point for most incumbents when habits begin to creep up on their ability to learn.

That point may come later in relation to some campaign activities than others. The more an activity produces clear-cut results—information about what is effective and what is not—the longer an incumbent's learning advantages will continue. For example, when a member of Congress is asked to help a constituent pry a check out of a reluctant federal agency, the results are easy to measure. The check either appears or it does not. The time it took to appear is easy to determine. The constituent's reaction is likely to be heard quickly. With more experience and some observational learning, the incumbent's staffers can learn which agency employees are helpful, what appeals will speed up the agency's response, what to tell the frustrated constituent in the meantime. Because the results are measurable, increasing experience with casework should improve an incumbent's capacity to perform it well.

In contrast, what Richard Fenno calls an incumbent's "home style"—the ways incumbents present themselves to their constituents and explain their activities—is a broad, diffuse set of behaviors whose impact is very hard to measure. It is difficult to tell which particular parts of that style are effective in winning voter support and which are not; the results of an incumbent's effort to seem trustworthy and sympathetic are harder to specify than are the results of calling employee A rather than employee B to locate a delayed social security check.

For that reason, it is difficult for incumbents to learn how to make specific changes in their home styles in response to changing conditions. It is harder, in short, for incumbents to learn from experience with respect to their home style. So once a new incumbent's style has been rewarded with election victory, it is likely to reach the "habit" phase fairly early in his or her career. As Fenno points out:

> Whereas, in the beginning, prospective House members are uncertain as to what kinds of home activities will work, once they have one or two testing elections behind them, they become more confident. They probably have no clear idea, as we noted earlier, of which element of home activity was responsible for how much of their support. But they do know that the sum of the elements contributed to victory. So the temptation is to keep the support they had "last time." Maintaining an established home style becomes part of the protectionist perspective.[32]

The stability of home styles is also encouraged by the expectations of constituents; once people have gotten used to an incumbent's style, they come to expect it and may punish him or her for acting "out of character."

This does not mean, of course, that home styles and other aspects of an incumbent's behavior inevitably "harden," like a clay sculpture drying into permanence. But it does mean that in many aspects of campaigning (such as self-presentation), we cannot expect innovation to come from long-time incumbents unless they have experienced a major change in circumstances, such as the near loss of an election, a sharp change in issues, or a major redrawing of their district's boundaries. At the aggregate level, then, innovations in political campaigning are much more likely to be introduced by newcomers and by moderately experienced campaigners who have not yet nailed down a series of comfortable election victories.

INTERACTIONS: CANDIDATES AND SITUATIONS

The learning environment of a campaign, like other environmental forces, is not a one-way influence. The case of incumbency is just one example, though an important one, of the ways in which campaigners' personal characteristics interact with the learning environments of campaigns. The characteristics and behavior of campaigners can affect the situations they face, by activating some parts of the environment and not others, by provoking certain kinds of reactions, by calling forth certain expectations in other people. In that way, campaigners have a hand in creating their own environments.

For example, consider a candidate who believes strongly in "right-to-work" laws—legislation that, despite its name, is designed to undercut the power of labor unions. Simply by making that position known, he or she helps to shape the environment of the campaign organization. Among the many Political Action Committees and other groups that might *potentially* get involved in the race, the candidate's right-to-work stance will surely activate certain groups and discourage others. It will probably assure the candidate of contributions from the National Right-to-Work Committee and other antiunion fund raisers. It will undoubtedly increase labor's interest in the candidate's opponent. It will draw certain key activists to the candidate's side and turn off others who might have considered working for the candidate of their party under other circumstances. The candidate's positions on issues, then, can help to shape the environment in which he or she runs.

A candidate's personality characteristics can also shape the influence of environmental forces by affecting the candidate's learning skills—for example, his or her awareness of events in the race. The fact that an event occurs, or that some ideas are offered, does not necessarily mean that the campaigner will pay attention to or understand them. Some qualities, such as high levels of anxiety, can interfere with campaigners' attention to events. And people with a learned pattern of low self-esteem, even though they may want to respond effectively to other people's expectations, are more likely to misunderstand information directed at them.[33]

These influences on people's ability to receive and understand information are a central concern of one major study of American Presidents: James David Barber's *The Presidential Character*.[34] Barber classifies Presidents according to whether they are active or passive in the job, and positive or negative in their attitude toward politics and the uses of presidential power. Interestingly, those he terms "active-positives"—including Franklin D. Roosevelt and John F. Kennedy—were particularly good learners; they sought feedback on their behavior and made adjustments accordingly. "Active-negatives" such as Richard Nixon and Lyndon Johnson, in contrast, tended to be less flexible and more closed to stimuli. Their learning was deeply affected by qualities such as low self-esteem and high anxiety, which restrict a learner's attention and ability to grasp new information.

These same influences operate in campaigns. As Barber's book shows, people with "learning deficits" can act effectively enough to win office. They may even keep winning as long as their environment does not change very much. But because their attentiveness to new stimuli is limited, they will probably keep repeating the strategies learned in earlier campaigns, oblivious to subtle changes in circumstances. When the environment does change, a candidate whose learning skills are heavily burdened might miss the change altogether or misunderstand what it means. His or her behavior, then, might appear oddly inappropriate—as Nixon's sometimes did during the Watergate crisis—when in fact it simply reflects the impact of personal characteristics on learning and then on environmental events.

The campaign's environment in turn affects campaigners' beliefs and expectations. Recall, for example, the presidential campaign of John Anderson in 1980. Anderson was a long-time Republican congressman from Illinois who had always run to win. Having faced and beaten back a bitter primary challenge in 1978, Anderson decided to retire from Congress and run for President; he held the fond (if quixotic) dream that once he won the Republican nomination, he would attract enough Democratic and independent votes to defeat Jimmy Carter. But the primaries proved disappointing; the largely conservative Republican primary voters liked Ronald Reagan better. It became clear that Anderson would not be his party's nominee.

Some of his supporters urged Anderson to keep running as an independent candidate against *both* Reagan and Carter. Prompted by a growing distaste for both rivals and the policies they stood for, Anderson did enter the general election campaign as an independent. But the polls kept telling their mournful tale: Anderson's popular support was dropping, and he had virtually no chance of winning the election. As things got worse, Anderson's focus began to change. No longer really expecting to win, he turned more and more from election-oriented candidate to political visionary. Said one top aide, "He now has this vision and passion about trying to wake America up, about freeing it from political myopia." A newsmagazine reported:

> Privately, Anderson and his advisers have begun talking about their campaign as the first step to "something different" in American politics—perhaps a new party or a realignment of the Democrats. . . . "The country is not quite willing to accept what I am saying, but I think someday they will." That future vindication, more than anything else, keeps Anderson in the race, a martyr for a noble cause.

Another aide admitted, "There is a certain amount of Joan of Arc in this campaign."35

The expectations of Anderson about the impact of his candidacy had been changed by events—by primary results, by polls, by the difficulty of raising money. His strategy shifted as a result. By election day, his earlier dreams had given way to the hope that he would win at least 5 percent of the vote, the minimum necessary for him to receive public funding to repay most of his campaign debts. (He did.) His lifelong Republican loyalty had given way as well. Even after the 1980 elections Anderson showed no interest in returning to the party fold; in fact, in 1984 he endorsed the Democratic presidential nominee, Walter F. Mondale.

John Anderson was changed by the events of his presidential campaign. At the same time, some of Anderson's own characteristics—his stands on some issues, his appeal, his decisions—helped create those events. Political campaigns have some fascinating, even unique features as learning situations. But the learning experience of a campaign also depends on the interaction between those features and the campaigner's characteristics as a learner.

CAMPAIGN LEARNING: SUMMARY

This chapter has developed a sketch of political campaigns as learning experiences, drawing on the social-learning principles presented in chapter 2. The sketch pictures a learning environment populated largely by political activists—other campaigners, party and interest-group leaders, reporters. The information and reactions coming into campaigns are often *about* voters, but very seldom directly *from* voters. This activist "filter" colors that incoming information, and frequently reinforces the candidate's own beliefs and expectations.

The voters' main opportunity to convey their preferences comes on election day; the election result is the main response consequence in a campaign. But as a teaching tool the election result is vague; it does not say which of a candidate's strategy decisions, issue positions, or personal qualities it is rewarding, which it is punishing, and to what extent. It is difficult for most campaigners to learn, in specific and practical terms, what the voters meant. Yet the importance of the election result as a response consequence means that activists will *try* to learn what caused it. Typically, a plausible explanation for a candidate's win or loss originates with campaign insiders, spreads rapidly to other active observers, and is diffused more widely and given credibility by media people. It quickly becomes established as the dominant "explanation" of the vote and influences what campaigners learn from the race. Again, campaigners' learning depends primarily on the explanations constructed by other activists, rather than on direct contact with the voters.

Because the learning situation of a campaign is so difficult, those who have had experience with it and won—the incumbents—normally hold an advantage. Repeated victories can dull that advantage, however, leading incumbents to cling tenaciously to earlier patterns of campaigning even when conditions change. The case of incumbency shows that although the learning environment of campaigns is distinctive and powerful, its impact depends in part on the actions and characteristics of individual campaigners; they are not only affected by that environment, but in turn help to shape it.

Before we carry these ideas into the real-life struggles of Senate campaigns targeted by the pro-life movement, there is one other relationship to be considered. As American campaigns have become more candidate-centered, political party organizations have become part of the campaign environment rather than part of the campaign itself. The relationships between campaigns and party organizations are important to examine; they have implications for the governing and the coherence of a democratic society as well as for the nature of campaigns as learning experiences. The next chapter explores those relationships and considers their meaning.

NOTES

1. See, for example, Norman R. Luttbeg, *Public Opinion and Public Policy,* 3rd ed. (Itasca, Ill.: Peacock, 1981); and W. Lance Bennett, *Public Opinion in American Politics* (New York: Harcourt Brace Jovanovich, 1980).
2. Larry J. Sabato, *The Rise of Political Consultants* (New York: Basic Books, 1981), 74; see also 92-104.
3. See Philip E. Converse et al., "Electoral Myth and Reality: The 1964 Election," *American Political Science Review* 59 (June 1965): 333-36.
4. In *Home Style* (Boston: Little, Brown, 1978), 234 and 90.
5. Ibid., chap. 1.

6. Xandra Kayden, *Campaign Organization* (Lexington, Mass.: Heath, 1978), 65.
7. Quoted in John H. Kessel, *Presidential Campaign Politics* (Homewood, Ill.: Dorsey, 1980), 162.
8. Richard H. Stewart, quoted in Ernest R. May and Janet Fraser, *Campaign '72: The Managers Speak* (Cambridge, Mass.: Harvard University Press, 1973), 114. Note that, in this case, at least one of the two campaigns had polling data available very quickly to gauge voters' reactions; but the counsel of the advisers traveling with the candidate overrode the poll results for some time.
9. See, for example, Sidney Verba and Norman H. Nie, *Participation in America* (New York: Harper & Row, 1972), esp. chap. 6; and John S. Jackson III et al., "Herbert McClosky and Friends Revisited," *American Politics Quarterly* 10 (April 1982): 158-80.
10. Charles Guggenheim, quoted in May and Fraser, *Campaign '72*, 257.
11. An example of a rational-choice argument on this point is in Anthony Downs, *An Economic Theory of Democracy* (New York: Harper & Row, 1957), 88-93.
12. See Crouse's *The Boys on the Bus* (New York: Ballantine, 1972).
13. In fact, that is probably a happy misperception for a democratic system; if House challengers, for instance, were completely realistic about their chance of winning (in a typical election, over 90 percent of them lose), most would not bother to run. These supportive environments help protect people with "deviant" views against pressures to merge with the majority. See Louis Sandy Maisel, *From Obscurity to Oblivion* (Knoxville: University of Tennessee Press, 1982), chap. 1.
14. Quoted in Fenno, *Home Style*, 11.
15. I do not mean to imply that a winner will necessarily become resistant to any change. Rather, he or she will not be motivated to substitute a new strategy as long as the current approaches are getting good results.
16. Brian Werth, "Politicians on Parade," *Bloomington Herald-Times*, Sunday, 4 July 1982, A-14.
17. Quoted in Marjorie R. Hershey, *The Making of Campaign Strategy* (Lexington, Mass.: Lexington, 1974), 118-19.
18. Interview by the author.
19. Polling and simulation partisans might argue that these questions are, in theory, resolvable. Even if that were so, they are unlikely to be resolved in practice; very few campaigns, especially below the presidential level, are well-heeled enough at the end of the race to be able to afford the sophisticated analyses that would be required.
20. See *Newsweek*, 15 November 1982, 34-37.
21. Ibid. According to *Newsweek*, 78 percent of Democratic identifiers who voted for Reagan in 1980 supported a Democrat for Congress in 1982.
22. David Broder, "GOP Governors Warn Reagan Team," *Bloomington Herald-Times*, Sunday, 21 November 1982, A10.
23. Rowland Evans and Robert Novak, "Returning to 1980 Theme," *Bloomington Herald-Telephone*, 6 November 1982, 6.
24. Elizabeth Drew, *American Journal* (New York: Random House, 1977), 239.
25. Jonathan Moore and Janet Fraser, eds., *Campaign for President* (Cambridge, Mass.: Ballinger, 1977), 4.
26. Jules Witcover, *Marathon* (New York: Viking, 1977), 398.

27. Ibid., 402.
28. Quoted in Moore and Fraser, *Campaign for President,* 47.
29. In fact, several studies show that incumbents often become more selective in their campaigning over time; they tend to cut down on minor campaign activities and concentrate on two or three big projects, while challengers are more likely to spread themselves thin. See David A. Leuthold, *Electioneering in a Democracy* (New York: Wiley, 1968), 75-76, 110, 123.
30. Thomas E. Mann and Norman J. Ornstein, "The Republican Surge in Congress," in *The American Elections of 1980,* ed. Austin Ranney (Washington, D.C.: American Enterprise Institute, 1981), 265.
31. Interestingly, a 1978 survey found that incumbent members of Congress were more likely than their challengers to say that there had been little or no change in their district during the past few years. See Eugene J. Alpert, "Candidates' Perceptions of District Opinion" (Paper presented at the annual meeting of the Midwest Political Science Association, 1979).
32. Fenno, *Home Style,* 189.
33. See Paul M. Sniderman's *Personality and Democratic Politics* (Berkeley: University of California Press, 1975).
34. 2nd ed. (Englewood Cliffs, N.J.: Prentice-Hall, 1977).
35. David M. Alpern et al., "Playing for Posterity," *Newsweek,* 13 October 1980, 41.

5. Do Political Parties Matter in Campaigns?

The theory is now in place. But before sending it out to confront the real world — at least the real worlds of Senate campaigns targeted by the pro-life movement in 1980 — let us draw on it once more. There has been a lively debate over the present status and likely future of political parties in American politics. The dominant view during the 1970s was that the parties' strength was rapidly fading; the insightful columnist David Broder, for example, titled his book on the subject *The Party's Over.* Many researchers agreed, armed with a variety of findings: fewer voters than ever before call themselves Republicans or Democrats or are guided by the party label when they vote; candidates rely increasingly on their personal organizations, the media, and interest groups to win office, rather than their party organization; the parties themselves do not stand for much in terms of issues. In short, the argument goes, political parties are no longer an important part of the campaign environment.

Yet some party organizations seem not to have heard of their own decline. Take the example of the Republican National Committee in 1980; along with two other national Republican groups, it spent $9.4 million to put party-boosting ads like these on national television:

> PASSENGER IN CAR: Congressman, I think we're running out of gas.
> ANNOUNCER: It's not as if the Democrat Congress didn't have a warning. The last three Presidents warned them.
> PASSENGER: Congressman, we *are* running out of gas.
> ANNOUNCER: But the Democrats, who have controlled Congress for 25 years, ignored them. They just went blindly down the road.
> DRIVER *(an actor bearing a strong resemblance to Democratic Speaker of the House Thomas P. O'Neill):* Hey! We're out of gas!
> ANNOUNCER: The *Democrats* are out of gas. Vote Republican. For a change.

In 1982, the Republican party mounted an even more extensive series of ads costing $15 million, with the theme "Stay the Course." If this slick, expensive ad campaign were the work of a dead party, then millions of American television watchers might be justified in wondering what a live party organization does.

Are political parties really fading out of the campaign environment? The perspective developed in the last two chapters should give us some answers. This chapter uses the learning approach to shed light on the roles of political parties in campaigns, to examine the conditions in which parties will have greater or lesser influence on campaigners' behavior. Let us begin by considering the thesis of party decline and the dissenters from that thesis and then approach the question in a new way.

The Thesis of Party Decline—And Its Critics

PARTY INFLUENCE ON VOTERS

One prominent analyst of party decline sees "an astonishingly rapid dissolution of the political party as an effective intervenor between the voter and the objects of his vote at the polls." To others, "the figures indicate a clear erosion of the strength of party affiliation in the American public."[1] Note the focus of their concern: the parties are fast losing their capacity to guide a *voter's* choice of candidates, to give structure to the *citizen's* political world. The trend has been called by many names: party decomposition, dealignment, electoral disaggregation.

The supporting evidence is convincing. Ever since the major voter surveys began in the early 1950s, the proportion of citizens who consider themselves Democrats or Republicans has generally been dropping. The proportion calling themselves *strong* partisans has also decreased (see chapter 1). Especially among younger voters, more and more people prefer to see themselves as independent of any party loyalty. Increasing numbers vote a split ticket—a Republican candidate for one office, a Democrat for another—rather than accept one party's entire slate of nominees.[2] New evidence confirms that party identification is not the stable determinant of voters' choices it was once thought to be, but is subject to change in response to changing political circumstances.[3]

Some observers see even worse trouble for the parties: not just a drop in party loyalty but an increase in public dissatisfaction with the whole party system. One reporter argues:

> There was a time—it probably ended during the early 1960s—when many people felt, as political analyst Michael Barone put it, that "anybody in your party was terrific and everybody in the other party was a skunk."
> No more. More likely, everyone is a skunk.[4]

Indeed, when asked by University of Michigan pollsters in 1980 whether there was anything in particular they liked about the Democratic party, only 46 percent of the respondents said yes; only 34 percent could think of anything they liked about the Republican party.[5] About half agreed that "it would be better if, in all elections, we put no party labels on the ballot."

Not all analysts interpret these numbers in so damning a fashion. For one thing, though fewer citizens now identify with a party, those identifiers are still a majority; about six in ten of the Michigan respondents called themselves either Republicans or Democrats. For another, criticism of the parties is nothing new in American politics. In a 1964 sample of Wisconsin adults, at a time when strong partisanship was more prevalent than it is now, 64 percent of those surveyed agreed that "the political parties more often than not create conflicts where none really exists."[6] And at least one study suggests that for many Americans, there is still a balance between criticism and approval in their evaluation of one or both parties, that the movement in public attitudes has been from strong partisanship to neutrality, rather than to a complete rejection of the parties.[7]

There is room for discussion, then, about the nature of public attitudes toward political parties; the extent of the damage done in recent years is not entirely clear. But the overall picture is gloomy. Perhaps it can best be captured by the conclusion that voters are more independent of party ties than they used to be; they are less willing to be guided by party labels when they think about particular candidates. In that sense, at least, political parties *are* less important parts of the campaign environment.

PARTY ORGANIZATIONS

Political parties are more than just collections of voter sentiment. What about the parties as organizations? Are they as weak internally as they are in relation to the voters?

Many observers say yes: there has been a downhill slide in party organizational strength since the heyday of the late 1800s.[8] Many reasons have been proposed, but the direct primary, which first made its way into state laws just after the turn of the century, is often regarded as the chief cause. The direct primary was promoted by the Progressive movement as a means of taking nominations out of the hands of party elites. It did so to a remarkable degree. As the use of primaries became widespread, control over nominations — the key to party control over candidates and elections — largely passed into the hands of people who vote in primary elections. In many states, in advance of the primary, parties are forbidden by law (and in many other states, unable or unwilling) to endorse the candidates they prefer. So the bulk of American party organizations, quite simply, has lost the power to choose its own candidates.

In fact, at times a party organization finds itself saddled with a candidate who was actively opposed by the party's leaders before the primary. In 1980, for example, San Diego Democratic leaders were in the awkward position of campaigning against their party's candidate for Congress. He also happened to be the head of the state's Ku Klux Klan and had won the Democratic nomination on an openly racist platform.

Acts of government deprived party organizations of other functions, often in reaction to the parties' own excesses. The party machines of the last century, whose power rested in large part on their ability to provide government jobs to party loyalists, lost much of that ability when the civil service system substituted exams for political pull. By the middle of this century, even the remaining patronage jobs had lost much of their earlier appeal; a job with the streets department or the sewer commission simply did not excite as much enthusiasm in a white-collar world. Public assistance programs were greatly expanded by the Roosevelt New Deal, providing many people with an alternative to the traditional party functions of favors and food baskets.

More recently, a spate of new technologies has permitted candidates — candidates who can afford them, that is — to bypass their party altogether. With the availability of television spots, sophisticated polling, computerized direct mail, and other tools, candidates no longer need the party's organizational help to reach voters. As long as they have the money, insurgent candidates can target direct mail or buy television time as easily as party-backed candidates can. Crotty and Jacobson sum it up:

> Parties are no longer the principal funders of campaigns. PACs are. Television has replaced the party as the dominant communicator of political information and, as a consequence, the preeminent influence on voter attitudes. Parties are no longer the major organizers of campaigns. Media consultants, public relations and professional experts can create "instant" parties for candidates with the funds to pay for them.[9]

All these changes have taken their toll on personnel and mechanisms of party organizations. Big-city parties today are often no more than skeletal remains of the party machines they replaced. And there are many cities and towns in the United States where a party structure is simply nowhere to be found.

In short, we see evidence of party weakness. But again there is an alternative view. The alternative suggests that instead of declining steadily from some early peak of power, American party organizations have *always* had to struggle for survival in an inhospitable environment. Ever since the founding of the Republic, there has been a strong antiparty strain in American political thought and practice. From the debates over the adoption of the Constitution to the present, political parties have been viewed as fractious influences to be watched carefully, rather than as vital forces to encourage and maintain.[10]

The widespread acceptance of the direct primary, in fact, is a legacy of that time-honored antiparty feeling. It shows that even in the glory days of boss rule, party organizations in large sections of the country were not strong enough to conquer antiparty reformers; state parties fought the reforms one by one, and lost one by one. But during their history of struggle with the American political environment—with decentralized authority, waves of party reformers, ambivalent public attitudes—party organizations have won some victories too; the history of party organizational strength is better represented by a wavy line than by an arrow pointed downward.

That varied pattern continues today. Some party organizations have found ways to deal with their environment and have grown stronger in the process. The two national party organizations, especially the Republicans, developed established patterns of activity and staffing during this century and have recently taken on more functions, improved their fund raising, and increased their provision of services to state and local parties. Many state-level parties, too, have gotten richer in staff and budgets since 1960 and gained in institutional strength—leading the authors of a recent large-scale study to conclude that "the parties as institutions have been getting stronger as popular support for them has declined."[11]

PARTY IN GOVERNMENT

The party organizations' power over elected and appointed officials has also had its ups and downs. Party influence in the House, for example, probably reached its peak in the 1890s and the early part of this century.[12] But party cues have remained an important influence on legislators' behavior, not so much because congressional party leaders are powerful as because legislators' contacts with their supporting coalitions and their colleagues reinforce party differences.[13] Recent reforms in the House could permit even greater party influence.[14] So do the relatively few periods when a party-minded President occupies the White House, as has been the case during the Reagan administration.

Party power in state governments ranges from substantial—in Indiana, for instance—to nonexistent. There is even some evidence of party influence on judges' decisions in certain kinds of cases, though it reflects the tendency for judges who share similar values to share a party affiliation as well, rather than any direct power of party organizations over the courts.[15] It serves as a reminder, however, that people who are highly involved in politics are often more sensitive to partisan values, and more frequently in contact with other activists who reinforce those values, than other citizens are.

In short, the thesis of party decline weighs in with *some* compelling evidence. Its strongest and most elaborate argument is that the parties are increasingly irrelevant to voters' thinking and behavior. But a drop in citizen support does not necessarily go hand in hand with a decline in party organization (just as an increase in voter support does not necessarily make a party stronger in an organizational sense) nor with a weakening of party influence over people in public office. Perhaps the best answer to the question "Are the parties in decline?" is that maddening old standby of social science: in some ways yes, and in other ways no.

How does this uneven picture affect political campaigns? How much influence do parties have on campaigners' behavior, and what are the results?

A Social-Learning Approach to Party Influence

In social-learning terms, party "influence" would mean that the party is an agent of campaigners' learning, a force capable of affecting their attention, symbolization, and expectations about the results of their behavior. To do so, the party would have to operate through one or both learning processes described in chapter 2: response consequences and observational learning. In other words, party can affect campaign behavior by affecting the *results* of campaigners' choices (and thus their expectations about what will happen if they act in a given way), and by providing *models* from whom campaigners can learn.

The approach requires that agents of learning be identified explicitly. "Party" is not specific enough. Three aspects of the term "party" have been explored in this chapter: parties as they exist in public attitudes, party organizations (including party leaders and activists), and the party in government. But since public attitudes normally affect campaigners only indirectly (as we have seen), through the filter of activists' understanding, we focus here mainly on party organizations and other members of the campaigner's party who are public officials or candidates themselves, as agents of campaign learning.

We must also take into account that different *levels* of party—national, state, local—may differ in their levels of influence. It is entirely possible, for example, that a given state party organization may have resources to offer that can materially affect the campaigner's chance of winning, while the national party's campaign committee provides fewer of these resources, and local and congressional district parties have nothing to offer the candidate at all. Party influence gained through the provision of campaign resources, then, might be strong at the state level and nonexistent at the local level.

Finally, keeping in mind the interactive nature of learning, we should expect that party resources and models matter more to some campaigners than others. New candidates, challengers, those whose campaign environment has become more hostile—these people should feel a greater need for models, and a greater dependence on resources other than their own, than should secure incumbents. So we pay special attention to the chances for party influence on these campaigners. Now let us look at the evidence: to what extent do party organizations make use of these avenues of influence?

RESOURCES: TO WHAT EXTENT DO PARTIES
AFFECT CAMPAIGNERS' OUTCOMES?

If campaigners expect that the party organization (or some other aspect of party) influences the results they want, then (according to the principle of response consequences) they should be more likely to respond favorably to party requests and to act in harmony with what they think are the party's interests. How much, then, do parties control or influence the things that candidates want?

It is a fair assumption that the great majority of campaigners want to win more than they want any other outcome that campaigns can provide. Party organizations may control or affect that outcome in several ways. The surest effect occurs when the party organization can simply *decide* who wins. Imagine, for example, a situation in which the party organization names its nominee for an office, and a majority of voters is sure to accept the party's choice in the primary and general elections. At the height of the Cook County Democratic machine's power in Chicago, that is how it worked. The machine chose the full slate of Democratic nominees for local offices and some other offices (at one time, even statewide posts) for which Cook County votes could sway the outcome. The machine could normally guarantee that its precinct work (and, if necessary, a little creative vote counting; the slogan Vote Early and Often was not always uttered in jest) would bring out enough supporters to assure victory for its slate. The machine had the resources to make its nominees into winners; it held all the cards. Thus it is not surprising that Democratic campaigns in Chicago at those times bore the very heavy imprint of the Cook County Democratic organization. The candidates were the machine's creatures.

There are still some places where party organizations hold similar levels of power. Candidate selection in Britain, for instance, is almost entirely a party-controlled matter. Party organizations also control most of the resources used by those candidates; the parties employ and train campaign managers (called "party agents") and provide money and workers. The result is an impressive degree of party loyalty in candidates' behavior and in their voting patterns once elected to Parliament.[16]

By contrast, most American party organizations now have to struggle with the vagaries of primary elections if they hope for that kind of control. Because the power to nominate candidates is vital to a party organization—for its prospects in the general election, its ability to reward party loyalists with nominations, its chance to discipline elected officials if they disregard the party's interests—some state and local parties do try to control the primary's outcome. Some do so by endorsing a slate of candidates prior to the primary, formally or informally, and with varying degrees of success.[17] Some give assistance to the party's preferred candidates, in the form of money or organizational support. A few go straight to the source and try to talk potential challengers out of running.

But a party's ability to "guide" primary elections has its limits. For one, party regulars may be unwilling to deny renomination to a rebellious incumbent if he or she is popular with the voters; parties, like candidates, want to win elections. In 1982, Connecticut Senator Lowell Weicker was challenged for renomination by Prescott Bush, a conservative Republican (and the brother of Vice-President George Bush). Bush charged that Weicker had deserted the Reagan administration time after time on important votes and that Weicker was a maverick, not a true Republican. The state Republican organization clearly agreed, but voted to renominate Weicker anyway. The reason was clear: polls showed that Weicker would run a stronger race in the general election than Bush would.

Even the strongest party organizations must face the possibility that they could lose a primary fight: a political maverick may put together a personal organization that out-votes the party's regulars; or a complete unknown with a popular name (someone named Kennedy in Massachusetts, for example), running against the party's choice, may render the party's efforts useless on primary day. Candidates know, then, that in most areas the party's backing is not the only route to nomination and election victory. It is one route among many.

The result is that this avenue of party influence on campaigners—control over nominations and elections—has not been available to most American party organizations. But in those few areas where party organizations have succeeded in taming the primary elections, parties retain an important source of influence on campaigners' behavior.

RESOURCES: MONEY

Even if a party organization cannot control access to candidacy and assure its chosen candidates of victory, it may still gain some level of influence over their behavior if it controls (or at least helps provide) the resources campaigners need to win. First among these resources, and the key to many others, is money. Campaign spending is especially crucial for candidates who do not already hold office. An expert in campaign finance writes about congressional challengers:

Nonincumbents, in contrast [to incumbents], usually begin the race in obscurity; the campaign is crucial because it is the only means for grabbing the attention of voters. An effective campaign costs money; the more nonincumbents spend, the better they are known, and the better they do on election day.[18]

Moreover, it is harder for challengers than for incumbents to *raise* money. Thus, the greater the extent to which a party organization can funnel money into a challenger's race, the more influence it is likely to have over these indebted campaigners.

To a lesser extent, party money should matter to incumbents too. Generally, at least in congressional races, incumbents' campaign spending has rapidly diminishing returns; it does not add much to the support they gain *between* elections.[19] Nevertheless, incumbents are often more insecure about their election chances than, objectively, they need to be. In such circumstances, party organizations with a lot of money to spend should be able to "buy" at least some influence with incumbents.

Here the figures tell us three important things about the prospects for party influence. First, party organizations provide only a small portion of the money raised by the average candidate—in the neighborhood of 5 to 17 percent in federal-level races. Increasingly, party money is overshadowed by contributions from PACs, particularly business PACs. Second, the parties' weakness is especially apparent at the local level and in many states. But third, the difference between Democratic and Republican party fund raising is profound—and has profound implications. When a reporter for *Congressional Quarterly* wrote, just before the 1980 election, that "campaign spending by political parties this year is a Republican-dominated extravaganza in which the Democrats are only bit players,"[20] he was describing a situation in which one party's influence over its campaigners had the potential to vastly outstrip that of the other party. Let us take a look at the details.

PARTY MONEY: THE NATIONAL REPUBLICANS

The national Republican party during the 1970s underwent one of the quietest reconstructions in history. While the national Democrats fought loudly and publicly over party rules, their Republican counterparts were working almost unobserved to build the financial and organizational power that is now bringing greater party influence over Republican campaigners.

The impetus came from defeat at the polls. After President Nixon was forced to resign because of the Watergate scandal, the Republican party lost 44 House seats in the 1974 elections. Its incoming national chairman in 1976, former Tennessee Senator Bill Brock, saw the need for two kinds of responses. Organizationally, he established plans to rebuild the party apparatus from the ground up. Financially, he worked to broaden the party's substantial program of computerized direct-mail fund raising.

The direct-mail appeals paid off handsomely. By 1979, Brock claimed that about half a million contributors were giving up to $20 each to the Republican National Committee annually. By late 1982 the mailing list had swelled to 1.7 million names.[21] In the 1981-82 election cycle the RNC netted $83.5 million, the vast majority of it raised in small sums through direct mail (see table 5.1). The two Republican "Hill committees"—the National Republican Senatorial Committee (NRSC) and the National Republican Congressional Committee (NRCC)—also moved eagerly into direct mail. Each cultivated its own set of contributors, and each raised impressive sums. In 1981-82, for example, for every dollar its Democratic Hill counterpart raised, the Republican Congressional Committee raised seventeen.

TABLE 5.1
NATIONAL PARTY COMMITTEES' FUND RAISING AND SPENDING,
1981-82
(in millions of dollars)

	Raised (net receipts)	Spent
Democrats		
Democratic National Committee	$16.2	$16.4
Democratic Senatorial Campaign Committee	5.6	5.6
Democratic Congressional Campaign Committee	6.5	6.5
Other national-level committees	3.1	2.7
TOTAL	$31.4	$31.2
Republicans		
Republican National Committee	$83.5	$84.3
National Republican Senatorial Committee	48.9	47.7
National Republican Congressional Committee	58.0	57.1
Other national-level committees	.5	.7
TOTAL	$190.9	$189.8

SOURCE: Federal Election Commission.

For party organizations, these are big bucks indeed. The result was that the three national Republican committees could spend lavishly on a wide variety of campaigns. Their direct contributions were imposing enough; ever since 1978, Republican party committees have frequently approached the legal ceilings on direct party donations to federal candidates.[22]

Even more important for party influence, the committees have put the bulk of their money into "coordinated spending"—paying directly for services used by a campaign, such as polling and television time. Paying for these services gives the party committee a bigger voice in the shaping of a campaign and, because of the higher ceilings on coordinated spending (especially in Senate races), a bigger opportunity to contribute. In 1982, for example, national-level Republican committees put about sixteen times as much money into coordinated spending in an average Senate race as they gave directly to the candidate (see table 5.2).

The two types of party money added up fast in some races where the spending ceilings were high. Seven Republican Senate candidates each received more than $400,000 from their party in direct and coordinated funds in 1982; one, Pete Wilson (now Senator Wilson), got more than $1.3 million for his race in California.[23] These levels of party spending are unprecedented. As the Senatorial Committee's communication director put it, "We Republicans have made the party role very important."[24]

TABLE 5.2
AVERAGE CONTRIBUTIONS AND SPENDING BY NATIONAL PARTY COMMITTEES IN HOUSE AND SENATE RACES, 1981-82

	Democratic Candidates	Republican Candidates
Senate Races		
Direct party contributions to the campaign	$16,077	$16,828
Party "coordinated spending" on the candidate's behalf	$58,038	$263,865
House Races		
Direct party contributions to the campaign	$1,479	$10,625
Party "coordinated spending" on the candidate's behalf	$456	$13,095

SOURCE: Computed from Federal Election Commission data.

The national Republican committees also work to channel PAC funds into selected campaigns. In 1982, for example, Republican officials held briefings encouraging PAC representatives to give to the House and Senate candidates targeted for support by the Republican committees. A White House aide estimated that the party was able to guide between $75,000 and $250,000 in

PAC money into each of the selected House races late in the campaign—vitally-needed "last-minute money."[25]

The party came through on Brock's promise to help state and local candidates as well, partly as a means of grooming attractive candidates for later congressional races. By 1980, the RNC's new Local Elections Division had a budget of almost $3 million, of which $1.7 million went directly to 775 state legislative candidates. The division shifted focus in time for the 1982 elections, providing technical advice to help targeted candidates campaign more effectively.[26]

The national party even set up an independent PAC to funnel additional money into campaigns such as those targeted by the RNC's Local Elections Division. Called GOPAC, it began by raising $1.5 million in time for the 1980 races, relying on the same direct-mail approaches that had proven so effective for its national party brethren.[27] In these ways, the national Republican party has expanded its role in thousands of carefully selected campaigns.

PARTY POVERTY: THE NATIONAL DEMOCRATS

In comparison with the Republicans' fund-raising muscle, the national Democrats have been aptly described as "a political version of the 98-pound weakling."[28] The Republican party's financial edge over the Democrats is nothing new, of course. But the disparity deepened and widened in the 1970s, largely because the two national parties took very different developmental paths. Both parties became more influential relative to their state and local organizations during that decade. But while the Republicans did so by concentrating on the systematic provision of money and services to state parties and candidates, the Democrats were more concerned with reform of the party's rules for selecting delegates to presidential nominating conventions.

The national Democrats did virtually nothing to improve their fund-raising capability during the 1970s—a remarkable fact, considering that in 1968 the Democratic National Committee mortgaged its future by agreeing to accept the $9.3 million debt incurred by the presidential campaign of Hubert Humphrey. The debt hung like a millstone around the party's neck; until it was finally paid in 1982, the DNC was not in a position to secure even the slightest visibility, much less influence, in Democratic campaigns through its contributions. The Democrats continued to rely on the traditional device of large fund-raising dinners and other events to raise cash. Interestingly, the party's presidential candidate in 1972, George McGovern, made very effective use of direct mail to raise money for his campaign. But the national party did not take the hint; even when changes in the campaign finance laws made direct mail the fund-raising method of choice, the Democrats continued to rely on the big givers and to lag farther and farther behind the Republican national committees.

One Hill committee staff member blames Democratic complacency for party differences in fund raising. The Democrats, after all, had long been the majority party in Congress and in voters' attachments. And Democratic candidates had benefited greatly from Watergate fallout; in 1974, Democrats picked up even some very safe Republican congressional seats. "Winners never innovate," the staffer says.

> Losers innovate. And after '74, the Republican party innovated. They turned themselves on their ear, and they really started building. And the Democratic party was to a certain extent fat and sassy, and it simply didn't do the innovation that was necessary. And it got picked off.

The results could easily be seen in the 1980 elections. The DNC netted $15 million, most of it in large individual gifts ($500 or more). The RNC had taken in five times as much. The Democratic Senatorial Committee, by the last month of the campaign, had raised a grand total of $500,000 — about 1/25 of its Republican counterpart — in a year when the Democrats had an unusually large (and, as time soon proved, unusually vulnerable) number of incumbents up for reelection.[29]

As Neil MacNeil pointed out, the Democratic Congressional Campaign Committee "was a feeble, ill-financed rival to [the Republican congressional committee]. With only a handful of staffers and a budget of less than $1.5 million, the Democratic committee had no capacity to match the depth and variety of assistance the Republicans could offer their candidates."[30] The Hill Committee staffer fills in more details:

> The Republican Congressional Committee had more people on a radio and TV production division than we had on our entire staff! For example, they had a guy whose job was basically to help match up Republican candidates with PACs who are likely to give to them. And he'd look over the PAC records and see what kind of PACs gave to what kind of candidates. And then their candidates would come through, and he'd say, "Okay, judging from where you're from, and your ideology, and your voting record in the legislature, or whatever, we would recommend that you go to this one, this one, this one, and this one," and in some cases would literally take them by the hand to see some PAC. We had nobody that could do that. We would hand them a list and say, "Here are all the labor guys in town. Good luck!" Or, "Here are the ten biggest PACs. Go to it!"

MacNeil concluded that "plainly, every House Democratic candidate had to find his own campaign funds, and that did nothing to lessen his independence from, or increase his loyalty to, the party leaders."[31] In the words of the California congressman who took over the leadership of the DCCC in 1981, "there was even less to the campaign committee than met the eye."[32]

Moreover, while the RNC was putting its money into hundreds of state legislative races, the DNC made no contributions to state legislative candidates. In fact, when one reporter inquired at the DNC about the number of Democrats and Republicans in each state legislature, the committee's research department searched for an answer and finally came up with a list—produced by the Republican National Committee.[33] Totally absorbed in the struggling campaign of President Carter, the DNC had no spare resources with which to influence important state and local races.

Even the Democrats' effort to develop an independent PAC, modeled on the Republicans' GOPAC, fell flat. The Democrats certainly tried to learn from the Republicans' success. A fund-raising letter launching the new DEMPAC literally cribbed the opening paragraphs of the letter used to raise money for GOPAC, and paraphrased others.[34] But a combination of poor planning and a lack of DNC cooperation doomed DEMPAC's chances in 1980; its direct-mail effort brought in a mere $30,000 to $40,000.[35]

Election night 1980 brought stunning Democratic losses; recall that Republicans picked up the Presidency, 33 additional House seats, 12 Senate seats (and control of that body for the first time since 1952-53), four governorships, and 222 state legislative seats—a sweep that few observers had expected. As we would anticipate, the Republican victories were seen as a generalized reward for that party's new directions in campaigning and fund raising. Thus the national Republican committees looked forward to more of the same in 1982, with particular attention to races for the Democratic-dominated House. Letters headed "Ronald Reagan, Washington" called upon contributors to help support the "GOP Victory Plan" that was thought to have worked so well in 1980:

> This GOP Victory Plan carefully blends direct cash contributions, national TV advertising, issue research and up-to-date survey information into one overall campaign program for candidates. . . .
> This same Plan, used in 1980, was the prime reason we cut the Democrats' majority from 267 to 234 seats by increasing Republican seats from 158 to 192. This was the single largest gain for our Party in 14 years. . . .

Just as these new directions in the Republican party had been stimulated by Republican losses in 1974, so the Democrats were affected by the devastation of 1980. Losing, we have seen, is a poor teacher; it motivates change, but does not explain what the change should be. Everyone, it seemed, had a reason for the Democratic losses: Ronald Reagan's popularity, Jimmy Carter's unpopularity, the hostages in Iran, anti-incumbent feeling, conservative trends, New Right spending. But one thing was certain: the national Republican commit-

Do Political Parties Matter in Campaigns? 127

tees had gone into direct mail in a big way and were raising money hand over fist for their candidates. Well-known Democrats began to call for similar efforts by their party committees. Democratic House Speaker Tip O'Neill said to his party's caucus in the House,

> ... candidates need the financial and technical support of the party. The preoccupation of the Democratic National Committee with presidential politics must cease. The congressional campaign committee must serve as a genuine political and financial resource for Democratic incumbents and challengers alike in 1982.[36]

O'Neill and others made the same point to candidates for the position of DNC chairman. Their advice was heeded. New national chairman Charles T. Manatt took a page from Bill Brock's book and declared that his priorities would be fund raising and grass-roots party building, as well as stronger ties with Democratic elected officials and organized labor. The DNC's direct-mail drive was launched in 1981, warning prospective contributors of the growing strength of the "New Right Republicans and the Moral Majoritarians."

These DNC efforts were soon joined by the party's congressional campaign committee, which substantially expanded its own direct-mail program in 1981. Taking note of the New Right's success with "single issues," the Democratic mailings centered on issues of concern to environmentalists, women's rights advocates, people concerned with social security, and civil rights. They sounded the note of alarm that seems to be peculiarly effective in direct mail; consider this DCCC mailing signed by Representative Peter Rodino of New Jersey:

> If the Republicans win just half as many seats in 1982 as they won in 1980, they'll capture the House. And progressive ideals could become a memory. . . . Right Wing zealots—the people who in TV ads last year accused George McGovern of advocating the killing of babies—are now targeting the House Democrats.

Results for the Democrats were not immediately rewarding. Direct mail has high start-up costs; much of the initial "take" must be reinvested in new mailings in order to build a list of regular donors. Thus in 1981–82, for every dollar the national Republican committees raised, the Democrats raised 16 cents —and their mailing list remained only one-eighth as large as the Republicans'. There was hope that the investment would pay off. In the meantime, the Democrats would pay the price for their late start.

During the 1970s, then, the Republican party clearly made more effort than the Democrats to adapt to environmental changes in campaigning. When campaign finance reforms put a premium on small contributions, the national Republicans moved quickly into direct-mail fund raising. Their success with

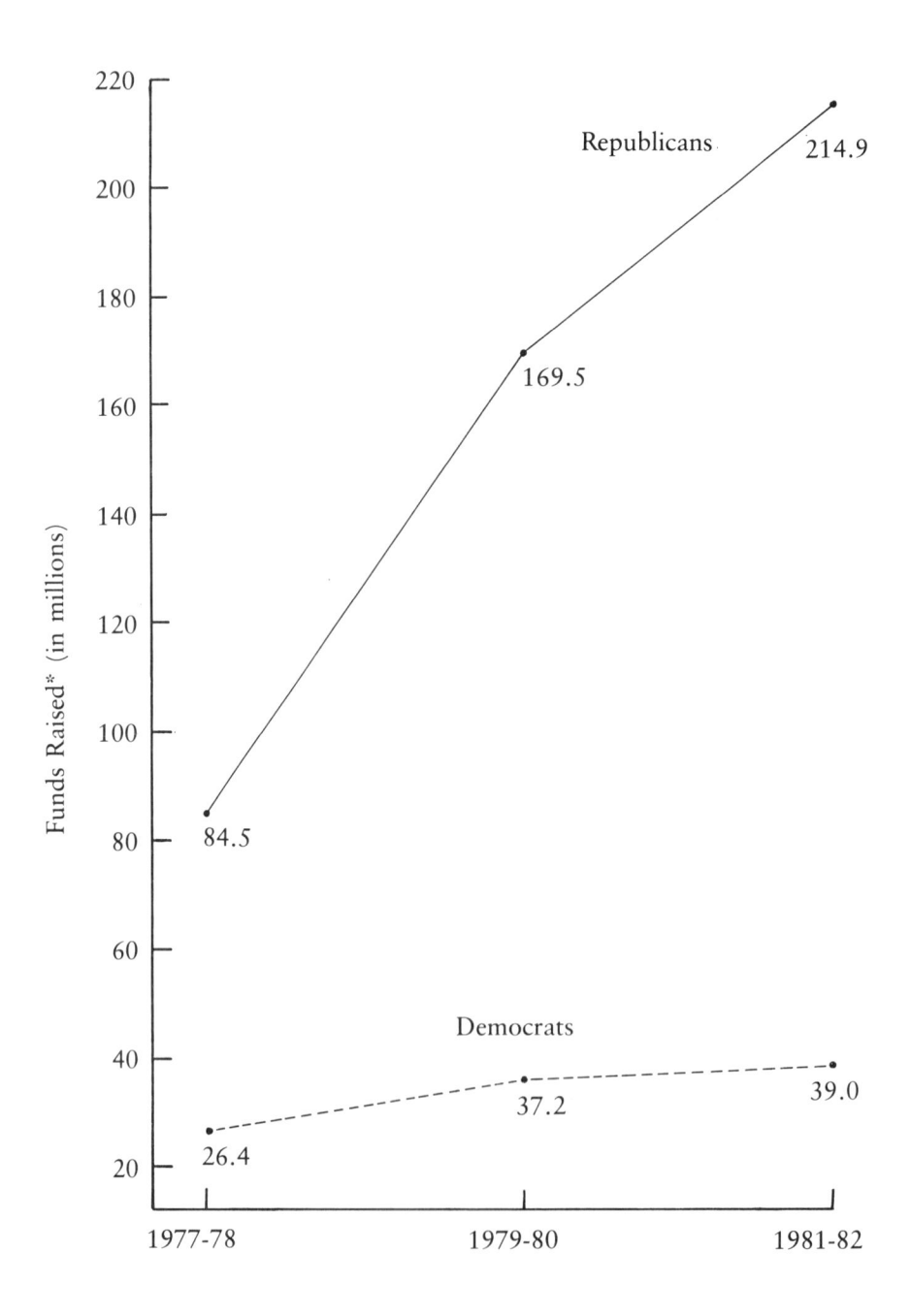

FIGURE 5.1
PARTY FUND RAISING, 1977-82

SOURCE: Federal Election Commission.
*by party committees at all levels (though most funds were raised by national-level committees).

direct mail produced bigger and bigger party budgets (see figure 5.1). The spending of that money was carefully designed—through the targeting of races and the emphasis on coordinated funds—to expand the party's role in House and Senate campaigns. And that spending was meant to help strengthen the party in Congress. As a Reagan aide put it: "The best way for us to encourage [party] discipline is for us to make it clear that the President is more likely to raise funds for you if you support him than if you do not."[37] The national Democrats, during the 1970s, acted as though these important changes in campaign finance simply did not exist. Democratic candidates were managing to raise money, of course, and often in large quantities—but almost entirely from nonparty sources, at considerable cost to any possible party role in their campaigning.

SELECTIVE INFLUENCE: STATE PARTY MONEY

The most systematic recent look at state parties shows that they are gaining strength as organizations; since 1960, more state parties have begun to operate continuously (rather than just at election time), with more professionalized staffs and expanded budgets and activities.[38] As might be expected, Republican state organizations have moved faster and farther along this path than the Democrats. But this increasing institutionalization does not seem to have improved the parties' ability to contribute to campaigns. Indeed, state parties are less active in contributing to party candidates now than they were in the early 1960s.

When state parties *do* give, they give selectively. Just as the national party committees put most of their money into races for the House, Senate, and the Presidency, the state parties concentrate their funds—and thus their potential influence on campaigns through the medium of contributions—on state elections. Their biggest contributions go to gubernatorial and state legislative candidates; almost half of the state parties give to these races and to U.S. House candidates. Only a quarter of the parties open their pockets to U.S. Senate campaigns, and a comparable percentage do not take out their wallets for any candidate.[39]

SELECTIVE EXISTENCE: LOCAL AND CONGRESSIONAL
DISTRICT PARTIES

In analyzing local parties, the first question is not how much money they spend on campaigns, but whether they exist at all. In a large study of local parties conducted in the late 1970s, only 26 percent claimed to have a regular annual budget, no matter how small.[40] Perhaps worst-off are party organizations at the congressional district level, which are often marginal to the party's precinct-to-county-to-state structure.

The result is that parties at the substate level vary more in resources — and thus in campaign money as a potential influence over candidates — than do party organizations at other levels. In many localities, especially rural and less-populated areas, those that are less industrialized, and where the workforce is less unionized, party organizations are weak and low in resources.[41] That fact is not generally lost on candidates; listen, for example, to these congressional challengers:

> The Republican party in this district is virtually nonexistent. Out of 350 precincts that are entitled to elect precinct delegates, last year there were 54 elected. Prior to that time there were only 25.
>
> They could do a lot just supporting the candidate's effort to raise funds. But they don't bother. . . . They're just totally inept. . . . A lot of people think somehow or other magically the party gives you plenty of money, and that you actually make a little from the campaign. The party . . . in total donations in my campaigns, gave me zero dollars.[42]

Clearly, then, the term "party money" conceals a tremendous range of resources, from the multimillionaire national Republican committees down to the impoverished (or simply invisible) organizations of both parties in many precincts, counties, and even states. Potential party influence over campaigns, then, should range widely too. But before reaching any conclusions, let us examine party money in context. What alternative sources of campaign money do candidates have?

PARTY MONEY IN CONTEXT

Even when a party organization gives substantial sums to campaigns, we have to ask, "substantial compared to what?" The larger the party money looms as a proportion of the candidate's total budget, the better the party's chances of influence over his or her campaign. Good answers to this question, unfortunately, are available only for U.S. House and Senate campaigns; for lower-level candidacies, we can only guess. But in congressional races, all party organizations combined are the source of no more than one campaign dollar in six or seven — even, on the average, in Republican Senate campaigns.

The biggest part of a typical congressional campaign budget — about two-thirds — comes from donations made by private individuals.[43] That might not offer the parties much competition for influence; each donor, after all, is limited by law to a maximum contribution smaller than that which a party organization is allowed to give.

But the remaining campaign money comes mainly from a source that does rival party influence: Political Action Committees. PACs are steadily surpassing party organizations in campaign contributions. Consider these facts. During the last decade, political parties have never contributed more than 17 percent of House and Senate candidates' campaign spending, and this peak in direct party contributions was reached in 1972. In each election year since then, Democratic party organizations contributed less than 5 percent, a level unlikely to inspire much gratitude or bring much clout.

Most ominously for the parties, PAC money continues to grow as a proportion of the total. For example, PAC contributions accounted for 14 percent of House campaign funds in 1972; in the 1982 House elections, more than 30 percent of the candidates' dollars came from PAC treasuries.[44] Even when the parties' coordinated spending—money spent on a candidate's behalf—is considered as well, party money is overshadowed by contributions from PACs. The contrast has been particularly sharp in Democratic campaigns (see table 5.3 below).

These figures may not show the full extent of party influence through the provision of money. As the Republicans' PAC briefings indicate, a party organization's judgment about a candidate may have influence beyond its contribution; party money is often a signal to PACs and other contributors that the

TABLE 5.3
AVERAGE PARTY AND PAC MONEY IN THE CAMPAIGNS OF HOUSE AND SENATE GENERAL ELECTION CANDIDATES, 1981-82

	Democratic Candidates	Republican Candidates
Senate Races		
Direct party[a] contributions	$17,556	$18,189
Party "coordinated spending" on the candidate's behalf	68,509	264,114
Total party money	$86,065	$282,303
PAC contributions	$325,996	$329,876
House Races		
Direct party contributions	$2,411	$11,764
Party "coordinated spending" on the candidate's behalf	1,584	13,359
Total party money	$3,995	$25,123
PAC contributions	$73,718	$64,630

SOURCE: Computed from Federal Election Commission data.

a. Includes national, state, and local party committees (in contrast to table 5.2, which includes national party committees only).

candidate stands a chance and is worth supporting. And we have no reliable figures on state and local campaigns (though the relative poverty of so many local parties would suggest that the party's *proportion* of campaign funds is likely to be less than impressive).

But from all the evidence available, we can conclude that with the possible exception of national-level Republican committees, party money is not ample enough to bring much party influence over campaigns. Still, the campaigns that are lavishly supported by national Republican committees should show the imprint of those committees' preferences in campaign techniques, choice of issues, or any other areas in which the committees press their concerns. More generally, whenever a party organization can affect the flow of money into a campaign—when the RNC channels money into a state legislative race, for instance—it improves its ability to influence the campaign's behavior.

Influence Through the Provision of Resources: Party Services

Campaigns use their money to buy services: professional managers, television time and production, direct mail, telephones, and electricity and rent for campaign headquarters. So even if a party organization does not give much money to a campaign, it may still preserve some influence by contributing a substantial proportion of these needed services.

As a general rule, most party organizations do not have the staff or the money to provide many services to candidates; this means of influence, like party money, is more often noted for its absence than its presence. As one researcher found in House races, "it is not simply that parties provide only a small proportion of the necessary campaign funds . . . ; they give relatively little assistance of any kind to most congressional candidates."[45] A losing congressional challenger captured the same thought: "It wasn't what they [party organizations] didn't do for me, it's what they don't do for anybody."[46]

But there has been a recent change in the direction of more party services to candidates. As in the case of party money, it comes largely from the Republican national party, with the national Democrats just beginning to follow suit. By 1980, for example, the RNC was offering help to candidates in conducting surveys, producing radio and television ads, scheduling the events of a race, and providing policy and opposition research.[47] Then-chairman Bill Brock set up a program in which state parties could use the national party's computer facilities for help with anything from redistricting to office bookkeeping. These computer services were used in 1980 to analyze polls taken for candidates and process the results of a massive voter registration drive. All these services were especially valuable to candidates because the national party could often provide them at cost—much cheaper than the prevailing commercial rate.

The RNC put special emphasis on providing services to state legislative campaigns. Its local elections division, which Brock called "the top priority of the RNC since I've been here,"[48] sent staffers into the field to work directly with state legislative races—some 4000 races in 1980. In addition to helping recruit and train candidates, the division helped design surveys, taught local volunteers how to conduct those surveys, and analyzed the data they collected. It showed them how to raise funds through direct mail. It provided them with precinct targeting—analyses of voting patterns and party registration figures in order to pinpoint where the campaigns should concentrate their time and resources.

Many candidates were impressed with the party's help. Take the example of a Pennsylvania state legislator who received advice and services from the RNC in 1980. He commented, "From the start, I was very skeptical of a group of people coming in from outside of the district, outside of Pennsylvania even, and providing a three-term legislator with advice about how to run in a district that he knows pretty well." But when a direct-mail fund-raising letter, which the RNC suggested and helped to develop, began to pay off and the candidate began to rise in the polls, a journalist reports that "he became a believer in the suggestions of his Washington-based Republican consultants."[49]

By providing these services, the national party gets its share of rewards in return. The promise of these services helps the party recruit the kinds of candidates it wants to run. Moreover, making the services available, especially at low cost, greatly increases the chance that they will be used. That in itself gives the party some level of control over the way targeted candidates run their campaigns. It helps bring many campaigns and state parties "up to speed," giving them access to the newest and most sophisticated campaign technologies. If the party's advice and services are effective, then it can receive a good return on its investment: a lot of winning candidates. Most important, effective advice should increase the value of the national party organization in the candidate's eyes—and that should heighten the party's influence over campaigners who win office with party help.

What were the national Democratic committees doing to match these Republican services? Not much. The DNC and the Democratic Hill committees have had little help to offer House and Senate campaigners. In interviews with the author, one Senate campaign aide described the services provided by Democratic party committees in 1980 as "fairly minor. I mean, they provide legal analysis and stuff like that. But it's not overwhelming." And a Hill committee staffer summed up the party difference in these words: "They've [the national

Republican committees] got crews to go out and film commercials for candidates. The Democratic Senatorial Campaign Committee doesn't even have facilities to look at a tape!"

Republican successes in 1980 shook the national Democratic committees out of their lethargy. The Democratic Congressional Campaign Committee set itself an ambitious list of goals for 1982: to concentrate its resources on 80 House races and shower these campaigns with consulting help, polling, precinct targeting, research, media spots, and targeted mailings, as well as $25,000 apiece in cash. The results were much more modest, since the Campaign Committee's fund raising fell short of its hopes, though a Democratic Media Center was finally established in 1983 to tape and edit ads for radio and television.

But the DNC, under new chairman Charles Manatt, did try to redress the national party's previous inattention to state and local Democratic organizations. Beginning in 1981, a State Party Works program was developed with the help of political consultant Matt Reese; the Reese team began visiting state Democratic organizations to train staff members in fund raising, organization, and communication. The purpose was to help state parties provide more services to campaigns and thus to increase the parties' influence over Democratic candidates. The result, one writer observes, was to change state parties' view of the DNC from "a foreign power that did not dispense foreign aid" to "a well-intentioned, if under-funded, ally."[50]

There is no question, however, that the national Democrats are running years behind the national Republicans in party services. This does not mean that Democratic candidates were running for office with no polls, no television, and no telephone lines. It does mean that the average Democratic campaigner received a larger proportion of his or her services from PACs, individual donors, and other sources, and a smaller proportion from the party, than the average Republican candidate did. As a result, the national Democratic committees lost another chance to gain real influence over Democratic campaigns.

STATE AND LOCAL PARTY SERVICES TO CANDIDATES

As is the case with party money, there is a wide range among state and local party organizations in the levels of services they provide. State Republican parties are more involved than Democratic parties in assisting candidates and are generally more highly developed and active, at least in part because of the national Republican program of party building. But nearly all state parties have something to offer to campaigners.

Most state parties operate some form of voter identification, registration, or get-out-the-vote program, and a majority conduct public opinion polls during election years. Most of the parties also run seminars to teach people how to campaign. About half the state parties give other aid to candidates: research assistance, help with media and other advertising, staff assistance, direct mail, guidance in complying with election laws. Only one in five organizations, however, offers to help candidates with fund raising. Levels of services are frequently modest, but they do help the more active state parties make their presence felt in candidates' organizations.[51]

A majority of the county parties included in one large-scale study[52] engaged in several campaign-related activities, at least during the campaign's active phase: distributing campaign literature; organizing fund raisers and other events; providing phone campaigns, newspaper ads, and press releases; putting up lawn signs; and helping to coordinate the various campaigns being run in the county. These county-level parties seem more active now than they were 20 years ago — even the Democrats, for the Republican edge that was so obvious at the state and national levels is not found among county party organizations.

PARTY RESOURCES: THE RICH GET RICHER

To this point, we have seen tremendous variation in party organizations' ability to provide money and services to candidates and thus have a means of influencing their campaigns. National Republican committees and several state Republican parties could be expected to have substantial (and growing) impact on many congressional and state legislative races; at the other extreme, some state Democratic organizations might be expected to be completely ignored by congressional and state candidates.

There is an irony that touches all these findings, however, and it stems from a perfectly logical premise. Parties, like candidates, want to win races. So they usually put their money and services into campaigns that have a chance. In congressional elections, for example, party committees tend to concentrate on helping their own incumbents (especially when they are thought to be in danger) and candidates for open seats.[53] In fact, incumbents in Congress have a striking advantage in getting party money: they control many of the party committees that dole out the donations. Thus in the 1980 elections the two parties' congressional committees gave about 60 percent of their money to incumbents, while fully 75 percent of the Democratic Senatorial Campaign Committee's money went to incumbents.[54]

The parties' problem is that these are the very races where the candidate is least likely to need the party's favors. Incumbents, in particular, have many other sources of money and services. They can usually count on donations from a variety of PACs and interested individuals. And they have impressive resources right in their own offices. For members of Congress, these resources — paid staff members (who routinely campaign for their bosses), free use of the mails, office space, telephones, travel allowances, and other paid advantages — have been estimated as worth the equivalent of $567,000 in a campaign.[55] Incumbents get more free media exposure because they hold public office. Compared to these resources, the money and services that most party organizations can muster are likely to seem pretty paltry.

The same holds true for attractive candidates in races where there is no incumbent. Their chance of winning tends to attract more dollars and services from givers of all kinds. So in the two kinds of races where party resources are usually most heavily concentrated, party organizations are most likely to face stiff competition for the candidate's attention.

Candidates running against incumbents, especially when their chances do not look good, normally get little help from party organizations. Ironically, the party's money is probably more highly valued in these campaigns than in most others, because these candidates do not get much help from PACs or other groups either; thus the party's contribution may be a sizable portion of the candidate's resources. Too, these are races where party organizations are most likely to have been responsible for recruiting the candidate; in races where there is a better chance of winning, candidates are more likely to have been self-starters.[56]

Even in these needy races, party help will probably be rewarded with some criticism. Losing candidates frequently believe that they *could* have won if only they had had more money. Their party organization often seems a logical place to ask for that money. If the party is unwilling to provide more help — and it almost certainly will be — the campaigners may find their party friends to be a great disappointment.

In sum, party organizations face a predicament when they contribute money and services to campaigns. The candidates most likely to win are least likely to need the party's help in doing so. Thus party contributions to incumbents and candidates for open seats may bring relatively little influence in return — a painfully selfless result for a party organization. Party help may be most keenly appreciated, and most influential, in campaigns with the slimmest chances of success.

THE IMPACT OF PARTY REFORM: TWO
CONTRASTING DIRECTIONS

With party influence on campaigns so precarious, one might assume that any party reform movements would be designed to strengthen that influence. Yet the assumption is only half correct. The national Republicans' movement into high-powered fund raising and campaign services does seem very likely to expand the party's influence, especially in Senate and state legislative races. But although the national Democrats have put even more intensive effort into party reform during the last 15 years, the results may well have *weakened* party influence on campaigns.

The Democratic reforms did give the party's national organization greater power over the state parties (see chapter 1). But the national party's victory was hollow. The new rules made it easier for issue-oriented enthusiasts and candidate loyalists, rather than party regulars and public officials, to control the party's nominating machinery. And because of the rules' complexity, more and more state parties turned to primary elections as the means of choosing their convention delegates. In these low-turnout primaries and participatory caucuses, the influence of well-organized interest groups, or even fringe groups of various kinds, could more easily compete with that of the regular party organization. Listen to the complaint of one activist about the party platform devised by her county Democratic caucus under the new participatory rules:

> I can remember speaking [on the platform at the county party caucus] at 7 on a Sunday morning—hadn't gone home since 10 A.M. Saturday. But at 10 P.M. Saturday night, all the businessmen, all the housewives, all the *reasoned* electorate had gone home, and all the pot-smoking kids were sitting there at seven in the morning with me. . . . And it was very unfair, because they railroaded through all the garbage that they wanted onto the platform. . . . It was not what the rank-and-file electorate person who was paying the taxes in this state thought![57]

The party regulars in counties throughout the nation would doubtless say "amen." Clearly the reforms had alienated many of the older organization loyalists and Democratic elected officials.

So in 1981, when a commission began rewriting the Democratic party's rules for the fourth time in 12 years, loyalists and officeholders set out to recapture control. An important result was the addition of a group of about 550 "superdelegates" to the voting membership of the convention—party and elected officials who would attend as uncommitted delegates and thus assure themselves of some role in the nomination process.[58] At the same time, the national Democratic committees were starting to implement their born-again interest in fund raising and grass-roots party building, concerns that a decade of participatory reform had obscured.

THE EFFECTS OF CAMPAIGN FINANCE REFORM

Another set of recent reforms has also changed the political environment in ways that challenge the parties to either shift their focus or lose influence over campaigners. The Federal Election Campaign Act Amendments of 1974 and 1976 (with the unfortunate acronym FECA), described in chapter 1, were designed to limit the flow of private money into presidential and congressional campaigns. But in reality these reforms have limited the *parties'* campaign spending while funneling still-plentiful private money into campaigns through PACs.

FECA's provision for public funding of presidential campaigns, for example, capped the amount that the national parties can spend (the limit was $4.6 million in 1980) in behalf of their nominee in the general election. And the law cut down on the parties' grass-roots activities. Presidential candidates who accepted the federal funding had to stay within the law's strict spending ceilings. To maximize the effects of that spending, candidates tended to use their limited funds to buy the most efficient media available, especially television, and to drop the traditional campaign paraphernalia (bumper stickers, yard signs, posters, and buttons) that had made so many local party activists feel a part of the race. That, many complained, restricted the state and local party committees' role in presidential races.

FECA was amended in 1979 to undo the damage. Now, state and local parties are allowed to spend unlimited amounts of money on volunteer activities to promote federal candidates: voter registration and get-out-the-vote drives, campaign paraphernalia, and other expenses connected with volunteer activities. In fact, some writers feel that the correction may have gone too far. Reporter Elizabeth Drew estimates that national party committees, which are permitted to raise this "soft money" for the state parties, pumped at least $10 million of it into the 1980 election—including money (corporate treasury funds, individual contributions beyond the legal limits) that cannot be directly contributed to federal campaigns.[59] This may be a promising loophole for the parties— or at least for the Republicans, who raised 90 percent of the soft money in 1980.

But the aspect of the reforms that has probably done the greatest damage to party influence—the ceilings on party contributions to congressional campaigns—remains in force. In House races, the national party committee, the state party, and the relevant Hill committee are each limited to $10,000 in *direct* contributions to a candidate ($5000 per party committee in the primary and again in the general election), for a total of $30,000 in direct contributions by the three party committees; more can be contributed in case of a run-off.

National party committees can add to that amount through coordinated spending (of up to $18,440 per candidate in 1982 in most states; this limit, unlike that for direct party contributions, is adjusted in time for each election to reflect changes in the cost of living). The state's party organization is allowed to spend an identical amount. If the state party does not have the money (and most do not), the national party can pick up the state's share, thus doubling the total allowable for national party committees. So in 1982, the national-level party committees could give or spend a maximum of about $67,000 for each House candidate—while it is estimated that a challenger needs between $200,000 and $300,000 to beat an incumbent House member.[60]

Restrictions are less severe in Senate races. While direct contributions are limited to a total of $17,500 per candidate from all national party committees combined, limits on a party's coordinated spending depend on the size of the state; the ceilings ranged from $36,880 to $655,874 in the 1982 election—two cents multiplied by the state's voting-age population and adjusted for inflation. If they also contribute the state party's share, national-level parties can put big money into Senate races in the largest states—the party limit in California in 1982 was more than $1.3 million. (In practice, of course, this mattered only for the Republicans; the Democratic party was in no danger of spending a million dollars in one place.)

Even with these opportunities, the bottom line is this: party giving is limited by law, but candidate "receiving" is not. When candidates want to spend more —and frequently much more—than the parties can offer, there are alternative sources of money: PACs and the solicitation of individual donations through direct mail. To the extent that FECA has encouraged the growth of PACs and the use of direct-mail fund raising, it has encouraged powerful competitors for party influence over campaigns.

Party Influence Through Modeling

Parties have another potential source of influence over campaigners. People do not learn from response consequences alone; in fact, learning from models is more common. So by controlling (or at least providing) the channels of observational learning—by guiding campaigners' attention to certain models—party organizations could have an impact on what campaigners learn and thus on how they behave.

Recall that in observational learning, an individual forms an idea of how a model's behavior is constructed and performed; that idea, or symbolic coding, can guide the individual's own action at some later time. The first step involves attracting the individual's attention to the model. Party organizations have developed "campaign schools" for that purpose. These are meetings at which models selected by the party—successful candidates, managers, or professional consultants—teach campaigners the strategies that the party regards as effective.

Party campaign schools have been run for decades, but their use has greatly increased since the mid-1970s. Republican party committees have been responsible for most of that increase. The Republicans have also extended the schools' reach—previously limited to congressional campaigns—to state legislative races. In 1980, for example, the RNC held about 100 training seminars for state legislative candidates and managers to convey the party's ideas about polling, precinct targeting, media, scheduling, and staffing.[61]

To get a feel for the nature of campaign schools as learning situations, let us examine a set of them. In preparation for the 1980 elections, the RNC and the Republican congressional committee held 16 Regional Campaign Management Workshops in various parts of the country from late 1979 to June 1980. The participants—about 70 per workshop—included a number of campaigners recruited by the RNC's regional political directors and local elections' field people. Each workshop, geared toward House candidates and managers with limited campaign experience, provided three days of basic training in campaign techniques. An organizer tells what happens in each:[62]

> In the regional school, we more or less define political strategy and the need for a campaign plan itself, and take them through the mechanical steps of what a strategy is. Basically, that strategy answers the questions, "Who are you going to get to vote for you? What groups are you going to go after, to get those votes, and why?" . . . And then the planning part answers the questions, "What is it that you're going to do to get those groups to vote for you? When are you going to do it? And how are you going to carry it out?"
>
> And then we just take them—a very mechanical process—take them step by step through the kinds of research that you need to do, the various organizational structures to be considered. . . . Basic requirements for developing good press relations. Various elements of media communications. Radio, television, newspapers, tabloids, bumper stickers. What each one of those media is good for. How to make the decision which of those media you're going to choose, to deliver which message.

The purpose, in short, is to provide models for many of the strategic responses that campaigners need.

The RNC followed up these regional workshops with a longer and more intensive Campaign Management College: six days of study for groups of 20 workshop "graduates" and other experienced congressional campaigners. Perhaps the most interesting segment of the college was its use of computerized campaign simulations, or what the staff called "war games." These were designed to let campaigners rehearse what they had learned—a vital component of effective modeling—in a situation set up to resemble a real race. Participants were divided into teams and given a case study of an actual 1978 congressional campaign where the Republican candidate got 48.5 percent of the vote. Each team then rewrote the campaign plan to show how they would have picked up the additional 2 percent needed to win. The data from these redesigned plans were fed into a computer program along with pertinent details of the election district and its voters. While the teams watched, the computer calculated how each plan would have fared.

Most of the teachers at these RNC sessions were party staffers; others were outside consultants. Interestingly, candidates were *not* used as teachers in these schools; some had formed the bad habit of winning without following the party's approved program of research and planning, and the school's organizers did not want to risk the presence of such models.

Other Republican campaign schools were run exclusively for candidates. These schools put little emphasis on the "nuts and bolts" of campaign techniques and much more emphasis on presentation of self: issues and images. A staffer explained:

> Well, in a nutshell, we would give them issue briefings on the issues that we felt were important at the time. Each time, we had a discussion by members of Congress and sometimes outside people. Defense issues, energy, economics—those were the main ones we tried to have in each of the sessions. We would have, oh, say, Congressman Brown from Ohio spend an hour talking with them about energy issues as *he* saw them, from his role on the [House] energy committee, and discussing the legislation that was up that he thought was critical, and talking pro's and con's on the points that were being raised. The same thing on economic issues.
>
> And then we would have a discussion of what the pollsters were finding were the issues of concern, and what the mood of the country was, and we would try to do that each time.

On issues that pollsters identified as major public concerns, the campaign school provided detailed models: information about the dimensions of the issue, the nature of current legislation, and ways to answer questions about it. On issues that did not rank high in the polls, the school's intent was to help the candidate develop his or her own position and communicate it effectively. The overall message, however, was that candidates should be emphasizing issues that ranked high in the polls, and on which the party's position was thought to have majority support. In 1980, that meant energy, the economy, and defense. In this way, issue agendas recommended by the party organization were diffused to many congressional campaigns by means of the Republican candidate schools. The same teaching device had been used in 1978, as a reporter indicates:

> In 10 targeted districts across the state, Republican congressional challengers trained in special "candidate schools" in the East are waging nearly identical campaigns against their Democratic opponents. They promise to "take the spirit of Proposition 13" to Washington, to slash taxes and cut government programs.[63]

In addition to an issue agenda, the candidate schools taught styles of self-presentation. The key to this part of the "curriculum" was a series of simulated press conferences in which school staff members, playing the role of reporters, fired questions at each of the candidates. These mock press conferences were videotaped and critiqued by the school's instructors. The critics paid special attention to

> their mannerisms, not answering questions directly, their presence—all those kinds of things that most candidates don't have the opportunity to ever see. They don't see how they look to other people. So by using videotape, we are able to work with candidates on appearance: How do you look? Do you stutter? Do your glasses make you look strange, especially on TV? Your clothes, the colors—those sorts of things; mannerisms, scratching your head, fidgeting, eye contact, and then the substantive responses.

The ordering of priorities is revealing: image first, then the substance of issues. As one congressman-model stated in a candidate school session entitled "What Really Worked for Me": "We ignored issues a lot. Most people in your district are not going to vote for you because of whether or not you want to go back to the gold standard, they're going to vote for you because they like you: you smile a lot, you have a good personality, or they feel they can trust you." A Reagan adviser put it more succinctly: "Issues are simply a vehicle to build images."[64]

The Democrats ran campaign schools too, but less frequently and without the flash and sophistication of simulated elections and videotaped press conferences. The Democratic Congressional Campaign Committee held several two-day schools on the basics of campaign management and techniques. The Senatorial Committee organized two sets of seminars: a series for nonincumbents, and another for the staff members of senators up for reelection in 1980. As even one of the school's own organizers admitted, however, "Our training schools are not nearly as sophisticated as the Republicans."

In sum, campaign schools are an explicit effort by both parties to influence candidates' learning and behavior—a means by which a party committee teaches campaign innovations to its candidates. The models, after all, were not selected by the "students" (as models would be under other circumstances); they were chosen by the party committee because their approach to organizing or polling or articulating issues is one that the party's leaders want its campaigners to learn. The Republican staffer who says that he does not ask candidates to speak at his seminars because they may admit that they won without having done much research or polling is really saying, quite understandably, that he chooses speakers who will promote the party's vision of an effective campaign.

While much of the instruction at these schools involves questions of style and technique, they are just as capable of teaching the party's position on substantive issues. In this way, the party organization can affect the issue agendas of campaigns and public officials; when the NRCC candidate school teaches congressional challengers to emphasize the need for tax cuts or increasing defense spending, it affects the issue message of those campaigns and (by influencing voters' expectations about the candidate, and making a difference in the kinds of people who join his or her supporting coalition) affects their likely behavior in office as well. Not all campaign schools choose to deal with substantive issues. But many of the Republican schools do.

The schools can be very effective learning situations; they are designed to make learning as easy as possible for their "students." By bringing campaigners to Washington or some other central site, the organizers take them away from the distractions of their usual environments and focus their attention on models. The sessions are concentrated, often lasting for up to ten hours a day, with little opportunity for participants to do anything other than attend to the curriculum. The models, in short, are readily available, and little else is.[65]

Besides, the campaigners have a lot of incentive to pay attention. They are not forced to come, and those recruited by party leaders are likely to be attracted by the encouragement and flattery they receive. Most are moving into a campaign environment that differs from their previous experience and want to know how to respond effectively to it. Because they are inexperienced, or because their environment has changed enough to make their prior experience inapplicable, they have reason to look for models. They are urged to do just that. In the words of one Republican campaign school instructor, "There is lots of material out there. You do not have to develop the exquisitely virgin concept on tax policy. There are things out there that you can use."[66]

Finally, these schools provide the kinds of information that campaigners *can* use most easily: explicit instructions on how to construct a strategy, how to organize, how to advertise, how to behave. The students do not need to ponder what makes a successful model tick; they are told how the model's strategy works and how it might be applied to their own race. By constructing such inviting and effective settings for observational learning and by filling them with predigested information about approved party models, party organizations, especially those of the Republicans, are developing what may be their most effective means of influence on campaigns.

Party-Based Learning Without the Party Organization's Help

Parties may play another role in campaigners' observational learning, but in a special sense. Even if party committees do not hold training schools, campaigners may simply be more likely to choose their models from among their own party's candidates than to use models from the other party. In that way, the networks of campaign learning and diffusion of innovations would remain largely inside party lines. Then the actions of Republican campaigners could differ systematically from those of Democratic campaigners, even in the absence of any efforts by party *organizations* to affect those behaviors.

The influence is not that of the party organization, but of the shared party tie.[67] And that influence will probably be frequent because same-party models are likely to be more available to a campaigner, to capture his or her attention, and to seem likely to work in his or her own race, than should potential models from the other party. Consider, for instance, the impact of a campaigner's experience. As Frank Sorauf reminds, being active in a party's organization or campaigns is a logical place for people to learn the skills and establish the connections that are so important in campaigning:

> In most parts of the country the party still remains a likely source of . . . the skill, experience, connections, approval, and resources that any candidate needs. It is, of course, possible for the candidate without party ties to seek election, but for every one who does, there are dozens of successful office seekers who have party ties.[68]

In contrast to the trend among voters generally, people who run for office (and those who work actively in their behalf) are often strong partisans.[69] Varieties of forces bind campaigners to some aspect of their party: contacts and friendships with other party activists, positive feelings toward the ideals or group symbols they associate with their party, and the kind of closeness forged by voluntary effort under stressful conditions.

The sharing of partisan attachment, in short, should increase campaigners' attention to same-party models. That tendency will probably be reinforced by the fact that the people who are most readily available to the campaigner—the volunteers, staffers, and contributors who provide a large part of the reactions he or she receives—are frequently more partisan than the general public. So the important qualities of availability and attractiveness are more likely to characterize models of the campaigner's own party than those of the other party.

Similarity between the model and the observer is a key factor in observational learning. And the chances are that campaigners of the same party will share other important characteristics as well. On the average, two Republican congressional candidates are likely to have more in common with one another—in the groups supporting them, their sources of campaign contributions, the issue orientations of activists involved in their campaigns—than with a Democratic congressional candidate.

The point should not be pushed too far. Both parties are diverse internally. The Democratic party, especially, has several distinct "issue groups" within it, which attract different supporting coalitions and contributors.[70] A liberal Democrat in an eastern university town, whose partisanship is tied to a strong dedication to social welfare principles, is not very likely to see a conservative southern Democrat as an attractive potential model. There should be several different networks of observational learning within the Democratic party, each with its own distinctive models and campaign approaches.

But the Republican party has become more ideologically homogeneous in recent years. That makes the use of same-party models even more likely among its campaigners. And it means that observational learning is more likely to produce a distinctive party-based similarity in the campaigns of Republican newcomers than in the case of Democratic newcomers. The Republican party's campaign schools, services to candidates, and campaign contributions should make that party distinctiveness even more pronounced in its campaigns.

The Parties' Rivals for Influence on Campaigns

PAC POWER

Under certain conditions, then, party organizations can and do influence campaigners' behavior. But they have a lot of competition. Among the most formidable competitors are Political Action Committees.

We have already seen that in terms of campaign spending, PACs rivaled party organizations for influence throughout the 1970s. By the early 1980s, with the exception of the national-level Republican committees, the parties had clearly lost the race. Increasingly, PACs are offering campaign services and expertise to candidates as well.

A number of PACs, particularly those on the New Right, have learned that if they can provide vitally needed electioneering activities to a campaign (such as voter targeting, precinct organizing, direct mail), they can affect the directions the campaign takes. The Committee for the Survival of a Free Congress, for instance, offers to pay for a precinct organizer in the campaigns of New Right candidates, but only if the organizer conducts the precinct voter mobilization plan that CSFC regards as necessary for an effective campaign. As its director stated, "If they want our help, they do it our way."[71]

Many of these groups also work to expand their influence through the provision of models by holding campaign schools of their own. The CSFC's school, for example, featured the kind of simulation exercise that won the national Republican campaign schools such high marks for effectiveness.

One might argue that PACs such as the CSFC do not really rival party influence; rather, they enhance it, since their efforts are usually confined to one party's candidates. They could be regarded, then, as intraparty influence networks. But in fact, most of these groups are offering an alternative to the party organization's own influence, and especially in the case of the Democrats, an alternative that excludes some parts of the broader party coalition. The liberal PAC Democrats for the 80's, for instance, made clear in its 1982 mailings that its help was intended for "Democrats who seek a reasoned and responsible position on nuclear weapons reduction," by which it meant supporters of a nuclear freeze. Another, the Democratic Study Group Campaign Fund, went further, proclaiming that when it offered money and services to congressional candidates in 1982, conservative "boll weevil" Democrats need not apply. And New Right groups such as NCPAC acknowledged that while their contributions went mainly to Republicans, they had nothing but contempt for the Republican party and hoped to destroy its influence and substitute their own. With those kinds of friends, neither party needed enemies.

POLITICAL CONSULTANTS AND OTHER HIRED GUNS

The high price and complexity of many of the newer campaign-related technologies (computers, direct mail, sophisticated polling) propel growing numbers of candidates to get expert advice on how to use these tools effectively. In some European democracies that expert advice comes from campaign consultants employed by the candidates' parties. But American parties were too weak when these technologies were developing to monopolize knowledge about their applications to campaigns. Other groups stepped into the breach—and came to rival the parties for influence on candidates.

At first, advertising agencies offered the much-wanted advice. Then independent entrepreneurs came in to fill the growing demand with counsel and services in polling, direct mail, personnel management, computerized data processing, market research and broadcast advertising, image making, campaign accounting, canvassing, and any other activity on which a campaign might want to spend its money.[72] The result is that with enough funds, a candidate can create the equivalent of a party organization without the party. It is not very cost effective in a broader sense, since this expensive "party equivalent" is geared up for only one candidate, rather than a whole range of candidates (as the party's machinery could be). But it is effective in giving candidates the means to run independently of their party—to remain, if they choose, a party of one.

Professional consultants vie with parties not only in the provision of services but also in the provision of models, as chapter 3 suggested. So far, as our later examination of Senate races shows, many of these firms have tended to work in the campaigns of one party only; they act as agents, then, of intraparty observational learning. But that can change; if the circumstances of a race developed so that the most relevant models were in the other party, then consultants could be one of the means by which observational learning could cross party lines rather than reinforce them. For several reasons, then, the rise of independent consultants gives the candidates a way to sidestep party influence.

Conclusion: The Conditions of Party Influence

For the American parties to influence campaigners' environments, they must first deal effectively with their own environments. When a party organization can muster significant amounts of the resources candidates need—money, volunteers, services—then the influence of that organization will grow. National-level Republican committees are following that pattern in the 1980s, at least with respect to House, Senate, and selected state legislative candidates. The national Democratic committees and many parties at local and state levels, Republican as well as Democratic, have been much less successful.

Party organizations can also influence campaign behavior by providing models for candidates to follow. Again, the national Republicans are working actively to develop that avenue of influence through campaign schools and other means. Again, the national Democrats lag far behind. So far, the increasing role of professional consultants has strengthened the tendency for campaign innovations to diffuse mainly within party lines. So does the tendency for candidates and managers to prefer same-party models. But except for the national Republicans, few party organizations have made themselves active sources of observational learning.

To some extent, the uphill struggles of American party organizations are inherent in the design of the nation's political system. With separation of powers comes the fact that there is no necessary bond between party members in Congress and their colleague in the White House. If there were, as in a parliamentary system—if cabinet ministries were awarded to members of the majority party in the legislature, and fear of a no-confidence vote required a substantial level of party cohesion—then the party organization would have a very valuable set of rewards for loyal candidates, rewards that no PAC or professional consultant could provide. To the extent that such rewards are made contingent on the candidate's acceptance of party discipline, they should be a mighty source of influence on the candidate's campaigns. But the separation of powers deprives American parties of this plum, just as the direct primary system deprives parties of the vital function of nominating their standard-bearers.

The parties' problems are not in institutional design alone, however. Popular suspicion of parties and of centralized power—the source of those institutional choices—has dogged the parties from the beginning. The tremendous expansion of the mass media and other new campaign technologies need not have weakened party organizations; if the parties had been firmly rooted in public opinion when these technologies emerged, party organizations might have captured those tools and used them to cement party influence on candidates' campaigns. If the national party organizations had been powerful when television was in its infancy, then they might have been able to claim time for political broadcasts as part of their rightful turf, and been able to distribute that time to loyal candidates. They might have been able to organize such effective polling outfits that private pollsters would find little market potential in politics.

Some party organizations *have* succeeded in making themselves centers of expertise on the new campaign technologies and thus becoming indispensable to candidates.[73] Most parties have not. The result is that in many campaigns around the country, nonparty actors such as PACs, single-issue groups, and independent experts have been able to obtain these tools, offer them to candidates, and further erode party influence.

The forces limiting party influence on campaign behavior are formidable, but not out of reach. The story of the national Republican committees shows clearly that those forces can be harnessed—that with effort, the usually hostile environment of American parties can be tamed. The interesting question is whether the national Democrats and party organizations at state and local levels will be able to follow suit—and if not, how the nature of the party competition in American campaigns will be changed.

NOTES

1. The first commentator is Walter Dean Burnham in *Parties and Elections in an Anti-Party Age,* ed. Jeff Fishel (Bloomington: Indiana University Press, 1978), 333; the second is Norman H. Nie et al., *The Changing American Voter,* enlarged ed. (Cambridge, Mass.: Harvard University Press, 1979), 49.
2. See Nie et al., *Changing American Voter,* chap. 4.
3. Charles H. Franklin and John E. Jackson, "The Dynamics of Party Identification," *American Political Science Review* 77 (December 1983): 957-73.
4. Robert J. Samuelson, "Fragmentation and Uncertainty Litter the Political Landscape," *National Journal,* 20 October 1979, 1726.
5. Data from the American National Election Study by the Center for Political Studies.
6. Reported in Jack Dennis, "Support for the Party System by the Mass Public," *American Political Science Review* 60 (September 1966): 605.

7. See Martin P. Wattenberg, "The Decline of Political Partisanship in the United States," *American Political Science Review* 75 (December 1981): 941-50.
8. See, for example, Leon D. Epstein, *Political Parties in Western Democracies* (New Brunswick, N.J.: Transaction, 1980), 209-15.
9. In *American Parties in Decline* (Boston: Little, Brown, 1980), 249.
10. See Samuel J. Eldersveld, *Political Parties in American Society* (New York: Basic Books, 1982), chaps. 2 and 4.
11. Cornelius P. Cotter et al., "State Party Organizations and the Thesis of Party Decline," (paper presented at the annual meeting of the American Political Science Association, 1980), 38.
12. See Robert L. Peabody, "House Party Leadership in the 1970s," in *Congress Reconsidered,* ed. Lawrence C. Dodd and Bruce I. Oppenheimer, 2nd ed. (Washington, D.C.: Congressional Quarterly, 1981), 140-41.
13. See John W. Kingdon, *Congressmen's Voting Decisions,* 2nd ed. (New York: Harper & Row, 1981), chap. 4.
14. Norman J. Ornstein and David W. Rohde, "Political Parties and Congressional Reform," in Fishel, *Parties and Elections,* 280-94.
15. See Frank J. Sorauf, *Party Politics in America,* 4th ed. (Boston: Little, Brown, 1980), 364-69.
16. See Epstein, *Political Parties,* 215-25.
17. See Sorauf, *Party Politics,* 214-17.
18. Gary C. Jacobson, *Money in Congressional Elections* (New Haven: Yale University Press, 1980), 146.
19. Ibid., esp. 36-50.
20. Larry Light, "Republican Groups Dominate in Party Campaign Spending," *Congressional Quarterly Weekly Report* 38 (1 November 1980): 3234.
21. Elizabeth Drew, "Politics and Money," *New Yorker,* 6 December 1982, 54-149.
22. These legal ceilings are discussed later in this chapter.
23. FEC data.
24. Larry McCarthy, quoted in Light, "Republican Groups," 3237.
25. Drew, "Politics and Money," 68.
26. Rob Gurwitt and Tom Watson, "Democrats Recoup State Legislature Losses," *Congressional Quarterly Weekly Report* 40 (13 November 1982): 2849.
27. Christopher Buchanan, "National GOP Pushing Hard to Capture State Legislatures," *Congressional Quarterly Weekly Report* 38 (25 October 1980): 3192.
28. Rhodes Cook, "Democrats Develop Tactics," *Congressional Quarterly Weekly Report* 40 (3 July 1982): 1591.
29. Charles O. Jones, "The New, New Senate," in *A Tide of Discontent,* ed. Ellis Sandoz and Cecil V. Crabb, Jr. (Washington, D.C.: Congressional Quarterly, 1981), 102.
30. Neil MacNeil, "The Struggle for the House of Representatives," in Sandoz and Crabb, *A Tide of Discontent,* 74.
31. Ibid., 75.
32. Fund-raising letter from Tony Coelho, 29 January 1982.
33. Buchanan, "National GOP," 3188.
34. See chapter 3, page 77, in this volume.
35. Buchanan, "National GOP," 3192.

36. MacNeil, "The Struggle," 82.
37. Drew, "Politics and Money," 102.
38. See James L. Gibson et al., "Assessing Party Organizational Strength," *American Journal of Political Science* 27 (May 1983): 193-222.
39. Ibid., 203-4.
40. See James L. Gibson et al., "Whither the Local Parties?" (paper presented at the annual meeting of the Western Political Science Association, 1982), 15.
41. Ibid., 24-28.
42. Quoted in Thomas A. Kazee, "The Decision to Run for Congress" (paper presented at the annual meeting of the Midwest Political Science Association, 1979), 14 and 15.
43. Jacobson, *Money in Congressional Elections*, 56.
44. FEC figures and Gary C. Jacobson, "Money in the 1980 Congressional Elections" (paper presented at the annual meeting of the Midwest Political Science Association, 1982), table 1.
45. Jacobson, *Money in Congressional Elections*, 35.
46. Quoted in Kazee, "The Decision," 13.
47. Policy research helps the candidate bone up on major issues. Opposition research is designed to locate unfavorable information about the opposing candidate (such as previous votes cast that might prove to be damaging). On the development of RNC services to candidates and parties, see "Bill Brock Concentrates on Grass Roots," *CQ Guide to Current American Government* (Washington, D.C.: Congressional Quarterly, Fall 1979), 79-82.
48. Ibid., 79.
49. Buchanan, "National GOP," 3189.
50. Cook, "Democrats Develop Tactics," 1594.
51. See Gibson et al., "Assessing Party Organizational Strength," 202-4.
52. Gibson et al., "Whither the Local Parties?"
53. See Jacobson, *Money in Congressional Elections*, 93-94 and 101. The pattern varies according to the party's prospects in the coming election. When the party expects that its candidates will do well in November, it normally tries to capitalize on that trend by giving more help to its challengers. When it expects to do poorly, the party is likely to focus on protecting its incumbents.
54. The Democratic Senatorial Committee's action reflects the unusually large number of Democrats up for reelection in 1980 (Democrats held 24 of the 34 contested seats) and the expectation that national political tides favored the Republicans; for the same reasons, only 10 percent of the RNSC's contributions went to incumbents.
55. Ellen Hume, "Conservatives Foresee Big Gains in Congress This Year," *Louisville Courier-Journal*, 23 October 1978, A7.
56. Linda L. Fowler, "The Electoral Lottery," *Public Choice* 34, nos. 3/4 (1979): 410-12.
57. Interviewed by Darrell West, 1 July 1980.
58. See Rhodes Cook, "Democrats' Rules Weaken Representation," *Congressional Quarterly Weekly Report* 40 (3 April 1982): 749-51.
59. See Drew, "Politics and Money," 63-64.
60. Alan Ehrenhalt, "Campaign 'Reform' No Boon to Challengers," *Congressional Quarterly Weekly Report* 41 (11 June 1983): 1191.
61. Buchanan, "National GOP," 3189.

62. Unless otherwise cited, the quotations below are from interviews with RNC and NRCC staff members.
63. Hume, "Conservatives Foresee Big Gains," A7.
64. Bill Moyers' Journal, Campaign Report no. 4, "See How They Run" (WNET transcript), 3 October 1980, 12 and 17.
65. Recall that the availability of models is an important determinant of learning. In a parallel discussion of legislative cue giving, Kingdon argues (*Congressmen's Voting Decisions,* 73) that one reason why legislative colleagues are such prominent sources of cues on congressional votes is that they are readily available at the time of decision.
66. Moyers, "See How They Run," 6.
67. Kingdon makes a similar argument (*Congressmen's Voting Decisions,* chaps. 3 and 4) when he notes that cue giving can explain the voting cohesion of party blocs in Congress. Even though members of Congress do not regard the congressional party leadership as a very important influence on their votes, they do normally take their cues from other members of their party when deciding how to vote on a bill.
68. *Party Politics,* 85.
69. See, for example, Jeff Fishel, *Party and Opposition* (New York: McKay, 1973), 129-30 (on new members of Congress); and Epstein, *Political Parties,* 117 (on campaign staffers and activists).
70. See John H. Kessel, *Presidential Campaign Politics* (Homewood, Ill.: Dorsey, 1980), 66-84.
71. Quoted in Crotty and Jacobson, *American Parties in Decline,* 147.
72. See especially Larry J. Sabato, *The Rise of Political Consultants* (New York: Basic Books, 1981).
73. See, for example, Robert Agranoff, ed., *The New Style in Election Campaigns* (Boston: Holbrook, 1972), chap. 4.

6. A Tale of Six Races: The Abortion Issue Enters Campaign Environments

So far in these chapters we have traced the roots of social-learning theory and examined how it helps us understand political campaigning and the role of political parties in campaigns. But the proof of the pudding is yet to be tasted. The theory must be put to the test to see whether it can predict and explain events.

This book began with a discussion of change: in the political parties, in political issues and the groups that promote them, in election laws—change, in short, throughout the environment of political campaigning. One of the most intriguing changes has been the rise of single-issue politics in the last decade. The phenomenon is not new; it could fairly be said that during the course of the nation's history, single-issue politics has been as American as apple pie. But as chapter 1 suggested, a number of conditions in contemporary American politics give single-issue appeals a distinctive force. Their intensity has become a real source of concern to many candidates and staff members—an insistent challenge demanding their response. That gives us a particularly interesting arena in which to look at the interaction between campaigners and their changing environment.

This chapter begins by exploring the nature of that change, the character of single-issue politics and the controversy that is so often cited as the quintessential single issue: the drive to make abortions illegal again. It traces the process by which groups supporting a ban on all abortions (here to be identified by the term they have chosen for themselves: "pro-life" groups) became active participants in political campaigns during the late 1970s and early 1980s. It introduces the six Senate campaigns targeted for defeat by pro-life organizations in 1980. In so doing, it lays the groundwork for a partial test of the theory. But let us begin with single-issue politics, its character and its power.

THE SPECIAL NATURE OF SINGLE-ISSUE POLITICS

To call a group "single-issue" conjures up images of fanatics, zealots, people obsessed with a particular issue to the exclusion of the broader public interest. Yet single-issue politics has played a persistent and important role in American political history, giving many issues a place on the political agenda that they might not otherwise have attained. From the abolitionist movement of the last century to the civil rights marches of the 1960s, the effort to gain rights for black Americans has often taken on a single-issue tone; indeed, if it had not, very little might have been achieved. In fact, many who hotly criticized single-issue politics in the early 1980s were themselves politically active a decade earlier in another single-issue movement: the protests that made American involvement in the Vietnam war a central political issue.

Single-issue politics, then, is not a pathology. Rather, it is simply a way of defining a political issue, and a style of activism, adopted by many people and interest groups at various times. And for good reason: it is a style that has proven effective in the American political environment.

A given issue—abortion, for example—can be defined or symbolized in various ways.[1] Some people might define the issue *referentially*—in other words, in a specific and concrete way, focusing on its objective elements so as to limit the scope of meaning and the depth of emotion that it will evoke. A physician giving a speech at an American Medical Association convention, for instance, might discuss abortion as a matter of routine medical practice, offering suggestions on the available procedures and statistics as to their use. The presentation is dry, clinical, affectively neutral. The speaker's definition of the issue does not invite the expression of strong feelings or the recollection of deeply personal experiences and emotions. The approach does invite calm, unemotional, uninvolved acceptance. It is often used to contain a potential conflict, to quiet a rebellious voice.

Another political actor might define the same issue *condensationally*—with very different effects on the audience. Condensational symbols refer to things in a more ambiguous, emotionally provocative way. They expand the scope of the issue to a level that encourages listeners to respond intensely, affectively, and very personally. Here is an example, again with reference to abortion:

> The important issue is the holocaust of 1.5 million babies, and doctors getting rich off it. . . . Women's bodies are being torn apart. Hostility is being put between the mother and her child. It is a straight due process question, when a group of people are defined as less than human and preyed upon by somebody else. Anyone, any group that has as the objective the killing of innocent preborn children is not a legitimate group, period.[2]

The definition of the abortion issue contained in this second approach has a very different purpose from that of the first. The second speaker wants to arouse strong emotions with her words; the images in her language—holocaust, babies, people being preyed upon, innocent children — are power references to people and events that reach into our deepest feelings, our private values. Issues defined in condensational terms, then, draw on beliefs and experiences that touch nerves in people. They have the power to incite; they can be used to fan conflicts, to create political attachments in individuals whose nerves have been touched.

Characteristically, the issues that drive single-issue politics are defined in the condensational mode. Handgun control, to its opponents, is not defined as an effort by government to regulate the distribution of potentially unsafe products, but as a conspiracy to deprive Americans of their God-given right to defend their homes and families, a drive to emasculate law-abiding citizens while criminals do as they please. As theater, the latter definitions are certainly more compelling, more likely to engage the individual's fears and hopes, than the former. In the language of those fertile fields of condensational symbols, the Western movies, "them's fightin' words."

And in the world of political campaigns, them's motivatin' words. Because they make use of condensational symbols, single-issue groups have the ability to mobilize people. In the American campaign environment, where public apathy is pronounced, voter turnout is low, and candidates usually find themselves searching for "people" to whom to respond, the dramatic message of a single-issue group is not easily ignored.

In short, single-issue politics involves a very intense, emotional concentration on a policy area or concern that has been defined in condensational terms. Because the issue arouses such strong feelings, it is regarded by its proponents as fundamentally different from all the other, more mundane concerns of a campaign. To its partisans, the issue cries out for priority; there can be no hedging permitted, no compromise, no allowance made for a candidate's other commitments or qualifications.

A single-issue group works to engage and attach its members to the political world *through that issue alone*. The group cannot ask candidates to show the same singlemindedness. But it can (and does) put candidates on notice that the group's support will be given or withheld exclusively on the basis of their stance on that issue. And it can (and does) demand that candidates accept the group's position on the issue without exception or equivocation, or forfeit that support. For candidates, this produces a real dilemma. If they accept the group's position, they will alienate voters who do not share it, as well as limit their own maneuvering room. If they reject the group's position, they will draw the fervent opposition — the *singleminded* opposition — of its highly motivated activists and supporters. One campaign manager, whose candidate had been targeted for defeat by several such groups, complained:

A Tale of Six Races: Abortion Issue Enters Campaign Environments

> As far as the single-issue people are concerned, [our opponent] could be sleeping with a sheep and they wouldn't give a damn, just so long as he continues to toe the line on their issue. And the irony is that on other issues, the senator [the manager's candidate] probably agrees with them on nine out of ten, but they don't seem to care. How do you deal with people like that? I wish I knew.

Single issues, then, and single-issue activism can be very troublesome elements in a campaign environment. The demands they make on candidates pose difficult strategic choices. Single-issue politics has a similarly intrusive effect on the making of public policy; the larger the number of groups that refuse to accept compromise on a given issue, the harder it will be to craft the majorities needed to make and implement policy decisions.

As we have seen, a number of factors have increased the prominence of single-issue politics recently. Sophisticated new technologies such as computerized direct mail help single-issue groups to identify and reach likely supporters. The political parties' declining hold on voters' affections and behavior gives single-issue groups an opening. As one state pro-life leader put it,

> I think that the parties have declined because they've become, I don't know, sort of untouchable; they don't respond to the people. I think everybody is looking for a way to make their voice heard, and they would rather work on specific issues than work on the party.

And the campaign finance reforms of the 1970s gave these groups more channels—PACs and independent expenditures—through which to make their mark on campaigns.

A raft of groups concerned with "single issues" took advantage of these environmental changes and became politically active in the 1970s and 1980s. Among the most prominent, and the most interesting as well, are groups that want abortions made illegal again. Two political scientists have written: "Many political observers believe the antiabortionists to be the most successful of the new single-issue groups, and without question they have accomplished much more than anyone would have predicted."[3] In its brief existence the pro-life movement has prompted congressional legislation to limit the impact of a major Supreme Court ruling, increased media attention to the question of abortion, and made it an issue in campaigns all over the nation. How did this remarkable demonstration of political strength come about? How did abortion become a concern of American politics?

HOW ABORTION CAME TO BE A POLITICAL ISSUE

Laws and public attitudes toward abortion have changed dramatically in the last two centuries, for religious reasons and some very secular reasons as well.

Historically in English common law, upon which so much of the American legal tradition is based, abortion was not considered a proper concern of government until the midpoint of pregnancy: the time known as "quickening" when a pregnant woman begins to feel movement in her womb. After "quickening," abortion was a criminal act, though it was not punished as severely as was the killing of a "born" person. Even the Catholic church saw reason to treat the early days of a pregnancy differently from the middle and later periods; until 1869, the church's canon law stated that only after 40 days of pregnancy had passed did the "inanimate soul" in the womb become an "animate soul," and thus a person.[4]

More restrictive abortion laws were passed in England in 1803, and in the United States beginning in 1821. By 1900, virtually every American state had moved to make abortion illegal throughout pregnancy, except in cases where it was felt necessary to save the life of the mother. A number of arguments had been offered in favor of the change. Some legislators were concerned about the safety of the operation; any surgery, in the days before antibiotics and sulfa drugs, was dangerous. Many physicians wanted to tighten up the standards for medical practice and get rid of the medically untrained abortionists then active. Industrialists anxious to open up the resource-rich western frontier wanted to make sure that the population would grow rapidly enough to support that expansion. And some activists were determined to write into the law a strict standard of sexual morality; restricting the availability of abortion, they felt, was a blow against illicit sex.

Pressures then built to modify these restrictions. By the mid-1900s, population growth had been rapid enough to result in overcrowded cities. The development of medical knowledge had made abortion techniques much safer than they once were; illegal abortions, however, were still taking place in unsanitary, even life-threatening conditions. Feminists argued that the issue at stake was no less than the right of women to control their own bodies and futures. Movements to reform abortion laws grew.

State governments had made abortions illegal, and so it was to state governments that reformers turned. The American Law Institute published a model reform statute in 1958 that would permit abortions under some conditions.[5] In 1967 Colorado became the first state to liberalize its abortion law to resemble the model statute. After that, change came swiftly; in the six years following Colorado's action, 17 other states and the District of Columbia relaxed their restrictions on abortion.

While this rush of legislative change was taking place, several challenges to other states' restrictive laws were wending their way through the courts largely unnoticed—that is, until two such cases reached the U.S. Supreme Court and

A Tale of Six Races: Abortion Issue Enters Campaign Environments

produced a decision that altered the course of American politics. In the cases of *Roe* v. *Wade* and *Doe* v. *Bolton* (1973),[6] the Court struck down a state law that had outlawed abortion except to save the mother's life. A pregnant woman, the majority ruled, has a constitutionally derived right to privacy in choosing whether to bear her child.[7] A state can limit that right only at certain times and for certain reasons. During the first trimester, or first third, of pregnancy, the state cannot intervene. During the second trimester, states can regulate how abortions are performed in order to protect the mother's health. Once the third trimester of pregnancy begins, the Court declared, the state can act to protect the fetus or unborn child by restricting or even banning abortions. But at no time, even during that final trimester, can the state ban abortions deemed necessary to preserve the mother's life or her health.

It was a sweeping decision. With these two companion rulings, the Court took abortion policy effectively out of the hands of the state legislatures. And it redefined the government's role in abortion policy in a manner that went beyond the fondest dreams of many pro-choice reformers. It stated that a fetus or unborn child is not a "person" within the meaning of the Fourteenth Amendment—which prohibits states from depriving any person of life, liberty, or property without the due process of law—and so has no "right to life" under that amendment.

The reaction to the decision was immediate and intense. Thousands of letters poured into the Supreme Court, many of them angry and personal. Even former Justice Hugo Black was the target of more than a thousand enraged letter writers, though he had died 16 months before the ruling. Religious leaders went public with their criticism. Terence Cardinal Cooke of New York demanded, "How many millions of children prior to their birth will never live to see the light of day because of the shocking action of the majority of the United States Supreme Court today?" The president of the National Conference of Catholic Bishops stated, "It is hard to think of any decision in the two hundred years of our history which has had more disastrous implications for our stability as a civilized society."[8]

Abortion was catapulted onto the national political agenda. The context as well as the content of the Court's ruling contributed to the making of the issue. Recall that by the time the decision was handed down, only 18 states had taken steps to ease their restrictions on abortion, and even some of these changes fell short of the Court's new standards. Thirty-two states had not liberalized their laws. So this was an unusually abrupt move for the Court, which normally prefers to let a controversial question evolve in lower courts, and to let political debate on the question come to a peak before agreeing to rule. Moreover, its decision prevented even the most conservative states from enforcing antiabortion laws about which many state and church leaders felt very strongly.

The ruling, in short, challenged the moral and religious beliefs of a lot of people. Their feelings about abortion had suddenly become politically relevant. Many were propelled into political action. Shortly after the decision was published, while pro-choice groups were still stunned and delighted at their unexpected gain, groups of pro-life supporters were forming all over the country. One leader of a state pro-life organization explained,

> I had eight chapters [in her state pro-life organization] the day the decision came down, and within a week I had eleven; I mean, it was the reaction to the decision and the injustice of it. We would have *never* had abortion on demand in Iowa, without the Court's decision, because I was lobbying at the time, and we had all the votes to keep the existing law as it was. And this state just was not a pro-abortion state. We would have never, ever had it. I know that. The people were indignant. And so that's one of the reasons we grew to the size that we've grown, because there was a lot of indignation there.

ABORTION AS A "SINGLE ISSUE"

> In a town used to heavy lobbying and rough legislative fights, the abortion issue stands out in the capital as one of the most emotional.[9]

We have seen that a given issue can be defined in many different ways. The shape of any particular issue, and the meanings it takes on, depend on the circumstances of its entrance onto the political agenda and the nature of the groups or individuals who put it there. In the words of one writer,

> ... issues are not preordained problems that have to emerge in the political arena in particular forms and at particular times. Political issues are constructed by political actors for public consumption. The substance and the public impact of issues depend a great deal on how they are symbolized.[10]

The nature of the abortion issue in the 1970s and 1980s was shaped in large part by the groups that expressed outrage at the Supreme Court's 1973 ruling and that acted on their outrage by vowing to have the ruling overturned. Their approach to the issue was highly condensational, and its result was to make abortion a very compelling "single issue" in American politics.

Even before the Supreme Court's ruling, pro-life groups had become active in several states to prevent liberalization of state abortion laws. Many of these groups were church-related, and many were Catholic. The fervent and well-reported reactions of church leaders to *Roe v. Wade* left many with the impression that abortion was a "Catholic issue" in which the church hierarchy would play an important role. The impression was misleading. True, a number of Catholic bishops and priests have actively supported and assisted pro-life groups. But the pro-life movement was not composed only of Catholics when it began, and increasingly, since the mid-1970s, its leadership and membership have included members of fundamentalist Protestant churches and other "theological conservatives" such as Mormons and Orthodox Jews.

No matter what their denomination, these pro-life activists tended to be active church members, people for whom a full religious life was a high priority. And they tended to belong to churches whose doctrine taught that life begins at conception and that after conception, the life thus created was as human as that of any Supreme Court justice. To end a pregnancy at any point, then, would be seen as the killing of a human being. To someone who accepts that premise, a judicial decision that legalizes all abortions done within the first three months of pregnancy and that prevents a state from placing an absolute ban on abortion is a decision that sanctions murders. As one pro-life leader put it, "The right to choose is the right to kill."

Many pro-life partisans see themselves as 1980s-style abolitionists — similar in goals to the people who fought for the abolition of black slavery before the Civil War. Their purpose, as they see it, is to speak for human beings who cannot speak for themselves. Thus, like the abolitionists, they consider it vital to destroy the idea that an individual has the right to choice on abortion — the idea, in *Roe* v. *Wade,* that the continuation of a pregnancy ought to be a private decision made by the woman involved, in consultation with her physician. That "right to choice," pro-lifers argue, has two flaws. First, it ignores the other human being in question — the fetus, or unborn child — whose interest is to live and to be born. Second, they contend, it wrongly grants women and their doctors the power of life and death over the fetus or unborn child, when that power rightly belongs only to God. In the words of one pro-life law professor: "The real issue is whether life is a gift of God or of the State. Innocent life is nonnegotiable precisely because it comes from God."[11]

To these pro-lifers, the abortion issue involves no less than the protection of human life against those who would destroy it. Even if they went no further, it would be clear that their definition of the issue is condensational to its core. But many people in the movement *did* go further. Many (though not all) saw abortion as a graphic indicator that something was very wrong with the society itself.

That "something" was what has been called "secular humanism." The close church ties of most of these pro-life activists had nourished certain strongly held values. Central to those values was the belief that the moral order of society should derive from God's laws, and that those laws are absolute. Many felt that a radically different doctrine held sway around them: the belief that moral values are relative and situational, rather than absolute; that people ought to develop their own individual standards of conduct on the basis of their own reasoning and needs, rather than on the basis of religious morality. This "secular humanism," exalting human needs over God's laws, was viewed by many as the root of the so-called abortion mentality that they saw in the media, in pro-choice organizations, and now in government policy. And the root had produced many other branches, they feared: sexual permissiveness, the decline of the traditional family, Planned Parenthood, perhaps even planned euthanasia. One state pro-life leader explains her concern in these terms:

> There's a movement in this country that life is not of value, in and of itself. Only if it's productive, only if it can contribute. And I don't agree with that. I think that life, no matter what kind of condition or state of dependence, I think life is of value. . . . *Every* life—because God wouldn't have created a life if it wasn't valuable. . . . *We* have to try to make people understand what the problem with this anti-life mentality is. It will destroy this country, if we don't stop it.

Another pro-life official describes the "issue web" of the movement—the context in which she feels the drive to ban abortions is embedded—as "a very basic battle between the secularists and the religious people, the God-believers and the humanists. Frankly, that is *the* bottom-line issue."[12]

Thus the abortion issue has a very broad and very personal meaning for pro-lifers; it refers not only to what they see as the destruction of innocent lives but also to the importance of the family, the order of society, the meaning of life, and the authority of God. The other parties to the defining of the issue see it very differently, but in equally condensational terms. Pro-choice groups have stressed the terrible personal costs that would result if government policy were to require women to continue pregnancies against their will. They have warned that women would not stop seeking abortions if antiabortion laws are passed, but would fall prey to unsafe, back-street procedures and dangerous efforts to abort themselves. They have reminded listeners that if abortions are banned, victims of rape and incest will face not only the psychological damage resulting from the attack but the prospect of bearing and bringing up the attacker's child. The principle of choice on abortion has become closely linked with the movement for women's rights in this and other nations.

The language of the debate itself is highly charged. What pro-choice advocates call a "fetus" or the "products of conception," pro-lifers term an "unborn baby" or a "preborn child." Some pro-life activists have referred to their opponents, and to elected officials who support the pro-choice position, as "baby-killers." Those favoring the pro-choice side have accused pro-lifers of advocating "compulsory pregnancy," of valuing the "potential life" of the fetus more than the actual life of the mother.[13]

Consistent with our expectations about single-issue politics, the pro-life movement defines the abortion issue as nonnegotiable; compromise, they feel, is out of the question on an issue so fundamentally important. "Our issue is totally and absolutely different than any other issue," one national pro-life group leader contends:

> You can't compromise with human life. . . . Compromise is the name of the game for many issues because unfortunately, it's the only way to get things done. If I compromise with someone over the size of the budget, I'm not bothering anyone. But if I compromise on abortion, the compromise harms human life. And life is sacred.

The issue, they argue, takes precedence over all other matters of public policy. As one state organizer explained her single-issue position,

> I'm concerned about a lot more issues than abortion, but this is the primary one, because I think so many issues hinge on this type of thing; anybody who would go for taking the life of little ones is not going to look out for my interests in anything else either, you know.

In short, the composition of the pro-life movement and the circumstances of the abortion issue's emergence onto the political agenda have produced a very potent "single issue." But the issue did not erupt in campaign environments right away. First, the pro-lifers took their case to Congress.

THE PRO-LIFE MOVEMENT'S LEGISLATIVE ACTION

After *Roe* v. *Wade,* the hundreds of state and local pro-life organizations continued to sponsor slide presentations to educate other citizens and to lobby the state legislatures. But since the Supreme Court had made abortion a national question, Congress took on a new importance. Right on the heels of the Court's ruling, several members of Congress introduced bills to prevent the use of federal funds in paying for abortions[14] and to overturn *Roe* v. *Wade* by constitutional amendment.

The funding restrictions, termed "Hyde amendments" after one of their original sponsors, Republican Congressman Henry J. Hyde of Illinois, first became law in 1976. Since then, Hyde amendments have passed Congress every year—usually after agonizingly long debate, and with ever more strict application.[15] The effect of the amendments is to make it much more difficult for lower-income women to get abortions; those who can pay for the procedure are not affected by the law. Nevertheless, the legislation has had a big impact; by one estimate, the amendment has reduced the number of abortions paid for by federal Medicaid funds from over 300,000 a year to about 2000.[16] Perhaps even more important, pro-life legislators have put Congress on record numerous times as stating that paying for abortions is not a proper function of the federal government.

But the effort to overturn *Roe v. Wade* by constitutional amendment met with repeated failure. Dozens of amendments were introduced in Congress to grant legal "personhood" to the fetus from the moment of conception. Each of these "Human Life Amendments" (HLAs) failed to gain the two-thirds support necessary to pass the amendment and send it to the state legislatures for consideration. In a movement driven by a sense of urgency, this delay in achieving its primary goal brought frustration — and a change in strategy. A national pro-life organizer recalls:

> After a period [of time], everyone began to realize that we could educate and lobby till doomsday, but if people representing us in Congress didn't feel the same way we did, then we would never achieve a Human Life Amendment. And that's when we began to turn to [electoral] political action.

THE MOVEMENT INTO CAMPAIGNS

Pro-lifers had made some early forays into campaigns and elections. In 1975, the National Conference of Catholic Bishops adopted a "Pastoral Plan for Pro-life Activities," calling on pro-lifers to become active in congressional races around the country. The following year, pro-life leader Ellen McCormack declared herself a candidate for the Democratic presidential nomination; with no electoral base outside the pro-life movement, she managed the impressive feats of raising enough money to qualify for federal matching funds and running in 18 of the 30 primaries.

National pro-life groups began to position themselves for the 1978 elections, forming PACs so that they could become directly involved in (and contribute to) House and Senate races. The Life Amendment PAC (known as LAPAC) was launched in 1977, and was soon joined by the National Pro-Life PAC, Life-PAC (which concentrated on state legislative races) and other organizations with an interest in abortion, such as the Moral Majority Inc. and The Christian Voice. The National Right to Life Committee (NRLC) — the biggest of the national groups, claiming 1800 chapters and 11 million members — would later set up its own PAC.

Pro-life electoral efforts also increased in 1978. In Minnesota, which had one of the most highly organized state pro-life movements, the results were striking. Not only did U.S. Representative Donald Fraser, a pro-choice leader favored to win the Democratic Senate nomination, lose his primary, but by November the state had elected two pro-life senators and a pro-life governor. In Iowa, the senior senator and a front-running candidate for statewide office, both pro-choice Democrats, were unexpectedly defeated after a pro-life group campaigned against them. Three other pro-choice senators—Republican Ed Brooke of Massachusetts and Democrats Tom McIntyre of New Hampshire and Floyd Haskell of Colorado—met a similar fate.

Were pro-life groups responsible for their defeats? The answer is elusive. Many experts say no;[17] the pro-lifers themselves must admit that even if they had not lifted a finger, these candidates—most of them liberal Democrats—would have faced tough races in the conservative tide of 1978. But in politics, what is *perceived* to be real is likely to have very real consequences. And after the 1978 elections, it was widely perceived that pro-life groups had made a difference in these races. Some of the defeated candidates claimed in postelection interviews that pro-life opposition had done them in. Newspaper and television reporters beat a path to pro-life leaders' doors, asking how they "won" these elections and what they planned to do next time, in 1980.

LAPAC's executive director, Paul A. Brown, was quick to capitalize on this newfound media attention. He announced soon after the 1978 election that LAPAC was targeting six senators and six House members for defeat in 1980; borrowing a strategy used earlier by an environmental group, Brown called his targets "the Deadly Dozen."[18] The senators on LAPAC's list were Democrats Birch Bayh of Indiana, Frank Church of Idaho, John Culver of Iowa, Patrick Leahy of Vermont, and George McGovern of South Dakota, and Republican Bob Packwood of Oregon.[19]

Brown's announcement came as a shock to many pro-lifers. Leaders of several other antiabortion groups were uncomfortable with the idea of a public "hit list." Brown's knack for controversy and confrontation was the source of one of many internal rifts plaguing the antiabortion movement. Nevertheless, the hope of defeating the six senators on LAPAC's list was widely shared among state and national pro-life groups—and it was the state groups, whether affiliated with LAPAC, NRLC, or independent, on which most of the burden would fall. LAPAC's announcement, then, was the opening gun for pro-life efforts in 1980.

In choosing its quarry, LAPAC used the time-honored strategy of targeting incumbents who seemed to be in trouble with voters anyway. Brown explained:

> We based our decision mainly on vulnerability. We are not naive enough to believe we can beat everyone. We will concentrate on the close [Senate] races: those with a margin of 8 percent or less in the last election. None of our targets won his last race by so large a margin that our 5 to 10 percent of the vote couldn't make the difference in 1980, and we have good pro-life groups in all these states.[20]

By doing so, he felt he could guarantee the pro-life movement at least some success in 1980 and thus add to the "giant-killer" reputation pro-lifers had begun to build in 1978. Five of LAPAC's Senate targets were liberal Democrats representing conservative Republican states; the sixth, Packwood, was a Republican in a state whose voter registration leaned Democratic. The biggest winning margin among the six in 1974, their last Senate race, was a less-than-luxurious 56 percent. And there were other reasons why the pro-lifers could expect to be taken seriously as new forces in these six campaign environments.

THE POTENTIAL CLOUT OF THE PRO-LIFE CHALLENGE

First, in spite of its newness to electoral politics, the pro-life movement was organizing and learning fast. Both LAPAC and the National Right to Life PAC (NRTL-PAC) had good lines of communication with their grass-roots supporters through newsletters and personal contact. By 1980, LAPAC was also offering a series of campaign training schools and political action workshops to local chapters, and packets of information to help its members win delegate seats at the Republican and Democratic national conventions. Several state pro-life groups, affiliated with a national organization or independent, had weathered campaigns in 1978 and gained valuable experience.

Second, there was the "extraordinary passion of the anti-abortion cause."[21] As one campaign staffer put it: "Right-to-life types will quit their jobs and go to work for you 40 hours a week. Their help is probably greatly disproportionate to their numbers."[22] People willing to cast their vote on the basis of a single issue are likely to attract notice in a race; and although surveys suggest that most Americans want abortions to remain legal in at least some circumstances,[23] the bulk of singleminded concern about the abortion issue in 1980 was coming from the pro-life side. A Culver aide remarked sadly that "the pro-choice constituency is fairly amorphous; they're not as dedicated to their cause, by and large, in terms of single-issue dedication, as are the pro-life people." Analysis of a 1980 *New York Times*-CBS poll confirmed this:

> Supporters of the anti-abortion movement do seem more likely to make the abortion issue a central concern in choosing candidates. About one-third of those who consistently favored the anti-abortion [constitutional] amendment said abortion views would affect their vote this fall, compared with just under one-fifth of those who opposed the amendment.[24]

Pro-life leaders in 1980 estimated that no more than 5 to 10 percent of voters viewed abortion as a "disqualifying issue," a reason for voting against a pro-choice candidate regardless of his or her positions on other issues. But in a close race—and all six of the targeted senators were expected to be in close races—that highly motivated group of pro-life voters could count on having an impact.

Further, the symbolism of the movement seemed capable of swaying many people whose feelings about abortion were ambivalent or undecided. Consider one fascinating finding of the *New York Times*-CBS poll mentioned above. When respondents were asked, "Do you think there should be an amendment to the Constitution prohibiting abortions, or shouldn't there be such an amendment?" 62 percent said no. Only 29 percent of those polled took the pro-life position. Later in the list of questions, that same issue was rephrased: "Do you believe there should be an amendment to the Constitution protecting the life of the unborn child, or shouldn't there be such an amendment?" This second question employed the symbolism of the pro-lifers, referring to "protection" and "unborn children," rather than the symbolism of the pro-choice position and its emphasis on the amendment as a "prohibition." Significantly, this time 50 percent said they would support such an amendment; only 39 percent were opposed.[25]

Both questions referred to an antiabortion amendment. But when the issue was phrased as the pro-lifers do, the support for their position increased by more than 20 percent. The same process could occur in a campaign. Abortion is not a pressing matter to most people. If pro-life groups succeeded in defining the terms of campaign debate about the issue, they could be expected to capture the hearts of at least some undecided voters. That possibility made pro-choice candidates very nervous. They could not be sure how important the abortion issue would become in the race, nor whose definition of the issue would hold sway. Under those circumstances, it would not be surprising if many elected officials, even those who felt fairly sure of reelection, viewed the possibility of a pro-life crusade against them as a serious threat.

The potential impact of the pro-life targeting also had to do with the *kinds* of people likely to be pro-life voters. All but one of the targeted senators were Democrats. The people to whom pro-life groups appealed were also likely to be Democrats: Catholics, southern fundamentalists, blue-collar workers. So the abortion issue could hurt pro-choice Democratic candidates by cutting into their traditional bases of support. That possibility loomed larger in 1980 when the Democratic platform took a clear pro-choice stand, while the Republican platform endorsed passage of a Human Life Amendment. The effect on long-time Democrats who were also pro-life activists was marked. The campaign manager for one of the targeted senators complained:

> [Pro-life groups] were able to go in, and with that right-to-life issue, really take the heart out of the Democratic party. Many, many, *many* of our workers who

worked for us in past elections sat on their hands or worked against us because of the abortion issue. And that was *very* devastating in terms of trying to put an organization together—just like taking the core out of an atomic bomb; the damn thing doesn't work!

Many Republican and New Right leaders saw the pro-life movement's potential for deepening the splits within the Democratic party. Conservative columnist Patrick J. Buchanan wrote after the election:

> The abortion issue is not just a social issue; it is the overriding social issue that split the FDR coalition and sent millions of Southern evangelical Christians and Northern Catholics into the camp of a Republican President [Ronald Reagan] with whom they may disagree on a dozen other issues.[26]

New Right organizer Richard Viguerie put it more bluntly: "If abortion remains an issue, and we keep picking liberals off, this movement could completely change the face of Congress."[27]

Finally, the abortion issue was expected to have special force in Senate races. It would take a brave group to announce its intention to defeat one-sixth of the *House* members up for reelection; during the past decade, at least 90 percent of all House incumbents who ran for reelection won their contests. Groups aiming at senators seem to have had a clearer shot; only 60 percent of senators seeking reelection in 1978 were successful, and in 1980, 55 percent.[28]

Recent research has identified several reasons why senators have been more electorally vulnerable than House members are.[29] For one, the media cover senators differently from members of the House. Coverage of a senator's actions puts more emphasis on national policy issues; thus, senators' stands on controversial issues are likely to be better known, and to be a factor in their public images. House members are less visible in the media; there are more of them, and their office is less "elevated." For the average House incumbent, the media spotlight is off most of the time. Because of that, House members can hope to become known to their constituents primarily through the pork-barrel projects they bring home and the constituent services they provide. They are better able to set the terms of their own coverage, since they are of interest primarily to local newspapers and radio stations, rather than the feistier (and less easily impressed) statewide and national press and broadcasters.

Senators have other problems too. Just as they receive a lot of media attention, so do their challengers—and that gives challengers a boost in gaining name recognition among voters. In contrast, reporters frequently treat House challengers like surprise packages at rummage sales: potentially interesting, but not worth the effort or the cost to investigate.

For all these reasons, the pro-life targeting loomed as a threat of some potential significance to these six Senate campaigns in 1980. It became even more threatening as the conservative mood on social issues appeared to deepen at the close of the decade. Even the Supreme Court seemed to be responding in its own way; in the summer of 1980, the Court narrowly upheld the constitutionality of the Hyde Amendment. Pro-lifers had come a long way in the short time since *Roe v. Wade*. With eager anticipation, they turned their attention to the Senate races on LAPAC's list.

The Campaign Settings

THE LEARNING ENVIRONMENT OF SENATE CAMPAIGNS

Throughout this book we have been talking about "campaigns" in general, with occasional references to the ways that campaigns differ. That reflects the book's main purpose: to draw some fundamental insights about the nature of campaigning as a learning process. But as we begin to test these insights, we enter the world of specific campaigns, not general ones. So let us move from the general to the particular in three steps: first, by examining the special characteristics of *Senate* campaign environments, then the special features of those environments in the 1980 elections, and finally, by getting to know the six targeted races in more detail.

In discussing why senators seemed to make especially attractive targets for pro-lifers, the last section suggested some ways in which Senate campaign environments differed from House campaigns. Several of those differences can have a big impact on campaigners' learning. The simple fact that senators have a six-year term means that their last race—and the learning they derived from its experiences—is no longer very vivid in their memories by the time the next campaign comes. In some aspects of the campaign, participants will have forgotten what decisions were made or what the consequences of those decisions were; in others, circumstances will have changed so much that their earlier learning will seem irrelevant.

One party staffer points out, regarding the senators up for reelection in 1980:

> All of the technology and the situation changes about every two to four years. So their whole world had changed since 1974. In '74, political polling was still relatively primitive. Television was relatively primitive. A lot of the names were different. Talents were different. The situations were different. I mean, we had a situation back in '74 where an incumbent could simply run on seniority, on bringing home the bacon. No longer.

Senate incumbents, then, cannot rely on the patterns of past successes as easily as House incumbents can; more decisions must be made anew. That is especially true because Senate campaigns, it has been suggested, usually revolve more around issues than House campaigns do. With six years between campaigns, there is little reason to expect the big issues to remain the same. In short, campaigning is a discontinuous process for Senate members. Their specialized campaign learning, like their campaign organization, is more likely to get rusty between elections than that of a House member, who gets more regular practice in electioneering.

Besides, the six-year term can encourage newly elected senators to concentrate their attention on Washington—at least in the first part of their term—rather than on the voters of their home states. Their environment is dominated by committee meetings, legislation, and their Senate colleagues. When the next race approaches, these senators may find that they have not touched bases with their active constituents as often as they should have. A reporter quotes a defeated senator:

> A lot of senators vote like statesmen for the first four years of their terms and in the process alienate a lot of people. Then in the last two, they vote like politicians. A House member is more apt to be political the entire time he is in office since he is always running.[30]

The difficulty of senators' learning environments is increased by the size and diversity of their constituencies. In terms of sheer complexity, the constituencies of most Senate candidates are rivaled only by candidates for statewide office (who share the same constituents, of course) and the Presidency. So it is not surprising that, as a particularly insightful observer finds, Senate campaigners do not seem to have as intimate or detailed a "feel" for their constituencies as most House candidates, or at least House incumbents, do.[31]

These great challenges in the Senate campaign environment have some compensating advantages. In particular, Senate candidates can expect to raise more money than most other campaigners can. And money buys information: professional polling, media advice, organizational expertise. The quality of that information and advice is not always high, but at least in some cases it offers Senate campaigners a way out of the dilemma so often faced by their House and state legislative counterparts: too little information about the reactions of the district as a whole, and too much information about the responses of the campaigner's closest associates.

The learning environment in Senate campaigns has another prominent element: media people. Senate candidates normally cannot expect to reach more than a small part of their big constituencies without the use of television and radio and the attention of newspapers.[32] They are much more media dependent than are campaigners in smaller districts, and much less dependent on the face-to-face campaigning so common in local, state legislative, and even many House races. Further, reporters and broadcasters have more reason to pay attention to Senate campaigns than to lower-level races.[33] The actions and reactions of media people, then, play a larger role in affecting Senate campaigners' behavior than they do in all but presidential (and perhaps gubernatorial) campaigns.

In 1980 the media were calling attention to some new forces in these Senate campaign environments—almost all of them troublesome to LAPAC's targets. First, there was the strong conservative tone of many new political movements: the tax revolt that was spreading from California, the growth of evangelical Right groups such as the Moral Majority and others. Then there was the big problem at the top of the ticket; Jimmy Carter's unpopularity was expected to do some damage to the electoral prospects of the five Democrats on LAPAC's list.

Most obvious was the independent spending, used to mount savagely negative ad campaigns, that confronted many liberal Senate candidates in 1980. As chapter 1 indicated, the most fearless of the independent spenders was the National Conservative PAC (NCPAC), which began pummeling five Democratic senators with a well-financed television drive fully 18 months before the election. Four of those senators were LAPAC targets: Bayh, Church, Culver, and McGovern. NCPAC's director, John T. ("Terry") Dolan, was very open about the organization's intent. "There's no question about it—we are a negative organization that wants to get rid of five bad votes in the Senate. . . . We're not interested in respectability. We're going to beat these five and send a shiver down the spine of every other liberal Senator and Congressman."[34]

LAPAC, then, found itself in the company of several New Right groups—NCPAC, the Gun Owners of America, and many others—when it trained its fire on these six senators. And not surprisingly, since LAPAC's target list included a major portion of the liberal leadership of the Senate. Five of LAPAC's targets were liberal Democrats, with 72 years of Senate votes and voices among them. Each of the five represented fairly conservative states where more Republicans than Democrats won public office, where much of the population was rural or lived in small towns, and where the targeted senator had been sustained in the past by his campaigning skills and constituent service rather than by his agreement with most constituents on the big issues of national defense and social welfare. By focusing the state's attention on "hot button" issues such as abortion, gun control, and national defense, the New Right organizations hoped to hit these senators at their most vulnerable point, neutralize the impact of their casework and political savvy, and propel people out to vote.

The six targeted senators, in short, had many troubles in common. So did the state pro-life groups charged with defeating them. Each race had its own special features as well.

THE BAYH RACE IN INDIANA

Democrat Birch Bayh was an especially attractive target for the pro-life movement. All constitutional amendments—including any Human Life Amendment—have to begin their long route to ratification in the Senate Judiciary Committee's Subcommittee on the Constitution. Bayh chaired that subcommittee. He had held hearings on the HLA but did not support the amendment. Removing Bayh from that key position was of highest priority for LAPAC.

In his eighteen years in the Senate, Birch Bayh had gained considerable power. He had authored three constitutional amendments, which the Senate then passed: the Twenty-fifth, on presidential succession; the Twenty-sixth, giving eighteen year olds the vote; and the Equal Rights Amendment, which later died in state legislatures. He chaired the Senate Intelligence Committee and played a vital role in congressional supervision of the Central Intelligence Agency.

Despite his national prominence, Bayh never had smooth sailing at election time in Indiana. His largest winning margin in three Senate races was a not very robust 51.7 percent. And in 1980 he faced the traditional "fourth term jinx"; no one had ever won a fourth Senate term in Indiana. In fact, Bayh first got to the Senate by convincing a slim majority of the voters that "18 years in Washington is long enough for one man," the man being former Republican Senator Homer Capehart, Bayh's opponent in 1962. That slogan came back to haunt Birch Bayh in 1980. It was repeated with great glee by his Republican opponent, two-term Congressman Dan Quayle.

The contest between the liberal Bayh and the conservative Quayle drew the interest of a number of New Right groups. In addition to NCPAC, Bayh was attacked by the Committee for the Survival of a Free Congress (CSFC), the Gun Owners of America, the John Birch Society, and the Moral Majority.

Several pro-life groups joined the attack. Most prominent among them was the Political Action Committee of the Indiana Right to Life Committee (IRTL-PAC), one of the more experienced and well organized pro-life groups in these targeted races. The PAC had cut its teeth on congressional elections in 1978. By the fall of 1980, IRTL claimed a base membership of 20,000, chapters in most of the state's counties, and a Voter Identification Program that had located 200,000 pro-life households. As one reporter commented, "They have a very sophisticated operation going on over there. It's computerized; they have found out who the people are who are sympathetic and they have zeroed in on them."

Bayh was no slouch either. A very folksy, personable politician, he was known as one of the best campaigners in the state. "He's as skillful a campaigner as you would ever want to see," said one journalist who had followed his career. Those skills had won him support even in some of the most conservative parts of his rock-ribbed Republican state. And he could count on strong backing from organized labor, which had given Bayh its highest marks for his Senate voting record in 1980 (see table 6.1 on page 172).

A year before election day, Bayh was running about 20 points ahead of his opponent. But Quayle, a very photogenic young man for whom the National Republican Senatorial Committee had great hopes (and an open wallet as well; national-level Republican committees spent more than $215,000 on Quayle's behalf in 1980), quickly made big inroads into Bayh's lead. Focusing on a call for "a new generation of leadership," Quayle drew even with the incumbent by mid-1980.

Bayh mounted a vigorous campaign in response, contrasting his accomplishments with Quayle's rather modest record in the House, and objecting to the growing presence of "right-wing hate groups from the outside." Quayle disavowed the support of several such groups, but worked closely with IRTL. It was a battle of contrasts — a pro-choice liberal Democrat against a pro-life conservative Republican — and as the fall campaign began, it looked as though the race might be decided by a percentage point or two.

THE CHURCH RACE IN IDAHO

The Idaho Senate race had several features in common with the contest in Indiana. Frank Church was the first Democratic senator ever to be reelected in Idaho. And reelected again; by 1980 he had served a full 24 years in the Senate. During those years he paid special attention to foreign policy, finally achieving, in 1979, his lifelong dream of chairing the Senate Foreign Relations Committee. He had also taken several foreign policy stands that were very unpopular in his state: most recently his support of the Panama Canal treaties. Idaho, with its fairly small (and overwhelmingly white) population, more rural than most states, was a very conservative constituency for Frank Church.

But clearly he had not won four previous Senate races by antagonizing his constituents on foreign policy. Church's campaigning skills were legendary. He was a very persuasive debater. His expert constituency service had touched most of the state's families during his four Senate terms. His seniority, he argued, brought many benefits to Idaho.

TABLE 6.1
THE CAST OF CHARACTERS

Target and Opponent	Current Office	Percent of Total Vote in Last Senate Race[a]	ADA 1978	ADA 1980	COPE 1978	COPE 1980
Indiana						
Birch Bayh (D)	Senator since 1962	50.7	85%	61%	94%	100%
Dan Quayle (R)	House member since 1977	—	15	0	11	13
Idaho						
Frank Church (D)	Senator since 1956	56.1	70	50	74	71
Steven D. Symms (R)	House member since 1973	—	10	0	5	13
Iowa						
John C. Culver (D)	Senator since 1974	52.0	85	78	89	89
Charles Grassley (R)	House member since 1975	—	5	17	10	17
Vermont						
Patrick J. Leahy (D)	Senator since 1974	49.5	65	83	79	83
Stewart Ledbetter (R)	Former state Banking and Insurance Commissioner	—	(Record: generally moderate)			
South Dakota						
George McGovern (D)	Senator since 1962	53.0	75	56	86	88
James Abdnor (R)	House member since 1973	—	20	11	22	6
Oregon						
Bob Packwood (R)	Senator since 1968	54.9	45	56	69	44
Ted Kulongoski (D)	First-term state senator and labor lawyer	—	(Record: liberal)			

a. From "The 1980 Elections," *Congressional Quarterly Special Report* 38 (11 October 1980).
b. ADA (Americans for Democratic Action) is an interest group supporting liberal legislation; COPE (Committee on Political Education) is the political arm of the AFL-CIO labor federation. Their ratings indicate the percentage of the time a Senate or House member voted or was paired in favor of the group's position on selected congressional votes. From *Congressional Quarterly Weekly Report* 37 (2 June 1979): 1067-69 (for 1978 ratings); and *Congressional Quarterly Weekly Report* 39 (21 March 1981): 516-18 (for 1980).

A Tale of Six Races: Abortion Issue Enters Campaign Environments

He had also been careful to stay on the safe side of several "hot button" issues in the state. Despite his generally liberal voting record in the Senate, he opposed gun control and had supported a measure to allow prayer in the public schools. On abortion, his position matched that of the Mormon church, which had a large membership in the populous southeastern part of Idaho: no abortions except in cases of rape, incest, and when the mother's life or health were at stake, and no federal funding of abortions.

But Church did not favor the more restrictive language of a Human Life Amendment; instead, he preferred a states' rights version that would allow any state to ban abortions within its borders. Ironically, that stand produced what all politicians fear: attacks by activists on both sides of the issue. Pro-lifers targeted him for defeat because he refused to support an HLA (and because he appeared to be beatable). And the targeting brought him no compensating help or contributions from pro-choice groups because he was on record for a states' rights amendment on abortion.

The state pro-life group was a fledgling organization: the Idaho Pro-Life PAC did not form until the summer of 1980, though a state Right to Life group had existed for several years. Its head had no previous political experience. In organization and resources, it was far behind its Indiana counterpart.

But the Idaho Pro-Life PAC had plenty of company in opposing Church. Among the alphabet soup of antagonists was ABC (Anyone But Church), an arm of NCPAC, which had begun attacking Church in television ads a full year and a half before the fall of 1980—at times with somewhat less than perfect accuracy. ABC claimed that Church had "almost always opposed a strong national defense" and had taken "influence-buying money" from several lobbyists. The tone of the campaign can be seen in the remarks by the ABC chairman that Church "can lie faster than a dog can trot. He lies by omission, by half-truth, by talking like a conservative at home and voting like a liberal in Washington."[35]

Church's Republican opponent, four-term Congressman Steve Symms, was ABC's kind of candidate. He opposed the Panama Canal treaties, the SALT II arms limitation agreement, and the Equal Rights Amendment. He was a co-sponsor of an HLA in the House. (Interestingly, he had entered the House a pro-choice supporter. A first-term letter from Symms to his constituents had contended that decisions on abortion "must be solved between the people involved. Between a man[!] and his God."[36] He later changed his mind and moved to a pro-life position.)

Symms was a formidable challenger. He had already won four House races in a district containing half the state's people. The 1980 election was expected to be Church's toughest race. By January 1980 the senator had raised more campaign money than any other candidate in Idaho history. But by early fall, polls showed the two contenders running dead even.

THE CULVER RACE IN IOWA

The Iowa Senate race was a conservative-liberal battle on a grand scale. John Culver, a Democrat first elected to the Senate in 1974, was not known for doing things partway. A former record-setting Harvard fullback, he had spent three years in the Marines, then won his law degree from Harvard. He became legislative assistant to his close friend Senator Edward Kennedy before winning a House seat in the Democratic landslide of 1964. After five House terms, he moved to the Senate in a similarly Democratic election year.

His record in the Senate was unabashedly liberal. He played a key role in preserving the Endangered Species Act. He fought to kill the B-1 bomber. He took a clear pro-choice stand on abortion. And although he was a first-termer, Culver was regarded as a very effective advocate for his legislative positions. To reporter Elizabeth Drew, Culver had a reputation in the Senate for

> brains, tenacity, integrity, shrewdness at picking his issues and skill at pushing them, and an ability to work with his colleagues. He was usually among a handful who voted against proposals that played to the crowds but that he dismissed as "demagogic." And what he accomplished he did in part through the sheer force of his personality and style.[37]

His reaction to having been targeted by the New Right was characteristically blunt, calling it a "poison in the political bloodstream."[38]

> I have searched the Scriptures but I can't find anything saying that Jesus Christ opposed the Panama Canal Treaty or favored the Kemp-Roth tax cuts. Yet I get a zero in Christian morality from the Moral Majority because I didn't. They're trying to manipulate sincere people on religious grounds. Well, the Scriptures aren't political weapons and the New Right is not the New Testament.[39]

Culver's opponent was Republican Congressman Charles E. Grassley, a three-term House member. The two were opposites in almost every way, as the interest-group ratings in table 6.1 show. In contrast to Culver's liberalism, Grassley was a down-the-line conservative favoring increased defense spending, less spending on social programs, and a greater role for the private sector in economic and social policies. Compared to Culver's forceful speaking style, Grassley was customarily depicted as an earnest but not very articulate speaker, an "easygoing" and "slow-speaking" candidate.

Grassley's rise in the polls, however, was anything but slow. By June of 1980, the respected Iowa Poll reported Grassley ahead of Culver by 17 percentage points. Although that was disturbing news to the Culver campaign, it was not really surprising. No Democrat had ever won a second Senate term from Iowa. Culver himself had been elected in 1974 with only 52 percent of the vote. In the next senatorial election in 1978, Culver's liberal Democratic colleague Dick Clark had been upset by a conservative Republican with a record very similar to Grassley's—and Clark had gone into the race with higher poll ratings than his friend John Culver did in 1980.

Many observers expected the Culver-Grassley race to be a replay of Clark's race. Included among them was the Iowa Pro-Life Action Council, the group that had received so much coverage in 1978 for its stand against Dick Clark. It was by far the most experienced pro-life group in the six states that we are considering—well-organized, politically sophisticated, and led by a dynamic activist. And it was determined to obtain a second pro-life senator for the state of Iowa.

THE LEAHY RACE IN VERMONT

Under normal circumstances, elections in Vermont do not get much national attention. But the Senate elections in 1980 were not "normal circumstances." New Right groups had concentrated their efforts on Senate races in small states on the logical premise that a small state has as many senators as a large state and is much easier to blitz with mailings and other advertising. So the New England Conservative PAC (an affiliate of NCPAC), the National Right to Work Committee, pro-lifers, and others had all taken an intense interest in Vermont's junior senator, Patrick J. Leahy.

Like many of the pro-life targets, Leahy represented the minority party in his state. The only Democrat in Vermont's congressional delegation, he was in fact the first Democrat ever to be elected to the Senate from that state. He was also the first Catholic. That made his pro-choice stance (although he described himself as *personally* opposed to abortion) all the more objectionable to many pro-life activists. Moreover, he chaired the Senate committee in charge of the Washington, D.C., budget, and supported the use of District funds to pay for abortions.

He was plainly vulnerable. A first-termer, he had won his seat in 1974 with only 49.5 percent of the vote. Leahy had responded to that slim victory by working hard to shore up his political base. He had returned to the state almost every weekend for six years, stressing his constituent service and accessibility. It was an approach that worked well in Vermont, the most rural state in the nation, with only half a million people and a long tradition of personal-contact campaigning. That tradition helped protect Leahy against the televised assaults mounted by outside groups.

A further advantage was the lateness of the Vermont primary; Leahy's Republican opponent would not be selected until September, with only two months remaining before the general election. And in the primary, pro-life efforts met with frustration. The Vermont Pro-Life Political Action Committee, like its Idaho counterpart, had just formed in time for the 1980 race. It was a small group, with little evidence of widespread local organization. It began by endorsing a little-known Republican, who then ran poorly in the primary.

The Republican primary winner, former state Banking and Insurance Commissioner Stewart M. Ledbetter, resisted pro-lifers' efforts to put him on record in support of an HLA. He opposed Medicaid funding of abortions but said he would vote to allow abortion in cases of rape, incest, and to save the mother's life. He never received (nor apparently wanted) a pro-life endorsement.

Ledbetter started the race well behind Leahy. His efforts to become better known were hampered by a strike at the *Rutland Herald,* the Vermont newspaper that normally devoted the greatest attention to state politics. But the contest heated up very quickly, in part thanks to the activities of New Right and single-issue groups. Media spending far surpassed the levels that Vermont had ever experienced. By October, Leahy's staff began to fear that his comfortable lead was slipping away.

THE MCGOVERN RACE IN SOUTH DAKOTA

An entire brigade of conservative groups viewed George McGovern as 1980's juiciest target. An early opponent of the American involvement in Vietnam, Democratic presidential candidate in 1972, an 18-year veteran of the Senate, and a symbol of liberal Democratic stands while representing a small, rural Republican state, McGovern seemed to many observers a man whose time had come — and gone. He was the only Democrat who had won three Senate terms in South Dakota's history, and each of his elections had been a squeaker. In 1974 he had come from behind to win with 53 percent of the vote. He began the 1980 race badly behind.

Moreover, McGovern had to face something in 1980 that he had never faced before: a Democratic primary opponent. To many in the state, McGovern was the architect of the South Dakota Democratic party; he had almost singlehandedly taken it from invisibility to viability. Later, when he himself sought the Democratic nomination for office, he ran unopposed. But in 1980 a conservative Democrat with pro-life backing filed against him. The opponent had no real political constituency on his own; he had just returned to South Dakota after 20 years of residence out of state. When McGovern was held to 62 percent in the primary by a political newcomer, the McGovern staff knew that things were tougher than they had realized.

The primary campaign was a taste of events to come. NCPAC's television ads had arrived in the state in early 1979, accusing McGovern of close friendship with Cuban dictator Fidel Castro, among other things. NCPAC was soon joined by a remarkable array of McGovern antagonists, including one group (called Target McGovern) whose emblem was a caricature of the senator with a rifle sight drawn over his heart. Independent spending against McGovern overflowed the state's airwaves into mass mailings and literature drops. In fact, mailings overflowed the state; New Right leaders saw the McGovern race as the lure to attract contributions from across the nation into New Right coffers.

Many of these groups attacked McGovern for his pro-choice stand. But his main adversary on the abortion issue was the Life Amendment PAC of South Dakota, an affiliate of the national LAPAC. The group was not as extensively organized as those in Iowa and Indiana, but neither was it inexperienced. And LAPAC had a trump card in its 1980 campaign: several LAPAC members were former McGovern campaign workers. When they withdrew their support from the senator, they weakened his campaign's organizational base.

Yet the campaign had reason to hope. McGovern had many loyal supporters in the state. He was a master of fund raising through small contributions, and the highly successful national mailing list developed in his presidential race was still in use. He held an important Senate position for his relatively rural state: he was the second-ranking Democrat on the Agriculture Committee, whose chairman, Herman Talmadge of Georgia, was also in a close race for reelection. If Talmadge lost, McGovern could head the committee. And although he was often regarded as too liberal for South Dakotans, McGovern was respected for his forthrightness and consistency.

But his opponent, Republican Congressman James Abdnor, would be hard to beat. A farmer in a farm state, Abdnor had represented the western half of South Dakota in the House since 1973. He was seen as a strong conservative: for a balanced federal budget, for more defense spending, against the Equal Rights Amendment. He was an HLA co-sponsor with enthusiastic pro-life support (though as a lifelong bachelor, he seemed somewhat incongruous as a "pro-family" candidate). Perhaps most important, he was well liked in South Dakota. While his House record was short on substance,[40] Abdnor was generally described as affable, folksy, and an effective, down-to-earth campaigner. He began the race with a big lead, estimated by some polls at 25 percent in June. By fall, the race looked too close to call.

THE PACKWOOD RACE IN OREGON

Senator Bob Packwood differed from the other LAPAC targets. He was the only Republican, and the only target who did not temper a pro-choice position with a statement of *personal* opposition to abortion. To a greater extent than the other five, Packwood had been out front on the issue; *Congressional Quarterly* described him as the "Senate's leading advocate of the 'pro-choice' position on abortion."[41] Very early in his campaign planning, Packwood worked to activate national pro-choice support for his reelection.

But like the other targets, Packwood was vulnerable. He had served two Senate terms, after six years in the state House of Representatives, but his last reelection had been won with only 55 percent of the vote. He represented a state where his party was in the minority. And he had been under attack from both ends of the ideological spectrum; conservatives had not forgiven him for supporting the Panama Canal treaties, and liberals felt he was too conservative, too closely allied with business interests.

Still, Packwood seemed to be in better political shape by the summer of 1980 than did the other LAPAC targets. One reason was his skill as a strategist. Knowing his vulnerabilities, Packwood's first priority was to scare away any potentially attractive challengers who might be able to exploit those weak points. Even before the 1978 elections, he had begun amassing a huge war chest for use in 1980. This early show of strength worked; the people expected to have the best chance of defeating Packwood declined to run against him.

As further protection, Packwood had sought and won the chairmanship of the National Republican Senatorial Committee during the 95th Congress; this is the group that doles out money and other help to Republican Senate candidates. The chairmanship gave his staff a lot of exposure to other campaign professionals and campaign-management techniques. He put a very high value on campaign expertise, even to the extent of personally instructing his staff on the fine points of yard sign construction. He was also able to attract the support of a wide range of interest groups with a Senate voting record often described as "eclectic."

In the primary race, only one of Packwood's several opponents seemed to be a viable candidate. Conservative and pro-life, she had the support of the Life Amendment PAC of Oregon (a group independent of the national LAPAC). The PAC, formed in 1979, had only limited resources and a small volunteer organization. Its candidate soon found herself the object of harsh personal attack by a conservative, pro-life Republican rival. Right-wing groups that had previously set their sights on Packwood, including NCPAC and the Moral Majority, turned their attentions elsewhere. Packwood had an easy primary victory.

Opposing Packwood in the general election was labor lawyer Ted Kulongoski, a freshman member of the state senate. Kulongoski began the race a distinct underdog. But he proved to be an attractive and energetic candidate, building on labor and environmentalist support to become a serious challenger.

His hopes increased that the state's Democratic majority would return to the party fold and that conservative Republicans, unhappy with some of Packwood's votes, would take a pass on the Senate race.

The Life Amendment PAC had fewer hopes. Kulongoski declared himself *personally* opposed to abortion, but refused to support a Human Life Amendment. There was no endorsable pro-life candidate in the Senate race. Nevertheless, the PAC's leaders reasoned that a Packwood defeat was very much in their interest because it would replace a nationally known pro-choice senator with one who had no seniority and might be more "educable" to the pro-life cause.

The Research Hypotheses

How could we expect these Senate campaigners to behave in response to the threat posed by the LAPAC targeting in 1980? And how would the state pro-life groups behave in turn? Let us draw on the learning approach to derive some hypotheses—some predictions about these campaigners' behavior—that will structure and guide our investigation of the six targeted races.

To do so, we must consider the political environment at the time. The pro-life targeting seemed a real threat to these six incumbents. Moreover, the dimensions of the threat were unknown; most of the pro-life groups were fairly new, and the effectiveness of their actions was not yet clear. Nor could the Senate campaigners be sure how the use of the abortion issue by NCPAC and other New Right groups would change the situation; whether NCPAC's tender mercies would increase the impact of the state pro-life groups' efforts or would backfire and hinder those efforts. But whether they expected the targeting to hurt them a little or a lot, most of the Senate campaigners did guess that the issue would hurt them.

The incumbents were not likely to run short of other problems either. None was electorally secure. Recall that each senator represented a state in which the party registration favored his opponent, and where the dominant political sentiment was believed to reject some of the incumbent's positions on major issues. In particular, the five Democrats were accused by many of being too liberal for their constituents. Each had already come under attack by New Right groups spending unprecedented sums. They each faced the hazards to which Senate campaigns are typically prone; although all of the incumbents had had a lot of campaign experience, it had been six years since their last race. Much had changed during that time.

The state pro-life groups faced a changing and uncertain environment too. They were all political newcomers to some extent; two of the groups had formed only months before, and even the most well established had less than a decade of campaign experience to draw upon. Their leaders were volunteers—many with no previous political involvement outside the pro-life movement—rather than political professionals. They, like the senators' organizations, had to contend with new laws governing their activities and campaign spending. And they were charged with a difficult task: to carry out a national pro-life leader's public pledge to defeat a U.S. senator.

The new elements, the unknowns, the discontinuities—all these factors work to limit the usefulness of one's previous learning. In such a situation, the theory would say, a campaigner would be likely to look for models, for people similar to him or her who seem to have some answers. And as suggested above, there *were* some potential models. The pro-life groups in various states faced many of the same problems. They shared a central concern with the abortion issue. The Senate campaigners also had a number of problems in common, not least of which was their presence on LAPAC's list. Here, then, are the specific hypotheses.

1. If these campaigners and pro-life leaders believed that their political environment had changed substantially—or found themselves in a relatively new situation—then they would try to learn observationally in order to respond to that environment. In areas of the campaign where they did not see big changes from the last race, or in which they had some successful previous experience, they would draw from their prior learning and build on expectations developed in situations most nearly similar to the present one.

2. From the theory's discussion of modeling, these campaigners and pro-lifers would be most likely to learn observationally from actors similar to them in important respects: from other campaigns in the same party, from the campaigns of senators with a similar ideological orientation, from pro-life groups in similar states and with similar situations. They would pay special attention to models whose actions have previously been rewarded—who won their races or met their goals—and use recent losing campaigns as "negative models."

3. There are two reasons why the pro-life groups should rely more on observational learning, and use it more effectively, than their Senate targets. First, since so many of the pro-lifers were new to politics and campaigns, they had fewer relevant experiences of their own to draw upon. That left many of them no alternative to the use of models.

They also had more relevant models that met the criteria of success and similarity. In the 1978 elections, all the senators targeted by pro-life groups lost their races. Several of those losing incumbents complained that pro-lifers had beaten them. Remember that election results are a generalized form of reinforcement, and so the "meaning" of an election depends on the interpretations offered by candidates, activists, consultants, and reporters as to what really mattered and what did not. Pro-life efforts may or may not have made any *real* difference in those 1978 races. The important point is that many activists, reporters, and candidates *thought* they did, and the aura of victory generalized rapidly to include the campaign tactics used by those pro-life groups.

In the same rush of events, the targeted senators running in 1980 were left with a trail of only "negative models"—senatorial campaigns targeted and then unseated in 1978. In the absence of more specific and reliable detail, the strategies followed by the 1978 targets were assumed to have failed. That made observational learning more difficult for their colleagues in 1980. If those 1978 strategies were not effective, what *would* be effective in response to the targeting? "Negative models" do not say. They can indicate what to avoid, but not necessarily what to substitute. So while observational learning would seem an obvious choice for those senators targeted in 1980, the lack of successful, similar models should make the use of that learning problematic.

4. From the discussion about the behaviors most likely to be learned from models, we can most readily expect the diffusion of strategies whose effectiveness is easiest to demonstrate (fund-raising appeals, for example, with their quick and concrete returns), those that are especially compelling (and therefore likely to attract people's attention), those that cost relatively little, and those that require the least radical changes in the actor's thinking and behavior—for example, because at least some of their components are already in his or her repertoire.

What findings would lead us to reject these hypotheses? Finding, for example, that campaigners and pro-lifers were aware of big changes in their political environments, but did not derive their responses to the changes from observational learning; that they did learn by observing models, but not models that met the criteria of success and similarity; or that the campaigners and pro-life groups, though differing in their access to successful models, did not differ in the extent to which they used observationally learned strategies.

We tested these ideas in interviews with the principal actors in these six races. In each state we spoke with the person(s) we identified as having the clearest decision-making authority in the senator's campaign organization, the leader(s) of the main pro-life group active in the race (and in some states where more than one group was making a substantial effort, the heads of these groups as well), and one or more political reporters covering each race for the major newspaper(s) in the state.[42] The study had a three-wave design; one wave of interviews with each participant was conducted right after the spring primaries, another at the beginning of the fall campaign (mid-August to early September), and the third immediately after the November election (sometimes followed by more conversations to clarify any ambiguities).

Our aim was to learn the behavior of the campaigns and pro-life groups at each time point, to identify any changes in their behavior, and to determine the source of each behavior: whether it had been learned observationally (and from which models), stemmed from the campaigner's or pro-lifer's own personal experience, or had come from some other source that the theory had not specified. The interviews covered a wide range of subjects: questions about specific campaign behaviors and techniques, perceptions of single-issue politics, previous experience with various styles of campaigning, beliefs about the activities of the opposition, feelings about the role of the political parties, and other matters. We supplemented these interviews with newspaper accounts of the six races, conversations with other campaign insiders and observers (to get the fullest possible view of the campaigns' behavior), the newsletters published by each of the major national and state pro-life groups, and other printed materials developed by the campaigns and the pro-lifers specifically for use in these elections.

The interviewing was like detective work. The issues were sensitive, and the conversations took place in the heat of a hard-fought campaign. Our respondents had plans, expectations, and worries that they did not always want to share with us—at least not until the election was over. Our task was to ferret out those sensitive bits of information by using several sources of data, by following up on brief comments and partial disclosures, and by using the three-wave nature of the study to flesh out earlier answers with later questions. We were, in short, putting together the pieces of a very interesting puzzle. As the campaigns wore on, more pieces began to appear, and the placement of earlier pieces was confirmed or changed. By the time of our postelection interviews, the puzzle seemed largely complete. We were in a position to determine whether our expectations had proved accurate. In the next chapter, let us see what actually happened.

NOTES

1. See Murray Edelman's *Politics as Symbolic Action* (Chicago: Markham, 1971); and W. Lance Bennett, *Public Opinion in American Politics* (New York: Harcourt Brace Jovanovich, 1980), chap. 9.
2. Nellie Gray, head of March for Life Inc., quoted in Nadine Cohodas, "Abortion Prompts Emotional Lobbying," *Congressional Quarterly Weekly Report* 39 (28 February 1981): 384. Quotations in the rest of this chapter, unless otherwise identified, come from the study to be described below.
3. William J. Crotty and Gary C. Jacobson, *American Parties in Decline* (Boston: Little, Brown, 1980), 140.
4. On the history of abortion law and policy, see James C. Mohr, *Abortion in America* (New York: Oxford University Press, 1978).
5. The ALI sample statute would allow abortion where pregnancy had resulted from rape or incest, where there was "substantial risk" that the baby would have grave physical or mental defects, or where pregnancy was likely to result in serious physical or mental health damage to the mother.
6. 410 U.S. 113 (1973) and 410 U.S. 179 (1973), respectively.
7. "Privacy," in this context, refers to an individual's right to be free from unwarranted intrusion by government; it was also used as the basis for earlier Court decisions striking down state laws against the sale of birth control devices.
8. Quoted in Bob Woodward and Scott Armstrong, *The Brethren* (New York: Avon, 1979), 282-83.
9. Cohodas, "Abortion Prompts Emotional Lobbying."
10. Bennett, *Public Opinion*, 249.
11. Charles E. Rice, *The Human Life Amendment: No Compromise* (Washington, D.C.: American Life Lobby, 1980), 8.
12. Several other writers see the abortion issue as a form of class conflict: a growing division between the change-oriented, upper-middle-class "new intelligentsia" and a more traditionally oriented, "embourgeoised" working class. See Everett Ladd, "The New Lines Are Drawn," *Public Opinion* 1 (July/August 1978): 48-53.
13. As in the bumper sticker that interprets the pro-life position as follows: "Life begins at conception and ends at birth."
14. After the Supreme Court in effect legalized abortions, the federal Medicaid program covered the cost of abortions for low-income women. In practice, between one-fourth and one-third of the legal abortions each year have been performed on women who receive welfare assistance. See Kenneth A. Weiss, "Supreme Court Upholds Hyde Amendment," *Congressional Quarterly Weekly Report* 38 (5 July 1980): 1860.
15. As of mid-1984, Hyde amendments allow Medicaid to pay for abortions only when the procedure is deemed necessary to save the mother's life.
16. See Weiss, "Supreme Court Upholds Hyde Amendment."
17. The most thorough analysis can be found in Michael W. Traugott and Maris A. Vinovskis, "Abortion and the 1978 Congressional Elections," *Family Planning Perspectives* 12 (September/October 1980): 238-46.
18. In 1970, Environmental Action began targeting a "Dirty Dozen" each election year, composed of Congress members it hoped to defeat. As a means of making Congress more sensitive to environmental issues, the practice seemed to have some effect;

the targeting got a lot of free publicity, and may have claimed some scalps as well, since 24 of the targeted House and Senate members were defeated in the course of five elections.
19. The targeted House members got substantially less attention from LAPAC in the 1980 campaigns; they were Republicans John Anderson of Illinois and Harold Hollenbeck of New Jersey, and Democrats Robert Drinan of Massachusetts, Robert W. Edgar of Pennsylvania, Joseph Fisher of Virginia, and Morris Udall of Arizona.
20. Interview with Paul A. Brown by Darrell West, 20 December 1979.
21. Roger M. Williams, "The Power of Fetal Politics," *Saturday Review,* 9 June 1979, 13.
22. *Congressional Quarterly Weekly Report* 40 (23 October 1982): 2713.
23. See, for example, Judith Blake and Jorge H. Del Pinal, "Negativism, Equivocation, and Wobbly Assent," *Demography* 18 (August 1981): 309-20. Note, however, that most survey respondents do not favor abortion on demand; the most commonly accepted position is that abortion should be legal only in cases where pregnancy or childbirth would endanger the mother's life or health.
24. E. J. Dionne, Jr., "Abortion Poll," *Louisville Courier-Journal,* 20 August 1980, A11.
25. Ibid.
26. In "Nomination to Court 'Political Adultery,' " *The O'Connor Report* 1 (August 1981): 4.
27. Quoted in *Action Line* (the newsletter of the Christian Action Council, a predominantly fundamentalist pro-life group) 5 (7 May 1981): 3.
28. Incumbent senators had much greater success in 1982; only two of the 30 seeking reelection lost. Perhaps this suggests that incumbency is now becoming as much of an advantage in Senate as in House elections. But an equally plausible explanation is that 1982 was an anomaly; single-issue attacks on Democratic incumbents, who held almost two-thirds of the Senate seats up for election that year, were counterbalanced by very high unemployment rates, which hurt Republican candidates.
29. See the discussion in Richard F. Fenno, Jr., *The United States Senate: A Bicameral Perspective* (Washington, D. C.: American Enterprise Institute, 1982). But not all Senate races are hard fought; see Mark C. Westlye, "Competitiveness of Senate Seats and Voting Behavior in Senate Elections," *American Journal of Political Science* 27 (May 1983): 253-83.
30. Christopher Buchanan, "Senators Face Tough Re-election Odds," *Congressional Quarterly Weekly Report* 38 (5 April 1980): 908.
31. See Fenno, *The United States Senate.*
32. Keep in mind that Senate constituencies vary; senators from Wyoming or Alaska face very different conditions—in terms of the geographical size and population of the state and the range of its media markets—than do their colleagues from New York and California.
33. Fenno, *The United States Senate.*
34. Quoted by Bernard Weinraub, "Million-Dollar Drive Aims to Oust Five Liberal Senators," *New York Times,* 24 March 1980, B5.
35. See Bernard Weinraub, "Oust-Church Drive in Idaho Stirs Smear-Tactic Charges," *New York Times,* 11 May 1980, K20.
36. Rod Gramer, "Abortion Injected into Senate Race," *Idaho Statesman,* 17 August 1980, 1A.

37. Elizabeth Drew, *Senator* (New York: Simon & Schuster, 1979), 12.
38. Warden Moxley, "A New South in a New Republican Senate," *Congressional Quarterly Weekly Report* 38 (13 December 1980): 3561.
39. Seth S. King, "Ideologies Clash Sharply in Iowa Senatorial Contest," *New York Times,* 24 October 1980, A18.
40. McGovern's advertising tried carefully to take advantage of this fact; one radio ad began by announcing a discussion of Abdnor's record and then followed with ten seconds of silence.
41. *Congressional Quarterly Weekly Report* 38 (23 February 1980): 499.
42. The "we" in this case includes Darrell West, now of Brown University, who was a graduate student at Indiana University at the time of this study. Since several of the interviews were conducted "on background"—with the stipulation that their names not be used—we will identify our respondents in terms of their general roles in the campaign or pro-life group. Interviews (ranging in length from 20 minutes to several hours) were conducted by telephone, taped, and transcribed.

7. Pro-Life Groups Act in 1980: The Importance of Observational Learning
with DARRELL WEST

I never knew that much about the abortion issue. I probably wouldn't have had an abortion myself, but I wouldn't have stopped anyone else from doing it. But when I saw the slides and pictures [of actual abortions] on educational television, I was just amazed that in this country where we have such strong rights, that we actually were destroying our own kind!

It took me a matter of months before I actually got involved in the movement. It wasn't until I read some things in the paper and saw information about right-to-life organizations in my own city that I was prodded to get involved and do something about the way I felt.

Initially, you look on right-to-life as just another organization or club that you belong to. It's not your main thing in life, so to speak. But you finally reach a point where you become more committed to the movement, and it does change your lifestyle. . . . When I began to realize what attitudes were creeping in [to public opinion] after abortion became legalized, it just solidified my involvement, and I realized I couldn't turn my back on it.

—Director of a national right to-life PAC, May 1981

We worked our hearts out.

—Chairman, Iowa Pro-Life Action Council, November 1980

When reporters look for the sources of campaign innovations, they usually turn their attention to Washington, D.C. or New York City, where the big-time political consultants ply their trade. But the pro-life strategies that unnerved so many Senate campaigns in 1980 were born in more modest surroundings: in Des Moines, Iowa, where our story begins.

THE IOWA MODEL

Pro-lifers were active in Iowa politics even before the Supreme Court legalized abortion in 1973. They concentrated on the state legislature, lobbying its members to hold firm against the pressures to liberalize Iowa's abortion law. Their neighbors in Minnesota were active as well; the Iowans honed their lobbying techniques with advice from the Minnesota Human Life Alliance.

But in the early 1970s the indefatigable leader of Iowans for Life became convinced, as so many other state groups would later become convinced, that lobbying was not enough; electoral action was the necessary next step. If the voters would send pro-life candidates to the state legislature—and, once *Roe v. Wade* had made abortion a national matter, to Congress—then the pro-lifers' policy goals would be within reach.

How, then, could voters be influenced? By 1974, the Iowa pro-life leader had begun developing a small but useful tool, one that would later become the calling card of pro-life action in other political campaigns. First used in some local races and special elections, it was refined and expanded when she formed the Pro-Life Action Council in 1978 and set out to change the cast of Iowa state politics.

The Iowa group's strategy was a variation on a traditional campaign theme, not a path-breaking invention. Yet the special features of that strategy tell us a lot about the nature of the pro-life movement and its single-issue character. By 1978, when the Pro-Life Action Council became active in several statewide races, five main features or "fingerprints" characterized its involvement.

Above all, these Iowa activists were determined to confront their fellow citizens with the real meaning of abortion as pro-lifers saw it. They could not afford television or other high-priced mass teaching tools, but leafletting was within their means. They looked for a device that would grab people's attention and arouse their concern—a device capable of convincing people that the object of an abortion was not just a bunch of cells but a human life whose shape and looks resembled their own. For the leaflet's cover page, then, they chose a vivid photograph of a human fetus in the womb, apparently sucking its thumb.[1] The photo's caption read, "This little guy needs your help." They hoped it would produce a shock of recognition and move the abortion issue from abstraction to personal reality.

Inside, the leaflet carried a very distilled presentation of the candidates' stands on abortion law and funding. There was no mention of the personal qualities of the group's endorsed candidate nor of the candidates' views on other issues. There was only one issue for the Iowa Pro-Life Action Council. The tone of the portrayal, then, was much more issue-oriented and much more narrowly focused than that found in brochures typically distributed by candidates and other groups.

Third, the leaflet concluded its brief presentation with an interesting argument about the worth of one person's vote. In her travels leading up to the 1978 primaries, the Iowa group's chairman was struck by a high level of apathy around her; people simply were not interested in the primary election. The Iowa Secretary of State's office was predicting a very low voter turnout. If that were so, she reasoned, then a highly motivated group of voters, even though small, could make a big difference in the outcome. Calling the brochure back from the printer's, she added in big letters, "YOUR VOTE IS CRUCIAL," followed by this plea:

> Your vote . . . will have the impact of 10 votes or more since it is expected that less than 10 percent of the eligible voters will go to the polls. Don't pass up this unique chance you have to speak out loud and clear for pro-life.

Campaigners usually distribute their literature wherever they find people: in shopping centers, at factory gates and county fairs, door-to-door. But the pro-lifers were interested in a more carefully targeted audience; they wanted to reach potential supporters without alarming and activating those opposed to their cause. Their definition of the abortion issue suggested that potential pro-lifers could be found most easily among committed churchgoers. The leafletting, then, would be done only at churches, including, but not limited to, denominations whose leaders had taken a stand against legalized abortion. For the Iowa group's chairman, it was a case of hunting where the ducks were. "It's my philosophy or theory," she said, "and it's why we decided to do it, that people who go to church, no matter what faith it is—if they're going to get up on Sunday and go to church, they're going to have moral standards that will probably make them concerned about something like [abortion]."[2]

In this way as in others, she saw her issue as completely different from all other political interests. A *church* leafletting strategy would make no sense for environmental groups or those concerned about the rights of gun owners, she felt, because neither these nor other political groups were defending a principle so fundamental—and therefore, in her view of the world, so clearly church-related—as the right to life. Another state pro-life leader phrased it more pragmatically: "You see, churches are the key, because that's where the people are who think like we do."

The fifth fingerprint was the timing of the appeal; the Iowa group would leaflet only on the Sunday immediately before election day. That morning, they distributed leaflets in church lobbies after services, and put them under the windshield wipers of cars in church parking lots. Some campaigners try to schedule their advertising earlier in the election period in the belief that voters are so tired of the campaign by election day, and so overloaded with last-minute political stimuli, that they block out new messages. But again, the pro-lifers had a special purpose. Their issue, they believed, was vital and urgent. They wanted their message to carry a powerful emotional punch. But emotional messages have a short shelf life. Thus they hoped to stir churchgoers with a single-issue appeal late enough so that it would not have worn off by election day. The Iowa leader explains:

> You're hitting them *right* before the election, before they can forget it, on an issue that concerns them, and if they're in any type of frame of mind, which they probably *are,* because they've gotten up to go to church, they're going to see it [and] maybe be concerned enough to go to the polls the following Tuesday.

This strategy of distribution had other advantages for the Pro-Life Action Council. For one, it was relatively inexpensive; as the Iowa leader pointed out, "our brochure is the biggest bang for the buck, is what it amounts to, and we can take our money and put it into the development of a brochure and the printing of it, and the manpower is just volunteer." This was not a trivial consideration; the group, like many of its sister organizations in 1978 and 1980, had more volunteers than money.

The Iowa group made its statewide debut in the 1978 primaries by opposing the front-runner for the position of lieutenant governor: pro-choice state senator Minnette Doderer. The Pro-Life Action Council swung into action on the Sunday before primary day, distributing 50,000 copies of its leaflet; all five fingerprints of the leafletting strategy were in evidence. As the group's chairman had expected, turnout was light; only 17 percent of the eligible voters went to the polls. Doderer was unexpectedly and narrowly defeated.

What caused her defeat? As with most elections, the signs were unclear. But accurately or not, some key political actors called attention to the pro-life group's leafletting strategy. The candidate herself went public with her claim that pro-lifers should be held responsible for her defeat. Newspaper and television accounts featured the highly visible leafletting—its suddenness and drama, after all, made it "newsworthy"—and spread Doderer's claim nationwide, giving it even greater believability. The pro-lifers were happy to accept all that credit, especially since it was their first statewide campaign. Here is the Iowa leader's account of what she learned from the experience:

> . . . we defeated her. And we did it with our leafletting. The *New York Times* came out to interview me, and the very first sentence in the *Times* article said, "It was the right-to-lifers; they won every race they were in." And this quote was from her [Doderer]. We took that leaflet and we put inserts in it, giving the stands of the candidates in the different areas, and we won every single race. And that brought the national attention to us.

It was a heady introduction to big-league politics. Then came the general election. With Doderer out of the race, the group turned its attention to a bigger fish: Democratic U.S. Senator Dick Clark, a first-term liberal with a pro-choice record. Though the stakes were higher, the situation was very similar to that of the primary: another statewide race, the same electorate, the same election year, the same party. A learning approach would predict that the pro-life group would generalize its learning and expectations from the Doderer race to the Clark contest; with so many similarities, there was good reason to expect the strategy that seemed to have worked in the primary would work again in November. That was exactly what the pro-life leader assumed. When reporters asked her, right after the primary, what her group would do in the general election, she reports answering, " 'Well, we're going to do the same thing to Dick Clark.' And of course nobody believed we were going to. But they watched and we did the same thing, only we expanded it to 300,000 fliers instead of 50,000!"

Democratic leaders found the circumstances harrowingly familiar. Clark had been expected to win. His opponent, conservative Republican Roger Jepsen, had not impressed many reporters with his acumen. In October 1978, polls showed Clark fully 30 points ahead of Jepsen; as late as the Sunday before the November election, the *Des Moines Register* published a poll showing Clark 10 percent ahead. That day, the Pro-Life Action Council blanketed Iowa churches with its 300,000 leaflets. The following Tuesday, Clark was unexpectedly and narrowly defeated. Clark's campaign manager said, "We lost by about 26,000 votes. Peter Hart, who did our polling, found in a postelection survey that four percent of the voters switched because of the abortion issue, and that was the margin of victory."[3]

The pro-life group's role in Clark's loss is still being debated. Some observers felt, with a lot of justification, that Clark had alienated many Iowans for other reasons. Some argued that abortion was simply a "triggering" issue; the pro-life attacks increased people's suspicion of Clark, which led them to scrutinize his record more closely on other issues and find areas on which they disagreed with him. These other areas, they argued, finally influenced people's votes. Clark himself laid his defeat in part to a low turnout among Democrats and in part to the Republican party's organizational strength. But he, too, made postelection statements giving the pro-life group a share in the outcome. A political reporter agrees, suggesting that while the pro-life influence may have been exaggerated, it was clearly a factor:

> There is some indication from looking at the returns that Dick Clark did not do as well as he should have in some of the more traditional Democratic areas of the state . . . so yes, they had an impact. But it tends to be over-rated because when these politicians went around explaining why they lost, they pointed to these groups and gave them more credibility than I think they deserved. . . . I don't know.

But [Doderer] obviously wasn't going to stand up there and say that it was her crummy campaign that did it [caused her defeat] . . . so yes, I think that perhaps they're a *little* bit over-rated, but they're effective.

From their vantage point after the votes were in, the Iowa pro-lifers had reason to look at the consequences of their strategy with some satisfaction. The candidates they had worked to oppose were defeated. Even more, the results had come as a surprise to many seasoned political professionals. In the rush to explain why, reporters for such respected publications as the *New York Times* had cited the pro-life leafletting as a major factor. These reports were then retailed by other news outlets and soon became part of the "instant wisdom" about the 1978 elections. And the pro-lifers' main adversaries, Clark and Doderer, had agreed.

Were those reports right? Looking back at the many liberal defeats across the nation in 1978, observers might feel that the media, in their enthusiasm for a colorful news story, greatly exaggerated the pro-lifers' importance in the Iowa race. But if there *is* a "real" answer to that question, it is, to a great extent, beside the point. In the conditions that prevailed after the 1978 elections, the leading voices among political activists judged that the pro-life group and its leafletting strategy had made a difference in the election result, and that judgment changed the expectations of virtually everyone involved.

The Iowa group felt richly rewarded for its efforts. How should these experiences affect the group's actions in 1980? The theory suggests that as long as the two election environments are similar, the group should derive its expectations about 1980 from its experiences in 1978. In fact, the two elections shared many of the same features. The 1980 Senate campaign, as chapter 6 noted, was John Culver's first race for reelection; the same had been true of Dick Clark in 1978. Culver, like Clark, was a liberal Democrat and a pro-choice stalwart. His Republican opponent, like Clark's, was a strong conservative and a supporter of the Human Life Amendment. Culver and Clark had the same constituents, the same kind of supporting coalition, and many of the same strategic problems.

With such striking similarities between their two opponents, it is not surprising that leaders of the Pro-Life Action Council generalized from their successes in 1978 and used the same strategy against John Culver. The church leafletting strategy in fact emerged twice in 1980. In the primary, the group distributed 300,000 copies of a leaflet backing U.S. Representative Charles Grassley for the Republican Senate nomination, against a moderate Republican allied with the state's governor. All five fingerprints of the leafletting strategy were present in the primary: the three main characteristics of the leaflet, with distribution at churches on the Sunday before election day.

With Grassley the winner in the primary, the Action Council had to decide whether the now-familiar church leafletting was its best move in the general election between Grassley and Culver. Some pro-lifers argued that the strategy had lost its surprise value; perhaps it was time for a new approach. But another view dominated the group's discussion, just as the learning approach would argue; it was the feeling that the church leafletting was linked with successful results and that given the uncertainties of politics, change was needless.

The group continued on its proven path. Four of the five parts of the leafletting strategy were repeated in the general election, with the brochure expanded to a four-page tabloid discussing pro-life issues in greater detail. The only real change in the strategy, a minor alteration in one fingerprint, reflected the Action Council's great success as a model. So many other groups, having learned observationally from the pro-lifers' presumed effectiveness in 1978 and 1980, were expected to leaflet at churches on the Sunday before election day that the Action Council decided to leaflet one Sunday earlier, to avoid having its message lost in what the Council's chairman called "a paper campaign like had never been seen before!" Her expectation turned out to be right on target; on that final Sunday, cars in church parking lots were buried under leaflets from anti-ERA groups,[4] a "pro-family" organization called FaithAmerica, a smaller pro-life group named Iowa Democrats for Life, and several other groups and candidates.

The second tactic the group had used against Clark in 1978 was also carried forward into the Culver-Grassley race. The Pro-Life Action Council began a Voter Identification Program (Voter ID) in 1978. In it, pro-life volunteers telephoned people on lists of registered voters to ask which were pro-life, which were opposed to federal funding of abortion, and which would vote solely on the basis of the candidate's stand on abortion. The results were entered into a computer file and used later to mobilize volunteers, to target direct mail (including the church leaflet, which was mailed directly to some voters identified by the project), and to make get-out-the-vote phone calls just before the election.

Interestingly, the tactic had been learned from one of the group's intended victims. "Actually, Dick Clark is the guy who developed it," the pro-life chairman noted. "We had actually worked with it in the Democratic party in this state, and Clark is one of the gentlemen who devised the Voter Identification Project." Its main virtue, she felt, was that it could be so much more carefully targeted than the shotgun-style leafletting. It enabled the pro-lifers to concentrate their messages on people who are already registered to vote, and who already support the group's position. Its main disadvantage was its cost, not only in money and computer time but in volunteer efforts. She explains:

The mailing [to those identified by the program], if zeroed in, I'd say, could be really, really dynamite, because you go right in to a registered voter, into their home with this brochure, in to somebody who really believes in your side. The difficulty with that is expense. The mailing expense is prohibitive and we never have money. So that's why we go to the leafletting, the mass type of thing, so that we can get to as many as possible.

Clearly, the Iowa Pro-Life Action Council's strategies in 1980 against John Culver were drawn from its leaders' experiences in the 1978 Senate race. It is a classic case of learning from response consequences; the group's expectations were built on the satisfying results of its behavior in earlier races under similar conditions. As a political reporter observed, "Politicians are like generals: they fight this war on the lessons they learned in the last one, and the tactic worked, and as far as the pro-life people are concerned that I've talked to, this is just more of the same: identify more voters, get out more brochures, try to make [abortion] more of a public issue."

Moreover, the group's strategies, especially the much-remarked church leafletting, bore the earmarks of a single-issue movement. The leaflet distributed at churches did not discuss John Culver's liberalism or Charles Grassley's homespun background. It focused only on abortion, and only on the candidates' contrasting stands on that issue. Its tone was fervent and emotional; the leaflet left no doubt of the group's belief that abortion was the central issue in the election. There was no hint of compromise. There had been no effort to form coalitions, to join forces with other groups opposing Culver or supporting Grassley. It was single-issue politics in pure form.

By mid-evening on 4 November 1980, John Culver had become the former senator from Iowa. Again, the Iowa Pro-Life Action Council felt the thrill of accomplishment. In October 1978, Iowa had been represented by two pro-choice senators. When the Senate convened in 1981, both Iowa members would be pledged to vote for a constitutional amendment banning abortions. That meant a gain of two Senate seats out of 100 for the pro-life movement, in two short years, in one state alone. And a number of reporters and other observers had laid that result, rightly or wrongly, to the Action Council, its church leafletting and its Voter ID.

THE LEARNING SPREADS

The Iowa pro-lifers were now acknowledged leaders in the electoral activities of the pro-life movement. They had been even in 1978, when their reputation for campaign success had far surpassed the efforts and the presumed impact of pro-life groups in most other states. That perceived success made the Iowa group a prime model for pro-life organizations with less experience in the world of campaigns and elections. These newer groups sought out the Iowa chairman for help. She joked that when she arrived at the National Right to Life convention the year after the 1978 races, her workshop on campaign strategies was crowded with pro-lifers wondering how people from Iowa could have been so politically savvy:

> I always say [when I give a workshop] that "if a girl from East Overshoe, Iowa, can do this, you can do it too!" [laughs] I don't think we've ever been touted in the movement as being totally sophisticated. I mean, they can never *spell* Iowa right, much less know where it is! And so they figure, "My gosh, if *those* people can do it, well we can too."

She also offers a more pragmatic explanation for her role as a model for other pro-life groups. "Everybody said it couldn't be done [when we targeted Dick Clark in 1978], and we were able to do it, and the national press gave us the credit for it, so . . . it's a shot in the arm for the movement. And then naturally, other states were eager to find out how we ran it."

She was a willing teacher. Her group's leaflets and strategies were widely disseminated throughout the pro-life movement in 1979 and 1980. The learning took place through several channels. One important channel, as she indicates, was the national convention sponsored each year by the National Right to Life Committee. At this and other meetings, she met informally with interested pro-lifers from other states as well as giving workshops on her group's activities in the 1978 race against Clark. At each workshop she distributed copies of the Iowa leaflet, which were always eagerly received.

Between conventions, several national pro-life groups requested more copies and passed them along to activists in their state organizations. The Iowa representative on the board of the National Right to Life Committee took a stack of leaflets along to national board meetings, distributing some to each of the other state Right to Life directors. The executive director of LAPAC asked for a hundred copies, shipping them in turn to his own operatives in targeted states. In many cases, pro-lifers in other states contacted the Iowa chairman directly for advice. Upon requests from groups in Louisiana and California, she acted as a consultant in a primary and a special election where pro-lifers had endorsed a candidate for Congress.

But her experience was of special importance to the pro-life groups in several of LAPAC's 1980 target states. In reality the target list that LAPAC's Paul Brown had announced was more like the suggestion "let's you and him fight." Although Brown selected and publicized the list, he did not intend the national LAPAC to do most of the actual campaigning. Instead, he hoped to motivate a variety of state pro-life groups to move into the breach and work to defeat the incumbents that LAPAC had fingered. Only one of the six targeted states, South Dakota, had an active LAPAC organization. In Indiana, the major anti-abortion group was a Right to Life PAC. Independent PACs had formed in Oregon and Iowa. But there were no pro-life PACs in two of the six states at the time of Brown's announcement. Pro-lifers in these states and others bridled at Brown's tactics; they recognized with panic that the media would now hold them responsible, no matter how unprepared they were, for carrying out LAPAC's well-publicized threats. The Iowa chairman pointed out with some exasperation that Brown's flamboyance "put them on the line [in the six targeted states], and now these people have to produce, and so where do they turn? They go to people like myself, and I'm sure they go elsewhere, and ask, 'What did you do?'"

Her answer to that question always included a caution: it would be necessary to adapt her advice to the particular circumstances of the learner's own state and campaign. Simply applying the Iowa strategy in another state might not work:

> You have to deal with the makeup of the state, the strength of the pro-life movement in the state, the strength of the parties in the state, the strength of the candidate himself, the strength of the opponent . . . it's all got to be taken in, and there's just no flat answer to it.

The kind of learning she recommended, then, was abstract modeling: learning the rules underlying her group's behaviors. Those rules could then be applied to another Senate race so as to produce a strategy comparable to Iowa's, taking account of differences between the states' political environments.[5]

Thus it is interesting that so much of the Iowa strategy was adopted in whole by several of the other pro-life groups in 1980, rather than adapted to meet any specialized conditions or needs. One reason was surely the inexperience of some groups; with little or no prior campaign participation to guide them, with the pressure of Brown's public claims, and with a strategy available that seemed to have been a huge success in Iowa, it would be entirely understandable if their learning took a very direct form. As the Iowa leader described it, "Somebody sees somebody do something effectively in one state, and they copy it, you know." We have more to say later about the form of these pro-life groups' learning. For now, let us see what was happening in the other five targeted states.

OBSERVATIONAL LEARNING: IDAHO, OREGON, AND VERMONT

The Idaho Pro-Life PAC, newly formed in midsummer 1980, began life with a problem. At the time that Paul Brown had announced the targeting of Frank

Church, there had been no pro-life PAC in Idaho. Now the new PAC was expected to launch its career not just by recruiting members and raising money but by defeating a nationally known senator who also happened to be an expert campaigner. Moreover, the new PAC's leader was a newcomer to politics. What could she do? Promptly, she and her colleagues got in touch with the Iowa group's chairman, as well as other pro-life leaders.

As a result of their contacts, the Idaho pro-lifers adopted the leafletting strategy. The leaflet, prepared over a dining-room table, closely followed the Iowa model. On the cover was a photo of a newborn baby. At the end was the admonition, "Your vote on November 4 is CRUCIAL!" On the weekend before the general election,[6] more than 100,000 copies of the leaflet were distributed at churches, as well as at shopping centers and other public places.

There was one important difference between Iowa '78 and Idaho '80, a difference that called for abstract modeling. Senator Church, unlike the Iowa targets, described himself as pro-life. Unlike Clark and Culver, he had voted to cut federal funding for abortions. Unlike any of the other targets, he supported a states' rights amendment that would allow states to ban or restrict abortions. He joined Bayh and others on LAPAC's list because he did not support a Human Life Amendment. So the Idaho Pro-Life PAC had to do more than report Church's position on abortion; it had to explain why it did not define that position as pro-life.

One way to do that was to explain that a states' rights amendment would not prohibit abortions across the nation, but would allow any state to adopt a pro-choice policy for its own citizens. "So then that had to be part of our brochure," the Idaho leader commented, "to say what's wrong with the states' rights amendment and why we need a Human Life Amendment."

Another way was to contrast Church's position with the rest of the Idaho congressional delegation; the state's junior senator and both members of the House (one of whom, of course, was Steve Symms, Church's Republican opponent) were all HLA supporters. The intent was to portray Church as out of step with the mood of the state (a theme other groups that wanted to "separate Church from the state" had also stressed), even though he called himself "pro-life."

These two messages were variations on the Iowa model; they were not radical departures from it. Rather, they are examples of rule learning or abstract modeling: efforts to apply the Iowa lessons in a somewhat different campaign environment. The heart of the Idaho strategy had developed through modeling. As the Idaho PAC's leader confirms, "Well, of course, our leafletting idea came from what happened in the state of Iowa. Our feeling was that if it worked there, maybe it would work here."

Vermont pro-lifers had the same hope. Though the state had an established Right to Life Committee, no PAC had been formed until shortly before the 1980 campaigns. The new Vermont Pro-Life PAC quickly gave its public backing to a long-shot among the six Republicans competing for the right to face Senator Patrick Leahy in the fall. The National Right to Life PAC cautioned the Vermonters to wait, to cultivate one of the more viable candidates instead. As an NRTL-PAC leader explained, "We tried to recommend to Right to Life people, especially those getting involved in politics for the very first time, that sometimes you have to turn your back on someone who may be extremely pro-life but simply is not an electable candidate, and doesn't have the broad-base support. And this is one of those instances." The state PAC, however, held its ground.

Now the Vermont Pro-Life PAC, with minimal organization and resources, had to show that its support meant something; it had to shepherd its endorsed candidate through the Republican primary in September. Like the Idaho group, the Vermont pro-lifers learned and followed the leafletting strategy. In the familiar style, they distributed 75,000 leaflets for their candidate, primarily at Catholic churches, on the Sunday before the primary.

This time, the leafletting was not followed by victory. The long-shot candidate remained just that. The winner of the Republican Senate nomination, Stewart Ledbetter, endorsed Hyde but not the Human Life Amendment; later, even his support for the Hyde Amendment seemed to be somewhat less than totally consistent. There would be no pro-life Senate candidate in the November election.

After the September primary, then, the Vermont Pro-Life PAC found itself in a situation to which the Iowa model was not very applicable: the targeted senator's opponent refused to take a clear pro-life stand. The PAC was tempted to endorse Ledbetter anyway, as the "lesser of two evils," and to leaflet on his behalf. But there were strong objections from state Right to Life leaders about such an endorsement; the Human Life Amendment was their goal, they said, and they could not compromise on it. Moreover, the PAC had very little money, and in the absence of a pro-life Senate candidate, very little prospect for getting more from national pro-life groups. In the end, for lack of an endorsable candidate, the PAC did not use the church leafletting strategy in the general election.[7]

The president of the Life Amendment PAC of Oregon had had a little more time than her counterparts in Idaho and Vermont to prepare for the 1980 races. Two years earlier, she had headed a group supporting an initiative on the Oregon ballot that would have ended state funding of abortions. As a result of this experience, she had become acquainted with a number of other pro-life activists, who grew interested in doing more pro-life campaign work. She felt satisfied with the initiative campaign; it did not pass, but the vote was closer than many had expected.

When she began to think about the race against Packwood, however, she saw the limits of her own experience. The initiative campaign had been helpful preparation in some ways, but it had addressed a different question: abortion *funding,* rather than abortion itself. Especially in the current economic climate, she felt, it was easier to persuade people that the government should not pay for abortions than that the government should not permit abortions. When questioned, she found little in the 1978 experience from which she could generalize.

To fill the void, she sought a model. Months before the 1980 primary, she made contact with the Iowa group's chairman and with Minnesota and national pro-life leaders. The Iowa situation was similar to her own, she felt, in that there would be an endorsable pro-life candidate opposing Senator Packwood in the spring primary. She said, "Well, we found a circular in the state of Iowa that has been *very* effective, and also it was effective in Minnesota. We put out a comparable circular." The strategy was indeed comparable. The Oregon leaflet began with a photo of a newborn baby over the caption "This little guy needs your vote" and ended with the same phrase used in the 1978 Iowa version: "Your vote in the primary is CRUCIAL." Again we see the fingerprints of the Iowa model. The only difference was in numbers; as the Oregon leader stated, "We didn't have money enough to put out enough of them. We should have probably put out 350,000, and all we did was 60,000."

The primary voters, however, behaved more like Vermont's than like Iowa's. The pro-life Republican challenger, under attack from another pro-life Republican, soon lost her standing as a viable opponent for Packwood. The senator won renomination with ease. On the Democratic side, the Senate nominee was pro-choice. As in Vermont, the PAC had no endorsable candidate for the Senate in November. The results of the primary had been negative for the group, and the situation in the general election campaign was not promising. So, as in Vermont, the PAC's campaign behavior changed. There was no church leafletting in the Packwood race in November—at least, none by the Life Amendment PAC of Oregon.[8] Instead, the PAC concentrated on a House race against Democrat Al Ullman, where the Republican challenger was an HLA supporter.

MODELING PLUS PREVIOUS EXPERIENCE:
SOUTH DAKOTA AND INDIANA

The South Dakota and Indiana pro-life PACs were somewhat more experienced than the previous three; each had taken part in congressional campaigns before. Neither had targeted a Senate race before, however. In their preparation for 1980, although the leaders of these groups felt they had some relevant experiences of their own to draw upon, they also expected some new challenges to appear. The result, in both campaigns, was a very interesting mix of modeling and learning from response consequences.

The state coordinator for the Life Amendment PAC in South Dakota, a state unit of the national LAPAC, was something of a political pro. She had been active in Democratic politics for more than 15 years—many of those years, in fact, as a McGovern volunteer. Her group had worked on congressional campaigns in 1978.

Despite her experience, however, this was not only the state group's first Senate race but also her own first campaign *against* the man she had supported for so long. As a further spur toward observational learning, her group's campaign activities were planned with the help of LAPAC's national director, Paul Brown, who brought to bear his extensive knowledge of pro-life models from other states. She was particularly well informed about Iowa, and she agreed that in her preparation for the 1980 races, "we, possibly, draw on some of that information."

In fact, the Iowa model was closely applied in the South Dakota primary election through the offices of the national LAPAC, which printed the leaflets used in South Dakota. Recall that in 1980, Senator George McGovern had opposition in the Democratic primary for the first time in his career, from a conservative Democrat endorsed by LAPAC. This was expected to be the real test of McGovern's vulnerability in the general election; if a political unknown could run at all respectably against the three-term senator, then it would be clear that McGovern was in trouble in November.

The church leafletting strategy emerged fullblown in the Democratic primary. On the leaflet's cover was the photo originally used by the Iowa PAC—Lennart Nilsson's photograph of a fetus in the womb—followed by the charge that Senator McGovern "continuously votes your tax dollars to kill preborn children," and a brief comparison with the antiabortion stance of McGovern's challenger, Larry Schumaker. One hundred thousand of these leaflets were handed out, chiefly in church parking lots, on the Sunday before primary day.

The results looked like Iowa's. McGovern won the primary, as expected, but he was held to 62 percent of the Democratic vote. That was a slimmer margin of victory than most reporters and political activists had predicted. The outcome was widely interpreted as proof of McGovern's shaky prospects in the fall, when he would face a Republican who was much better known than Schumaker had been. For LAPAC in South Dakota, the primary election was a real "moral victory," a positive reinforcer. The group had another endorsable candidate in U.S. Representative James Abdnor, an HLA supporter who would face the senator in November. Like the Iowa Pro-Life Action Council, South Dakota's pro-lifers had an opportunity to generalize from their experience in the primary: a satisfying experience, followed by similar conditions in the general election campaign.

The group *did* generalize its strategy from the primary. Another hundred thousand leaflets in the same format were distributed on the Sunday before the election in church parking lots and, where permission for that was refused by pastors and ministers, house-to-house. There was only one small modification; the leaflet emphasized the positive aspects of Abdnor's pro-life record, instead of focusing only on McGovern. As a political reporter pointed out, LAPAC had been criticized after the primary for indulging in "negative campaigning."

The Indiana Right to Life PAC was even more experienced than South Dakota's by the time of the 1980 races. Its extensive campaign background would rank second only to Iowa's among the six state groups. It had, for example, adopted the Voter Identification Program (indirectly from Iowa and Minnesota by way of the National Right to Life Committee's workshops) in 1978; by the beginning of the 1980 campaign, its Voter ID was well established.

It also had successes of its own to learn from. In 1978, the group had endorsed Republican challenger Joel Deckard against U.S. Representative David Cornwell, a pro-choice Democrat, in a race followed by a Deckard victory. The IRTL-PAC's leader felt that pro-lifers had clearly played a role in that victory, especially through the means of the new Voter ID. She saw some resemblances between the campaign environment of 1978 and the 1980 race. Most voters were against abortion but still politically apathetic, she argued; that was true in 1978, and it remained true in 1980. Therefore it was necessary to motivate the pro-life supporters to vote by contacting them directly about the campaign. "That's what we did in the Deckard race, and that's what we'll be doing in the Bayh race, and in many other races this year," she said. Her reasoning in that decision shows evidence of learning from response consequences: "Well, we look at what we've done in the past, and decide whether or not it was effective."

But the IRTL-PAC was also a part of the communication network connecting many state and national pro-life groups. It worked with a pro-life consultant whose services were also used by pro-lifers in other states. The models, in short, were available. And the current campaign setting in Indiana had some new features. The 1978 pro-life victory had come in a congressional rather than a statewide race; the increased size of a Senate constituency was an important strategic element in the 1980 campaign.

This combination of some relevant prior experience with some new circumstances produced variations on the now-familiar theme. It gave the PAC's leader more confidence in adapting the Iowa model to the special characteristics of an Indiana campaign. In the early summer of 1980, she described her planning for the general election (since neither Bayh nor his opponent, Republican U.S. Representative Dan Quayle, had a primary contest):

> Well, I see the brochures that some other states have used during the last phase of the campaign. But I can't say that we're going to use them; we can look at it, and listen to what they say about why they think it was effective, and then try to judge it in terms of Hoosier voters and our credibility, and see if that's the same kind of message that we want to get out.

The PAC did produce an early brochure on the Bayh race, comparing the senator's position with that of his PAC-endorsed opponent, Quayle. The leaflet was mailed during the summer to households that the Voter ID had tagged as being pro-life.

Just before the November election, 300,000 copies of IRTL's newsletter, "Communicator," were distributed around the state with inserts carrying the PAC's endorsements in congressional races as well as endorsements of Quayle and Ronald Reagan. Prominent in this insert was an emphasis on turnout:

> Q: Does my vote make a difference?
> A: YES! Many elections are won or lost by a small percentage. Your vote is *extremely* important.

Brochures on the abortion issue, contrasting Bayh's stance with that of Quayle, were handed out at churches on the Sunday before the general election—but by the Quayle campaign itself, with the advice and consultation of IRTL-PAC.[9] Differences between these tactics and the Iowa model are worth noting, for they reflect the broader learning opportunities that the Indiana PAC's own campaign experience provided. But the imprint of observational learning can still be seen, even though the fingerprints might be smudged: the church leafletting, the Sunday-before-the-vote timing, the way in which candidates' records on abortion were presented, the central stress on turnout in the message. The strategy arrived in pieces, and at times through intermediaries, but it arrived nevertheless.

Pro-Life Campaigning: How Helpful Was the Learning Approach?

In the last chapter we hypothesized that where they had previous experience of their own, state pro-life groups' approaches would be structured by the results of that experience. But our interest was drawn even more strongly to the effects of inexperience and environmental change. While some groups had been involved in very similar Senate and House campaigns in the recent past, others had come into existence just a few months before the 1980 election, and were led by people whose campaign background was limited or nonexistent. Where groups had little personal experience to draw upon, we predicted they would depend heavily on learning the strategies provided by successful, similar models.

The predictions proved to be accurate. The most experienced state group, the Iowa Pro-Life Action Council, derived its expectations and strategies in 1980 from its own well-publicized (and, pro-lifers thought, effective) role in the defeats of Dick Clark and Minnette Doderer in 1978. The primary election in 1978 had marked the Iowa group's first statewide use of strategies evolved in earlier local and special elections. The nature of those strategies, especially the church leafletting, but also the contents and uses of the Voter Identification Program, reflected the single-issue character of the pro-life campaign. The drama and novelty of the leafletting attracted media coverage throughout the nation. In the uncertainty that normally surrounds election outcomes, and unexpected outcomes in particular, media people and other activists saw the pro-life leafletting as a plausible explanation for Doderer's unexpected defeat. That explanation had all the makings of a good news story—intense conflict, surprise, action, human interest—as well as an arguable basis in fact. It spread widely, for both reasons, and gained general acceptance.

This explanation also served as a powerful reward for the Pro-Life Action Council. We have seen how difficult it is to use election results as a basis for learning how to make one's strategies more effective—how election victory, then, has blunt and conservatizing effects. So it did for the Iowa pro-lifers. The Action Council tried the same strategies again when the general election of 1978 seemed to resemble the conditions of the primary. Once more, when it came time to explain the unexpected defeat of Senator Dick Clark, reporters pointed to the church leafletting and the Voter ID. The pro-lifers' strategic behaviors had been rewarded twice, exactly as they had hoped. In six months' time, the Iowa Pro-Life Action Council had developed a reputation for political expertise.

The Iowa group's leader approached the 1980 races with the expectation that as long as the situation remained comparable, the strategies would work again. The campaign itself brought no marked environmental change, no sharp turn that might cause her to reevaluate that belief. A small change—the extensive imitation of the church leafletting strategy by other single-issue and campaign organizations, causing concern that the pro-life leaflet would be lost in the shuffle—brought a small improvisation in response. But in the main, the Action Council's behavior in the primary and general elections of 1980 was a replay of 1978. The pro-lifers' strategies were firmly rooted in the expectations they developed from their experience in the Doderer and Clark races.

The same sense of effectiveness in an uncertain environment that had led the Iowa group to repeat its strategies also made it a model for other groups facing similar situations. In states where the pro-life PAC had little or no relevant experience of its own to draw upon—Idaho, Oregon, and Vermont—we saw striking evidence of observational learning from the Iowa model. The three groups' leaders all had access to the details of Iowa's strategies. They studied those details. With the Iowa group's reputed successes foremost in their minds, they adopted various aspects of the leafletting and the Voter ID, within the limits of their own resources.[10] Where they saw some differences between Iowa's 1978 campaign environment and their own in 1980, they adapted parts of the Iowa strategy to the special character of their race: the discussion of a states' rights amendment in the Idaho brochure, for example. When they faced a situation that no longer resembled the Iowa model—when the primary election left the Oregon and Vermont groups without an endorsable pro-life candidate—their actions changed.

The pro-life PACs in South Dakota and Indiana are not as pure types as these. Both had prior campaign experience, and both faced new elements in the 1980 elections. The South Dakota group had drawn early on the Iowa model. Its own experience with "moral victory" in the 1980 primary led it to continue using that strategy. The Indiana Right to Life PAC applied many elements of that strategy as well. But because of its more extensive experience, its greater organizational resources, and its access to models other than Iowa's (through the services of a consultant), the Indiana PAC blended those elements with others to create the only distinctive variation on the leafletting strategy that we have seen in these six 1980 races. It is an example of the process by which observational learning can lead to the creation of new patterns of behavior, rather than just the spread of existing patterns.

Two conclusions stand out at this point. First, the use of models was vitally important to these state pro-life groups as they prepared for action in the 1980 Senate elections. Through observational learning, a set of intriguing strategies spread across the six races, originating in the Iowa group's experience and diffusing to the others. These pro-life groups were not foot soldiers carrying out orders, or creatures of some national machine, but independent entities making independent campaign decisions, each with its own sources of ideas, funds, and talents. Yet the result was a great similarity in behavior, brought about by observational learning from a shared model.

The similarities are especially striking because so many of the groups were new and inexperienced; they had neither the time nor the background to learn from other models or from the results of their own initial actions. The nature of the learned strategy is also a factor. The church leafletting was to take place only when the campaign was almost over. To keep its shock value intact, groups could not experiment with the leafletting in advance, and learn from the responses to such an experiment. The newer pro-life groups had little alternative to adopting the Iowa strategy in whole — or at least as much of it as they could afford — and then waiting to see the results.

A second important conclusion is that election victory plays so vital yet so blunt a role in guiding people's choice of models. We have said much about the special qualities of campaigns as learning situations. Like so many other campaign actors, these pro-life groups did not have access to good, detailed polling data or other means of monitoring citizens' responses to various events, issues, or candidates. Like virtually all campaign actors, the pro-lifers had to deal with the pervasive uncertainty of campaigning, with the lack of certain knowledge about the relationships between individual campaign actions and the outcome of the race on election day. Victory, under such circumstances, is a powerful reward but a rather vague teacher.

What does victory teach? In Iowa, 1978, it suggested that the Pro-Life Action Council must have been doing *something* right when it leafletted at churches on the Sunday before election day and used volunteers to identify potential pro-life voters. No one could be certain that this was so. But it was a plausible assumption at a time when observers and participants were searching avidly for plausible assumptions. When asked what she had learned from the election of 1978, a national pro-life PAC leader said simply, "We learned that our methods worked."

The assumption was strengthened by the fact that the victory had not been expected; Doderer and Clark had both been front-runners, and the pro-life opposition had not been seen as a grave threat during the campaign. "We did it with tremendous odds against us," the national leader emphasizes. Compared to the results that most observers anticipated, then, the defeats of the two pro-choice candidates took on added value as rewards for the pro-life group's behaviors. In turn, the Iowa strategies took on added attractiveness as models for other pro-life groups.

Its success in 1978 was not the only reason that Iowa became the model for the 1980 pro-life campaigns. Other groups had also come out of the 1978 elections with a reputation for effectiveness, without also becoming models for the pro-lifers. The national Republican party had a lot to celebrate in 1978; it targeted a number of races and experienced many more wins than losses. The National Rifle Association made its customary claims of potentcy after election day. The New Right claimed many of the same scalps as did the pro-life groups, including Clark's. With all these potentially successful models, why did pro-life groups in 1980 rely so heavily on the Iowa group's strategies alone?

The answer bears out the second hypothesis we offered in the last chapter: in addition to a model's apparent effectiveness, the other important criterion for the choice of models is that he or she resemble the learner in important respects. Recall that one reason why similarity is a primary determinant of the choice of models is that people are often drawn to others like themselves, to people who share their interests, values, and daily activities. So similar models will probably be more readily available to a learner than will models with very different values and habits. Moreover, a sense of similarity or shared values should make the model more attractive to the observer, more likely to get his or her attention.

These effects of similarity—making a model more available and more attractive to the observer—were clearly operating in this case, leading newer pro-life groups to choose a pro-life model. In terms of availability, pro-life leaders in Idaho, Oregon, and Vermont were not regularly involved with other sources of political information; they were not active in Republican circles or environmental groups or pro-gun networks. But they did receive news and ideas from other pro-life PACs, through newsletters, national conventions, and personal contact. Those ideas engaged their attention because the senders shared one of their most deeply felt goals: a ban on abortions.

We have seen the intensity of these pro-lifers' feelings about abortion and its centrality to their personal beliefs. For people with so deep a commitment to a single issue, the shared value of pro-life activism is likely to be an overriding source of similarity. Set apart from their nonactivist friends and neighbors by the strength of their single-issue beliefs and behavior, the pro-life leaders become an important source of support, empathy, and encouragement for one another. Their shared values and experiences let them speak the same language. The leader of a national antiabortion PAC put it well:

> The fact that our [National Right to Life Committee] board of 50 people could come together out of such different backgrounds, philosophies, incomes, you name it—we may have a housewife from Wyoming and an attorney from Washington state and a doctor from Maryland, and yet the one thing that they all have absolutely in common in the pro-life movement is the issue of right-to-life. It doesn't matter what state you're in. That's the unique part of the whole movement, that we break down all the fences that still remain on most other issues. There is no political affiliation that can't be broken down on this issue.

This vital source of similarity, in short, has made these pro-life leaders into a community based on beliefs and behavior, rather than on geography, which their other political ties cannot match. It has made them into a learning network. And it has directed their attention to models within that network, rather than those outside it; their observational learning, then, has given the pro-life movement's strategies a distinctive character.

We can see the signs of an insular learning network in the Iowa leader's comments about her group's strategy. Earlier we relayed her feeling that the church leafletting would not work for other political groups, even for other single-issue groups, because the supporters of other organizations are not plainly identifiable by their involvement in churches, whereas the pro-life constituency (in her view) is. She elaborates on that argument:

> [Abortion] is a moral issue, so it's going to hit church-going people, whereas I don't think any other interest [such as pro-gun groups, for example] that's been given credit for any political savvy at all could probably use the same tactic. They could use direct mail. Anybody could poll—*any* group could, you know. Our opponent could do the same thing. They could go to the voter survey and find out which people are on their side and see that they get their message to them. But they'd be hard-pressed to go to *churches* and do leafletting.

Her words make clear her belief that pro-lifers are unique—set apart from other political activists. So when pro-lifers needed models from which to develop campaign strategies, their attention was first attracted to the learning network provided by other pro-life groups, rather than to parties, candidates, or consultants outside the pro-life movement. The most experienced pro-life group facing similar circumstances was the Iowa Pro-Life Action Council. Its presumed successes, as well as the values it shared with other pro-life groups, engaged their interest, led them to retain what they had learned from Iowa's experiences, and motivated them to use that learning in their own states.

National pro-life organizations were quick to see the vital role of observational learning in the growth of their new movement. The major national pro-life groups and their newsletters were an obvious means by which state and local groups could learn what other pro-lifers were doing. In issues of *LAPAC Reports* during the 1980 campaigns, for example, LAPAC's leaders offered a steady stream of campaign updates on the races in which various state pro-life groups were involved. It also offered direct instruction in preferred campaign techniques. One issue included a sample survey with which local groups could set up a Voter Identification Program. Another advertised a guide to politics and parties written by a congressional aide expressly for pro-life groups.[11] And LAPAC announced its intention to provide models in person, by running How to Win Seminars at national Right to Life conventions and for local groups upon request.

The National Right to Life Committee was similarly tempted to teach, and to serve as a communication channel among state and local pro-life groups.

In 1980 it adopted a three-year plan for work toward acceptance of a Human Life Amendment, in which the NRLC would distribute information about fund raising, media use, and other political activities to the various state groups. At its national and regional meetings, the NRLC scheduled workshops at which an expert on Voter ID would tell other activists how to set up their own program. Just before the general election in 1980, NRLC sent its state affiliates an outline of a postelection press release they could use in dealing with their own media, adding prudently, "with various suggested statements depending on the outcome [of the vote]."

When state pro-life groups saw their targets defeated in 1980, the glow of victory seemed to touch not only the church leafletting strategy and the Voter ID but also the use of pro-life models. Learning from those models had been central to many groups' preparation for the 1980 campaigns. In the aftermath of the election, pro-lifers concluded that this approach must have worked. Strategies developed for use in Iowa and Minnesota had been transplanted into other states in the East and West, and apparently flourished—at least that seemed to be what the election returns were saying.

If the church leafletting and the Voter ID could be transplanted so easily, many pro-life leaders reasoned, so could other activities. Increasing efforts were made to locate good pro-life models and to teach other state and local pro-life groups how to use them. The director of NRTL-PAC explained in mid-1981:

> Iowa and Minnesota were the forerunners in campaign strategy. Another state organization might take the lead in some other area. For example, an Illinois pro-life group came up with a newspaper ad to counteract the messages, spread by NARAL and NOW, that a Human Life Amendment would outlaw birth control in addition to abortion. Illinois came up with a flier which lists what those groups [NARAL and NOW] are saying about the HLA, and then lists the truth: that a Human Life Amendment will have absolutely no impact on the pill and the IUD. And Illinois has already sent out the flier to the other 49 state groups, so if they want to copy it, there it is.

She concluded that modeling is an important part of the movement's development: "We spend a lot of time exchanging information so that we never have to reinvent the wheel. If you want to do something new in your state, it's probably already been done in some other state. There are very few things that have not already been done. So you simply get in touch with that state and find out how they did it."

Her enthusiasm for encouraging state groups to learn from pro-life models is shared by many of her state-level counterparts. Newsletters, ads, brochures, and other materials produced by one state group are frequently sent to other states' pro-life organizations, and are sometimes reprinted by them. This readiness to share materials helps compensate for a major problem faced by a movement with virtually no paid workers: the lack of time and money to explore many alternatives. Even the Iowa group, the model in this story, has taken advantage of other pro-life models when its own experience was limited or its resources scarce. The group's chairman recalls:

> In our [party] caucuses [in the winter of 1980, during the presidential nominating season], Minnesota had an excellent caucus pamphlet and we had nothing. I had struggled and struggled to put something down on paper, and I was just too busy, because we had the first caucuses, and I had presidential candidates stumping and knocking at the doors [laughs], and it was just a zoo. . . . And I needed *something* to get into their hands. Human Life Alliance in Minnesota had an excellent caucus pamphlet, and I called and asked them if we could use it. Of course we changed it to what we wanted in it. But this is done a lot in the movement because we're a volunteer movement, and what works for somebody else that we think will work for us, we go with that, and find out if they'll let us, and that saves an awful lot of time.

The tendency to use pro-life models has been further strengthened by the feeling among pro-life leaders that many secular communication channels are hostile to their cause. Newspapers, television, and radio are common sources of observational learning in politics. But these channels are not trusted by many pro-life activists, on the assumption that reporters and editors are usually pro-choice and do not portray the activities of pro-lifers fairly and accurately.

One state pro-life leader complained, "The press has not been very honest with us at all, I don't think. They haven't tried to tell the story as it is." Another argued that reporters paint pro-lifers as extremists, "simply because they don't agree." A third stated, "The media people who were assigned to cover us . . . tended to be liberal in nature. Their own political beliefs were very different from my own and therefore, whether they were meaning to or not, they were very biased on the issue, just because they were very, very uninformed as to what the issue was all about."[12]

There is some evidence that this concern about media coverage is not unjustified. One political reporter said, "Those [pro-life] people have been burned an awful lot by [the media] . . . obviously a pro-choice bias among many media people has shown up in a lot of stories, and these people are real leery." The director of NRTL-PAC, citing survey data showing that media people are much less likely than other citizens to feel that abortion is morally wrong, pointed out:

> We know from our own experience too, which comes out loud and clear on this particular survey, that the major media are definitely on the other side of this issue. The latest example was the hearings held in Congress on when life begins. What

was put out on the AP wire was not the testimony that was given in the hearing. The headline that appeared in my paper said, "Six Women Protest Hearing," and the entire article was written about the six pro-abortion women who stood on their chairs and screamed during the hearing. That was what was covered. Nothing about what was really going on in that hearing [i.e., testimony by witnesses that human life begins at conception]. It's been very frustrating to us.

One can still learn from a hostile communication channel by applying a systematic correction factor to the information it conveys. But that sort of cool calculation is made less likely by the intensity of the pro-lifers' beliefs and the sense, widespread in the pro-life movement, that media coverage misinterprets their activities in order to turn public opinion toward the pro-choice position.

These attitudes toward the media carry a certain irony. As chapter 6 indicated, there is little systematic evidence that the abortion issue (or any other issue, taken alone) actually turned the tide in any of these elections. Yet because the pro-life campaign activities in 1980 were such an interesting story, they were heavily reported. That coverage probably exaggerated the pro-life groups' impact on election results, and in so doing, gave pro-lifers a better chance of influencing campaigners.

Whether justified or not, these suspicions about the media—and the resulting tendency *not* to use media coverage as a dependable source of observational learning—made pro-life groups depend all the more on models found within the movement. The result was a striking similarity among the six pro-life groups' strategies in 1980, in spite of the Iowa leader's warning that her strategies should be adapted to fit each state's special environment.

Finally, the pro-lifers' behavior bears out our predictions about the kinds of strategies most likely to diffuse to other groups. The church leafletting strategy has many of the characteristics we named as likely to promote diffusion. Its central element—the leaflet—is attention attracting and easy to transmit. The logic of the strategy is clear and simple. Its cost is minimal, as political advertising goes. And it was available as a model, since it was distributed (through national pro-life channels) to groups in every state. Besides, the church leafletting does not bend the social or moral values of other pro-life activists. The strategy centers on churches and people who attend them, institutions that have been so important to pro-lifers. It provides a dramatic means of expressing the deeply felt values that pro-life activists share. All these factors made the strategy easier to *learn*. Its reputed success encouraged its *use*.

In contrast, the Voter Identification Program has diffused to a more limited extent. That, too, is understandable in learning terms. Though this program may be as easy to explain as the church leafletting and as readily available for learning, it is not nearly as attention getting as is the distribution of pro-life leaflets in public places. It requires contact with an undifferentiated group of citizens, including many who might be expected to react negatively or even abusively to being telephoned by pro-lifers, rather than the more sympathetic reactions that could be expected among congregations of particular churches. It costs more than the church leafletting would; a full-scale Voter ID demands a great deal of time and effort over a long period and, optimally, the use of a computer. Perhaps most important, its long-term, behind-the-scenes character makes it less likely to get credit as a possible cause of the election results. These factors restricted its use by most state pro-life groups.

So far, our social-learning hypotheses have held up very well. They have led us to observe the extensive diffusion of the Iowa strategies among state pro-life groups in 1980, the reasons for that diffusion, and the adoption of those strategies in more complete form by some state groups than others. They have helped us understand why one of the Iowa strategies—the church leafletting—was adopted by more groups and used to a greater extent than was the other strategy (the Voter Identification Program). And the hypotheses have drawn our attention to the insular nature of pro-lifers' learning network in 1980, the fact that their models were almost always internal to the pro-life movement.

Can we expect that insularity to continue, and the distinctive character of the pro-life campaign strategies to be seen year after year? Chapter 9 has more to say on this point, with the advantage of information about pro-life campaigning in 1982 and beyond.

But first, let us turn to the other set of main characters in this story. How did the targeted senators and their staffs deal with the pro-lifers' charges and tactics? How well does social-learning theory help us understand what they did? Chapter 8 tells what happened.

NOTES

1. The photo used by the Pro-Life Action Council in the 1978 Iowa elections (and by many other pro-life groups thereafter) was part of the Lennart Nilsson series published by *Life* magazine almost a generation ago, showing a living human fetus inside the womb. But it was not always reported as such. Apparently expecting that an antiabortion group would display pictures of an aborted fetus rather than a live one, some reporters and columnists described the photo on the Iowa brochure as that of a dead fetus. The description was probably reinforced by reports of pro-life actions in other states; one national pro-life group did mail several thousand color photos of dismembered aborted fetuses to political activists in at least two states, and these gory pictures had become a frequent feature of the educational slide presentations sponsored by pro-life groups.
2. These statements, unless otherwise identified, come from our interviews with state pro-life leaders, in the study that chapter 6 describes.
3. Quoted in Lisa Cronin Wohl, "Decoding the Election Game Plan of the New Right," *Ms.* 8 (August 1979): 96.
4. A state Equal Rights Amendment was also on the general election ballot. It was defeated.
5. An example can be seen in the Iowa chairman's experience with a special election in California. She had been asked to advise state pro-lifers in their campaign for a congressional candidate. She noted that the resulting leaflet improvised on the Iowa model in some ways. The characteristic admonition to go to the polls, for instance, was modified because the turnout rate in the special election was expected to be higher than Iowa's was in 1978: "We had, at that particular time [in the Iowa leaflet], 'Your vote will count 10.' Well, theirs said, 'Your vote is worth several,' or something like that"—a small change, but characteristic of rule-learning rather than direct imitation.
6. There was no pro-life activity in the Idaho primary. The PAC had not yet formed at that time, and neither Church nor his Republican opponent, U.S. Representative Steve Symms, had a primary challenger.
7. It did, however, send out 1500 copies of a one-page newsletter just before election day. The newsletter announced the PAC's endorsements in other races and contented itself with pointing out that Senator Leahy's voting record was "anti-life," while Ledbetter was at least in favor of the Hyde Amendment.
8. The leafletting strategy did appear, however, and it had been learned observationally. But its use in the general election was by a Christian Right group called Moral Response, which had drawn on the Oregon pro-lifers for advice and information about leafletting at churches.
9. Apparently, IRTL-PAC ran out of money after distributing its summer brochures and "Communicator" inserts. But the Quayle campaign saw the advantages of the abortion issue, as did FaithAmerica, which also leafletted on the issue at churches on the Sunday before election day.
10. The Idaho PAC did not attempt a Voter ID Program, although its leader knew of the program and wished to use it, because of a lack of time and volunteers. In social-learning language, then, she had learned the behavior by observation but had not performed it. Because of similar constraints, the Vermont and Oregon

groups had only begun to set up a Voter ID by the time of the November election. South Dakota's program was only slightly more advanced. The reasons why the Voter ID was slower to diffuse than the church leafletting strategy are discussed later in this chapter.

11. Robert G. Marshall, *Bayonets and Roses: Comprehensive Pro-Life Political Action Guide* (privately published, 1976).

12. Some pro-life groups attribute the biases they see in media coverage to motives more sinister than ignorance. Consider this comment by Mrs. Judie Brown, president of the American Life Lobby, about media treatment of the proposed Human Life Statute (a bill stating that human life begins at conception and abortion is, therefore, prohibited): "Isn't it odd how, all of a sudden, the press is promoting the uncertain concepts like the Human Life Statute while it, at the same time, venomously attacks those leaders in the movement who support the protection of every single human life from the moment of fertilization, without exception?

"Well, ISN'T IT? Of course not! The press always presents only that portion of the issue with which it can carefully mesmerize the public with scare tactics, back-room saloon slogans and 'statistical manipulation.' " See *A.L.L. About Issues* 3 (March 1981): 1.

8. The Senate Campaigns Respond

with Darrell West

> He ran for President once. The television crews came around, then, and the police escorts and the cheering crowds.
> Then he lost. The scent of power vanished as fast as it had come. And now, eight years later, he was back home, walking the streets and shaking the hands and making the small talk, practically alone, a figure out of history trying to win one more chunk of the future.
>
> —Steven V. Roberts, September 1980

With this stark image, a reporter for the *New York Times* described the re-election campaign of Senator George McGovern seven weeks before election day 1980. McGovern's was very much an uphill fight; the prospect of defeat stalked the campaign's every decision. Though McGovern was in deeper trouble than most Senate incumbents, one of the reasons for his campaign's despair—the efforts of pro-life groups to mobilize voters—was also in the minds of other Senate campaigners around the nation.

The abortion issue entered campaign environments in 1980 with a media escort. Television and newspaper reporters questioned candidates about the issue and speculated about the impact of the targeting. Churches, which had long played a role in campaigns in some parts of the country, were now an important force in many other campaigns. As these environmental changes took place, the behavior of Senate campaigners changed also.

Our main characters in this chapter are the people in charge of the six Senate campaigns targeted by pro-life groups in 1980.[1] Where did they derive their expectations about the pro-life challenge and the possible results of the moves they might make? What did they learn, if anything, from the senatorial campaigns targeted by pro-lifers in 1978? How much effort did they make to learn from one another's experiences, as opposed to their own experiences in previous races?

At first glance, these six Senate campaigns seemed to resemble one another in some important ways, a condition that should make them more "available" to one another as potential models. The targeting was a threat they all shared. The tactics used against them by pro-life groups were strikingly similar. Recall from chapter 6 that all the targeted senators were thought to be vulnerable at the polls, and all had aroused the opposition (at least to some degree) of the New Right. Most of the six represented fairly small, predominantly Republican states, though five of the six incumbents were unreconstructed liberal Democrats. And they had these characteristics in common with Dick Clark, the main pro-life target in 1978.

In addition to this possible opportunity for learning from models, these campaigners had a motive to do so. The 1980 race looked as though it might be very different from their last campaign in 1974. The political climate had changed; in 1974, Democrats were helped by Watergate and a discredited Republican President, while in 1980 they had Jimmy Carter like a weight around their necks. Voters were reputed to be more conservative now. There was a profusion of PACs, new laws governing campaign finance, and a new generation of techniques for reaching voters since the senators' last race. The pro-life targeting had not been part of their campaign environments in 1974. Moreover, the attacks they were now facing from pro-life groups, NCPAC, and others were considered unusually harsh; listen to these campaigners:

> Oh, I don't think there's been anything comparable to this. Here's a group [NCPAC] that comes in and isn't even supporting his opponent, [but] just wants to get Bayh.
>
> I think the abortion issue itself and the way it's used in this campaign, the way it's used as a camouflage issue, kind of a shadow issue for the New Right on the East Coast, is a new element for South Dakota.
>
> I've never seen a campaign like this before in Idaho, a campaign where a single group has been attacking one man's integrity for a year and a half, just stabbing away.

These two conditions—threatening changes in the environment and potential models who resemble the campaigners in important ways—should encourage efforts at observational learning. But as we suggested in chapter 6, two other factors should hinder those efforts. For one, while models were available, *successful* models would not be easy to find. Dick Clark lost in 1978; in fact, so did all the senators who were thought to have been pro-life targets that year. And when the 1980 campaigns were being planned, it was not at all clear how the current crop of senatorial targets would fare. In this important respect, the circumstances of the state pro-life groups—with an apparently successful model to follow—differed dramatically from those of their senatorial quarry in 1980.

Besides, there was a big exception to the similarities among the Senate races in 1978 and 1980. In contrast to the pro-life groups, which shared a singleminded focus on the abortion issue and held the same position on that issue, the six senatorial campaigns (and others that might be potential models for them) had to respond to a large number of issues, from balanced budgets to bombers. The senators differed in their stands on many of these issues; in particular, they did not all take the same position on the question of abortion.[2] These differences should limit a campaigner's confidence that the experiences of the other targeted Senate campaigns would also be relevant to him or her.

The alternative to learning from models would be to generalize from their own previous experience. And in each campaign, that experience was extensive. The six Senate incumbents and most of their top staff members had each been involved with campaigns, controversial issues, and hostile groups throughout their adult lives; unlike many of the pro-life leaders, they were steeped in responses to political situations.

The problem was that the situation in 1980 had some new elements. If their opportunities for modeling were limited, would these campaigners' past experience be applicable enough to give them the basis of an approach to their current dilemma? Would they be able to get enough information to help them fine-tune that approach successfully? Or would they be left acting out the scenes of an old play, unable to be sure whether the 1980 audience would approve? To answer those questions, we must start the story while the 1980 races were still very young, just after election day 1978.

THE SENATE CAMPAIGNERS: EARLY DAYS

November 1978 was not a pleasant month for the six Senate incumbents and their top staffers. Dick Clark's defeat and those of Democrats Tom McIntyre of New Hampshire and Floyd Haskell of Colorado came as chilling news. The three incumbents should not have lost, according to the polls, but they *did* lose. And the abortion issue kept turning up in postelection analyses. Pro-lifers had made a difference, many commentators said; in particular, the targeting had hurt liberal Democrats.

No sooner had the bad news sunk in than Paul Brown of LAPAC called on media representatives, announcing the names of his six Senate targets for 1980. Had pro-life groups really taken away Clark's lead in 1978? Could they do so again in other states? The Senate campaigners could not be sure. But without a doubt, Brown's target list, which might have attracted little attention in those Senate offices in October 1978, was not so easily dismissed in late November.

The response was prompt; representatives of the five Democratic targets joined with colleagues to open a channel for observational learning. In December 1978, on the heels of Brown's "hit list" announcement, the Democratic Senatorial Campaign Committee (DSCC) in Washington convened a discussion group of aides to Democratic senators up for reelection in 1980. Out of this group developed a smaller seminar, meeting every ten days to two weeks to share ideas about dealing with single-issue influence in the 1980 campaigns. Regular members of this group were aides to Senators Bayh, Church, Culver, Leahy, and McGovern. Staffers of other Democratic senators worried about single-issue targeting, such as Gaylord Nelson of Wisconsin and John Durkin of New Hampshire, also took part.

The start of these informal meetings was just what we would have expected, given the learning approach. They were prompted by a threatening change in the campaign environment. They were designed to develop some potentially effective models for responding to the pro-life targeting and other single-issue attacks. As one of the group's charter members explained its origins, "Well, I think everyone had a jolt, after the McIntyre and Clark loss, and everyone felt very threatened and felt the need to get together and discuss various approaches and this kind of thing." A DSCC consultant added, "It was designed primarily to give political advisers to people running in 1980 a chance to exchange war stories, and to figure out whether something that was happening to them might also be happening to somebody else, and whether they could learn from other people's experiences."

Note that in this search for models, the campaigners were drawn to people who were similar to themselves in important respects. The participants all shared the same party affiliation and all faced single-issue opposition. No effort was made to include the one targeted *Republican* on the LAPAC list, Bob Packwood, nor did he try to become a part of this learning network.[3] Though a number of House members also expected trouble from single-issue groups, the meetings never expanded beyond Senate campaigners. And no Senate *challengers* were part of the group; only Senate incumbents. It was, in the words of a McGovern aide, "an opportunity for people under like challenge to sit down and talk informally about the problems they were facing and how they were responding." The potential models discussed at these meetings, in addition to the participants themselves, were other "people under like challenge": Clark, McIntyre, and other Democratic senators who had faced single-issue attacks in 1978.

Note, too, the importance of availability in this search for models. The frequent contacts among Senate staffers on the Hill—channels of communication that were already established and functioning for many other purposes—became a natural channel for observational learning. Although campaign staffers located in the various states might have been equally interested in getting together to talk about models, they didn't do so; there were no existing communication channels to link them to one another. So the only contacts among the state campaign staffs occurred when the Washington Senate aides, who had shared campaign information in the Hill meetings since December 1978, stayed in touch with one another when they moved back to their states for the fall campaign.[4]

WHAT WAS LEARNED IN THE "HILL MEETINGS"?

Discussions in the Hill meetings began with the events that had prompted them: the defeats of Senators Clark and McIntyre. Their aim, many participants said, was to explore what had happened in the 1978 races in order to derive expectations about what was to come in 1980. One aide said, "Certainly the McIntyre and Clark races were looked at very carefully. There was the feeling that here were two people who, in a normal year, should have been reelected, and why weren't they?"

The participants investigated that question with vigor, in the hope that Democratic Senate campaigners in 1982 and 1984 would not be asking the same question about *them*. They talked with Clark and former members of his and McIntyre's campaign staffs. Several participants read McIntyre's just-published book (*The Fear Brokers*, 1979) about his confrontations with the New Right and the pro-lifers; aides to Senators Bayh, Church, and Culver all reported that this "symbolic model" had affected their expectations about the 1980 race.

They drew a number of conclusions about the forces that brought Clark and McIntyre down. The shared feeling about McIntyre's race was that he had not taken the single-issue challenge seriously enough nor begun campaigning soon enough. One 1980 campaigner distills the consensus this way:

> Well, McIntyre's defeat was laid, I think in part, on Mr. McIntyre's belief that he was not really in trouble up there. It was only when they were ten days to two weeks out [from election day], and their opponent started using Boston TV (which was unprecedented in New Hampshire politics at that time), that he sensed he was in trouble, and by that time it was too late to put it back together.

Clark had the same problem, they believed; the polls had been showing a strong Clark lead, and his staff did not get a sufficiently early warning that their boss was in electoral trouble. Another shared explanation for Clark's loss was that the Democratic turnout in Iowa had been low in 1978; that gave single-issue groups a perfect opportunity to affect the election results by turning out in force. Had the Clark campaign placed more emphasis on voter turnout, the Hill meeting group agreed, he might have won.

Further, they drew some lessons that could be applied to their own campaigns in 1980. The low turnout in traditionally Democratic constituencies had been a problem in 1978, they concluded, and would likely be a problem in 1980. They all felt that McIntyre had been caught napping in 1978 and concluded that the single-issue problem would have to be addressed much earlier in their own 1980 races. Their observational learning had given them motivation as well; they had been prompted to use their learning in order to avoid sharing Clark's and McIntyre's fate.

THE DISADVANTAGES OF "NEGATIVE MODELS"

Chapter 2 drew the distinction between *learning* a model's behavior—forming ideas in one's mind as to how that behavior works—and *performing* a model's behavior. People normally *learn* many more behaviors and strategies than they actually *use*. We saw in the last chapter that much of the behavior pro-life leaders learned from the Iowa model was in fact put to work in their own states' races. The strategy that was learned but not fully used—the Voter Identification Program—was simply too costly for several of the state pro-life groups.

The Senate campaigners had a very different problem. The disadvantage of Clark's and McIntyre's strategies was not that they were too costly but that they were followed by defeat on election day. Studying those strategies left a vital question unanswered or answered only in a general way: What changes could Clark and McIntyre have made to turn their races around? What *would* have worked? The pro-life groups in 1980, following an apparently successful model, needed only to apply that model's behaviors. The Senate campaigners, seeking but not finding a winning model, had a harder time putting their observational learning to use.

A good example is the campaigners' conclusion that Clark and McIntyre had underestimated the danger of their situation in 1978. One reason, the Hill meetings suggested, was that the polls had not shown either to be in any trouble. A McGovern staffer pointed out that "in fact, when [pollster Pat] Caddell took a postelection poll [in New Hampshire in 1978], it showed that McIntyre had won! So McIntyre believed his polls, and did not work as hard as he wished he'd had. And I heard the same thing in regard to Dick Clark." On the abortion issue in particular, staffers felt that polls had consistently underestimated pro-life strength. As a Bayh aide stated, "In the campaigns of 1978, the poll data never showed how well [pro-life groups] would do."

That sounds like a valuable lesson. But how could the 1980 Senate campaigners put it to use? If they could not trust the polls to measure how well (or how poorly) they were doing against the targeting, what *could* they trust? The 1978 races did not seem to provide any answers. Several possible alternatives were considered in the Hill meetings: asking ministers and pastors about the strength of pro-life support in their congregations, establishing "contact people" in church congregations across the state to relay warnings of pro-life organizing activity, employing religious leaders to travel from one church to another to get a reading on the extent of pro-life backing. These were plausible alternatives, and they were each used by one or two of the campaign organizations. But they did not diffuse more widely for one simple reason: there was no clear evidence—yet—whether they would prove more effective than the polls had in 1978.

Another example involves the handling of the opposition. The Hill meeting participants generally agreed that single-issue groups had kept their targets on the defensive in 1978. Not only was that an uncomfortable position for a candidate but it inflicted serious damage as well; with the incumbent off balance, reeling under the vitriolic attacks of NCPAC and others, there was no one to remind the voters that this was a two-candidate race, that the incumbent's opponent had a record too. In more placid circumstances, incumbents usually prefer to ignore their opponents on the assumption that attacks on the challenger simply provide him or her with free publicity. But the consensus in the Hill meetings was that to ignore the opponent in 1980 was political suicide; it would enable single-issue groups to do even more harm by focusing attention on their caricature of the incumbent.

One campaign that took this lesson particularly to heart was that of Frank Church. Here is the reasoning of his staff, as expressed by a top aide, on responding to single-issue attacks:

> It is clear on the face of it that these [single-issue] groups have one common objective. That is, and they are very open about it, you make Frank Church the issue. Then, pretty soon, we're playing their game. And we're *not* going to play their game. Their game is that they say all the nasty things and Steve Symms [Church's opponent] says all the nice things, and runs the high road. And ergo, we're constantly on the defensive. That's what happened to Haskell; that's what happened to McIntyre.
>
> So, you know, our campaign will concentrate on Symms. Symms has a record, or the lack thereof, and is vulnerable. And our strategy is to keep our eyes on the idea that while we're not going to let these groups get away with distortions without correcting the record, at the same time we are not going to allow ourselves to become the issue. Steve Symms is the issue.

It is a reasonable inference. If single-issue attacks drew blood in 1978 because they put the senator on the defensive, then in 1980 the senator must not be put on the defensive. But again, the negative model does not tell *how* the learner should avoid being put on the defensive. The Church campaign inferred that the senator would have to go on the attack and lay bare his opponent's weaknesses. It was not the senator's customary campaign style. If one of the single-issue targets in 1978 had followed that aggressive approach and won, then his colleagues in 1980 might have built on this strategy with a certain amount of confidence. But that was not the case. Even for an experienced campaigner such as Frank Church, a new campaign style, in the absence of a successful model, would inevitably pose some risk.

LEARNING ABOUT THE PRO-LIFERS

If the Hill meeting discussions—eager as their participants were to learn—were inconclusive on how to respond effectively to single-issue targeting, they were even more inconclusive on the matter of responding to *pro-life* activities. The 1978 Iowa race was studied and debated. Numerous approaches were suggested. Each seemed to have serious flaws.

Frank Church's intention to go on the offensive, to make his opponent the issue, seemed hazardous when applied to the pro-lifers. The senator's opponent might often be on the attack, and NCPAC would surely be on the attack often, but the pro-life groups had been quiet through much of the 1978 campaigns. They made provocative public statements only through their church leafletting and perhaps an occasional media interview. To attack the pro-lifers when they were remaining quiet might seem unfair, particularly because antiabortion groups were frequently led by women and stressed their concern with saving babies. Even worse, to attack the opponent's pro-life voting record could backfire; it could activate people inclined toward the pro-life position but not aware that their senator held a different view.

Several Senate aides wondered whether they could "neutralize" pro-life support by getting at least as many pro-choice voters to the polls. One aide reports the results of those discussions:

> Well, there was great hope that the pro-choice people could be activated politically. The polling that was done seemed to indicate that the pro-choice people, however, were people who were interested in a variety of issues, and would *not* vote for a candidate specifically on the pro-choice position, whereas the right-to-life people were very singleminded and would vote by and large on that issue, and that issue alone.
>
> There was all kinds of discussion as to how to provoke the pro-choice people into a more activist role, and to make them as effective as the right-to-life people were, politically. And that issue, of course, was never really resolved.

It was an unhappy dilemma. Pro-choice people, the pollsters said, were more likely to be Republicans than Democrats. In a primary election, then, most of the pro-choice voters would be no help to a Democratic incumbent. In the general election, these pro-choice people were not singleminded enough to cross party lines and vote for a targeted Democrat. But pro-life supporters, who were

The Senate Campaigns Respond 221

thought to be mainly Democrats, *would* cross over and vote for a pro-life Republican. The targeted Democrats would lose both ways.

The Hill meetings at least provided information about the pro-life groups' activities in 1978, which became the basis for campaigners' expectations about what they would face in 1980. Consider the comments of a Culver staff member as to what pro-lifers were likely to do in 1980, clearly drawn from his knowledge of the Clark campaign in 1978: "They usually concentrate on intensive activities the last week of the campaign, even the last couple of days. In the past, in Iowa, on Sunday they've tried to leaflet churches and so forth, and that's kind of their big push." A McGovern aide's expectations were more picturesque: "I assume they are following their traditional pattern of laying low until the last ten days to two weeks, and then come storming out of their church basements on the attack, with leaflets and direct mail and melodramatic pictures and that kind of thing."

In short, the five targeted Democratic campaigns, and others who might be potential models for them, responded to the pro-life challenge by opening an avenue for observational learning. They were eager for information about the challenge and examples of effective ways to deal with it. Their meetings supplied some information. They studied what happened in the 1978 Clark and McIntyre races, talked with pollsters and other consultants, and pieced together a picture of the pro-life strategy; from that picture, they drew expectations about what the pro-lifers might do in their own 1980 campaigns.

But on the subject of the most effective responses to the pro-life targeting, the Hill meetings had a lot of ideas but almost no answers. Clark and McIntyre had tried to beat the targeting, but both lost; therefore, it was easy to assume that their approach to the pro-life challenge had failed. There were no successful models in sight. Since the *performance* of a modeled strategy depends mainly on that strategy's "functional value"—whether it seems to work—we have reason to suspect that the 1980 senatorial campaigners might not be able to make much use of all this observational learning when their races began.

TRYING TO LEARN FROM A NEGATIVE MODEL:
THE CASE OF JOHN CULVER

Similarity between the model and the observer, the theory says, improves the chances for observational learning. In one campaign in our study the environment bore a striking resemblance to one of the 1978 models. John Culver, as we pointed out, was running in the same state as Dick Clark had, under the same party label, against an opponent whose ideological orientation was similar to Clark's opponent, and against the same pro-life group that had been active in the Clark race. The theory would predict that Culver's campaign would learn more from the Clark race than would any of the other 1980 campaigns. And that is what happened.

One writer said of the Culver campaign that "the political landscape in this Senate contest has been shaped largely by the results of the 1978 race."[5] Our interviews with Culver staff members and others brought out a number of important ways in which this held true. The interviews also underlined the biggest problem of these targeted Democrats: the difficulty of applying what they had learned from a "negative model."

Clark and others targeted in 1978, the Hill group agreed, were complacent about the danger; they did not gear up soon enough. That point had immediate effect on the Culver staff. "I think to a certain extent the Clark defeat put us on notice about how tough it was," said a top Democrat in Iowa. "If there were any illusions about that, they were removed. When I signed on with the campaign, I guess my perception of the odds were less than 50-50 that we would win. I thought we were underdogs. And perhaps I would not have thought that if it were not for the Clark experience."

So Clark's loss put Culver's people on alert. The areas on which they focused their attention, after being thus alarmed, reflected the explanation they had constructed for Clark's defeat. One of those areas was voter turnout. The belief that Clark was hurt because traditionally Democratic groups did not turn out in large numbers—and that the Democratic party and organized labor had not done enough to increase the turnout—guided Culver's campaign efforts. "We were very conscious of the fact that there were substantial Democratic defections in the Clark race," a top aide stated. "And we tried very early on to pound them back in shape. That meant, at least early in the campaign, spending more time and having more concentration on Democratic constituencies than might have been the case otherwise. So Step One was to consolidate our base. And I think that was in reaction to the Clark race."

Labor union members were approached aggressively, through pro-Culver union leaders and letters from the senator himself, with fervent appeals for action. The campaign warned frequently and forcefully about the strength of the New Right—what Culver termed "the hate factories of the East"—in order to encourage liberals to vote. And like many other liberal Democrats, Culver argued that independent presidential candidate John Anderson ought to be included on the general election ballot, a move that President Carter's forces were trying urgently to prevent. Culver and others feared that many liberals, faced with a choice between Carter and Reagan, would stay home in disgust. With Anderson on the ballot, those liberals might have an incentive to go to the polls—and would probably vote for Culver as well.

Another of the accepted explanations for Clark's loss was that he had been too apologetic about his Senate voting record. He seemed to backpedal during the campaign, observers said; he tried to downplay his liberalism in order to improve his election chances. In the words of a top Democrat in Iowa, "People felt that Dick Clark danced around the issues a bit." He added,

> I think that might have been unfair. I think they felt he danced around issues because he's an urbane person and he uses precise language. But I think that for whatever reasons, in contrast to that, John [Culver] had a reputation for slugging it out head-on: a brass knuckles kind of guy. I think that contrast was there. I guess I was aware of that contrast, and thought that it might be beneficial [to Culver's chances].

Culver's "brass knuckles" approach to issues, his aggressive defense of liberal principles, was certainly consistent with his approach to serving in the Senate and with his actions in previous campaigns.[6] An aide explained:

> He is not the kind of person who sits down and reads the polls to find out what the people want to hear, and then crafts his views on that basis. He has very strong beliefs on things like arms control and economic policy. And he articulates them in as strong a fashion as he can. He might think about methods of communication, about what methods can best get his point across. But he really speaks what's on his mind, and he believes that's good politics.

It is entirely possible, then, that John Culver would have run as a "defiant liberal" in 1980 no matter what had happened to Dick Clark in 1978. But it was clear to insiders and reporters that Clark's loss strengthened the Culver campaign's predisposition to "come on strong." A top aide suggests that "the Clark experience reinforced some attitudes that John Culver had about politics." A political reporter confirms:

> [Culver's approach] is a more high-profile strategy. You know, stand up there and stick out your jaw and say, "Here's where I stand, by God, and if you don't like it, well, go out and vote for that other son-of-a-bitch."
>
> [*Question:* Why do you think he does that?]
>
> Well, I think *because* of what Clark did. It's the view among most politicians in this state that Dick Clark in 1978 ran from his record. . . . I think there are quite a few Democrats who are saying "By God, Dick Clark screwed up, and John Culver: you'd better not run from your record; you ought to stand up there and defend it."

Culver's staffers also drew on the Clark race in their decision to set up a heavy schedule of personal appearances by the candidate, rather than rely on media advertising alone. A top Democrat in Iowa recounts:

The Clark campaign was seen by party activists as being comparatively laid back, low-key. They didn't do aggressive scheduling and so forth. Clark was very TV-oriented. I mean, the campaign operation was basically to raise money and spend it on TV and radio. TV is good, but you don't get the same *intensity* of contact. You reach masses of people, but it's not the same as coming to some small town and going to a coffee with 50 people and really impressing the socks off somebody down there, who then spreads it all around the community.

And so we made a very real effort to contrast the Culver campaign with that, to stir up the troops, because we were trying to build a stronger organization than they did in 1978. We were trying to do a more balanced campaign in order to generate that organizational enthusiasm. In our view, there was no substitute for candidate activity.

And so we ran awfully aggressive schedules, meaning all kinds of events, long hours, small towns. We scheduled more appearances than Clark did, certainly, and . . . God, for a year, [Culver] was out here every weekend, tearin' across the state. I think it's fair to say that the Clark schedule involved a much higher concentration on large cities and airport press conferences—the media centers. We tried to reach out more.

He concludes, "That was a clear reaction, I think, to the Clark campaign."

Culver's staff also drew one lesson from Clark's experience with the abortion issue. Both senators' staffs saw abortion as primarily a "Catholic issue."[7] Clark had tried to soft-pedal media coverage of the issue by not campaigning in heavily Catholic areas of the state. Culver, on the other hand, campaigned extensively in predominantly Catholic counties and urged Catholic leaders to speak on his behalf. An Iowa reporter recalls:

Culver had some literature on that, and ads which he bought in Catholic papers that talked about how, on the 17 issues most important to the National Conference of Catholic Bishops, he voted right on 16 of them. The only one he *didn't* vote right on, with them, was the Human Life Amendment. And Grassley voted wrong on 12, right on one, and they didn't know where he was on four.

His top aides did not expect to convert what they called "hard core" pro-lifers with these messages. But they reasoned that a direct appeal to Catholic voters might give "soft core" pro-lifers, whose attitudes toward abortion might not dictate their choice of candidates, some reasons to vote for Culver despite his pro-choice stand.

In all these instances of learning, we can see signs of the explanation constructed for Clark's defeat. In reality, there may have been many reasons why Clark lost: his positions on foreign policy, his style of self-presentation, the state of the agricultural economy. But right after election day, activists and reporters judged other causes to be more important; Clark lost, they argued, because his campaign was not aggressive enough, not concerned enough with voter turnout, not straightforward enough about his record, and not effective enough in dealing with the pro-life targeting. Those shared judgments came to guide what Culver and his staffers learned from the 1978 race.

Culver's campaign, of the six targeted by pro-lifers in 1980, shows the most extensive influence of the Clark model. Packwood's campaign, on the other hand—the race whose characteristics and environment differ the most from Clark's—made no discernible effort to learn from the experiences of either Clark or McIntyre, or indeed from any Democratic model. These patterns support the hypothesis that similarity between model and observer is a key determinant of the choice of models. But success, the other key determinant, was not to be had here, and its absence made the learning situation difficult for the Culver staffers. A top member of that staff commented wistfully, after election day, "but in terms of any model of who best handled this thing, I don't think there was one."

LEARNING FROM OTHER 1980 TARGETS

In addition to the 1978 races, the six targeted campaigns could look to one another as possible models. The experiences of one campaign could help the others anticipate what might be coming; observing the results of one campaign's strategies could teach others some new ways to handle the pro-lifers.

Again, participants in the Hill meetings *tried* to learn from one another. Especially as the primary season drew nearer, they discussed one another's situations and strategies. An organizer of the meetings reports that a typical session was filled with comments like these:

> "This is what's happening [in our race] and this is what we're doing about it, and what do you think? What are *you* guys doing about it?" We talked about their advertising strategies; how they used the media consultants they selected and how they were getting along with them; how satisfied or dissatisfied they were with the product they were getting.
> We talked a lot about the New Right and how they were dealing with it. We talked a little bit about labor's role in assisting them; we had a representative of organized labor at one of the meetings, as I recall, to talk about what labor might be able to do for candidates in 1980.

In particular, they exchanged materials being used against them, including pro-life leaflets distributed in several primaries. A McGovern aide remarked, wryly:

> The camaraderie of despair is always beneficial, I guess. I would say, "My God, this is what they've done to us," and somebody else would say, "Well, yes, they're doing that in our state too," and then we discovered that because media were so cheap in South Dakota, relatively speaking, NCPAC and some of these other groups

would come out and try out their spots and their materials in South Dakota, to see how they went over; and if they went over well, they'd go into other states where the media were more expensive. So we were sort of serving as the off-Broadway of the media in South Dakota, and then we could alert others that it was coming, and in some instances I think they were able to take corrective steps ahead of time.

Understandably, the McGovern staff did not enjoy the distinction of serving as "the off-Broadway of the media," but their experience was very instructive for other targeted Democrats. In particular, it forewarned other campaigns that the church leafletting strategy was still in use. Consider the remarks of this Bayh aide:

We anticipate that they will act similarly [in Indiana] to what they did against George McGovern in the primary election a month ago. There, the Sunday before the primary, in a number of Catholic parishes throughout the state, they distributed pictures of dead fetuses on one side and George McGovern on the other, with an "X" across the picture, calling him a murderer. . . .

Bayh's aide was not speaking from his own experience, as his somewhat inaccurate description of the leaflet indicates.[8] He was drawing on what had been learned in the Hill meetings and from newspapers. This observational learning was very helpful to him; it let him develop expectations as to what the pro-lifers might have in store for Indiana. That, in turn, was the vital first step in his choice of responses to the targeting.

The Senate campaigners used one another as models in other ways. Several of the Democratic campaigns followed one another into legal action against the excesses of some pro-life and New Right groups.[9] All five Democratic campaigns, after debating Dick Clark's strategy of targeting messages to Catholics, found ways to do so in their own states; typically, these were ads in Catholic newspapers signed by prominent Catholics, stressing the senator's concern for the social justice and humanitarian programs favored by the Catholic leadership. These were cases in which campaigners not only formed ideas about the behavior of other targeted Senate races but actually *acted on* that learning.

But these cases were not very common, especially when compared with the pro-life groups, whose strategies in 1980 had almost invariably been borrowed from models. The Senate campaigners were much less likely to adopt the strategies learned from one another, even in responding to the blow they all expected to face: church leafletting. It was not for lack of trying. It was because some important problems, typical of the learning environment of campaigns, held them back.

One of the most important is that while a campaign is in progress, it is hard to find clear-cut indicators of a model's "success" with a particular strategy. The election result is not yet known. Even if poll data are available, they are not always specific enough to gauge the results of, say, a decision to attack the pro-life targeting rather than ignore it. Fund raising is an exception; the amount of money raised by a particular direct-mail appeal *is* a clear-cut measure of its success. But as a learning device, even the response to a fund-raising technique has its drawbacks.

Take the example of Bob Packwood's campaign strategy. It is one of the very few instances in which these 1980 campaigners had a successful model available. But information about that successful model came too late.

Chapter 6 pointed out that early in 1979, Packwood's campaign staff made a clever choice. Their boss was electorally vulnerable. He would have much less to worry about, obviously, if it were possible to discourage any potentially strong opponent from entering the race. To do that, they would have to make it appear that Packwood was much stronger than observers judged him to be, that anyone who was thinking about challenging him should expect a very tough and very costly campaign. Without election results to create this impression, and with poll data to the contrary, money was the answer. If Packwood's campaign was able to raise a massive amount of money by the time potential opponents were deciding whether to run, the most attractive prospects would try their luck elsewhere. The real challenge would be over before the active campaign had even begun.[10]

Packwood had long been a strong proponent of women's rights. He and his staff, as well as others, had come to feel that a feminist constituency was developing across the nation, ready to be mobilized. So the campaign designed a letter to be signed by pro-choice and feminist leader Gloria Steinem, warning that "Bob Packwood is in danger of drowning in a virtual sea of 'right-to-life' money and zealots." The Steinem letter was classic direct mail: it raised the specter of a dramatic threat and it was targeted to members of groups (pro-choice, feminist, civil libertarian) thought to be most sensitive to that threat.

It succeeded beyond even the campaign's expectations. By the summer of 1980, the Steinem letter had reportedly brought in over half a million dollars in contributions, and had motivated a whole raft of volunteers to staff campaign offices for Packwood around the state of Oregon. Reports of its success had the hoped-for effect: no strong Republican campaigner chose to oppose Packwood in the primary, and a series of prominent Democrats declined to run against him in November.

This kind of strategy is exactly the sort that would be expected to diffuse from one campaign to another. A fund-raising letter is easy to transmit and to understand. It falls within a class of behaviors familiar to campaigners. Its results are clear and tangible; its success can easily be measured and reported in the universal language of dollars. Few other campaign strategies are linked so clearly and so individually with a set of results.

There is good evidence that Packwood's use of the Steinem letter served as a model for other targeted 1980 campaigns. Later, both the McGovern and Culver organizations sent out fund-raising letters to feminists and pro-choice supporters, signed by another pro-choice leader, Karen Mulhauser, then head of the National Abortion Rights Action League. Of course fund-raising letters are sent out in droves by major campaigns, and a skeptic might argue that McGovern and Culver did not model Packwood's strategy, but responded independently to the same circumstances.

But the signs all point to observational learning. First, the Packwood strategy was widely reported in political circles because of its stunning results; indeed, the Packwood campaign encouraged the spread of that information, since it might enhance their efforts to scare off any remaining challengers. Culver aides remembered reading about the Steinem letter in a political newsletter by consultant Alan Baron.

Another channel for observational learning was available to Culver's and McGovern's staffs: they and Packwood shared the same direct-mail fund-raising specialist.[11] When asked about the origins of the Mulhauser letter, a top Culver aide said, "I was aware of the Packwood letter; that was one of the factors [in our decision]." When asked why, he answered, "We were aware that these letters had been successful."

Unhappily for the McGovern and Culver campaigns, however, it took time to learn whether the Steinem letter had worked for Packwood. The delay was costly. By the time the effectiveness of the strategy had become clear, it was too late for McGovern and Culver to achieve Packwood's goal: to raise enough early money to drive away any strong challengers. If Packwood had been part of the Hill meeting group, the other targeted campaigns might have been alerted when the Steinem letter was first mailed, and might have picked up indications of its success early enough to try it soon afterward. But Packwood was not part of that group; the communication channels through which ideas were spread early in the campaign (and, to a great extent, later in the race as well) did not usually cross party lines.

In short, it was difficult for the Senate campaigners to *act* on strategies learned from other 1980 campaigns because, in most cases, the consequences of those strategies were not yet known. The incentive for performing a model's behavior, which is normally provided by knowing that the behavior brought good results for others, was not present here. It was hard to know whether a particular strategy used in another campaign would improve the senator's chances or would make things even worse.

Consider the predicament of one of these targeted races when its polls showed that the senator's support was dropping, a situation that should encourage the campaign's attention to models:[12]

> When McGovern was getting tough, out in South Dakota, we had a sense that, you know, maybe we're doing the wrong thing; people were saying that McGovern was coming back; well, maybe *we* should get tough. But that was never anything that we sat down and talked about as a group to reach a strategy decision on. I think it probably ate at everybody individually, worried us a little bit, thinking that we'd done the wrong thing. But we never got to the point where we considered changing our strategy.

Why didn't this campaign "get tough" when they saw McGovern doing so and suspected that he might be on to something? Because they had no clear evidence that the strategy was working for McGovern, or that it *would* work. The election was weeks away. Public opinion polls on the McGovern-Abdnor race were reported occasionally in the media, but campaigners in other races had learned from the Clark and McIntyre defeats that polls could not always be trusted. Besides, most of these campaigners knew that poll results are political tools; most polls are commissioned by campaigns themselves or by groups with a stake in the outcome of the race, and these groups are likely to make public only those poll data that suit their purpose. So the campaign manager quoted above could only measure the effectiveness of McGovern's change in strategy by "what people were saying." That was not enough to motivate him to act on what he had learned from McGovern.

PROFESSIONAL CONSULTANTS: OTHER SOURCES OF MODELS

As the story of the Steinem letter shows, campaigners can also learn about new strategies through the consultants they hire. Much of the information that consultants provide comes from their experience with other campaigns. Frequently, a consultant will have several clients in any one election year. In 1980, for example, Peter D. Hart did polling for Church, Culver, and Leahy. He also worked on other races that resembled those of the pro-life targets in some ways. The range of possible models is further expanded by the fact that consulting firms often share information with one another, at least with other consultants who work for the same party's campaigns. Candidates who hire them can get access to a fairly large communication network, including not only the other races that their own consultants are working on but also the campaigns that other consultants are handling.

Gaining access to that wider network of models and information is a major reason why campaigners hire consultants. All six targeted campaigns in 1980 made extensive use of professional consultants, often contracting with six or seven specialists in various areas of electioneering, and each campaigner mentioned the advantage of learning what other comparable races were doing. Especially as the campaign wore on and staff members became increasingly preoccupied with their own races, there were fewer and fewer *direct* contacts among campaigns. At that point, consultants became the main channel through which the six targets learned about one another's actions and their possible impact.

But the consultants did more than that; most tried to offer some recommendations of their own with respect to single-issue challenges. In relation to the pro-life targeting, most of these specialists counseled caution. Rarely was any of the campaigns advised to attack the abortion issue head-on. The arguments were familiar: the issue was not important to most voters, or even to most pro-choice voters, and aggressive discussion would only make the pro-lifers work harder. Attack the New Right head-on, many consultants advised, because that will help liberal candidates raise money. But deal with the abortion issue through personal contact rather than media and speeches: approach "soft core" pro-lifers through people they know and respect, such as pastors and lay leaders; inform them of the senator's stands on other "life issues" such as poverty and social justice, and convince them the senator is a moral man.

Yet, as sources of observational learning, the consultants foundered on the same rocks as the campaigners did: they had no successful model either. As one prominent pollster expressed it:

> When you come to the abortion issue, to my knowledge there was no single idea [on how to deal with it]. I mean, I wasn't involved with [two of the targeted races], but I was getting total information on everything that those people were doing, and what they felt was working—and I didn't get any great messages that they were doing something unique or special in terms of abortion. I just think everybody was "doing their own thing."

They were "doing their own thing," of course, because they had no assurance that anybody else's "thing" was any more likely to work. So, despite all the advice given, no single strategy or set of strategies diffused across all the targeted campaigns as an effective response to the targeting.

OTHER LIMITS ON THE USE OF MODELED BEHAVIORS

A lack of successful models was a real problem for the targeted campaigners. Other factors also limited their ability to take full advantage of modeling—factors the state pro-life groups did not face, or faced to a lesser extent. Some of these factors were especially prominent in the 1980 political environment. Others are endemic to the nature of campaigning as a learning situation.

Time and channel constraints. Recall that in these 1980 races, the most intensive efforts at observational learning took place in the Hill meetings, among Senate staff members whose channels of communication were already well established. But as the summer of 1980 ended, most of these staffers began spending much of their time in their states, to help run the active phase of the campaigns. As the participants scattered, the Hill meetings came to a close, and so did the frequent contact among the Democratic campaigns. There were occasional phone calls from one staffer to his or her counterpart in another campaign. But there was no systematic effort to continue the conversations because there were no already established channels of communication linking state campaign staffs with one another.

Efforts to set up such channels fell victim to time pressures; in their active phase, campaigns usually run at a pace that prevents much reflective thought. One staff member reported that she had tried to set up telephone contact with the other targeted Democratic campaigns but that "after our initial round of contacts, there always seemed to be too much to do to spend much time calling around to see what everybody else was doing." Another agreed:

> We often talked from time to time about—why don't we find out how other people have responded to the issue? But you know, you never have the time to do that. So you end up just going with your own—which is probably the best way to do it.

The pro-life leaders were in different states too. But they had an important advantage: continuing communication channels and less time pressure. National pro-life groups continued to monitor the six targeted Senate races through election day, and to convey information and ideas to the various state groups. The state pro-life organizations did not move away from their established communication networks when the active phase of the campaign began; rather, they were able to call upon those networks even more. And they did not have to develop strategy in the midst of the noisy confusion of a candidate's organization, while making daily or hourly decisions about various issue appeals, scheduling, and tactics. The pro-lifers had a more narrowly focused agenda, dealing solely with the abortion issue. They could devote more time and attention to learning a modeled strategy.

A sense of uniqueness. Another factor limiting campaigners' use of modeled behaviors was the sense, widespread among campaigns, that their race was unique (no matter how similar to other races it appeared to be). When asked which other targeted races were similar to theirs, staffers typically responded:

> I think they are all very different. The constituency is different. You know, every campaign is unique. (Culver staff)

> Every race is different. Every voting population is different. (Bayh staff)
>
> It's my philosophy as campaign manager that every campaign is unique, and that you have to be *very* careful about making comparisons. (Packwood staff)

Surely these campaigns differed from one another in many ways. But with the exception of the Packwood race, they also had many important characteristics in common. Their exaggerated sense of difference may result from the extraordinary degree of personal involvement required when running a campaign; that involvement draws campaigners closer to other members of their staffs, but may sharpen their sense of distance from outsiders—even in other campaigns. And the tremendous pressure of the fall campaign, combined with the very limited contact among the staffs of various candidates, may reduce their attention to the similarities among their situations. One direct-mail specialist described campaigners as "too insulated and too proud" to talk freely with one another and recognize their similarities. To the extent that this sense of uniqueness prevents them from seeing the resemblances between potential models and themselves, it reduces their incentive to adopt a model's behavior.

Again, this constraint did not seem to affect the pro-life groups as much. When asked about their similarities with other states' groups, the answer was always the same: "well, they're pro-life too." The singlemindedness of the pro-life cause rose above all state boundaries and other political affiliations. It bound them together in a way that the Senate campaigners, buffeted by dozens of different issues and group demands, could never be.

Uncertainty about what works. The final constraint is the uncertainty of campaigning—the difficulty of learning, while a campaign is in progress, which strategies will prove effective and which will not. The most prominent reinforcer, we have said, is the election result; it acts like a blunt instrument, giving a winner's strategies the stamp of apparent effectiveness and a loser's actions the stamp of failure. That is why past election victory is so important in people's choice of models. The choices made by a winning campaign carry the promise of effectiveness to an extent that other strategies—with the exception of fund-raising techniques that bring in impressive sums of money—do not.

The existence of a winning campaign among the many potential models—a comparable candidate who won the last election or the most recent primary—helps reduce the uncertainty about the link between action and outcome in a campaign. The pro-lifers in 1980 had just such a model; the uncertainty of their environment was reduced by the apparent success of the Iowa Pro-Life Action Council in 1978. The Senate campaigners had none. Uncertainty is always a part of campaigning; but when the uncertainty is relieved only by "negative models," campaigns that tried several approaches and lost, it will be more difficult for campaigners to base their strategy decisions on observational learning.

The Big Strategic Decision: What to Do About the Church Leafletting

We have seen that all five Democratic campaigns tried hard to learn from comparable races in 1978 and from one another's experiences in 1980, even to the extent of getting together every ten days or two weeks for a full 21 months in order to share information. But in sharp contrast with the state pro-life groups, this extensive observational learning was not often put to use.

The best illustration of the Senate campaigners' learning predicament—a changed and threatening environment, but no successful models to follow—was their efforts to deal with the pro-life church leafletting. All six campaigns expected to be leafletted on the Sunday before election day. At several Hill meetings, representatives of the five Democratic campaigns had talked at length about possible ways to respond to the leafletting or head off its impact. But when the leafletting came, no single response or set of responses spread from campaign to campaign, nor was there much evidence that their observational learning figured heavily in the campaigns' reactions.

The Packwood and Leahy campaigns made no response to the leaflets distributed in the primary elections. Neither was leafletted in the general election (since these were the two cases in which the candidate selected to run against the senator in November was not a supporter of the Human Life Amendment).

The Bayh and Church campaigns, both leafletted in November, reacted by holding press conferences to denounce the tactic and its sponsors. Beyond that, their approaches differed. Bayh's manager criticized the leafletting on the day it appeared, warning that it distorted Bayh's views. But his staff had decided against any further action "because our feeling was . . . that we were better off being positive on *our* side and going after ticket-splitters [who would support Reagan, but would also vote for Bayh over Quayle]."

The Church campaign had learned of the leafletting in advance and had scheduled a press conference just before the first leaflets were distributed, in which the senator urged Idaho voters to disregard the brochures. It was "despicable," Church stated, that people would not be able to attend houses of worship that weekend without having to face political interference. The campaign went no further to try to discredit the pro-life strategy, but the staffers *had* seriously considered distributing a "counterleaflet" of their own. Those plans were halted at the eleventh hour by the senator himself; when he learned of the plans, he objected in principle to leafletting on a Sunday.

The McGovern and Culver campaigns responded more aggressively. Both had been leafletted in their primaries. Both decided to counterattack in the fall, though they chose very different ways to do so.

Culver's campaign planned a radio blitz for the week before the general election. Ads warned voters to be prepared for last-minute attacks on the senator by extremist and New Right groups. The campaign's purpose was twofold: to reduce the impact of the leafletting by taking away the element of surprise, and to encourage voters to see the brochures as a political tool that distorted the senator's voting record and as an unprincipled, unfair attempt to hurl charges when it was too late for the senator to respond to them.

The Culver staff decided not to counterleaflet the Pro-Life Action Council. Their decision was based in part on the results of an Iowa Poll, taken during the campaign, in which most respondents had said that they would react negatively if their minister became involved in endorsing candidates for office. Culver's staff concluded that most Iowans did not appreciate the injection of politics into their church services, might even be getting impatient with the pro-life church leafletting, and probably would resent any leafletting of churches by candidates themselves. The best solution, they agreed, was to respond to the pro-life brochures through a series of radio ads, rather than risk alienating churchgoers with a counterleaflet.

On the weekend before election day, an unexpected event changed that decision. Top staffers received news of yet another pro-life leaflet, produced by a smaller Iowa pro-life group,[13] charging that Culver had voted to support experimentation on live, aborted fetuses. That was the straw that broke the camel's back. Because the accusation was so shocking—"it was a really outrageous distortion of the senator's position," an aide stated—the decision was made to counterleaflet. The campaign manager drew up a flier denying the charge and explaining the exact (and highly complex) nature of the legislation in question. Staff members worked through the night to print 50,000 copies of the flier for distribution the next day—the Sunday before the election—in areas where the new leaflet appeared.

McGovern's staff took yet another approach. Three weeks after being leafletted in the primary, the campaign sent out an "Open Letter to My Fellow South Dakotans" to a number of opinion leaders in the state: newspapers, members of the clergy, and others. The letter explained that McGovern was personally opposed to abortion, even though he did not favor a Human Life Amendment. It warned that outside groups were using the abortion issue to defeat progressive members of the Senate. The letter was published in many South Dakota newspapers, and was distributed to national political leaders and media people as well.

As the campaign developed, top aides became increasingly concerned that the pro-life attacks could have a ripple effect, making McGovern appear to be not only an opponent of the Human Life Amendment but also of traditional family values. That was worrisome; the losses McGovern would take on abortion were bad enough, the staffers felt, but the impression that he was somehow "anti-family" could hurt him very badly among blue-collar Democrats. They asked the advice of ministers in the state as well as political consultants. The response they chose was a broad-scale advertising campaign to emphasize McGovern's close ties with his large family. In October 1980 frequent newspaper ads included pictures of the four McGovern grandsons, with the handprinted message "Please Re-elect Our Grandpa." The McGoverns' October wedding anniversary was celebrated with a lot of publicity. Later advertising carried large photos of the whole McGovern family with the caption, "Nothing saddens me more than to be accused of being anti-life and anti-family. I look at my wonderful children and grandchildren and wonder sometimes, even in the heat of a political campaign, how opponents can be so cruel."

The campaign had ruled out the use of a counterleaflet after it became apparent that the logistics would be difficult, perhaps impossible.[14] Instead, direct mail was used to reach "soft core" pro-lifers: blue-collar Democrats who opposed abortion and might be tempted to defect to McGovern's Republican challenger. On the Sunday before election day, newspapers ran a pro-McGovern ad signed by prominent South Dakota Catholics; in an insert to that ad, McGovern wrote he considered it offensive to invade the churchyard with political brochures, so his supporters had chosen this less-intrusive means of reaching voters.

In short, there was a wide range of responses to the church leafletting strategy. The range included a selective counterleaflet on the abortion issue, an aggressive pro-family advertising campaign, attempts to discredit the use of Sunday-before-the-election leafletting, denials of the pro-lifers' charges, and planned silence. Some of the campaigns' strategies showed common themes: warning of the leafletting in advance, for example, and stressing the senator's agreement with other social justice stands taken by the Catholic church. But in spite of staff members' efforts to learn an effective response at the Hill meetings, no particular strategy—nor even any general approach—was adopted by most or all of these Senate campaigns.

The striking contrast between these findings and the behavior of state pro-life groups can be seen in table 8.1. The upper half of the table confirms that the Iowa group's strategy, so apparently successful in 1978, was almost universally adopted by pro-life groups involved in the 1980 races. The Senate campaigners' avid efforts to learn from models, as the lower half of the table shows, produced fewer results.

TABLE 8.1
BEHAVIORS LEARNED FROM MODELS: A COMPARISON OF PRO-LIFE GROUPS AND TARGETED SENATE CAMPAIGNS

Pro-Life Groups: Modeling Elements	Iowa Model 1978	Iowa Model 1980	Idaho	Indiana	Modelers Oregon	S. Dakota	Vermont
Brochure	x	x	x	x	x	x	x
Contents							
picture of fetus	x	x	x		x	x	
candidate's voting record on abortion	x	x	x	x	x	x	
stress on turnout	x	x	x	x	x	x	
Mode of transmission							
leafletting at churches	x	x	x	x^2	x	x	
timing: prior Sunday	x	x^1	x	x^2	x	x	
Voter Identification	x	x		x	x	x	

Senate Campaigns: Modeling Elements	Clark Model 1978	Bayh	Church	Culver	Leahy	McGovern	Packwood
Pro-choice fund-raising letter				x		x	x
Complaints to regulatory agencies		x				x	
Ads targeted to Catholics	x	x	x	x	x	x	
Ministers as campaigners	x	x		x		x	
Response to leafletting							
no response					x		x
warned of it in advance			x	x		x	
attacked it afterward		x				x	
counterleafletted	x			x			
pro-family ad campaign						x	

KEY: 1. The Sunday-before strategy was used in the primary; for the general election, leafletting was done a Sunday earlier. 2. In the general election, church leaflets were produced and distributed by the Quayle campaign with advice from IRTL-PAC, which distributed its own leaflets earlier.

The campaigners' problem was *not* a lack of ideas. As one participant in the Hill meetings reported, there were plenty of suggestions as to what might be done about the church leafletting:

> There was a discussion of whether there should be counterleafletting, or *some* action taken to put that within the proper context. . . . There were people who said, "We ought to be prepared to go on TV the night before [the leafletting] and talk about it, and run newspaper ads. We ought to leaflet ourselves in those places where you *could* leaflet.
>
> "We ought to send letters to each Catholic family outlining our position on the thing. We ought to run radio commercials about it." [Laughs.] Almost every type of communication was suggested. "There ought to be a parish committee of people who believe in pro-choice, or a statement signed by a group of ministers, that we can run as an ad or use as a letter."
>
> Almost everything, no matter how outrageous, was discussed, and it just ran across every single way that you would have of getting in touch with the voter on this particular item.

Rather, the problem was a lack of *evidence;* with no successful models to guide them, and no "trial runs" of their own, none of the campaigners could be sure how any of these suggestions would affect voters.

If these Senate campaigns could make only limited use of modeled behaviors in dealing with the church leafletting, then how *did* they derive their strategies? Their only alternative was to draw upon their previous experience and search for information that would help them adapt that experience to the new problems. In looking at some examples of that process, the reader can see three things.

First, the campaigners' previous experience did not always prepare them well; there were enough differences between their earlier encounters with single-issue groups and the current pro-life targeting to make any generalization hazardous. Second, adapting that prior experience required good information about the targeting and its likely effects, and that information was often in short supply. Third, the result was a very uncertain, trial-and-error learning process, one that put these Senate campaigns at a real disadvantage in trying to cope effectively with the pro-life challenge.

Each of these senators and top staffers had faced single-issue attacks before, on matters ranging from gun control to busing to national defense. Each had developed certain styles of responding to those attacks, styles that had been reinforced by at least one election victory and often several. John Culver, for instance, was well known for meeting an attack head-on. A reporter described Culver's previous handling of single issues this way:

[*Question:* Can you think of any times that he's adopted a conciliatory approach to a controversial issue?]
No.
[*Question:* On the Panama Canal, or busing, or gun control . . . ?]
No. No, I can't. He's not very conciliatory on any of these issues.
[*Question:* How long has that been characteristic of his campaigning?]
Oh, a long time. He's been known to be that kind of speaker and politician for a long time.

This pattern of aggressive response, of turning an attack back on his opponent, had been associated with a lot of positive results for Culver as a campaigner. He had, after all, won six races for the House and Senate using that approach. When challenged by the evangelical Right, Culver drew on the approach again; he had his staff research the Moral Majority and Christian Voice "morality ratings," publicly attacked the standards these groups used in their ratings, and made the New Right a major issue in his campaign. Early in the election cycle he described his plans with this characteristic pledge: "This is one target that's shooting back."

Patrick Leahy's experiences with controversial issues had led him to take a different approach. By the time of his reelection race in 1980, Leahy had evolved a nonconfrontational style—and had been rewarded with election success in Vermont before becoming the first Democrat elected to the U.S. Senate in his state's history. A source close to the campaign explained Leahy's usual manner of dealing with controversy:

> Well, I guess the main ingredient is, he's not combative. On the abortion issue, he'd handled the question for six years [in the Senate] basically in a very low-key, person-to-person way, where he told people what his position was, and he didn't debate the issue. [On issues where people have disagreed with him,] Patrick will just say, "Well, that's your opinion and you're welcome to it; this is *my* opinion, and let the people decide whether or not they are going to re-elect me," and that's it.

In short, each had a learning history: a history of experiences with other single-issue attacks, responses to those attacks, and response consequences. That learning history could be used—in fact, in the absence of good models, *had to* be used—to develop an approach to the pro-life targeting, at least in general terms. But each campaign also had a sense, as we saw early in this chapter, that the pro-life challenge in 1980 was not exactly like past single-issue attacks, nor was this election year exactly like other elections they had experienced. Their earlier learning could not be dusted off and used again in its entirety; the current situation had unique qualities that must be taken into account.

To do that, the campaigners needed information. They needed to know a lot about the pro-life groups and about the ways that pro-life campaigning differed from that of other single-issue groups in these campaigners' experience. They needed to know how their own initial approach to the targeting was being received by a variety of interests: media people, the opponent, pro-choice people, potential pro-life voters, pro-life groups themselves. Without that information, these campaigns could not adapt their earlier learning effectively; they would be whistling in the dark, fighting the current battle with the battle plans of the last war.

Getting that information proved to be extraordinarily difficult. The normal uncertainty of campaigning was even more impenetrable on the matter of abortion. All the campaigns used professional polling. Most polled very regularly in October, using "tracking polls" in which a hundred or more people would be telephoned per day, and a rolling average of several days' results tallied, to pick up any developing trends. On many issues, the tracking polls were a good investment. The Church campaign, for example, learned from poll data that opponent Symms was becoming vulnerable on his advocacy of the "Sagebrush Rebellion"—the demand for state control over the large federal landholdings in the West—and redid some of their ads to take advantage of that information.

But one lesson of the Hill meetings, drawn from the experience of Clark and McIntyre, was that the polls could not be trusted on the abortion issue. If the nation's top pollsters had not been able to get an accurate reading of single-issue pro-life voting in advance of the 1978 elections, many campaigners reasoned, why should the polls be any more trustworthy on that issue in 1980? Polls and canvassing kept delivering one reassuring message to campaigners: the abortion issue was not a prime concern of most voters. But the nagging thought remained: wasn't that what pollsters had told Dick Clark?

Deprived of their most sophisticated means of getting believable information about the pro-life challenge, and feedback on their approach to it, the campaigners had to find alternatives to polling. Some sent field staffers to talk with ministers, lay leaders, and other church members in areas where pro-life sentiment was thought to be strong. Some consulted with local political activists and others thought to have a good "feel" for the issues in their communities. Some tried to set up meetings with supporters who were active in the pro-life movement; others, recalling meetings where they were confronted, as one campaign manager put it, "with somebody who has a fetus in a bottle, you know," chose simply to brainstorm the problem with their own staffers.

As we have seen before, campaign decision makers often valued the judgments of these supporters and activists—in spite of the obvious fact that they had biases of their own—at least as much as they valued the answers they were getting from high-priced pollsters. Listen to a campaign manager explain why he decided to run media ads on the abortion issue in several selected cities: "It wasn't just based on polling, but on word from the field. We never *ever* would have done anything like that based just on polling." What was this influential "word from the field?" The recommendations of the campaign's own field staffers, based on their conversations with local activists.

In addition, in the absence of more specific information, campaigners used their candidate's general standing in the polls as an indicator of their progress in dealing with the abortion issue. Culver, for example, had been well behind his challenger when the active phase of the campaign began; in June 1980, polls showed him trailing Grassley by 17 percent. But as the summer wore on, newspaper columnists increasingly began to praise Culver's forceful approach to issues, and by early October the polls had greatly improved; the Iowa Poll credited him with a five-point lead. These positive responses stiffened the campaign's resolve to continue its aggressive approach. When the time came to prepare for the expected pro-life leafletting, the "halo effect" of those poll results helped point the Culver staff toward a frontal assault. The details of the response depended in part on suggestions from advisers; the radio blitz warning of last-minute right-wing charges, for example, had been recommended by a consultant. But given Culver's learning history, and without an example at hand of some approach that had already proven effective in a campaign similar to Culver's, we would have been very surprised to see his staff do nothing at all about the church leafletting or respond in an indirect way by focusing on his close family ties.

In the same sense, Patrick Leahy's customary approach to his pro-life critics was reinforced by the generalized reward of his strong standing in the polls. Alone among the five targeted Democrats, Leahy had been running ahead of potential challengers since the beginning of the race. He had the further comfort of seeing the pro-life-backed candidate lose the Republican primary in September. In October his staff began to worry; they sensed some slippage in the senator's support, and they wondered whether a national wave of discontent with President Carter might wash over their own race as well. The campaign flirted briefly with some changes, in particular, with more aggressive criticism of Leahy's opponent. Our interviews gave us the feeling that this campaign might have been tempted to try something new if a successful and similar model had been available. But there was no such model; top aides could not be sure whether Culver's attacks on single-issue politics, for example, were the reason for his rise in the polls, and whether such an approach might also work in a campaign environment like Vermont's. In the face of so much ambiguity, it is understandable that the Leahy campaign held on to its nonconfrontational style with respect to abortion; without good information about their effects, the strategies Leahy's people had learned from models could not compete with a familiar approach that had been used in their own previous, successful campaigns.

In short, these campaigners had to beat the bushes for indicators as to whether their early approach to the pro-life challenge was working. But the bushes held very few good indicators, and almost no sophisticated ones. Fine-tuning their approach, then, was all but impossible. The best they could do was to piece together reactions from field staffers and other activists, make some adjustments in their earlier learning, and move ahead.

When the dust cleared on election day, four of the six Senate campaigners came up losers. Birch Bayh, Frank Church, John Culver, and George McGovern were retired by the voters; Patrick Leahy and Bob Packwood won, and by slim margins (see table 8.2). The abortion issue is not likely to have "caused" these results (though it is interesting that of the six races, Leahy's and Packwood's were the only two where there was no church leafletting in the general election). Nor is it likely that single-issue attacks, more generally, were responsible for the outcome. Several other powerful forces were at work: the landslide victory of Ronald Reagan, the economic decline, frustration over the continued holding of American hostages in Iran, even the fact that President Carter conceded defeat before the polls had closed in some states, which apparently led some Democrats in those states (including Idaho) to leave their polling places

TABLE 8.2
ELECTION RESULTS IN THE SIX TARGETED SENATE RACES, 1980

Percentage of the vote received by . . . [a]

State	Senatorial Target	Opponent	Jimmy Carter	Ronald Reagan
Idaho	Church 49	Symms 50*	25	67
Indiana	Bayh 46	Quayle 54*	38	56
Iowa	Culver 46	Grassley 54*	39	51
Oregon	Packwood 52*	Kulongoski 44	39	48
South Dakota	McGovern 39	Abdnor 58*	32	61
Vermont	Leahy 51*	Ledbetter 49	39	44

*denotes winning candidate

SOURCE: *Congressional Quarterly Weekly Report* 38 (8 November 1980): 3338-45.

a. The candidate's share of the total vote cast for all candidates for that office. Since minor-party and independent candidates (e.g., John Anderson) picked up a share of the presidential vote and, in some states, the vote for senator, percentages do not always add up to 100 percent.

without voting. Given the precarious standing of each of these six senators, any of these problems might have been enough in itself, or especially in combination with others, to tip the balance.

But it is clear that all six incumbents had been hurt by the pro-life targeting to some extent and that only Packwood's, among the six campaign staffs, felt reasonably sure that its responses to the targeting had been effective. The others, particularly the four losing campaigns, were left to contemplate the old question: what else could they have done to turn the situation around?

Conclusion

The social-learning predictions that accompanied us through these six races have emerged relatively intact. They show a few wrinkles from the experience, but no serious structural damage. The threat faced by the Senate campaigners, and the new circumstances confronting most of the state pro-life groups, led them to concentrate heavily on what could be learned from models. When the pro-life challenge first entered their campaign environments, Senate staffers from five of these races moved immediately to set up a channel for observational learning and invested quite a lot of time in an effort to find good models. They drew many of their expectations about the nature of the pro-life groups' strategies from these Hill group meetings. Many potential models were studied: the Clark and McIntyre campaigns of 1978, the ideas of political consultants, one another's plans for dealing with the targeting and the church leafletting in 1980.

Moreover, as predicted, these efforts at observational learning were focused on models who shared important characteristics with the learner. The five targeted Democratic campaigns tried to learn mainly from the other Democratic Senate campaigns targeted by conservative single-issue groups. The greater the similarities, the harder the campaign tried to learn from a potential model; compare, for instance, the effort made by the Culver campaign with that of the Packwood staff to draw lessons from Dick Clark's loss in 1978.

Third, and also as expected, the strategies most likely to diffuse were those whose effectiveness was easiest to demonstrate, those easiest to transmit, and those most consistent with the values and experiences of the adopter. The Steinem fund-raising letter is the clearest example. Information about the tactic was readily available to political activists during the latter part of the campaign. The letter was easy to transmit and explain (as opposed to a candidate's self-presentational style, whose components are not nearly as readily isolated, described, and explained). It was a variant on a familiar technique, one very much in keeping with campaigners' experiences and values. Most important, unlike most campaign activities, whose independent effects are so hard to measure, the Steinem letter brought an unusually large and very measurable "take" — a clear indicator of an effective strategy, available while the race was in progress. The result was that Packwood's tactic was *learned* by all five of the other targeted campaigns and was *used* by two of them.

Finally, and unhappily for most of the targets, these Senate campaigners proved to be less able to *use* observationally learned strategies than were the pro-life groups. First, there were several differences among the six campaigns that call into question whether one campaign's strategies might work in another campaign's environment. Pro-life groups, on the other hand, did not want for similar models; their single-issue stance made abortion, and the targeting of incumbents on that issue, an overriding source of similarity among them.

Second, the pervasive uncertainty of campaigning makes it very difficult for participants to be sure which strategies are working and which are not. An "effective model," then, is customarily defined to mean a model whose campaign has recently won an election; in the uncertain world of electioneering, one of the only clear reinforcers is the election result. Again, the pro-lifers had a big learning advantage; the defeat of Dick Clark in 1978 had given the strategies of the Iowa Pro-Life Action Council the aura of effectiveness that encouraged modeling. In sharp contrast, the Senate campaigners had only the wreckage of their targeted colleagues' campaigns in 1978, and one another's uncertain prospects in 1980 (with the important though belated exception of Packwood's successful fund-raising drive) as a basis for learning—not a very powerful incentive to use these models' strategies.

Thus restricted in their ability to use models' approaches to the pro-life targeting, the Senate campaigners were forced back on their own experience. Each senator had faced controversies and hostile groups before, and each had a history of election successes. Particularly when a campaigner's strategic choices have been strongly rewarded, those choices become part of his or her characteristic "style"; they can serve as a source of continuity (and expected success) in an insecure and rapidly changing campaign environment. Each campaign, then, had a basis—a predisposition—on which to build an initial approach to the targeting. What these campaigns did *not* have was a sophisticated, reliable means of finding out how to adapt their earlier learning to the dynamics of the current race. That increased the danger from another quarter; previous experiences, because they tend to color the campaigner's attention to new information, can "protect" him or her from the very cues that warn of environmental change and guide adaptation to that change.

These Senate campaigners, then, were at a learning disadvantage relative to their pro-life adversaries. Their efforts to learn from the available "negative models" were fraught with risk. These snags in their ability to *use* observational learning made their job, in an already troublesome election year, all the more difficult. Remember the words of a Culver staffer, frustrated and discouraged after election day: "But in terms of any model of who best handled this thing [the pro-life targeting], I don't think there was one."

The story has come to an end—for the 1980 elections. What implications can be drawn about campaigning and single-issue targeting in the future? What have *we* learned about the ways candidates behave and the ways they construct explanations for political events? Finally, what do these findings tell us about the opportunities and the hazards of campaigns as learning situations, and as integral parts of the representative relationship? The next chapter offers some answers to these questions.

NOTES

1. Campaigns differ in assigning decision-making power; in each of these races the campaign manager had the primary authority to make strategy decisions, while in state legislative campaigns it may be the candidate who has that power. When we use the term "campaigner" in relation to a particular behavior, we mean the person with the authority to make the final decisions about that behavior. The specific influences on a campaigner will vary, depending in part on his or her role in the campaign organization. But the same social-learning principles should govern them all.
2. Recall that Church was on record favoring a states' rights amendment to ban abortion. Packwood, in contrast, was pro-choice and favored federal funding of abortions. The other four, as well as Dick Clark and Tom McIntyre, supported choice on abortion and public funding, but declared themselves to be personally opposed to abortion.
3. Nor did the Republican party set up a comparable communication network to help its candidates deal with single-issue groups. A top Packwood aide explained: "They [the Republican party] try to stay out of that, because many of the single-issue groups are registering people for the Republican party and helping the Republican party out."
4. A McGovern Senate staffer pointed out: "As you meet with people over the course of a year [in Washington], you develop personal friendships and associations, and so while I'm out here [South Dakota], if I have a question or a problem, or I'm troubled about how to approach an issue, I'll pick up the phone and call somebody from Church's office or Culver's or Birch Bayh's or Pat Leahy's or somebody else's office and say, 'What are you guys doing on this?' To that extent, on a very informal basis, we do have that kind of communication, but it's certainly not very well-structured."
5. Election Outlook," *Congressional Quarterly Weekly Report* 38 (23 February 1980): 465.
6. See Elizabeth Drew's *Senator* (New York: Simon and Schuster, 1979).

7. That was an attitude that infuriated pro-life leaders. After the church leafletting had taken place in 1978, Clark's campaign distributed 50,000 copies of a "counterleaflet," in which a number of prominent Catholics expressed their support for the senator, at Catholic churches. The decision to focus only on Catholics "was an insult to the *huge* number of Protestants that we have in our organization," said the (Protestant) leader of the Iowa Pro-Life Action Council. "And it just shows the stupidity that he, as a United States Senator, had not informed himself any better than to realize that we *were* something more than a 'Catholic issue.'" Campaign strategists saw it differently; they needed to target any materials to the people who were most concerned about the issue, and they considered Catholic churches to have a particularly high concentration of such people. Only a few of the 1980 campaigns, such as Birch Bayh's, made a serious effort to deal with the abortion issue in fundamentalist and other Protestant churches as well.
8. The picture, as chapter 7 indicated, was of a live fetus in the womb. But Paul Brown had also mailed grisly color photos of dead fetuses to a lot of people in South Dakota, independent of the church leafletting.
9. Both Bayh and McGovern wrote the postal authorities to support NARAL's complaint against a letter sent by Americans for Life. The letter, mailed to 50,000 church members in 1979, called these two senators "baby-killers" and pleaded for money to "stop the baby-killers." Late in the race, McGovern supported a complaint filed by the South Dakota Democratic party charging that NCPAC had compromised its independent status (and thus its right to spend unrestricted amounts of money in the race) by becoming involved in the campaign of James Abdnor, McGovern's opponent. Several other Democratic campaigns kept informed about the progress of this complaint. Bayh took preliminary steps toward a subsequent official complaint; NCPAC, he said, had violated the law by failing to file reports of its income and contributions in 1980.
10. On this strategy, see Gary C. Jacobson and Samuel Kernell, *Strategy and Choice in Congressional Elections* (New Haven: Yale University Press, 1981).
11. The specialist was the consulting group of Craver, Mathews, Smith and Co. None of the other three targeted campaigns had hired this group. Nor did the other three wish to be open about soliciting pro-choice money. Church, of course, was not considered to be pro-choice by most pro-choice activists. Leahy, seeking to contrast his own Vermont roots with the fact that his opponent was a transplanted New Yorker, made a point of refusing help from any out-of-state groups. Bayh's staff was responding very quietly and cautiously to the pro-life challenge, to avoid driving "soft core" pro-life sympathizers into the Republican camp.
12. The campaign manager who related these feelings to the senior author also requested that the identity of the campaign be withheld in this instance.
13. The group was the Iowa Democrats for Life; it was not affiliated with the Iowa Pro-Life Action Council.
14. Antilitter ordinances in many South Dakota communities kept the campaign from leafletting on public property, and many churches that had allowed LAPAC to leaflet in their lobbies and parking lots refused to grant the same privilege to McGovern's staff. (LAPAC too was denied the right to leaflet in some churches.)

9. Campaigning and Representation: Learning to Run, Learning to Represent

The targeted races in 1980 were the crest of what many regarded as a historic tide. In addition to the defeats of Birch Bayh, Frank Church, John Culver, and George McGovern, eight other Senate seats moved from Democratic to Republican control. That gave Republicans, for the first time in almost three decades, a majority in one of the houses of Congress. In his inaugural address, Ronald Reagan sounded the theme of many of the successful Republican campaigns when he pledged to stop the expansion of federal powers and federal social programs. "In this present crisis," Reagan charged, "government is not the solution to our problem. Government is the problem." The theme made conservatives and New Right supporters feel they had come in from the cold.

Pro-life groups, too, felt that the political environment had warmed to their issue. The 1980 elections had increased pro-life strength in both the House and the Senate. Some observers even claimed to see a pro-life majority in Congress.[1] Were the electoral efforts of LAPAC and other groups about to bloom into policy change?

This chapter carries the story forward in two ways. First, we move forward in time. The campaign that led to these marked changes was not an isolated piece of history. It was part of the continuous learning process in which people's behavior and environmental events interact to produce new behaviors and new events. No sooner were the 1980 elections decided than participants and observers began to extract explanations and create expectations about 1982, 1984, and beyond. The chapter begins by exploring this learning. Then we move forward analytically by drawing together some themes about the nature of campaigns as learning situations, and by looking at the implications for representation in American politics.

LEARNING FROM 1980: CANDIDATES AND THE NEW RIGHT

Campaigns, as we have seen, are difficult learning situations. One main reason is that it is hard for participants to get good information about the relationship between their strategic behaviors and the results they want: in short, to know how they are doing. The ultimate answer does not come until election day, and then it is too late to go back and do things differently. And the vote on election day does not explain which specific strategies it is rewarding and which it is punishing.

Yet in order to learn from election results—the main response consequences in the race—campaigners seek explanations of that very sort. So the difficulties of campaign learning lead to a process in which participants *construct* explanations of the vote totals, for individual races and broader sets of elections as well. As chapter 4 suggested, a plausible interpretation of the meaning of a given election (attributing the results to one or both candidates' strategic choices, personal qualities, issue emphases, or to events beyond the candidates' control) spreads from one actor to another until it becomes accepted as "what really happened" in the race. From that explanation, campaigners derive expectations as to what is likely to work in a given situation and what is likely to fail. These expectations, this learning, can then be applied in later campaigns. Let us examine what was learned through that process in the 1980 elections.

New Right groups were quick to call themselves giant-killers after election day 1980. Many media people and campaigners accepted that view; the New Right's impressive fund raising, effective organization, and powerful issues had been the big "story" of the campaign. Elements of that story thought to be closely linked with election results quickly spread.

One such element was the use of negative campaigning. In the early to mid-1970s, candidates learned that they could tap the prevailing anti-Washington sentiment among voters—even if the candidates were incumbents themselves—by running against the "Washington establishment" and distancing themselves from the policies and agencies that were distrusted by so many. The approach seemed to work, and it was widely adopted.

The New Right carried that style of campaigning much further in 1978 and 1980. NCPAC and other groups found that they could markedly improve their fund-raising prospects if their mailings identified an "enemy" by name—not necessarily their candidate's opponent, but some well-known political figure who could symbolize the fears and dislikes held by potential contributors. Personal attacks were not unprecedented in campaigns, of course; nor was mudslinging. What *was* notable was the New Right's freewheeling style of explicit attacks on a broad range of elected and appointed officials, including their candidates' colleagues in the House and Senate.

For example, in 1980 several New Right groups and candidates raised a lot of money by focusing their supporters' frustrations on George McGovern and the tradition of social liberalism he represented; candidates from several states all acted as though McGovern were their opponent. The national-level Republican committees took the same approach, though using more temperate language, by featuring a look-alike of Democratic House Speaker Tip O'Neill as the villain in a commercial run nationwide.[2] Only some of the ad's viewers were in O'Neill's district and would thus have the opportunity to vote for or against him in 1980; O'Neill himself was not the point. Rather, he was a handy symbol on which to focus voters' discontent: a remote political figure whose record and character were not well known among the public, and who had the misfortune of bearing a close physical resemblance to everyone's image of a cigar-smoking political boss, with his imposing girth, his shock of white hair, and his florid face. When McGovern and many other Democrats lost, the slash-and-cut approach of the New Right seemed to be one likely cause.

By 1982, the style of explicit personal attack had crossed party and ideological boundaries. Direct-mail appeals from Democrat Ted Wilson, for example, who was running for the Senate seat of Republican Orrin Hatch of Utah, featured letters from Frank Church attacking his former colleague Hatch in no uncertain terms. A range of PACs followed the same model. One was PRO-PAC (Progressive Political Action Committee, begun in 1981 by political consultant Victor Kamber), a liberal PAC that specialized in applying NCPAC's tactics to vulnerable conservatives. Thus, when NCPAC made an early foray into Maryland in 1981 to savage Senate Democrat Paul Sarbanes, PROPAC retaliated with newspaper ads spotlighting some of the more fearless remarks of Terry Dolan, NCPAC's leader. (One memorable example: "A group like ours could lie through its teeth and the candidate it helps stays clean.")

In fact, the Democratic Congressional Campaign Committee advised candidates to draw on that style as a means of dealing with any New Right attacks. In 1980, many observers noted, John Culver had gained in the polls with a strategy of hitting back at his attackers; so had George McGovern, at least for a time. Frank Church, who had consistently responded (through press aides) to New Right charges, had missed victory by a percentage point, even while Ronald Reagan was winning Idaho in a landslide. The lesson was not completely clear, but the results seemed to point to the need for forceful action to keep New Right attackers from defining the terms of the campaign. Shortly after the 1980 election, then, the DCCC offered this advice: Anticipate what the New Right targeters are going to use against you and hit back quickly. Don't let the candidate respond personally to the attacks; find someone else—a staff member, a friendly group leader, or an elected official—to do it for you. Keep the targeters on the defensive: expose their tactics, question their credibility, denounce their motives. Campaigners worried about their 1982 races listened closely.

And they made their moves early. Another lesson from both 1978 and 1980 was that New Right targeters had again weakened a number of incumbents by attacking them very early in the election cycle, long before the active phase of the campaign had begun for most people, when the number of competing campaign stimuli were few. So in 1981, and even more in 1983, many candidates and interest groups were already moving into their campaign pace for the next election. In fact, the Democratic National Committee got a jump on all comers by targeting a candidate for the 1984 elections even before the 1982 races were over. In a fund-raising letter, DNC Chairman Charles T. Manatt picked Republican Senator Jesse Helms of North Carolina as his symbolic opponent. Referring to Helms as "the New Right's Prince of Darkness," Manatt explained his timing with these words: "Jesse Helms isn't up for reelection until 1984. But his removal from the United States Senate is so critical to restoring a basic sense of decency and compassion to our nation's political climate that I refuse to wait a single day more before beginning work on Helms's defeat." Manatt combined two elements of a model's behavior—the unusually early start and the targeting of a symbolic opponent—in his fund-raising strategy.

New Right techniques spread to a variety of pro-choice organizations as well. The normally cautious Planned Parenthood made a big move into direct mail and radio and newspaper ads (one showed a couple lying in bed with a cigar-smoking politician in the middle, captioned "The decision to have a baby could soon be between you, your husband, and your senator") to raise money to counter the expected push for a Human Life Amendment. NARAL, bolstered by a wave of new members after President Reagan's inauguration (as were other feminist groups), also studied the tactics of the New Right and the pro-lifers in order to try to match their clout.

New groups such as Americans for Common Sense, formed by George McGovern after his 1980 defeat, made it their mission to warn of the New Right threat. Norman Lear, who had earlier brought Archie Bunker to the television audience on "All in the Family," now produced People for the American Way, a group aiming to show how the New Right's agenda left no room for the traditional American values of tolerance and diversity. People on the mailing lists of liberal groups were showered with messages like this one, written by Frank Church in a fund-raising appeal on behalf of Democrats for the 80's: "The New Right now has a lock on one of the two major parties; the few Republican moderates who haven't been purged are on the hit list. The crusade against justice, reason and moderation is on the march—and this country is in deep trouble."

No matter how deeply felt these warnings were (and they *were* deeply felt), they reflected the political learning that liberals had drawn from the 1980 elections—not just learning about the New Right's strength and its aims, but the learning of its tactics. The use of direct mail displaying vivid emotional appeals on key issues, regarded as so effective by New Right watchers in 1978 and 1980, was now adopted by pro-choice and liberal groups. Only the targets were different. The New Right appealed to pro-lifers, pro-gun people, and other social conservatives; the newly awakened liberals mailed to feminists, environmentalists, and citizens worried about social security.

One could argue that this campaign learning had unpleasant results. It accelerated the trend toward the "continuous campaign," not just among House members, but among many senators as well. It prompted an increase in negative campaigning, leaving many to wonder whether candidates and groups who had attacked one another with such abandon during the campaign would be able to work together effectively after the election. Pleasant or unpleasant, these changes are perfectly understandable; they were derived from widely accepted explanations for the defeats of so many liberals and pro-choice advocates in 1980.

LEARNING FROM 1980: PRO-LIFERS

The Life Amendment PAC came out of the 1980 elections into a happier learning environment—for a time. National pro-life leaders crowed about the movement's remarkable progress since *Roe v. Wade*. As *LAPACtion* put it, reporters who had formerly ignored the pro-life movement were now giving it regular coverage: "In 1980 there was hardly an election for dog-catcher to president in which abortion was not mentioned, and thanks to LAPAC and a lot of hardworking local political action committees, there was *no* Federal Election in which the candidate did not take a stand on abortion! . . . That is real progress!"[3]

Not only had many candidates taken stands on abortion, but in a lot of well-publicized contests the pro-life candidate won in 1980. John Willke, president of the National Right to Life Committee, exulted that the election had produced a gain of ten pro-life Senate seats and at least 20 in the House, as well as the pro-lifer in the White House.[4] Pro-life leaders conceded that the big issues in 1980 were the economy and defense. But, as *Action Line* argued,[5]

> . . . abortion was clearly an important factor as well. Consider this: the storied National Conservative Political Action Committee (NCPAC) targeted a half dozen liberal Democratic Senators for defeat on November 4—Birch Bayh, Frank Church, John Culver, George McGovern, Alan Cranston, and Tom Eagleton. Of those six, only two were not similarly targeted by pro-life groups: Cranston and Eagleton. Both won reelection in spite of NCPAC's efforts.

The abortion issue, they felt, had to be cited as part of the explanation for the election results.

Clearly, LAPAC and other pro-life groups felt that their work in these 1980 races had been a success. By inference, they considered the strategies they used in those campaigns to have been successful. And at the beginning of 1981, the 1982 Senate races seemed similar enough to those just past to encourage pro-lifers to apply those strategies again. Of the 33 Senate seats up for election in 1982, about two-thirds were held by pro-choice advocates, most of them liberal Democrats. Further, it looked as though the political environment continued to be receptive to pro-lifers' efforts; the long-expected conservative realignment seemed to be happening at last, under the banner of a very popular and pro-life President.

Emboldened by its experiences in 1980 and its expectations of continuing success, LAPAC named a new "Deadly Dozen" for 1982 shortly after the 1980 election. This time, the targets were drawn from the Senate alone. Ten of the 12 were Democrats, including LAPAC's prime target: Senator Edward M. Kennedy of Massachusetts.[6] LAPAC hoped that Kennedy would take over George McGovern's role, that of a nationally known liberal challenged by a pro-life-backed political unknown and then badly weakened in time for the general election. To that end, LAPAC distributed a bumper sticker right out of NCPAC's book: "If Kennedy Wins—You Lose."

Many other aspects of LAPAC's campaign activity in early 1981 were also a virtual replay of its efforts in the previous election. "We know this strategy works," explained LAPAC mailings. For example, Brown announced that he would continue the political action training seminars and the advertising that had been run in 1980. LAPAC's direct-mail fund raising kept the condensational tone of its earlier mailings, for instance describing the aim of pro-choice groups as

> DEATH . . . DEATH to the most helpless of all human beings . . . the pre-born child . . . and covered with another lie called "freedom of choice" for everyone but the one killed by these butchers.[7]

The National Right to Life PAC chose to move more cautiously and quietly, as it had in 1980. But other pro-life organizations followed Brown into the fray with similar target lists of their own.

A LESSON IN HUMILITY

Within the year, Brown saw things very differently. "Political reality has come home to the pro-life movement," he complained to a reporter, "and it has been totally unpleasant."[8] By the summer of 1981 it was clear that the movement's electoral gains were not producing the expected change in abortion policy. The momentum of the previous fall's victories was all but lost. LAPAC's expectations and behavior began to change. By examining that change, we can be reminded of another vital interaction in campaign learning: interaction between what happens in the campaign's active phase and the learning that takes place *between* elections.

Several reasons influenced the shift in the pro-lifers' fortunes. First, there was the urgency of the nation's economic problems: high inflation, growing unemployment, skyrocketing interest rates. Press accounts of the 1980 elections frequently cited the view that the Republican victories could be traced in part to public disgust with President Carter's handling of the economy. Ronald Reagan had campaigned on a new set of economic proposals stressing cuts in social programs and taxes (but increases in defense spending). For most of 1981, then, Congress was preoccupied with these economic measures; debate on abortion and other matters was postponed.

Second, when the consideration of abortion legislation did begin, the pro-life movement's internal divisions cracked wide open. One segment of the movement (later to include LAPAC) announced its support of new pro-life legislation called the Human Life Bill, a statute designed to reverse *Roe* v. *Wade* by "finding" that human life begins at conception. If that were established in law, its authors claimed, then fetuses or unborn children could be protected against abortion by the Fourteenth Amendment.[9]

The HLB had another quality attractive to many pro-lifers; as a statute, it needed only a simple majority vote in Congress to become law—a majority that some pro-life leaders believed they already had—while a constitutional amendment required a two-thirds majority, plus approval of three-quarters of the state legislatures.

The pro-life chairman of the Senate committee to which the HLB had been assigned, Orrin Hatch, argued that such a statute would not survive challenge in the courts. Hatch insisted that a constitutional amendment was the only way to overturn *Roe* v. *Wade*. With the support of the National Conference of Catholic Bishops (and later, after a close vote, the NRLC), he proposed a new constitutional amendment stating that abortion is not a constitutional right and giving Congress *and the states* joint authority to restrict or ban abortion. Thus states, unless Congress overrode them, could choose to ban all abortions within their borders. By the same token, other states would be free to keep all abortions legal. Hatch suggested that his amendment was the best that pro-lifers would be able to pass. LAPAC accused Hatch of betraying the pro-life cause.

These public battles within the movement meant that members of Congress who wanted to cast a pro-life vote had no obvious way to do so. If they supported the HLB over Hatch's amendment, or Hatch over the HLB (and it was widely assumed that only one of the measures could be brought to the full chamber for a vote), they would draw the enmity of at least some pro-life groups. The resulting political risks gave even many pro-life members of Congress a motive to delay action on the abortion issue.

Then there was the question of President Reagan's commitment to the pro-life cause. Soon after the 1980 election, *Action Line* mused:

> We have wondered if Reagan will remain true to his commitment after his landslide win. . . . The problem we will face is getting through to the President. During his campaign his aides isolated and insulated him from pro-life influence. Will this continue after the elections?[10]

Ronald Reagan reaffirmed his pro-life beliefs in public statements and made several appointments (including that of the U.S. Surgeon General) that pro-lifers acclaimed. But he made little effort to follow up on his statements and push for congressional action against abortion. And in his first opportunity to nominate a justice of the Supreme Court—a vital concern of pro-lifers, who saw the high court as the chief obstacle to a ban on all abortions—Reagan confirmed *Action Line's* fears.

The President's nominee was an Arizona judge, Sandra Day O'Connor. To Reagan's staff, the appointment was a master stroke: their man, who had won a smaller proportion of women's votes than men's in 1980, could now tell women's groups that he had nominated the first female Supreme Court justice in American history. But in the ensuing media coverage pro-lifers learned that when O'Connor had been a member of the Arizona state senate, she had cast several votes against pro-life measures.

"We've been sold out," Paul Brown charged.[11] So did many New Right groups. After a flurry of organizing led by direct-mailer Richard Viguerie, the Religious Roundtable Rally for Life was formed to oppose O'Connor's nomination. It included LAPAC and most of the other major pro-life groups as well as the Moral Majority, the Conservative Caucus, and the Committee for the Survival of a Free Congress. The Roundtable's lobbying campaign was quick and intense. And unsuccessful. When the full Senate voted on the O'Connor nomination in September 1981, the tally was unanimous in her favor; every one of the new members elected with pro-life support had voted for the nomination. Brown's response:

> Since the election of Ronald Reagan, the pro-life movement has suffered far too many defeats and has had to spend too much time keeping an eye on our "friends.". . .
> The nomination of Sandra Day O'Connor was yet another devastating blow to our cause. . . aside from a few "token" invitations to the White House, the pro-life movement has been had.[12]

This pattern—symbolic rewards for the pro-lifers but no real policy change—continued throughout 1981 and 1982. Reagan spoke the language of the pro-life movement at several dramatic moments. In 1982 he wrote a widely circulated letter to the Christian Action Council expressing "my prayers for success" of "legislation that would restore protection of the law to children before birth." He supported other issues that mattered to individual pro-lifers: voluntary prayer in the public schools and tax credits for parents of children in private schools.

When the Senate took its next showdown vote on abortion, however, pro-lifers felt that Mr. Reagan's support was too little and too late. It was August 1982; both the Hatch amendment and the Human Life Bill were dead in the water. Senator Jesse Helms had recently introduced a "superbill"—actually a rider on a bill to raise the public debt ceiling—that would permanently ban federal funding for abortions and stipulate that the Supreme Court made a mistake when it failed to recognize the "humanity of the unborn." Another Helms rider on the same bill went further, stating that federal courts would not be allowed to review cases having to do with voluntary school prayer.

The President did not translate his support for the "superbill" into lobbying activity until shortly before the vote. By that time, pro-choice groups had been able to galvanize the opposition. They were helped by the fact that the court-stripping language of Helms's school prayer rider came to be associated with the abortion rider—not the wisest move in a Senate where 60 of the 100 members were lawyers. The American Bar Association opposed the legislation; even Mr. Reagan's attorney general expressed doubts about it.

In the end, the pro-lifers did not have the votes; the Senate voted to table (kill) Helms's abortion rider by a margin of 47-46. The movement's hope for new abortion legislation in the 97th Congress died with the bill. Even worse, the showdown had highlighted the weakness of pro-life forces in the Senate.

The pro-life groups' failure to turn their recent election gains into policy change had a big effect on their behavior. Frustrated and dispirited, antiabortion activists turned away from politics in droves. The disappointment even jarred some groups away from the insular learning patterns they had maintained, the go-it-alone style in which their primary sources of learning and encouragement had been other pro-lifers. Faced with an environment growing more and more unfriendly, some pro-lifers warmed to the advances of the New Right.

LAPAC was among the pro-life groups that began working closely with New Right and "pro-family" organizations on matters of shared concern. The O'Connor nomination was one spur to such a coalition; another was the Human Life Bill, which a number of New Right organizations supported. Paul Brown argued that working with New Right groups might help the pro-lifers in campaigns, too:

> Now that the pro-life movement has joined forces, at least in elections of common interest, with the "New Right," it is time to examine our position and make some decisions for 1982. We must always bear in mind that while not every member of the "New Right" agrees with our stand, the vast majority does! . . . We look forward to working with the "New Right" in those campaigns of mutual interest—it will bring the day of the Human Life Amendment that much closer![13]

Again, LAPAC's activities broadened the rifts within the pro-life movement. Several other pro-life groups were highly critical of Brown's interest in forming coalitions and of his choice of coalition partners.[14] In fact, the New Right was having no greater success in influencing Congress than were the pro-lifers in 1981 and 1982. As the active phase of the '82 campaigns approached, both movements felt their electoral strength slipping; their failure to push abortion, school prayer, and other issues to the top of the congressional agenda gave many incumbents the suspicion that pro-lifers and the New Right were not as strong as they appeared to be. Even NCPAC's Terry Dolan predicted that many senators who had voted against the New Right agenda would, in his words, "get away with it" at the polls.[15]

LAPAC shortened its target list to six, with Kennedy still at the top. It spent heavily in those campaigns, but abortion got major attention in only one Senate race—that of Democrat Jim Sasser of Tennessee—and in a handful of other campaigns for Congress. When the votes were counted, LAPAC had batted zero. Sasser sailed back into the Senate with 62 percent of the vote, Kennedy with 61 percent, and none of the other four races was even close. Moreover, while pro-life strength remained relatively constant in the Senate, pro-choice forces won a substantial increase in House seats.

Brown put at least part of the blame on the Reagan administration. The President's real support, Brown insisted, had developed out of his stands on social issues, not economic policy, yet Reagan was permitting those social issues to be shoved aside. But whatever the cause, the 1982 elections exacted a high price from pro-life organizations.

After 1982, the pro-life movement suffered even greater losses. In June 1983, the Supreme Court reaffirmed *Roe v. Wade* by overturning a series of city and state laws restricting abortions. (Interestingly, Justice O'Connor led the dissent.) Less than two weeks later, Senator Hatch brought an amended version of his proposed constitutional amendment to the Senate floor; it stated simply, "a right to abortion is not secured by the Constitution." This would be the first Senate vote ever held on an antiabortion amendment.

Some pro-lifers thought it was the wrong antiabortion amendment. "This puts in the Constitution that killing babies is all right until somebody tells you to stop," said Nellie Gray, the head of March for Life. "I can't go along with that."[16] LAPAC also opposed the Hatch amendment, arguing that it did not go far enough.

In one of the many ironies of this story, the four new senators backed by LAPAC in 1980 all voted for the Hatch amendment. But its supporters fell far short of the necessary two-thirds vote; the amendment did not even win a majority, with only 49 members in favor. Senator Bob Packwood, who led the fight against Hatch, stated that senators "want to be done with this issue. The bigger the vote against this, the stronger the message. The right-to-life forces have crested and are on the decline."[17]

These tides of pro-life activity call our attention to the central premise that campaigns are dynamic, interactive processes. Campaign behavior cannot be understood fully if it is examined in isolation from the learning that took place in previous campaigns, or from the learning that takes place *between* elections. LAPAC's experiences in the 1980 races created high expectations in its leaders. They saw the defeats of four of their targets as evidence that their issue was important and their methods of presenting it were effective. Their initial reading of the 1982 campaign environment—on the basis of indicators such as the "mood" of the country as journalists reported it, the President's popularity ratings, the party and pro-life or pro-choice stance of the senators up for reelection in 1982—was that it bore some striking similarities to that of the election just past. They expected that continued use of the targeting, leafletting, and styles of activity of the 1980 campaigns would extend the string of victories for the pro-life cause.

And they expected that, in the meantime, the currency of election success would purchase a big change in congressional policy making on abortion. The euphoria of pro-lifers after the 1980 elections—very few, after all, had the lengthy political experience that might have moderated their expectations—sent their hopes flying. The early congressional demurrals, the later defeats, and the crushing blows of the O'Connor nomination and confirmation were especially bitter outcomes. The political environment that had seemed so inviting now turned sour. So the strategies changed, the internal conflicts deepened, the focus of LAPAC's energies blurred. Even its learning networks began to shift a little. LAPAC and some other pro-life groups drew closer to the New Right, whose leaders had long seen the uses of the abortion issue in attracting working-class Democratic support. The pro-lifers learned; their approaches and behavior were modified in the continuing interaction among their experiences, their expectations, and the political environment of their actions.

This book has suggested that seeing campaigns as learning situations can bring dividends in understanding—not simply a new set of terms but a new way of viewing and evaluating an old and important institution. Investigating campaign learning opens our eyes to many things: the strengths and weaknesses of voters, parties, and other groups as teachers; the strengths and weaknesses of incumbents and challengers, winners and losers as learners; the distortions in the learning process that inevitably affect the nature of representation in American politics. Let us conclude, then, by considering the *quality* of campaign learning, and its implications for the representative process.

THE QUALITY OF CAMPAIGN LEARNING

Ever since Theodore H. White and Joe McGinniss wrote best-sellers about presidential campaigns in the 1960s,[18] one popular strand of political writing has pictured campaigns as finely tuned instruments for manipulating the emotions and beliefs of the average voter. In this view, experts combine survey research with media advertising to produce almost-irresistible public images for candidates. The cover blurb for McGinniss's book, for example, describes a highly placed adviser to Richard Nixon in 1968 as "the man who cast the image that sold America a president."

Descriptions like this suggest that campaigns provide very good learning situations for candidates and consultants, where they can find out how to adapt their strategies to move the voters like marionettes. Yet, curiously, that same Mr. Nixon, who began the 1968 general election campaign with an enormous lead over his Democratic opponent, and with the apparent wizardry of high-priced television experts, market researchers, and advertising specialists, came within half a percentage point of losing the race two months later. If campaigns are such good learning situations for campaigners, then how could Richard Nixon almost have, in the much-used phrase, snatched defeat from the jaws of victory?

In fact, the social-learning approach shows clearly that campaigns have systematic disadvantages as learning situations. Campaign environments distort messages. They make it easier for some kinds of information to spread than others. They give campaigners a much better picture of the views of other political elites—activists, media people, other campaigners—than of the great majority of voters, whose decisions will determine the outcome of the race. For many candidates, running for office has more of the atmosphere of a carnival fun house than a computerized learning exercise; people, lights, and sounds appear and disappear unexpectedly, openings turn into dead ends, and nothing is what it seems.

One reason has to do with the campaign setting itself. The fast pace of the action, the constant flow of stimuli, and the campaigner's great personal investment in the outcome can create anxiety and psychological arousal well beyond the level that promotes effective learning.

But the most important influence on the quality of campaign learning is the difficulty of determining the relationship between a campaigner's particular strategic moves and the vote on election day. Every campaigner, even a presidential candidate, must act in the presence of some level of uncertainty about this key question: what is the exact mix of issue positions, personal characteristics, and campaign activities that will win the hearts of a majority of voters on election day? Some campaigns will cope with that uncertainty more successfully than others will. But no campaign organization will ever be completely free of it. And the greatest uncertainty involves voters' reactions and behavior.

During the race, feedback from the majority of voters is simply not available to most campaigns. If all campaigners were to get frequent reports of the results of meticulously designed professional polls, then they might indeed be able to play the electorate like a violin; more on this later. But candidates for most offices in the United States — local offices, state legislative seats, even congressional races in many areas — make many or most of their campaign decisions without the benefit of high-quality poll data. Even candidates for higher-level office do not always have the frequency of feedback (or the inclination to pay attention to it if it contradicts the judgment of trusted advisers) to take full advantage of this learning device. As one candidate for Congress pointed out:

> Only rarely can congressional candidates afford to expend their limited resources to commission a professional poll of their district. Consequently, most make decisions concerning how the voters feel with only intuitive information. In some cases information gaps can be filled through reallocation of campaign resources. But in many cases the information that one would like in order to make a rational decision simply does not exist. One lasting impression from my campaign, despite the fact that I have had a good deal of political experience and tried to run my campaign in a professional manner, was the frequency of the need to make "seat of the pants" decisions.[19]

Quick and specific feedback from voters is a scarce commodity in most campaigns. Campaigners must do most of their learning from other sources.

One source frequently used because it is both available and trusted are the reactions supplied by campaign advisers, staff members, and other strong supporters. Chapter 8 contains several examples. Consider another illustration from the McGovern campaign in 1980. Working on the assumption that an aggressive style had improved McGovern's chances, the campaign began in early October to run "soft negative" ads questioning his opponent's competence. An aide tells what happened when some key McGovern supporters disapproved:

> This is such a small state; both the candidate and his campaign manager have been through it so many times that whenever, let's say, we put out the newspaper

ads and the radio ads and the TV ads, oftentimes just what telephone calls we get the next day from people are enough to affect a judgment . . . and we ran those [soft negatives] and got bad phone calls the next morning from a handful of people [who objected to the negative tone], and we jerked it right off the air.

The sense that the voices of staff members and other activists ring out louder in the campaign environment than do the voices of voters is also supported by stories of the other five targeted campaigns in 1980. Each of these campaigns was led by experienced people, each had ample funds, and each made a major effort to get information about voters' reactions. Yet many of the campaigns' key decisions about how to deal with the pro-life challenge were made in the absence of good data as to how the public might react. For instance, most of these campaigns chose their response to the church leafletting by giving the greatest weight to recommendations from staff members, political allies, and other activists. In some races, reports from field staffers and friendly ministers or lay church leaders played a pivotal role. In others, the perceptions of top staffers were the main influence (as, for example, when Culver staffers decided to counterleaflet, even though they had previously agreed not to do so, because they were stung by a last-minute pro-life attack).

In no case did staff members believe the decision on a response to the pro-life leafletting could be derived easily and directly from poll data. In fact, staffers from every one of the campaigns expressed at least some distrust of poll findings. Some were suspicious of the polls' track records in the 1978 Senate races. Others argued that on a highly charged issue such as abortion, polls do not measure attitudes reliably.

If the polls were regarded as suspect, these campaigners had no other means of getting input from a broad range of voters—at least until election day. "The people" (other than political activists) were hard to find, and just as important, were hard to learn from. The "voice of the people" was present in these campaign environments only in secondhand form: as it was translated by campaign staffers and other activists.

The learning environment of a campaign, then, is an environment populated by political elites. John Kingdon reports, for instance, that when candidates in his study were asked about the characteristics of voters, they often responded by citing the characteristics of people with whom they were more familiar: their volunteers, party activists, or people working in interest groups. They tended to measure voters' interest in their campaign in terms of activist behavior: the number of volunteers coming to work at their headquarters, for example. He concludes that "to a great extent, politicians operate in an elite cognitive world, largely isolated from rank-and-file voters."[20] They are hearing *about* voters, but not very often *from* voters.

Is this learning bias inherent in the nature of campaigning, or does it simply reflect the fact that most campaign organizations cannot afford frequent and high-quality public opinion polls? One can argue, at least to an extent, that the bias is inherent. Granted, well-designed surveys can give campaigners a much more accurate picture of the voters' views than would be possible without such polls. Survey research can, and did, tell these 1980 Senate campaigns which demographic groups regarded abortion as an important issue and to what degree, as well as a lot of other helpful information.

But public opinion polls do not make campaign decisions. Campaigners do. Even the most dramatic poll results do not necessarily point to one and only one strategic response by a campaign; often, several possible courses of action are available to deal with a problem or take advantage of an opportunity revealed by poll data. The people who select or recommend a course of action—pollsters themselves, campaign managers, other staffers, and activists who happen to be around when the findings are discussed—inevitably interpret those findings from the perspective of their own learning histories and skills. Public opinion data take on meaning in a campaign, then, as they are filtered through the understanding of political activists.

Poll results do influence these activists' judgments about the campaign, of course, and sometimes do so powerfully. Even if a manager is convinced that the abortion issue matters a great deal to most voters, it would be difficult (though not impossible) to sustain the point when several well-designed surveys show that few respondents claim to care about abortion.

The less frequent and detailed the poll results are, however, the more a campaign will depend on the activists' interpretations of what the voters want. And in most American campaigns—those for state legislative seats, city councils, school boards, county commissions—it may be some time before frequent, well-designed polls are available to contest the judgments of the activists involved.

Another reason why the learning bias may be inherent in political campaigning is the nature of the election itself. If citizens are to be the main teachers of people running for elective office—"my boss," as so many elected officials like to tell constituents—then the vote must be one of their primary teaching tools. It is not the only instructional device that the Constitution guarantees; the freedoms of speech and press let citizens try to teach their leaders, as does the right to assemble peaceably and petition the government for redress of grievances. But voting has taken on major importance in discussions of citizens' powers because it is almost universally available in the United States, and is safer and less costly than petitioning the government or taking to the streets to demand change.

Thus it is significant that as a teaching tool for citizens to use, voting in an election has some serious limitations. As Verba and Nie have suggested, the act of voting has less information-carrying capacity than other political acts do.[21] The citizen does not set the agenda of the balloting nor the occasion on which the election is held. Voters are not asked to write on the ballot the concerns that bother them the most or the policy preferences they would like to see implemented. In fact, except with referenda and initiatives, people cannot express their concerns and issue preferences directly at all by means of the ballot.

In the end, the voting choice is only a choice among candidates. An individual may cast a ballot for Candidate A as a means of expressing concern about one particular matter—may vote for Ronald Reagan, for example, as a means of making a statement about the need for a strong national defense. But the gesture is a silent one; the voting machine will register only the choice "Reagan," not the reason for it. Robert Goodin concludes: "Democratic procedures can be used either to choose policies or to choose people. The real trouble stems from thinking that they can do both at the same time."[22]

Thus, neither the winners nor the losers can be certain what the voters meant by their choice of candidates. In fact, given the great diversity of people's concerns, and the variation in their levels of information and perceptions of candidates' positions, it is probably safest to assume that "the voters" meant a great many different things by their vote. Taken independently, then, the election results are a blunt instrument—potent but not very specific. The nature of voting as a collective act makes it a frustrating teacher.

Despite the difficulties, campaigners do learn from election results. Chapter 4 described the process—a form of observational learning—in which candidates, other activists, consultants, and reporters construct explanations of what the voters were trying to say on election day. One or more of these explanations spreads widely enough to become accepted as the dominant interpretation of why a given candidate won or lost. This vital process of constructing explanations, then, shapes what campaigners learn from the vote totals. Recall the numerous examples shown in chapters 7 and 8 as pro-lifers, reporters, and campaigners derived what they thought were the reasons for 1978 election results and applied that learning to races in 1980.

Although the explanations may be self-serving, misleading, or downright wrong, they are likely to have far-reaching impact. They may, for instance, affect the making of public policy. After the 1982 elections, reporters and participants converged on the explanation that Democratic gains in the House of Representatives reflected voters' dissatisfaction with the Reagan administration's economic policies. That explanation has several policy-relevant implications. If voters were rejecting Reaganomics, then the incoming House would have reason to cast a suspicious eye on Reagan's heavy budget cuts in domestic spending and give top priority to proposals for reducing the high unemployment rate. As one reporter put it, "believing the November 2 elections gave them a mandate to do so, House Democrats plan to push a multibillion-dollar public works jobs bill and a housing stimulus measure."[23]

In reporting the explanation, the media affect voters' feelings as to which political problems are important and which are not.[24] Ironically, then, election results probably influence voters' views almost as much as the voters' views affect election results.

The important point is that when they learn from election results, campaigners are not learning directly from the voters but from activists' and reporters' interpretations of what the voters meant. That happens because activists have more effective teaching tools at their disposal than most other citizens do. They are more frequent sources of stimuli to candidates and their staffs. The rewards they have to offer—campaign contributions, endorsements, strategic information, and other support services—are more numerous and more valuable than those that most voters can provide.

And activists are often more explicit teachers: more clear and specific as to how a candidate can gain their support. A state legislator, for example, can much more easily form some expectations about the link between his or her legislative votes and a particular group's endorsement than about the relationship between his or her legislative record and the voters' choices on election day.

PARTY AND SINGLE-ISSUE INFLUENCE

Among the activists whose views and concerns are so important a part of the campaign environment are party leaders and workers. Recall from chapter 8 that although most of the targeted Senate campaigners clucked in dismay at the weakness of political parties, they nevertheless paid close attention to models from within their party and drew their closest advisers and workers from within their party's ranks. The shared party tie was an important guide to their lines of communication.

It was the Democratic Senatorial Campaign Committee that set up the main channel of observational learning among these 1980 campaigns—the biweekly Hill meetings—a channel that was never opened to campaigners from the other party. When asked whether they would consider using strategies developed by the other party's candidates in response to the pro-life targeting, all but one of the Senate campaigners said no.[25] As a top Democrat from Iowa put it,

> I think, by and large, there's not a lot of discussion back and forth between Republican and Democratic staff members. . . . I surely made no conscious decision *not* to talk to Packwood's people. . . . You know, you just socialize more with Democratic people, that's all.

Nor had the one Republican campaign manager considered using any of the targeted Democratic campaigns as a model:

> No. Not at all. No. I would imagine that one of the problems there is that they're in the other party, so there's no commiseration, and we just haven't done that.

Friendships and lines of communication often remain within party boundaries. As a result, campaigners' attention is drawn more easily to candidate-models within their party. That is especially true when members of the same party can expect to share a set of circumstances — to face opponents who were all trained in Republican campaign schools, for example. The tendency is deepened by the socialization of many campaigners; their association with a party's label and candidates is much closer than that of most other citizens, and gives them greater sensitivity to the party's cues. Thus in the elite environment of the political campaign, party persists not only as a label but also as a primary source of models and other stimuli for candidates and their staffs.

In the same way, interest-group activists are potentially important influences on campaigners' learning. And *single*-issue movements can be especially effective teachers. The sheer intensity of their demands and behavior call attention to their message. That intensity makes the learning situation for candidates rather clear-cut, at least initially: accept the group's position on its issue and gain its active support, or reject that position and face the group's censure. In contrast with the ambiguity of so many other aspects of campaigning, the clear link between action and reward in such cases must be enticing.

Single issues can be very visible in campaign environments because they are so emotionally provoking. As chapter 6 suggested, single issues are typically defined in the condensational mode; they draw upon the power of abstract, affectively potent symbols. Murray Edelman writes: "Condensation symbols evoke the emotions associated with the situation. They condense into one symbolic event, sign or act patriotic pride, anxieties, remembrances of past glories or humiliations, promises of future greatness: some one of these or all of them."[26] They convey threat and reassurance of the most engaging kind. Because of the special ability of religious questions to provoke threat and reassurance, many single issues become linked with religious figures and beliefs — and thus can bedevil political campaigners. Listen to a McGovern aide talk about the difficulty of responding to the abortion issue:

I think the distinction [between the pro-life movement and other single issue groups] is that gun control and the Panama Canal and some of these other wonderful things are basically secular, whereas the right-to-life [movement] has been able to wrap itself in a religious mantle, and that's what makes it especially harmful and especially difficult to respond to. Because if you have priests, as an example, having Right to Life Sundays, speaking from the pulpit, allowing right-to-life groups to use their facilities, providing coffee and putting their notices in the church bulletin, that is a very difficult thing for a political figure to respond to in a secular way, because you have to avoid attacking the church, and it's a very tricky thing.

So single issues can affect political campaigns because they are intensely expressed, emotionally explosive, and because they provide a dramatic learning situation for campaigners. Then why, one might ask, couldn't the pro-life movement keep its momentum after 1980? Why did pro-life measures fail in Congress, and why was the abortion issue weak or absent from the 1982 congressional campaigns?

Certainly the pro-lifers had a lot of competition in defining the political agenda after 1980. In particular, high unemployment and high interest rates competed effectively for public attention. When Congress and the President agreed to give priority to economic matters in 1981, and pro-lifers could not muster enough votes to change that priority, the handwriting was on the wall: members of Congress (and subsequently, campaigners) had reason to wonder whether the consequences of offending pro-life groups were worth worrying about.

But consider what the pro-life movement had achieved by 1980. It had motivated singleminded voting in a bloc of people who, though few in number, can claim to have had an impact in any of several very close elections. In many cases it weakened or even altered their party identification, pulling adherents from out of the Democratic ranks and sending them to the polls to vote for Republican candidates. It affected the behavior of many campaigners. It won enough news coverage to attract the attention of people who may not have thought much about the abortion issue before. It gained enough supporters in the Senate to make the language of the Hyde Amendment even more restrictive, sharply curbing federal spending for abortions. It came within one vote of passing the Helms rider stipulating that the Supreme Court's decision in *Roe v. Wade* had been wrong. In the end, it provoked the supporters of abortion rights to organize more effectively than they had felt the need to do since 1973.

Perhaps just as important, for people interested in campaign behavior, is the simple fact that the pro-lifers' activities in 1980 presented six experienced Senate campaigns with a learning dilemma that hardly any of the campaigners felt they had effectively solved. Single-issue politics may not be able to dictate the results of many elections. And when a particular single-issue movement makes a public claim that it cannot fulfill, its effectiveness in campaign environments will wane, at least for a time. But because of the compelling urgency with which it can dominate some activists' vision of the political world, single-issue politics will remain a continuing challenge for campaigners, easily visible in campaign environments, and a potentially important teacher.

CANDIDATES AS LEARNERS

The learning environment of political campaigns, then, is defined largely by activists. Campaigners hear the voices of the broader public mainly through an activist filter. Yet it is the votes of the broader public, not just the activists, that candidates must win on election day. For this reason and others as well, the campaign learning situation is a difficult one for candidates and their staffs. Winners and losers, incumbents and challengers, each have their own hurdles to overcome.

The story of the pro-life targeting in 1980 gives us special insight into the learning advantages and disadvantages of incumbents seeking reelection. The Senate incumbents on LAPAC's list shared several distinct advantages as learners. First, by virtue of having run before and won, they had each developed a package of campaign strategies that the voters had rewarded before. And they had developed some hypotheses as to *why* those strategies had worked. Their experience had given them a basis for responding to the Senate campaign environment—a basis for deciding where talented staffers could be found, how voters could best be approached, which media outlets were particularly important. These are advantages that their challengers could match only with a heavy investment of time and money.

In addition, incumbency had given the targeted senators exposure to more campaign-related stimuli, from a greater variety of sources, and at less cost than they would have been able to obtain as challengers. For instance, the Packwood campaign could tap into pro-choice groups throughout the nation because Packwood's activity on the abortion issue during his twelve years in the Senate had given him contacts in the pro-choice movement, and familiarity with pro-choice concerns, on which he could draw in heading off the pro-life challenge to his reelection. Incumbency, then, is a resource for gaining information and for fine-tuning one's expectations about various campaign situations.

But their status as incumbents was not all profit for the six pro-life targets. Chapter 4 suggested that repeated victory at the polls tends to produce layers of incentive to repeat the patterns of past winning campaigns. The incentive is strengthened by the uncertainty of campaigning; when information about the effects of various strategies is scarce, it is tempting to repeat approaches that have already brought reward. Moreover, it saves planning time; as Richard Fenno points out in his study of House members, the pursuit of influence in office allows less and less time and energy to be spent on exploring alternative home styles, so the incumbent grows more and more likely to keep doing "what we did last time."[27] Since the incumbent's staff and strongest supporters were probably first attracted to the campaign by one or more of those "characteristic" approaches, a repetition will probably trigger the positive feelings that attracted them to the incumbent in earlier races.

The repeated reward of election victory has its costs, however. It reduces a campaigner's incentive to try new tactics or adopt new issues. It weakens his or her motivation to search aggressively for information about possible changes in the constituency. It poses the risk that changes will sneak up on the incumbent, leaving perceptions outmoded and well-entrenched habits of campaigning outdated and ineffective.

The six senators whose campaigns we have examined did try to fight these dangerous tendencies. They were prodded to do so by several factors. One was their vulnerability; the reassurance of past victories was somewhat diminished for these incumbents by the closeness of their last race. Another was the distance in time from the last election; many staff members recognized that in at least some important ways, "the world had changed" since 1974—and the world of political campaigning with it.

The nature of the abortion issue itself—in particular, the church relatedness of the pro-life movement—also prompted some effort at new learning. Five of these campaigns saw the pro-lifers (and to an even greater extent, the evangelical community) as alien territory in many ways. All five sought to reconnoiter that territory. In the effort to establish contact and gain information, each was drawn into new learning channels. Several campaigns began to work more closely with ministers, pastors, and lay church leaders than they had done in the past. Several experimented with new campaign methods; Culver, for example, imported his minister from Maryland to speak on his behalf to church congregations in Iowa.

Thus the circumstances of the race as well as the campaigners' previous experiences led them to seek information about the pro-life challenge, to draw upon a big learning advantage they had as incumbents. The problem, again and again, was that the information was not to be had; the clues they needed— the keys that would tell them how to neutralize the abortion issue—simply were not there. Because no successful models were yet available, information gathering did little to help them predict what would happen if they tried one response rather than another. Except for Packwood's staff, whose preemptive fund raising seemed to work well against a relatively weak pro-life effort, the targeted campaigners were all but stymied.

In their frustration, most of these campaigns fell back on some of the patterns the senator had developed in earlier winning races. In its relentless position taking on abortion and other matters, the 1980 McGovern campaign acted very much like a "typical" McGovern race. "He campaigns that way," a journalist commented, "because I think he has won that way in the past. I think he's got a certain belief that perhaps people out here, although they might not particularly agree with everything he says, may vote for him because of his style and outspokenness." Similarly, in its pugnacious response to active opposition, the 1980 Culver campaign could have been mistaken for the 1974 Culver campaign or the 1972 Culver campaign.

One might wonder if these forthright styles were really the most effective approaches these liberal Democrats could have used in the conservative atmosphere of 1980. The important point is that they had little alternative. Styles of self-presentation are broad complexes of attitudes and actions, cues given and approaches taken, in which it is difficult to separate out the components for purposes of learning. Because of that, the experience of past victory tends to confirm the "rightness" of the style as a whole, at least in the mind of the campaigner.

Then when can we expect to see innovation in political campaigning? In these 1980 races we saw efforts at observational learning—which are, of course, efforts to innovate in a particular campaign—when the campaigners' environment took a hostile turn. Studies using different perspectives tell us similar things: innovations are a likely response to threat, and in particular, to the presence or the fear of electoral danger. David Mayhew, for example, suggests that candidates in marginal seats, who fear losing the next election, would be most likely to gamble on new issues or new approaches to old issues in a sort of "entrepreneurial position-taking." Other members of Congress can then learn which of these issue positions are salable by watching the election outcomes of these "issue pioneers."[28]

Theodore Lowi makes a similar point when he argues that, historically, innovation has been the function of the minority party.[29] And Austin Ranney reports that most of the changes in party rules governing nominations have been initiated by the out-party. "There is no mystery why," he writes. "A party which has just lost an election is more likely to be dissatisfied with procedures producing a loser than is a winning party with procedures that just produced a winner."[30] The losing party is motivated to seek change, and its freedom from well-rewarded patterns—no matter how much it might wish to be less "free" in that sense—enables it to do so.

Thus the insecurity built into the requirement of standing for elections serves the need for innovations: it is primarily parties and candidates who see themselves in danger of defeat who bring new ideas into political campaigns and new issues into political debate. The direct-mail fund-raising program that reaped such dividends for the national Republicans in 1980 was born largely in response to the party's humiliating defeats after Watergate. Similarly, after the heavy Democratic losses in 1980, there were cries from all corners of the party to define Democratic answers to the nation's problems in new and more politically attractive ways. These changes may benefit American politics, or they may fail. But without the spur to observational learning felt by campaigners who believe themselves to be in trouble, political debate would be impoverished. Measures to make elective offices more competitive, then—and measures that help minority parties to survive—take on special importance, for they help to sustain the development and spread of innovations in American campaigning.

LEARNING TO REPRESENT

In all these ways, the campaign learning environment affects the quality of campaigners' understanding of people's wants and needs. The quality of campaigners' learning, in turn, affects much more than their choices of strategies in an election. This book began with the contention that just as learning is central to campaigning, so is it central to representation; in fact, campaigning is an integral part of the representative process. Fenno puts it well when he writes that

> . . . there is no way that the act of representing can be separated from the act of getting elected. If the congressman cannot win and hold the votes of some people, he cannot represent any people. Further, he cannot represent any people unless he knows, or makes an effort to know, who they are, what they think, and what they want; and it is by campaigning for electoral support among them that he finds out such things.[31]

What, then, does the social-learning approach tell us about the nature and quality of representation?

We have already seen that incumbents have several advantages as learners; in particular, they have access to more sources of stimuli than challengers usually do. But even for incumbents, those sources of stimuli are very likely to be other activists. And there is no reason to expect that it is easier for most incumbents to learn the views of the rest of their constituents *between* elections than it is during the active phase of the campaign. In fact, since campaigning tends to put candidates in contact with larger numbers of constituents than at other times, learning the concerns of the majority of voters will probably be even *more* difficult during the interval between elections. So the lack of direct information about most constituents' preferences—the knotty problem that almost all campaign learners face—is likely to continue when the winning candidate takes office. The learning environment of an elected representative systematically amplifies the voices of organized groups, other officeholders, party leaders, and media figures at the expense of other voters.

The idea of representation has many different meanings,[32] but it does not stretch the imagination too far to suggest that an important part of "representing" people is being able to find out what they want, what bothers them, at least on matters that engage them. In other words, one important part of representing a constituency is being a good learner: deriving a fairly accurate picture of public wants. Since representatives do not hear directly from most voters on most matters, the challenge for an elected official is to determine how well the views he or she *does* hear reflect the real distribution of views in the constituency—or at least to determine from the available stimuli the boundaries of public policy decisions and other representative behaviors that the voters will accept.

In a learning environment heavily weighted toward the views of activists and organized groups, this is no easy task. Some elected officials, particularly well-established incumbents who have become less open to new sources of information, may simply be unaware that the activists they see are not typical of most other citizens. Others may conclude that learning the wants of political activists and responding to those wants is sufficient in itself. It is a sensible strategy in many ways; the active voices in the district belong to the people who will be watching a representative's behavior most carefully, who will try to affect that behavior, and who have rewards and punishments available to get the results they want.

Even if an elected official wants to hear from the rest of the constituency and understands that there are biases in the stimuli coming from the district, it is not easy to estimate with accuracy the degree and direction of the biases. That remains a worry for many officeholders. Fenno cites the concerns of several members of Congress that so many of their constituents are hard to reach, indeed unreachable through the social and organizational networks on which incumbents rely, and therefore "mysterious"—difficult to characterize in terms of their political concerns, their expectations of public officials, and their expectations of the incumbent in particular.

Who are these quiet constituents? What do they want from politics? Without some answers to those questions, an elected official's ability to learn how to represent them is very limited. The incumbent may respond by making some assumptions about the concerns of this (usually substantial) portion of the constituency. Perhaps, the incumbent muses, many of these quiet people do not expect much from government. Perhaps they are quiet because they are basically satisfied with the way they are being represented. In any case, an incumbent can still hope to win their support through advertising and other forms of visibility, even if the "communication" with these shadowy constituents is one-way.[33]

Or the incumbent-learner may assume that organized groups, other public officials, and activists are accurately transmitting all the wants and concerns of the quieter voters. Many incumbents, especially in the more visible offices, feel inundated with demands from organized groups, suggestions from staff members, information from activists, and editorial commentary. Sitting at the eye of this storm of activist stimuli, perhaps they might be forgiven for assuming that the concerns of their less vocal constituents must certainly be contained in there somewhere—how many more concerns, they must sometimes wonder, could possibly exist in their district?

With each of these choices, the concerns of large numbers of quiet constituents are present only as they are interpreted by a much smaller group of politically involved people. It is no wonder, given the nature of this learning situation, that as Fenno writes: "House members are more accountable and more responsive to their supportive constituencies than they are to the remainder of their constituents" and thus that "the congressman must be careful lest he reach, respond to, and represent only those who make it easy for him to do so."[34]

If the quality of representation, as discussed here, depends vitally on the quality of learning that the political environment makes possible, what would change that environment to improve campaigners' (especially incumbents') ability to learn from citizens? One approach is to make candidates into better learners: provide them with ample, accurate information about their districts and increase their motivation to pay attention to new information and sources.

Perhaps the best way to encourage candidates to seek out new information is to make elections more competitive. Steps toward that end would have two effects. Shaking up the political environments of secure incumbents should increase their interest in observational learning, in finding out what was changing in their constituency and how the changes might affect them. And giving challengers a better shot at victory would probably increase outside interest in the challengers' campaigns and thus expand the range and volume of stimuli directed at them. Incumbents and challengers are like mirror images as learners: the former have access to a lot of stimuli but tend to lose the motivation to absorb them; the latter tend to be long on motivation but short on access to a wide range of stimuli. More competitive races might help each group learn.

Public financing of all political campaigns *could*—if the legislation was written to provide challengers with at least the minimum funding necessary to compete effectively[35]—increase the competitiveness of elections. And free broadcast time on television and radio for all candidates might do a lot to improve challengers' chances.

But it is not enough to increase campaigners' motivation to learn; all other things equal, they would be motivated to learn mainly from other political activists. The trick is to make citizens into better teachers. A necessary part of that process is to turn up the volume of stimuli coming directly from citizens to campaigns, relative to the volume of stimuli coming from the politically engaged minority. It is intriguing, for example, to consider turning the tables on campaign debates; instead of giving citizens a chance to watch rival candidates offer their views on current issues, perhaps campaigners could be given incentives to watch citizens speak their minds. New England town meetings are good examples of a structure that permits a wide range of views to be expressed at little cost to the citizen; perhaps residents of condominiums and inner-city neighborhoods could also be induced to spend an evening expressing their concerns to a captive audience of political candidates.

Many candidates have spent well-publicized "workdays" taking the jobs of gas pumpers, factory workers, and other "regular folks" in order to show an apparent understanding of voters' real concerns. More widespread use of this strategy may have the side effect of strengthening (or creating) some of the understanding the candidate hopes to demonstrate. Political sabbaticals, in which officeholders rotate periodically into the spheres of other citizens— for example, by spending six months working in a welfare office, or as an aide in a day-care center or on a family farm—might teach them even more. These rotations into the world of everyday survival are now limited, ironically, to candidates who lose elections.

And there are the polls. Public opinion surveys, as Benjamin Ginsberg points out, transmit individual attitudes at almost no cost to the citizen.[36] That certainly is one way for stimuli from nonactivists to reach candidates and public officials. The transmission fails one of our tests in that it is not direct; pollsters and their clients select the topics on which questions will be asked, frame the questions, and interpret the results. Even so, survey data made available at cost (or below) to all candidates in a race could help improve their understanding of citizens' concerns.

In the end, officeholders and other campaigners will pay attention to these concerns to the extent that doing so is linked with electoral reward. If candidates can increase their chance of winning, if incumbents can make their seats more secure by listening to a broader range of voices from their districts, they will do so. Thus, citizens would have to punish at the polls those candidates who did not listen. Equally important, it would be necessary for those candidates to realize *why* they had been punished—or rewarded: in other words, for candidates to be able to learn the nature of the relationship between their actions and the election results.

That would require much more dramatic change. The act of voting would have to convey more information. In effect, voters would need to be able to say more than yes or no to each candidate. They would need some means of explaining the main reasons for each of their choices, and the system of elections would need some means of aggregating the reasons along with the choices. An election would then be structured more like the currently used "exit poll"—but one in which the individual voter sets the agenda, explains as many choices as he or she chooses, and registers his or her concerns directly rather than indirectly in a separate conversation with a pollster. In fact, some might argue that with two-way interactive cable systems, in which people can talk back to their televisions with the aid of a home console, we have the beginnings of such a teaching tool.[37]

Others might ask whether any of these changes is politically feasible. Is it feasible, for example, even to consider any change in the structure of the ballot? Probably not; to suggest that the vote convey citizens' explanations for their choice of candidates is to ask too much of a blunt instrument. Perhaps the most we can hope for is that exit polls, though one step removed from the act of voting (in more than a temporal sense; voting by secret ballot is a private act, whereas an exit poll involves social interaction between pollster and respondent), be conducted routinely and analyzed expertly, not only in presidential races[38] but in Senate, congressional, gubernatorial, and even state legislative and local contests as well.

Even more important, if voters were to become better teachers of candidates, would the effects on American politics, policies, and leaders be wholly positive? Two interesting problems arise. One is that if voters were able to convey their concerns more clearly, then prospective officeholders might become even more aware than they already are of the extent to which constituents want reassurance rather than substantive policy results from their representatives. Fenno points out that constituents "may want good access or the assurance of good access as much as they want good policy. They may want 'a good man' or 'a good woman,' someone whose assurances they can trust, as much as they want good policy. They may want communication promises as much as they want policy promises."[39]

The second problem is closely related: as candidates gain a better understanding of what their constituents want, in "extrapolicy" as well as policy terms, candidates may become more expert at manipulating voters instead of being more fully controlled by them. A more effective learning environment, in short, might increase the campaign emphasis on trust, on the appearance of accessibility, on reassurance and personal style, at the expense of what little discussion of public policies is now found in campaigning.

So what? some might demand. If large numbers of voters would rather have reassurance than substantive proposals, if the current level of policy debate has already told them more than they wanted to know about environmental policy and national defense, then why shouldn't political candidates learn more about how to be effective stylistically? Why would that not enhance the quality of representation, given that so many citizens want to feel that they can trust, and that they have access, even more than they want particular changes in the Clean Air Act or the military budget?

The point is worth making. Feelings of access and trust *are* vital to the working of governments and the job security of elected officials. Those feelings can give officials the maneuvering room to deal with the classic conundrums of a democracy: the unpopular decisions necessary to reconcile competing demands, the tax programs required to pay for beloved but expensive government programs, the time taken from constituent service in order to study and oversee complex legislation.

But in the end, the tedious details of public policies affect the lives of individuals, and the life of the polity, at least as much as the stylistic behavior of elected representatives does. David Mayhew has argued that several facets of the organization of Congress are well designed to help maintain the institution itself against the pressures of incoherence caused by Congress members' pursuit of their reelection.[40] Perhaps what amounts to "institutional maintenance" in political campaigning—the push for candidates to learn about and discuss viable answers to public policy problems in the district and the nation—has been the result of an activist-dominated campaign learning environment. The real challenge, then, is the long-standing job of any democracy—and fittingly so, since campaigning is so central to the democratic process—to create a learning environment in which the concerns of the quiet citizens can be more effectively understood, while providing incentives for leaders to learn and act in citizens' long-range interest and that of the nation as a whole.

NOTES

1. This assessment was disputed by several pro-life leaders; see Bill Keller and Nadine Cohodas, "Tactical Errors, Disunity Blunt New Right Social Legislation," *Congressional Quarterly Weekly Report* 40 (16 October 1982): 2676.

2. See chapter 5.
3. *LAPACtion,* June 1981, 11.
4. See Patricia McCormack, "Women's Groups Take a Look at Reagan Administration," *Bloomington Herald-Telephone,* 14 November 1980, 15.
5. Vol. 4 (21 November 1980): 1.
6. The others on the LAPAC list in 1981 were Democrats Lloyd Bentsen of Texas, Quentin Burdick of North Dakota, Senate Minority Leader Robert Byrd of West Virginia, Howard Cannon of Nevada, Lawton Chiles of Florida, Howard Metzenbaum of Ohio, Daniel Patrick Moynihan of New York, Paul Sarbanes of Maryland, Harrison Williams of New Jersey, and Republicans S.I. Hayakawa of California and Lowell Weicker of Connecticut.
7. *LAPACtion,* June 1981, 2; ellipses in the original.
8. Quoted in Leslie Bennetts, "Antiabortion Movement in Disarray Less Than Year After Election Victories," *New York Times,* 22 September 1981.
9. See John Hart Ely and Laurence H. Tribe, "Let There Be Life," *New York Times,* 17 March 1981, A17.
10. Vol. 4 (21 November 1980): 3. On 22 January 1981 *Action Line* repeated its concern: "There is no question that powerful figures in the new administration view the pro-life movement as merely one among an array of social issues which can be set aside."
11. Quoted in Patrick J. Buchanan, "Nomination to Court 'Political Adultery,'" *The O'Connor Report* 1 (August 1981): 4.
12. Paul A. Brown, "LAPAC: What Next . . . Statute or Destruction?" *A.L.L. About Issues,* September 1981, 3.
13. In "Pro-Life + New Right = Victory for Preborn," *LAPACtion,* April 1981, 13.
14. The Christian Action Council, for example, objected strenuously to what it considered a violation of the movement's single-issue stance. Action Line asked, "Can the abortion issue be won if it becomes the preserve of the conservative leadership of this nation, whether traditional or 'new right?' Obviously not. For the abortion issue to be downgraded and made part of a multi-issue agenda is dangerous. The primary value of human life may fall prey to unwitting compromise for the sake of other issues or to hasty resolution in order to get on with the rest of the agenda." Vol. 5 (22 January 1981): 1.
15. Keller and Cohodas, "Tactical Errors," 2678.
16. Quoted in Nadine Cohodas, "Senate Judiciary Ties on Abortion Measure," *Congressional Quarterly Weekly Report* 41 (23 April 1983): 801.
17. Quoted in Nadine Cohodas, "Senate Rejects Amendment Designed to Ban Abortion," *Congressional Quarterly Weekly Report* 41 (2 July 1983): 1361.
18. See White's *The Making of the President* series on presidential campaigns from 1960 through 1972 (published by Atheneum the year following each election); and Joe McGinniss, *The Selling of the President 1968* (New York: Washington Square Press, 1969).
19. Louis Sandy Maisel, *From Obscurity to Oblivion: Running in the Congressional Primary* (Knoxville: University of Tennessee Press, 1982), 11.
20. John W. Kingdon, *Candidates for Office* (New York: Random House, 1968), 31; see also 150-156.
21. Sidney Verba and Norman H. Nie, *Participation in America: Political Democracy*

and Social Equality (New York: Harper & Row, 1972), chap. 7, especially 110-14.
22. Robert E. Goodin, "Voting Through the Looking Glass," *American Political Science Review* 77 (June 1983): 432.
23. Andy Plattner, "Hill Leaders Whittle Agenda for the Post-Election Session," *Congressional Quarterly Weekly Report* 40 (13 November 1982): 2838.
24. See Shanto Iyengar et al., "Experimental Demonstrations of the 'Not-so-Minimal' Consequences of Television News Programs," *American Political Science Review* 76 (December 1982): 848-58.
25. In fact, one strategy *did* cross party lines: the Packwood campaign's "Steinem letter" prompted similar action by the Culver and McGovern campaigns (see chapter 8). But note that the strategy did not diffuse directly from campaign to campaign; rather, it diffused via reports in a political consultant's newsletter and by means of a direct-mail house used by all three campaigns.
26. In *The Symbolic Uses of Politics* (Urbana: University of Illinois Press, 1964), 6.
27. See Richard Fenno, *Home Style* (Boston: Little, Brown, 1978), chap. 7, esp. 220.
28. David Mayhew, *Congress: The Electoral Connection* (New Haven: Yale University Press, 1974), 67-71.
29. At least until the point where the minority comes close to winning, at which time it will probably begin behaving like a majority party and strengthen its existing commitments. See Theodore J. Lowi, "Toward Functionalism in Political Science: The Case of Innovation in Party Systems," *American Political Science Review* 57 (September 1963): 570-83.
30. Austin Ranney, "Changing the Rules of the Nominating Game," in *Choosing the President,* ed. James David Barber (Englewood Cliffs, N.J.: Prentice-Hall, 1974), 82. Innovations might also enter the campaign process when new "types" of candidates—people whose social background and personal characteristics differ from those of most other candidates, such as members of racial or ethnic minorities or women—develop their initial approaches to the race by drawing upon the unique aspects of their previous experience.
31. Fenno, *Home Style,* 233.
32. See Hanna Pitkin, *The Concept of Representation* (Berkeley: University of California Press, 1972).
33. See Fenno, *Home Style,* 237-41.
34. Ibid., 234 and 236.
35. See the discussion of public financing in Gary C. Jacobson, *Money in Congressional Elections* (New Haven: Yale University Press, 1980).
36. See Benjamin Ginsberg, "Polling and the Transformation of Public Opinion" (paper presented at the annual meeting of the American Political Science Association, 1982).
37. Given the costs of such systems, however, their use might be effectively limited to the same kinds of people who populate the ranks of political activists: people with higher incomes, higher educations, and a stronger sense of political efficacy.
38. See Stanley Kelley, Jr., *Interpreting Elections* (Princeton: Princeton University Press, 1983).
39. See Fenno, *Home Style,* 240-41.
40. See *Congress: The Electoral Connection,* esp. 141-58.

Bibliography

ABRAMOWITZ, ALAN I. "A Comparison of Voting for U.S. Senator and Representative in 1978." *American Political Science Review* 74 (September 1980): 633-40.

ABRAMSON, PAUL R., JOHN H. ALDRICH, and DAVID W. ROHDE. *Change and Continuity in the 1980 Elections.* Revised ed. Washington, D.C.: Congressional Quarterly, 1983.

AGRANOFF, ROBERT. *The Management of Election Campaigns.* Boston: Holbrook Press 1976.

―――, ed. *The New Style in Election Campaigns.* Boston: Holbrook Press, 1972.

ALDRICH, JOHN H. *Before the Convention: Strategies and Choices in Presidential Nomination Campaigns.* Chicago: University of Chicago Press, 1980.

ALEXANDER, HERBERT E. *Financing Politics: Money, Elections and Political Reform.* Washington, D.C.: Congressional Quarterly, 1976.

ALPERN, DAVID M., with RICHARD MANNING and TONY FULLER. "Playing for Posterity." *Newsweek,* 13 October 1980, 41.

ALPERT, EUGENE J. "Candidates' Perceptions of District Opinion: The 1978 Congressional Election." Paper presented at the annual meeting of the Midwest Political Science Association, Chicago, 1979.

AMERICAN POLITICAL SCIENCE ASSOCIATION, COMMITTEE ON POLITICAL PARTIES. "Toward a More Responsible Two-Party System." *American Political Science Review* 64, Supplement (September 1950); New York: Rinehart, 1950.

ARIEFF, IRWIN B. "Senate Republicans Using Incumbency to Advantage in Snappy Media Operation." *Congressional Quarterly Weekly Report* 39 (6 June 1981): 993-95.

ARTERTON, F. CHRISTOPHER. "Campaign Organizations Confront the Media-Political Environment." In *Race for the Presidency,* edited by James David Barber. Englewood Cliffs, N.J.: Prentice-Hall, 1978, 3-25.

―――. *Media Politics: The News Strategies of Presidential Campaigns.* Lexington, Mass.: Lexington, 1984.

——. "The Media Politics of Presidential Campaigns: A Study of the Carter Nomination Drive." In *Race for the Presidency*, edited by James David Barber. Englewood Cliffs, N.J.: Prentice-Hall, 1978, 26-54.

ASHER, HERBERT B. *Presidential Elections and American Politics: Voters, Candidates, and Campaigns Since 1952.* Revised ed. Homewood, Ill.: Dorsey, 1980.

BAKER, ROSS K., LAURILY K. EPSTEIN, and RODNEY D. FORTH. "Matters of Life and Death: Social, Political, and Religious Correlates of Attitudes on Abortion." *American Politics Quarterly* 9 (January 1981): 89-102.

BANDURA, ALBERT. "Analysis of Modeling Processes." In *Psychological Modeling: Conflicting Theories,* edited by Albert Bandura. Chicago: Aldine-Atherton, 1971, 1-62.

——. "Behavior Theory and the Models of Man." *American Psychologist* 29 (December 1974): 859-69.

——. *Social Learning Theory.* Englewood Cliffs, N.J.: Prentice-Hall, 1977.

——. "Social-Learning Theory of Identificatory Processes." In *Handbook of Socialization Theory and Research,* edited by David A. Goslin. Chicago: Rand McNally, 1969.

——, and FREDERICK J. MCDONALD. "Influence of Social Reinforcement and the Behavior of Models in Shaping Children's Moral Judgments." *Journal of Abnormal and Social Psychology* 67, no. 3 (1963): 274-81.

BARBER, JAMES DAVID. *The Lawmakers: Recruitment and Adaptation to Legislative Life.* New Haven: Yale University Press, 1965.

——. *The Presidential Character: Predicting Performance in the White House.* 2d ed. Englewood Cliffs, N.J.: Prentice-Hall, 1977.

——, ed. *Race for the Presidency: The Media and the Nominating Process.* Englewood Cliffs, N.J.: Prentice-Hall, 1978.

BELL, CHARLES G., and CHARLES M. PRICE. *The First Term: A Study of Legislative Socialization.* Beverly Hills: Sage, 1975.

BENNETT, W. LANCE. *Public Opinion in American Politics.* New York: Harcourt Brace Jovanovich, 1980.

BENNETTS, LESLIE. "Antiabortion Movement in Disarray Less Than Year After Election Victories." *New York Times,* 22 September 1981.

——. "Conservatives Join on Social Concerns." *New York Times,* 31 July 1980, A1.

——. "National Anti-Liberal Crusade Zeroing in on McGovern in South Dakota." *New York Times,* 2 June 1980, B11.

BERGER, SEYMOUR M. "Observer Perseverance as Related to a Model's Success: A Social Comparison Analysis." *Journal of Personality and Social Psychology* 19 (1971): 341-50.

BERRY, JEFFREY M. *The Interest Group Society.* Boston: Little, Brown, 1984.
BIERSACK, ROBERT W., and PATRICIA HAEUSER. "Political Party Organizations and Campaign Services to Candidates." Paper presented at the annual meeting of the Midwest Political Science Association, Cincinnati, 1981.
BLACKWELL, MORTON C. "The Right Campaigns: The Pro-Life Movement." *Conservative Digest,* February 1979, 6.
BLAKE, JUDITH, and JORGE H. DEL PINAL. "Negativism, Equivocation, and Wobbly Assent: Public 'Support' for the Prochoice Platform on Abortion." *Demography* 18 (August 1981): 309-20.
———. "Predicting Polar Attitudes Toward Abortion in the United States." In *Abortion Parley,* edited by James T. Burtchael. New York: Andrews and McMeel, 1980, 27-56.
BOSITIS, DAVID A., and ROY E. MILLER. "Authoritarianism and Socialization: Some Insights from Learning Theory." Paper presented at the annual meeting of the Midwest Political Science Association, Chicago, 1979.
BRAUNTHAL, GERARD. "The 1976 West German Election Campaign." *Polity* 10 (Winter 1977): 147-67.
BRITT, DAVID W. "Effects of Probability of Reinforcement and Social Stimulus Consistency on Imitation." *Journal of Personality and Social Psychology* 18, no. 2 (1971): 189-200.
BRODER, DAVID S. "Parties in Trouble." *Today,* 11 May 1979, 10-11.
———. "Women Working the Grass Roots but Top Campaigns Look Tough." *Washington Post,* 30 August 1982, A2.
BROH, C. ANTHONY. "Horse-Race Journalism: Reporting the Polls in the 1976 Presidential Election." *Public Opinion Quarterly* 44 (1980): 514-29.
BUCHANAN, CHRISTOPHER. "National GOP Pushing Hard to Capture State Legislatures." *Congressional Quarterly Weekly Report* 38 (25 October 1980): 3188-92.
———. "Senators Face Tough Re-election Odds." *Congressional Quarterly Weekly Report* 38 (5 April 1980): 905-9.
BULLOCK, CHARLES S., III. "Explaining Congressional Elections: Differences in Perceptions of Opposing Candidates." *Legislative Studies Quarterly* 2 (August 1977): 295-308.
BURNHAM, WALTER DEAN. *Critical Elections and the Mainsprings of American Politics.* New York: Norton, 1970.
CAMPBELL, BRUCE A. "Theory Building in Political Socialization: Explorations of Political Trust and Social Learning Theory." *American Politics Quarterly* 7 (October 1979): 453-69.
"The Case of the GOP Clones." *Newsweek,* 13 October 1980, 37.
CHAMBERS, WILLIAM NISBET, and WALTER DEAN BURNHAM, eds. *The Amer-*

ican Party Systems: Stages of Political Development. 2d ed. New York: Oxford University Press, 1975.

CLARKE, PETER, and SUSAN H. EVANS. *Covering Campaigns: Journalism in Congressional Elections.* Stanford: Stanford University Press, 1983.

CLAUSEN, AAGE. "The Accuracy of Leader Perceptions of Constituents' Views." Paper presented at the annual meeting of the American Political Science Association, Washington, D.C., 1977.

CLEM, ALAN L., ed. *The Making of Congressmen: Seven Campaigns of 1974.* North Scituate, Mass.: Duxbury, 1976.

CLYMER, ADAM. "If Winning Is Important, Winning First Is More So." *New York Times,* 7 October 1979, E4.

―――. "Kennedy to Tap Key Aides from Three Presidential Races in '80 Campaign." *New York Times,* 21 October 1979, 38.

―――. "Reagan: the 1980 Model." *New York Times Magazine,* 29 July 1979, 23ff.

COBB, ROGER W., and CHARLES D. ELDER. "The Political Uses of Symbolism." *American Politics Quarterly* 1 (July 1973): 305-38.

COHODAS, NADINE. "Members Move to Rein in Supreme Court." *Congressional Quarterly Weekly Report* 39 (30 May 1981): 947-51.

―――. " 'Pro-Life' Interest Groups Try a New Tactic in Effort to Crack Down on Abortion." *Congressional Quarterly Weekly Report* 39 (28 February 1981): 383-87.

COLLIER, DAVID, and RICHARD E. MESSICK. "Prerequisites Versus Diffusion: Testing Alternative Explanations of Social Security Adoption." *American Political Science Review* 69 (December 1975): 1299-1315.

CONGRESSIONAL QUARTERLY. "Bill Brock Concentrates on Grass Roots." *CQ Guide to Current American Government,* Fall 1979. Washington, D.C.: Congressional Quarterly, 1979, 79-83.

CONOVER, PAMELA JOHNSTON, and VIRGINIA GRAY. *Feminism and the New Right.* New York: Praeger, 1983.

CONVERSE, PHILIP E., AAGE R. CLAUSEN, and WARREN E. MILLER. "Electoral Myth and Reality: The 1964 Election." *American Political Science Review* 59 (June 1965): 321-36.

CONWAY, M. MARGARET. "Political Party Nationalization, Campaign Activities, and Local Party Development." Paper presented at the annual meeting of the Midwest Political Science Association, Cincinnati, 1981.

COOK, RHODES. "Democrats Develop Tactics; Laying Groundwork for 1984." *Congressional Quarterly Weekly Report* 40 (3 July 1982): 1591-95.

―――. "Democrats' Rules Weaken Representation." *Congressional Quarterly Weekly Report* 40 (3 April 1982): 749-51.

_____. "First Test for 1980 Presidential Contenders." *Congressional Quarterly Weekly Report* 38 (12 January 1980): 83-86.

_____. "National Mood for Change Boosted Republican Ticket." *Congressional Quarterly Weekly Report* 38 (15 November 1980): 3370-71.

_____. "New Democratic Rules Panel: A Careful Approach to Change." *Congressional Quarterly Weekly Report* 39 (26 December 1981): 2563-67.

COSTIKYAN, EDWARD N. *How to Win Votes: The Politics of 1980.* New York: Harcourt Brace Jovanovich, 1980.

COTTER, CORNELIUS P., and JOHN F. BIBBY. "The Impact of Reform on the National Party Organizations: The Long-term Determinants of Party Reform." Paper presented at the annual meeting of the American Political Science Association, Washington, D.C., 1979.

COTTER, CORNELIUS P., JAMES L. GIBSON, JOHN F. BIBBY, and ROBERT J. HUCKSHORN. "State Party Organizations and the Thesis of Party Decline." Paper presented at the annual meeting of the American Political Science Association, Washington, D.C., 1980.

CROTTY, WILLIAM. *Decision for the Democrats: Reforming the Party Structure.* Baltimore: Johns Hopkins University Press, 1978.

_____, and GARY C. JACOBSON. *American Parties in Decline.* Boston: Little, Brown, 1980.

CROUSE, TIMOTHY. *The Boys on the Bus.* New York: Ballantine, 1972.

CYERT, RICHARD M., and JAMES G. MARCH. *A Behavioral Theory of the Firm.* Englewood Cliffs, N.J.: Prentice-Hall, 1963.

DARCY, R., and SARAH SLAVIN SCHRAMM. "When Women Run Against Men." *Public Opinion Quarterly* 41 (Spring 1977): 1-12.

DAVIDSON, ROGER H. *The Role of the Congressman.* Indianapolis: Pegasus, 1969.

DENNIS, JACK. "Support for the Party System by the Mass Public." *American Political Science Review* 60 (September 1966): 600-615.

DEWAR, HELEN. "Three Senate Doves on New Right Menu Proving Tough." *Washington Post,* 26 October 1980, A8-A9.

DE WITT, KAREN. "Candidate Grooming Isn't Left to Chance." *New York Times,* 10 February 1980, E2.

DIONNE, E.J., JR. "Abortion Poll: Views Expressed Vary According to the Way Questions Are Phrased." *Louisville Courier-Journal,* 20 August 1980, A11.

_____. "On the Trail of Corporation Donations." *New York Times,* 6 October 1980.

DOWNS, ANTHONY. *An Economic Theory of Democracy.* New York: Harper & Row, 1957.

DOWNS, GEORGE W., JR., and LAWRENCE B. MOHR. "Conceptual Issues in the

Study of Innovation." University of Michigan Institute of Public Policy Studies, Discussion Paper no. 76, Ann Arbor, 1976.

DREW, ELIZABETH. *American Journal: The Events of 1976.* New York: Random House, 1977.

———. "Politics and Money." *New Yorker,* 6 and 13 December 1982, 54-149 and 57-111.

———. *Senator.* New York: Simon and Schuster, 1979.

EDELMAN, MURRAY. *Political Language: Words That Succeed and Policies That Fail.* New York: Academic Press, 1977.

———. *Politics as Symbolic Action: Mass Arousal and Quiescence.* Chicago: Markham, 1971.

———. *The Symbolic Uses of Politics.* Urbana: University of Illinois Press, 1964.

ELDERSVELD, SAMUEL J. *Political Parties in American Society.* New York: Basic Books, 1982.

ELY, JOHN HART, and LAURENCE H. TRIBE. "Let There Be Life." *New York Times,* 17 March 1981, A17.

EPSTEIN, LEON D. *Political Parties in Western Democracies.* New Brunswick, N.J.: Transaction, 1980.

ESTES, W.K. "Reinforcement in Human Behavior." *American Scientist* 60 (November-December 1972): 723-29.

ETHEREDGE, LLOYD S. *Can Governments Learn?* Elmsford, N.Y.: Pergamon, 1983.

EULAU, HEINZ, and PAUL D. KARPS. "The Puzzle of Representation: Specifying Components of Responsiveness." *Legislative Studies Quarterly* 2 (August 1977): 53-85.

FEIGL, HERBERT. "The 'Orthodox' View of Theories." In *Minnesota Studies in the Philosophy of Science, IV,* edited by Michael Radner and Stephen Winokur. Minneapolis: University of Minnesota Press, 1970.

FENNO, RICHARD F., JR. *Home Style: House Members in Their Districts.* Boston: Little, Brown, 1978.

———. *The United States Senate: A Bicameral Perspective.* Washington, D.C.: American Enterprise Institute, 1982.

FINIFTER, ADA W. "The Friendship Group as a Protective Environment for Political Deviants." *American Political Science Review* 68 (June 1974): 607-25.

FIORINA, MORRIS P. *Congress: Keystone of the Washington Establishment.* New Haven: Yale University Press, 1977.

———. "Electoral Margins, Constituency Influence, and Policy Moderation: A Critical Assessment." *American Politics Quarterly* 1 (October 1973): 479-98.

———. *Representatives, Roll Calls, and Constituencies.* Lexington, Mass.: Lexington Books, 1974.

FISHEL, JEFF. *Party and Opposition: Congressional Challengers in American Politics.* New York: McKay, 1973.

———, ed. *Parties and Elections in an Anti-Party Age.* Bloomington: Indiana University Press, 1978.

FLANDERS, JAMES P. "A Review of Research on Imitative Behavior." *Psychological Bulletin* 69 (1968): 316-37.

FLEISHMAN, JOEL L., ed. *The Future of American Political Parties: The Challenge of Governance.* Englewood Cliffs, N.J.: Prentice-Hall, 1982.

FOWLER, LINDA L. "Candidate Perceptions of Electoral Coalitions: Limits and Possibilities." Paper presented at the Conference on Congressional Elections, Houston, 10-12 January 1980.

———. "The Electoral Lottery: Decisions to Run for Congress." *Public Choice* 34, nos. 3/4 (1979): 399-418.

FRANCOME, COLIN. "Abortion Politics in the United States." *Political Studies* 28 (December 1980): 613-21.

FRANKLIN, CHARLES H., and JOHN E. JACKSON. "The Dynamics of Party Identification." *American Political Science Review* 77 (December 1983): 957-73.

FRIESEMA, H. PAUL, and RONALD D. HEDLUND. "The Reality of Representational Roles." In *Public Opinion and Public Policy: Models of Political Linkage,* 3d ed., edited by Norman R. Luttbeg. Itasca, Ill.: Peacock, 1981, 316-20.

GAUNT, JEREMY. "Money Flows to the Right in 1982 Campaign." *Congressional Quarterly Weekly Report* 40 (27 February 1982): 482.

———. "Senators' Fund Raising: Millions for Self-Defense." *Congressional Quarterly Weekly Report* 40 (13 February 1982): 278-79.

GERMOND, JACK W., and JULES WITCOVER. *Blue Smoke and Mirrors: How Reagan Won and Why Carter Lost the Election of 1980.* New York: Viking, 1981.

GIBSON, JAMES L., CORNELIUS P. COTTER, JOHN F. BIBBY, and ROBERT J. HUCKSHORN. "Assessing Party Organizational Strength." *American Journal of Political Science* 27 (May 1983): 193-222.

———. "Whither the Local Parties?: A Cross-Sectional and Longitudinal Analysis of the Strength of Party Organizations." Paper presented at the annual meeting of the Western Political Science Association, San Diego, California, 1982.

GINSBERG, BENJAMIN. *The Consequences of Consent: Elections, Citizen Control, and Popular Acquiescence.* Reading, Mass.: Addison-Wesley, 1982.

———. "Polling and the Transformation of Public Opinion." Paper presented

at the annual meeting of the American Political Science Association, Denver, 1982.
GOFFMAN, ERVING. *The Presentation of Self in Everyday Life.* Garden City, N.Y.: Doubleday, 1959.
GOLDENBERG, EDIE N., and MICHAEL W. TRAUGOTT. *Campaigning for Congress.* Washington, D.C.: Congressional Quarterly, 1984.
GOLDMAN, PETER, with HOWARD FINEMAN. "The War of the Wolf PAC's." *Newsweek,* 1 June 1981, 38-39.
GOODIN, ROBERT E. "Voting Through the Looking Glass." *American Political Science Review* 77 (June 1983): 420-34.
GOPOIAN, J. DAVID. "What Makes PACs Tick? An Analysis of the Allocation Patterns of Economic Interest Groups." *American Journal of Political Science* 28 (May 1984): 259-81.
GRAMER, ROD. "Abortion Injected into Senate Race." *Idaho Statesman,* 17 August 1980, 1A.
GRANBERG, DONALD. "Pro-Life or Reflection of Conservative Ideology? An Analysis of Opposition to Legalized Abortion." *Sociology and Social Research* 62 (Winter 1977-78): 414-29.
_____, and DONALD DENNEY. "The National Abortion Rights Action League and the National Right to Life Committee: Initial Report of Comparisons of Two Opposing Social Movement Organizations." Mimeo., n.d.
GRAY, VIRGINIA. "Innovation in the States: A Diffusion Study." *American Political Science Review* 67 (December 1973): 1174-85.
GREENSTEIN, FRED I. "The Impact of Personality on Politics: An Attempt to Clear Away Underbrush." *American Political Science Review* 61 (September 1967): 629-41.
GUTH, JAMES L. "The Politics of the 'Evangelical Right': An Interpretive Essay." Paper presented at the annual meeting of the American Political Science Association, New York, 1981.
HALL, CALVIN S., and GARDNER LINDZEY. *Theories of Personality.* 3d ed. New York: Wiley, 1978.
HEMPEL, CARL G. "The Theoretician's Dilemma: A Study in the Logic of Theory Construction." In *Aspects of Scientific Explanation and Other Essays in the Philosophy of Science,* edited by Carl G. Hempel. New York: Free Press, 1965, 173-226.
HERMAN, ROBIN. "Taking Up Political Arms Against the Right-to-Lifers." *New York Times,* 9 November 1980, E8.
HERSHEY, MARJORIE RANDON. "Incumbency and the Minimum Winning Coalition." *American Journal of Political Science* 17 (August 1973): 631-37.
_____. *The Making of Campaign Strategy.* Lexington, Mass.: Lexington, 1974.

_____, and DAVID B. HILL. "The President and Political Socialization: Applying Social Learning Theory to Two Long-Standing Hypotheses." *Youth and Society* 9 (December 1977): 125-50.

HERSHEY, MARJORIE RANDON, and DARRELL M. WEST. "Single-Issue Politics: Prolife Groups and the 1980 Senate Campaign." In *Interest Group Politics,* edited by Allan J. Cigler and Burdett A. Loomis. Washington, D.C.: Congressional Quarterly, 1983, 31-59.

HIBBING, JOHN R., and SARA L. BRANDES. "State Population and the Electoral Success of U.S. Senators." *American Journal of Political Science* 27 (November 1983): 808-19.

HILL, DAVID B., and NORMAN R. LUTTBEG. *Trends in American Electoral Behavior.* 2d ed. Itasca, Ill.: Peacock, 1983.

HINCKLEY, BARBARA. "The American Voter in Congressional Elections." *American Political Science Review* 74 (September 1980): 641-50.

_____. *Congressional Elections.* Washington, D.C.: Congressional Quarterly, 1981.

_____. "House Re-elections and Senate Defeats: The Role of the Challenger." *British Journal of Political Science* 10 (October 1980): 441-60.

HOFSTADTER, RICHARD. *The Idea of a Party System.* Berkeley: University of California Press, 1969.

HUCKER, CHARLES W. "Congress Fine Tunes Campaign Law." *Congressional Quarterly Weekly Report* 38 (5 January 1980): 31-33.

_____, ed. "Special Report: 1980 Elections." *Congressional Quarterly Weekly Report* 38 (23 February 1980).

HUCKFELDT, R. ROBERT. "Political Loyalties and Social Class Ties: The Mechanisms of Contextual Influence." *American Journal of Political Science* 28 (May 1984): 399-417.

_____. "Political Participation and the Neighborhood Social Context." *American Journal of Political Science* 23 (August 1979): 579-92.

HUCKSHORN, ROBERT J. *Political Parties in America.* 2d ed. Monterey, Calif.: Brooks/Cole, 1984.

_____, and ROBERT C. SPENCER. *The Politics of Defeat: Campaigning for Congress.* Amherst: University of Massachusetts Press, 1971.

IYENGAR, SHANTO, MARK D. PETERS, and DONALD R. KINDER. "Experimental Demonstrations of the 'Not-So-Minimal' Consequences of Television News Programs." *American Political Science Review* 76 (December 1982): 848-58.

JACKSON, JOHN S., III, BARBARA LEAVITT BROWN, and DAVID BOSITIS. "Herbert McClosky and Friends Revisited: 1980 Democratic and Republican Party Elites Compared to the Mass Public." *American Politics Quarterly* 10 (April 1982): 158-80.

JACOB, HERBERT. "Initial Recruitment of Elected Officials in the U.S.—A Model." *Journal of Politics* 24 (November 1962): 703-16.

JACOBSON, GARY C. *Money in Congressional Elections.* New Haven: Yale University Press, 1980.

———. "Money in the 1980 Congressional Elections." Paper presented at the annual meeting of the Midwest Political Science Association, Milwaukee, 1982.

———. *The Politics of Congressional Elections.* Boston: Little, Brown, 1983.

———. "Strategic Politicians and Congressional Elections, 1946-1980." Department of Political Science Working Paper no. 81-7, University of California, San Diego, 1981.

———, and SAMUEL KERNELL. *Strategy and Choice in Congressional Elections.* New Haven: Yale University Press, 1981.

JAFFE, FREDERICK S., BARBARA L. LINDHEIM, and PHILIP R. LEE. *Abortion Politics: Private Morality and Public Policy.* New York: McGraw-Hill, 1981.

JEWELL, MALCOLM E. *Parties and Primaries: Nominating State Governors.* New York: Praeger, 1984.

———. "The State Party Convention as a Device for Influencing Primary Elections: A Study of Five States in 1982." Paper presented at the annual meeting of the American Political Science Association, Chicago, 1983.

JOHANNES, JOHN R. "Explaining Congressional Casework Styles." *American Journal of Political Science* 27 (August 1983): 530-47.

KATZ, ELIHU, MARTIN L. LEVIN, and HERBERT HAMILTON. "Traditions of Research on the Diffusion of Innovation." *American Sociological Review* 28 (April 1963): 237-52.

KAYDEN, XANDRA. *Campaign Organization.* Lexington, Mass.: Heath, 1978.

KAZEE, THOMAS A. "The Decision to Run for the U.S. Congress: Challenger Attitudes in the 1970's." *Legislative Studies Quarterly* 5 (1980): 79-100.

———, and MARY C. THORNBERRY. "Can We Throw the Rascals Out?: Recruiting Challengers in Competitive Districts." Paper presented at the annual meeting of the American Political Science Association, Chicago, 1983.

KELLER, BILL. "Evangelical Conservatives Move from Pews to Polls, But Can They Sway Congress?" *Congressional Quarterly Weekly Report* 38 (6 September 1980): 2627-34.

———, and NADINE COHODAS. "Tactical Errors, Disunity Blunt New Right Social Legislation." *Congressional Quarterly Weekly Report* 40 (16 October 1982): 2675-78.

KELLEY, STANLEY, JR. *Interpreting Elections.* Princeton: Princeton University Press, 1983.

KESSEL, JOHN H. *The Goldwater Coalition.* Indianapolis: Bobbs-Merrill, 1968.

———. *Presidential Campaign Politics: Coalition Strategies and Citizen Response.* Homewood, Ill.: Dorsey, 1980.
———. *Presidential Parties.* Homewood, Ill.: Dorsey, 1984.
KEY, V.O., JR. *American State Politics.* New York: Knopf, 1956.
———. *Politics, Parties and Pressure Groups.* 5th ed. New York: Crowell, 1964.
———, with the assistance of MILTON CUMMINGS. *The Responsible Electorate.* Cambridge, Mass.: Harvard University Press, 1966.
KING, SETH S. "Ideologies Clash Sharply in Iowa Senatorial Contest." *New York Times,* 24 October 1980, A18.
KING, WAYNE. "McGovern, Long a Target, Finds Rewards in Taking the Offensive." *New York Times,* 19 October 1980.
KINGDON, JOHN W. *Candidates for Office: Beliefs and Strategies.* New York: Random House, 1968.
———. *Congressmen's Voting Decisions.* 2d ed. New York: Harper & Row, 1981.
KIRKPATRICK, JEANE J. *Political Woman.* New York: Basic Books, 1974.
KREHBIEL, KEITH, and JOHN R. WRIGHT. "The Incumbency Effect in Congressional Elections: A Test of Two Explanations." *American Journal of Political Science* 27 (February 1983): 140-57.
KUKLINSKI, JAMES. "Representativeness and Elections: A Policy Analysis." *American Political Science Review* 72 (March 1978): 165-77.
———, and RICHARD C. ELLING. "Representational Role, Constituency Opinion, and Legislative Roll-call Behavior." *American Journal of Political Science* 21 (February 1977): 135-47.
KUKLINSKI, JAMES H., and DONALD J. MCCRONE. "Electoral Accountability As a Source of Policy Representation." In *Public Opinion and Public Policy: Models of Political Linkage,* edited by Norman R. Luttbeg. 3d ed. Itasca, Ill.: Peacock, 1981, 320-41.
LADD, EVERETT CARLL. "The New Lines Are Drawn: Class and Ideology in America." *Public Opinion* 1 (July/August 1978): 48-53.
———. *Where Have All the Voters Gone? The Fracturing of America's Political Parties.* 2d ed. New York: Norton, 1982.
LAMB, KARL A., and PAUL A. SMITH. *Campaign Decision-Making: The Presidential Election of 1964.* Belmont, Calif.: Wadsworth, 1968.
LAWSON, KAY. *The Comparative Study of Political Parties.* New York: St. Martin's Press, 1976.
LEUTHOLD, DAVID A. *Electioneering in a Democracy: Campaigns for Congress.* New York: Wiley, 1968.
LIEBMAN, ROBERT C., and ROBERT WUTHNOW, eds. *The New Christian Right: Mobilization and Legitimation.* Hawthorne, N.Y.: Aldine, 1983.

LIGHT, LARRY. "Democrats May Lose Edge in Contributions from PACs." *Congressional Quarterly Weekly Report* 38 (22 November 1980): 3405-9.

———. "The Game of PAC Targeting: Friends, Foes and Guesswork." *Congressional Quarterly Weekly Report* 39 (21 November 1981): 2267-70.

———. "Republican Groups Dominate in Party Campaign Spending." *Congressional Quarterly Weekly Report* 38 (1 November 1980): 3234-39.

———. "Surge in Independent Campaign Spending." *Congressional Quarterly Weekly Report* 38 (14 June 1980): 1635-39.

———. "Will Money Preserve GOP Gains of 1980?" *Congressional Quarterly Weekly Report* 40 (10 April 1982): 814-16.

LOWI, THEODORE J. *The End of Liberalism: The Second Republic of the United States.* 2d ed. New York: Norton, 1979.

———. "Toward Functionalism in Political Science: The Case of Innovation in Party Systems." *American Political Science Review* 57 (September 1963): 570-83.

LUKER, KRISTIN. *Abortion and the Politics of Motherhood.* Berkeley: University of California Press, 1984.

McCRONE, DONALD J., and JAMES H. KUKLINSKI. "The Delegate Theory of Representation." *American Journal of Political Science* 23 (May 1979): 278-300.

McGINNISS, JOE. *The Selling of the President 1968.* New York: Washington Square Press, 1969.

McGOVERN, GEORGE. *Grassroots: The Autobiography of George McGovern.* New York: Random House, 1977.

McGUIRE, WILLIAM J. "The Nature of Attitudes and Attitude Change." In *The Handbook of Social Psychology,* vol. 3, edited by Gardner Lindzey and Elliot Aronson. 2d ed. Reading, Mass.: Addison-Wesley, 1969, 136-314.

McINTYRE, THOMAS J., with JOHN C. OBERT. *The Fear Brokers.* New York: Pilgrim, 1979.

MADDI, SALVATORE R. *Personality Theories: A Comparative Analysis.* 3d ed. Homewood, Ill.: Dorsey, 1976.

MAISEL, LOUIS SANDY. *From Obscurity to Oblivion: Running in the Congressional Primary.* Knoxville: University of Tennessee Press, 1982.

MALBIN, MICHAEL J., ed. *Money and Politics in the United States: Financing Elections in the 1980s.* Chatham, N.J.: Chatham House, 1984.

MANDEL, RUTH B. *In the Running: The New Woman Candidate.* Boston: Beacon, 1981.

MANN, THOMAS E., and NORMAN J. ORNSTEIN, eds. *The American Elections of 1982.* Washington, D.C.: American Enterprise Institute, 1983.

MANN, THOMAS E., and RAYMOND E. WOLFINGER. "Candidates and Parties

in Congressional Elections." *American Political Science Review* 74 (September 1980): 617-32.
MARCH, JAMES G., and HERBERT A. SIMON. *Organizations.* New York: Wiley, 1967.
MARGOLIS, MICHAEL, and KEVIN NEARY. "Pressure Politics Revisited: The Anti-Abortion Campaign." *Policy Studies Journal* 8 (Spring 1980): 698-716.
MARGOLIS, MICHAEL, LEE S. WEINBERG, and DAVID F. RANCK. "Local Party Organization: From Disaggregation to Disintegration." Paper presented at the annual meeting of the American Political Science Association, Washington, D.C., 1980.
MARSHALL, ROBERT G. *Bayonets and Roses: Comprehensive Pro-Life Political Action Guide.* Published by the author; no place of publication listed, 1976.
MARSTON, ALBERT R. "Imitation, Self-Reinforcement, and Reinforcement of Another Person." *Journal of Personality and Social Psychology* 2 (1965): 255-61.
MATHEWS, TOM, with JAMES DOYLE, HENRY W. HUBBARD, JOHN J. LINDSAY, JOHN WALCOTT, and MARTIN KASINDORF. "Single-Issue Politics." *Newsweek,* 6 November 1978, 48-60.
MATTHEWS, DONALD R. *U.S. Senators and Their World.* New York: Vintage, 1960.
_____, and JAMES A. STIMSON. *Yeas and Nays: Normal Decision-Making in the U.S. House of Representatives.* New York: Wiley, 1975.
MAY, ERNEST R., and JANET FRASER. *Campaign '72: The Managers Speak.* Cambridge, Mass.: Harvard University Press, 1973.
MAYER, ALLAN J. "End of the Democratic Era?" *Newsweek.* 18 August 1980, 21-25.
_____. "A Tide of Born-Again Politics." *Newsweek,* 15 September 1980, 28-36.
MAYHEW, DAVID R. *Congress: The Electoral Connection.* New Haven: Yale University Press, 1974.
MENZEL, DONALD C., and IRWIN FELLER. "Leadership and Interaction Patterns in the Diffusion of Innovations Among the American States." *Western Political Quarterly* 30 (December 1977): 528-36.
MERKL, PETER H. "Comparative Study and Campaign Management: The Brandt Campaign in Western Germany." *Western Political Quarterly* 15 (December 1962): 681-704.
MILEUR, JEROME M., and GEORGE T. SULZNER. *Campaigning for the Massachusetts Senate: Electioneering Outside the Political Limelight.* Amherst: University of Massachusetts Press, 1974.
MILGRAM, STANLEY. *Obedience to Authority: An Experimental View.* New York: Harper & Row, 1974.

MILLER, ARTHUR H., and MARTIN P. WATTENBERG. "Measuring Party Identification: Independent or No Partisan Preference?" *American Journal of Political Science* 27 (February 1983): 106-21.

MILLER, JUDITH. "Billy Carter Investigation Hobbles Bayh Re-election Drive in Indiana." *New York Times,* 17 September 1980, B14.

———. "Local Campaigners Now Pursue Funds Nationwide." *New York Times,* 23 September 1980, 12.

———. "Senator Leahy Expected to Be Re-elected in Vermont." *New York Times,* 17 October 1980, C20.

———, with MARTIN TOLCHIN. "Democrats Expected to Hold Their Majorities in Congress." *New York Times,* 26 October 1980, 40.

MIROFF, BRUCE. "Presidential Campaigns: Candidates, Managers and Reporters." *Polity* 12 (Summer 1980): 667-75.

MISCHEL, WALTER. "On the Interface of Cognition and Personality: Beyond the Person-Situation Debate." *American Psychologist* 34 (September 1979): 740-54.

———. "Toward a Cognitive Social Learning Reconceptualization of Personality." *Psychological Review* 80, no. 4 (1973): 252-83.

———, and BERT MOORE. "Effects of Attention to Symbolically Presented Rewards on Self-Control." *Journal of Personality and Social Psychology* 28, no. 2 (1973): 172-79.

MISCHEL, WALTER, EBBE B. EBBESEN, and ANTONETTE RASKOFF ZEISS. "Selective Attention to the Self: Situational and Dispositional Determinants." *Journal of Personality and Social Psychology* 27, no. 1 (1973): 129-42.

MOHR, JAMES C. *Abortion in America.* New York: Oxford University Press, 1978.

MOHR, LAWRENCE B. "Determinants of Innovation in Organizations." *American Political Science Review* 63 (March 1969): 111-26.

MOORE, JONATHAN, and JANET FRASER, eds. *Campaign for President: The Managers Look at 1976.* Cambridge, Mass.: Ballinger, 1977.

MOREHOUSE, SARAH MCCALLY. "The Effect of Preprimary Endorsements on State Party Strength." Paper presented at the annual meeting of the American Political Science Association, Washington, D.C., 1980.

MOXLEY, WARDEN. "GOP Wins Senate Control for First Time in Twenty-eight Years." *Congressional Quarterly Weekly Report* 38 (8 November 1980): 3300-3303.

———. "A New South in a New Republican Senate." *Congressional Quarterly Weekly Report* 38 (13 December 1980): 3556-65.

BILL MOYERS' JOURNAL. "Campaign Report no. 3," Transcript, 26 September 1980.

———. "See How They Run," Campaign Report no. 4, WNET Transcript, 3 October 1980.
MUIR, WILLIAM K., JR. *Legislature: California's School for Politics.* Chicago: University of Chicago Press, 1983.
NAPOLITAN, JOSEPH. *The Election Game and How to Win It.* Garden City, N.Y.: Doubleday, 1972.
NIE, NORMAN H., SIDNEY VERBA, and JOHN R. PETROCIK. *The Changing American Voter.* Enlarged ed. Cambridge, Mass.: Harvard University Press, 1979.
NIXON, RICHARD. *Six Crises.* Garden City, N.Y.: Doubleday, 1962.
O'BRIEN, LAWRENCE F. *No Final Victories: A Life in Politics—from John F. Kennedy to Watergate.* Garden City, N.Y.: Doubleday, 1974.
O'HARA, PEG. "Congress and the Hyde Amendment . . . How the House Moved to Stop Abortions." *Congressional Quarterly Weekly Report* 38 (19 April 1980): 1038-39.
PADGETT, JOHN F. "Bounded Rationality in Budget Research." *American Political Science Review* 74 (June 1980): 354-72.
PAGE, BENJAMIN I. *Choices and Echoes in Presidential Elections: Rational Man and Electoral Democracy.* Chicago: University of Chicago Press, 1978.
———, and RICHARD A. BRODY. "Policy Voting and the Electoral Process: The Vietnam War Issue." *American Political Science Review* 66 (September 1972): 979-95.
PALETZ, DAVID L., and ROBERT M. ENTMAN. *Media—Power—Politics.* New York: Free Press, 1981.
PATTERSON, THOMAS E. *The Mass Media Election: How Americans Choose Their President.* New York: Praeger, 1980.
PERRY, JAMES M. "Liberal Incumbents Are Main Targets of TV Ads As Political-Action Groups Exploit Court Ruling." *Wall Street Journal,* 25 January 1980.
PITCHER, BRIAN L., ROBERT L. HAMBLIN, and JERRY L.L. MILLER. "The Diffusion of Collective Violence." *American Sociological Review* 43 (February 1978): 23-35.
POLSBY, NELSON W. *Consequences of Party Reform.* New York: Oxford University Press, 1983.
———. *Political Innovation in America: The Politics of Policy Initiation.* New Haven: Yale University Press, 1984.
POMPER, GERALD M. *Voters' Choice: Varieties of American Electoral Behavior.* New York: Dodd, Mead, 1975.
———, et al. *The Election of 1980: Reports and Interpretations.* Chatham, N.J.: Chatham House, 1981.
PORTER, H. OWEN. "Legislative Experts and Outsiders: The Two-Step Flow

of Communication." *Journal of Politics* 36 (August 1974): 703-30.
PRICE, DAVID E. *Bringing Back the Parties*. Washington, D.C.: Congressional Quarterly, 1984.
PUTNAM, ROBERT D. *The Comparative Study of Political Elites*. Englewood Cliffs, N.J.: Prentice-Hall, 1976.
RAGSDALE, LYN, and TIMOTHY COOK. "Representatives' Actions and Challengers' Reactions: Limits to Candidate Connections in the House." Paper presented at the annual meeting of the Midwest Political Science Association, Chicago, 1984.
RAKOVE, MILTON L. *Don't Make No Waves . . . Don't Back No Losers*. Bloomington: Indiana University Press, 1975.
RANNEY, AUSTIN. "Candidate Selection and Party Cohesion in Britain and the United States." In *Approaches to the Study of Party Organization,* edited by William J. Crotty. Boston: Allyn and Bacon, 1968, 139-57.
_____. *Curing the Mischiefs of Faction: Party Reform in America*. Berkeley: University of California Press, 1975.
_____. *The Doctrine of Responsible Party Government: Its Origins and Present State*. Urbana: University of Illinois Press, 1962.
_____. "The Political Parties: Reform and Decline." In *The New American Political System,* edited by Anthony King. Washington, D.C.: American Enterprise Institute, 1978, 213-47.
_____, ed. *The American Elections of 1980*. Washington, D.C.: American Enterprise Institute, 1981.
REED, ROY. "George Bush on the Move." *New York Times Magazine,* 10 February 1980, 20-21ff.
REES, GROVER, III. "The True Confession of One One-Issue Voter." *National Review* 31 (25 May 1979): 669-80.
RIKER, WILLIAM H., and WILLIAM JAMES ZAVOINA. "Rational Behavior in Politics: Evidence from a Three Person Game." *American Political Science Review* 64 (March 1970): 48-60.
ROBERTS, STEVEN V. "McGovern in a New Battle—for Survival." *New York Times,* 14 September 1980.
ROBINSON, MICHAEL J., and MARGARET A. SHEEHAN. *Over the Wire and on TV: CBS and UPI in Campaign '80*. New York: Basic Books, 1983.
ROGERS, EVERETT M., with F. FLOYD SHOEMAKER. *Communication of Innovations: A Cross-Cultural Approach*. 2d ed. New York: Free Press, 1971.
ROSE, RICHARD. *Do Parties Make a Difference?* 2d ed. Chatham, N.J.: Chatham House, 1984.
RUSSAKOFF, DALE. "NCPAC Bid to Beat Him Proves Boon to Sarbanes." *Washington Post,* 16 November 1981, A1ff.

SABATO, LARRY J. *PAC Power: Inside the World of Political Action Committees.* New York: Norton, 1984.
_____. *The Rise of Political Consultants.* New York: Basic Books, 1981.
SAMUELSON, ROBERT J. "Fragmentation and Uncertainty Litter the Political Landscape." *National Journal,* 20 October 1979, 1726-36.
SANDOZ, ELLIS, and CECIL V. CRABB. *A Tide of Discontent: The 1980 Elections and Their Meaning.* Washington, D.C.: Congressional Quarterly, 1981.
SCHLESINGER, JOSEPH A. *Ambition and Politics: Political Careers in the United States.* Chicago: Rand McNally, 1966.
_____. "On the Theory of Party Organization." Paper presented at the annual meeting of the American Political Science Association, Washington, D.C., 1983.
SCHNEIDER, CARL E., and MARIS A. VINOVSKIS. *The Law and Politics of Abortion.* Lexington, Mass.: Heath-Lexington, 1980.
SCHRAM, MARTIN. *Running for President: A Journal of the Carter Campaign.* New York: Pocket Books, 1978.
SCHUMPETER, JOSEPH A. *Capitalism, Socialism and Democracy.* 3d ed. New York: Harper: 1962.
SIMON, HERBERT. *Administrative Behavior.* New York: Free Press, 1945.
_____. *Models of Man: Social and Rational; Mathematical Essays on Rational Human Behavior in a Social Setting.* New York: Wiley, 1957.
SIMPSON, DICK W. *Winning Elections: A Handbook in Participatory Politics.* Revised ed. Athens, Ohio: Swallow Press, 1981.
SINGH, B. KRISHNA, and PETER J. LEAHY. "Contextual and Ideological Dimensions of Attitudes Toward Discretionary Abortion." *Demography* 15 (August 1978): 381-88.
SKERRY, PETER. "The Class Conflict Over Abortion." *Public Interest* 52 (Summer 1978): 69-84.
SKINNER, B.F. *About Behaviorism.* New York: Vintage, 1976.
_____. *Beyond Freedom and Dignity.* New York: Knopf, 1971.
SMITH, PAUL A. *Electing a President: Information and Control.* New York: Praeger, 1982.
SNIDERMAN, PAUL M. *Personality and Democratic Politics.* Berkeley: University of California Press, 1975.
SORAUF, FRANK J. *Party and Representation: Legislative Politics in Pennsylvania.* New York: Atherton, 1963.
_____. *Party Politics in America.* 5th ed. Boston: Little, Brown, 1984.
SPIELBERGER, CHARLES D., and L. DOUGLAS DE NIKE. "Descriptive Behaviorism Versus Cognitive Theory in Verbal Operant Conditioning." *Psychological Review* 73, no. 4 (1966): 306-26.

SPRAGUE, JOHN, and LOUIS P. WESTEFIELD. "Contextual Effects from Behavioral Contagion." Political Science Paper no. 22, Department of Political Science, Washington University, St. Louis, 1979.

STEINER, GILBERT Y., ed. *The Abortion Dispute and the American System.* Washington, D.C.: Brookings Institution, 1983.

STONE, WALTER J. "Prenomination Candidate Choice and General Election Behavior: Iowa Presidential Activists in 1980." *American Journal of Political Science* 28 (May 1984): 361-78.

―――, and ALAN I. ABRAMOWITZ. "Winning May Not Be Everything, But It's More Than We Thought: Presidential Party Activists in 1980." *American Political Science Review* 77 (December 1983): 945-56.

STUART, REGINALD. "Bayh's Fourth Contest May Be His Toughest Test Yet." *New York Times,* 18 October 1980, 7.

SUNDQUIST, JAMES L. *Dynamics of the Party System: Alignment and Realignment of Political Parties in the United States.* Washington, D.C.: Brookings Institution, 1973.

SWERDLOW, JOEL. "The Decline of the Boys on the Bus." *Washington Journalism Review* 3 (January/February 1981): 14-19.

THOMPSON, VICTOR A. "Bureaucracy and Innovation." *Administrative Science Quarterly* 10 (June 1965): 1-20.

TRAUGOTT, MICHAEL W., and MARIS A. VINOVSKIS. "Abortion and the 1978 Congressional Elections." *Family Planning Perspectives* 12 (September/October 1980): 238-46.

USLANER, ERIC. " 'Ain't Misbehavin': The Logic of Defensive Issue Voting Strategies in Congressional Elections." *American Politics Quarterly* 9 (January 1981): 3-22.

VECSEY, GEORGE. "Catholics in Survey Endorse Abortion." *New York Times,* 11 November 1979, 43.

VERBA, SIDNEY, and NORMAN H. NIE. *Participation in America: Political Democracy and Social Equality.* New York: Harper & Row, 1972.

VIDAL, DAVID. "U.S. Image-Makers Put Stamp on Venezuelan Campaign." *New York Times,* 2 August 1978, 2.

VIGUERIE, RICHARD A. *The New Right: We're Ready to Lead.* Revised ed. Falls Church, Va.: Viguerie Company, 1981.

VINOVSKIS, MARIS A. "Abortion and the Presidential Election of 1976: A Multivariate Analysis of Voting Behavior." *Michigan Law Review* 77 (August 1979): 1750-71.

―――. "The Politics of Abortion in the House of Representatives in 1976." *Michigan Law Review* 77 (August 1979): 1790-1827.

WAGNER, JOSEPH. "Media Do Make a Difference: The Differential Impact of

Mass Media in the 1976 Presidential Race." *American Journal of Political Science* 27 (August 1983): 407-30.
WALKER, JACK L. "The Diffusion of Innovations Among the American States." *American Political Science Review* 63 (September 1969): 880-99.
WALTERS, RICHARD H. "Some Conditions Facilitating the Occurrence of Imitative Behavior." In *Social Facilitation and Imitative Behavior*, edited by Edward C. Simmel, Ronald A. Hoppe, and G. Alexander Milton. Boston: Allyn & Bacon, 1968, 7-30.
WARNER, KENNETH E. "The Need for Some Innovative Concepts of Innovation: An Examination of Research on the Diffusion of Innovations." *Policy Sciences* 5 (1974): 433-51.
WATSON, RICHARD A. *The Presidential Contest*. 2d ed. New York: Wiley, 1984.
WATTENBERG, MARTIN P. *The Decline of American Political Parties, 1952-1980*. Cambridge, Mass.: Harvard University Press, 1984.
———. "The Decline of Political Partisanship in the United States: Negativity or Neutrality?" *American Political Science Review* 75 (December 1981): 941-50.
WAYNE, STEPHEN J. *The Road to the White House: The Politics of Presidential Elections*. 2d ed. New York: St. Martin's Press, 1984.
WEBER, RONALD E. "The Political and Social Beliefs of Evangelical Protestants in the United States." Paper presented at the annual meeting of the American Political Science Association, Chicago, 1983.
WEINRAUB, BERNARD. "Bush Gets Lessons in Performing on TV." *New York Times*, 13 January 1980, 23.
———. "Million-Dollar Drive Aims to Oust Five Liberal Senators." *New York Times*, 24 March 1980, B5.
WEISS, KENNETH A. "Supreme Court Upholds Hyde Amendment." *Congressional Quarterly Weekly Report* 38 (5 July 1980): 1860-62.
WEISS, LAURA B. "Abortion Question Poses Constant Concern." *Congressional Quarterly Weekly Report* 38 (15 March 1980): 733-34.
WEST, DARRELL M. "Constituencies and Travel Allocations in the 1980 Presidential Campaign." *American Journal of Political Science* 27 (August 1983): 515-29.
———. *Making Campaigns Count: Leadership and Coalition Building in 1980*. Westport, Conn.: Greenwood, 1984.
———. "Rhetoric and Agenda-Setting in the 1980 Presidential Campaign." *Congress and the Presidency* 9 (Autumn 1982): 1-21.
WESTLYE, MARK C. "Competitiveness of Senate Seats and Voting Behavior in Senate Elections." *American Journal of Political Science* 27 (May 1983): 253-83.

WHITE, THEODORE H. *The Making of the President 1968.* New York: Atheneum, 1969.

———. *The Making of the President 1972.* New York: Atheneum, 1973.

WILCOX, CLYDE. "The New Christian Right and the Mobilization of Fundamentalists." Paper presented at the annual meeting of the Midwest Political Science Association, Chicago, 1984.

WILLIAMS, ROGER M. "The Power of Fetal Politics." *Saturday Review,* 9 June 1979, 12-15.

WILLIAMS, RUSS. "Heavenly Message, Earthly Designs: Pat Robertson, *The 700 Club,* and Right-Wing Politics." *Sojourners* 8 (September 1979): 17ff.

WITCOVER, JULES. *Marathon: The Pursuit of the Presidency 1972-1976.* New York: Viking, 1977.

WITT, ELDER. "Supreme Court Considering Cases Challenging Congress' Curbs on Abortion Funding." *Congressional Quarterly Weekly Report* 38 (19 April 1980): 1037-41.

WITTMAN, DONALD. "Candidate Motivation: A Synthesis of Alternative Theories." *American Political Science Review* 77 (March 1983): 142-57.

WOHL, LISA CRONIN. "Decoding the Election Game Plan of the New Right." *Ms.* 8 (August 1979): 57-59, 94-96.

WOODWARD, BOB, and SCOTT ARMSTRONG. *The Brethren: Inside the Supreme Court.* New York: Avon Books, 1979.

ZIMMERMAN, BARRY J., and TED L. ROSENTHAL. "Observational Learning of Rule-Governed Behavior by Children." *Psychological Bulletin* 81 (1974): 29-42.

Index

Abdnor, James, 172, 177, 185, 200, 229, 241, 245
Abolitionists, 159
Abortion, 11-17, 19, 32, 82, 152-67, 169, 173-80, 186-215, 218, 224, 230-31, 234-35, 238-41, 243-45, 250-56, 259-60, 263-67. *See also* Pro-life groups
Abstract modeling, 46, 50-52, 78, 195-96
Active phase of the campaign, 29-30, 227, 231, 249, 252, 255, 268
Activists, 31, 39, 51, 90-93, 96-97, 103, 109-10, 138, 144, 154, 165, 175, 180-81, 187, 191, 194, 198-99, 207, 209, 239-42, 254, 257, 259-62, 265, 268-71, 273
Advertising agencies, 146
Affirmative action, 27
Agenda, political, 1, 30, 92, 158
Agranoff, Robert, 151
Aldrich, John F., 56
Allen, Vernon L., 56
Alpern, David M., 112
Alpert, Eugene J., 112
American Bar Association, 254
American Law Institute, 156
American Life Lobby, 212
American Medical Association, 153
Americans for Common Sense, 249
Americans for Democratic Action, 172
Americans for Life, 245
Anderson, John, 108-9, 184, 222
Anyone But Church (ABC), 173
Armstrong, Scott, 183
Aronson, Elliot, 56

Baker, James A., 111, 76, 98
Baker, Tom, 10
Bandura, Albert, 38, 40, 42, 52-53, 57-58
Barber, James David, 60-62, 83, 108, 275
Baron, Alan, 228
Barone, Michael, 114
Bayh, Birch, 10, 64, 163, 169-72, 196, 200-201, 214, 216-18, 226, 232-33, 236, 241, 244-46, 250
Behaviorist theories, 37
Bennett, W. Lance, 110, 183
Bennetts, Leslie, 33, 274
Bentsen, Lloyd, 274
Biases in campaign environments, 87-93, 257-65, 268-71
Black, Hugo, 157
Blake, Judith, 184
Bounded rationality, 38, 56
Breslin, Jimmy, 2
Brock, Bill, 20, 121-22, 124, 127, 133
Broder, David, 28, 35, 111, 113
Brooke, Ed, 163
Brown, Mrs. Judie, 212
Brown, Paul A., 163, 184, 194-95, 199, 215, 245, 251, 253-55, 274
Buchanan, Christopher, 149-50, 184
Buchanan, Rev. John, 17-18
Buchanan, Patrick J., 166, 274
Buckley v. *Valeo*, 33
Bunker, Archie, 249
Burdick, Quentin, 274
Burnham, Walter Dean, 148
Bush, George, 21-22, 71, 75-76, 120
Bush, Prescott, 120
Byrd, Robert, 274

Cable television, 272
Caddell, Pat, 218
Campaign consultants, 5, 20, 28, 44, 69, 71, 74-77, 81, 88, 92, 95-96, 116, 133, 139, 141, 146-47, 180, 186, 194, 200, 203, 206, 221, 225, 229-30, 235, 242, 261, 275
Campaign finance, 2-11, 19-20, 65, 120-32, 145-46, 178, 214. See also Direct mail; Fund raising
Campaign Management College, 140
Campaign organization, 60-61, 65-66, 69, 90, 96, 168, 177, 181, 202, 219, 224, 258, 260
Campaign schools, 42, 44, 74, 79, 139-43, 145, 147, 164, 263
Campaign staffs, 1, 23, 61, 63, 65-66, 75, 79-81, 90-92, 94, 106, 140, 216-29, 231-37, 239-42, 244, 259, 260, 263, 266, 270
Cannon, Howard, 274
Canon law, 156
Capehart, Homer, 170
Carey, Hugh, 75
Carter, Jimmy, 4, 58, 68-69, 71, 73, 76, 79, 87-89, 91, 102, 108, 126, 169, 214, 222, 240-41, 252
Casework, 55, 104, 106
Castro, Fidel, 177
Catholic church, 156, 158-59, 235, 245
Central Intelligence Agency, 170
Challengers, 4, 8, 10, 30-31, 74, 80, 92, 104-6, 111, 166, 178, 219, 227-28, 257, 265, 270-71
Chase, Chevy, 100
Chiles, Lawton, 274
Christian Action Council, 184, 274
Christian Voice, 16-17, 162, 238
Church, Frank, 163, 169, 171-74, 196, 211, 216-17, 219, 229, 233, 236, 239, 241, 244-46, 248-50
Cigler, Allan J., 33
Civil rights movement, 14, 153
Civil service, 116
Clark, Dick, 175, 190-92, 194, 196, 202-4, 214-18, 221-26, 229, 239, 242-45

Clem, Alan L., 83
Coelho, Tony, 98-99, 149
Cognitive theories, 37, 55
Cohodas, Nadine, 183, 273-74
Committee for the Survival of a Free Congress, 15, 74, 145, 170, 253
COPE (Committee on Political Education, AFL-CIO), 172
Common law, 156
Condensational symbols, 153-54, 158-60, 251, 263
Congressional races, 5, 7-8, 69, 97-98, 121, 135, 140-41, 144, 146, 162, 170, 198-201, 255, 258, 272. See also House races; Senate races
Conservative Caucus, 15, 253
Contextual analysis, 38, 57
Contingency-learning, 48-50
Converse, Philip E., 110
Cook, Rhodes, 35, 149-50
Cooke, Terence Cardinal, 157
Coordinated spending, 123, 129, 131, 138-39
Cornwell, David, 200
Cotter, Cornelius P., 149
Crabb, Cecil V., Jr., 149
Crane, Phil, 71
Cranston, Alan, 10
Craver, Mathews, Smith and Co., 245
Cronkite, Walter, 79
Crotty, William J., 116, 151, 183
Crouse, Tim, 92, 111
Culver, John, 10, 13, 163-64, 169, 172, 174-75, 191-93, 196, 216-17, 221-25, 228-29, 231, 234, 236-38, 240-42, 244, 246, 248, 250, 259, 266-67, 275

Daley, Richard J., 16
"Deadly Dozen," 163
Dealignment, 114
Deardourff, John, 75
Debates, campaign, 64, 88, 271
Deckard, Joel, 200
Deficit, federal, 2
Del Pinal, Jorge H., 184

Index

Democratic Congressional Campaign Committee, 98, 122, 125, 127, 134, 142, 248
Democratic Media Center, 134
Democratic National Committee, 122, 124-27, 133-34, 249
Democratic National Convention, 34, 164
Democratic Senatorial Campaign Committee, 10, 122, 125, 135, 142, 216, 262
Democratic Study Group Campaign Fund, 146
Democrats for the 80's, 10, 146, 249
DEMPAC, 126
Dennis, Jack, 148
Diffusion of innovations, 47-48, 58, 78-79, 144, 147. *See also* Innovation
Dionne, E.J., Jr., 33, 184
Direct mail, 2, 5, 18-20, 27-28, 75, 116, 122, 124, 127, 129, 132-35, 139, 145-46, 155, 192, 206, 227-28, 232, 235, 248-51, 268, 275
Dodd, Lawrence C., 149
Doderer, Minnette, 189, 191, 202-4
Doe v. Bolton, 157
Dolan, John T. ("Terry"), 9, 33, 169, 248, 255
Downs, Anthony, 111
Drew, Elizabeth, 33, 111, 138, 149-50, 174, 185, 244
Drinan, Robert, 184
Durkin, John, 216

Eagleton, Thomas, 73
Edelman, Murray, 57, 183, 263
Edgar, Robert W., 184
Ehrenhalt, Alan, 150
Eldersveld, Samuel J., 149
Election result, 56, 89, 93-103, 109-10, 180, 202-4, 207, 209-10, 217, 227, 232, 238, 247, 261-62, 266, 272
Ely, John Hart, 274
Endangered Species Act, 174

Entman, Robert M., 34
Environmental Action, 183
Epstein, Leon D., 149, 151
Equal Rights Amendment, 14, 16, 170, 173, 177, 192, 211
Estes, W.K., 57
Eulau, Heinz, 59
Evangelical Right, 14-18, 55, 169, 238
Evans, Rowland, 98, 111
Exit polls, 96-97, 272
Explanations for election results, 95-103, 110, 189-91, 202-4, 217, 222-25, 244, 246-47, 261-62

FaithAmerica, 192, 211
Falwell, Rev. Jerry, 15-17
Federal Communications Commission, 15
Federal Corrupt Practices Act of 1925, 3
Federal Election Campaign Act of 1971 and Amendments, 3-5, 32, 137-39
Federal Election Commission, 4, 33
Fenno, Richard F., Jr., 29, 59, 61, 83, 85, 90, 106, 111-12, 184, 266, 268-70, 272, 275
Ferraro, Geraldine, 72
First Amendment, 9
Fishel, Jeff, 85, 148-49, 151
Fisher, Joseph, 184
Ford, Gerald, 77, 91, 100-101
Foreign policy, 11, 48, 68, 100-102
Fourteenth Amendment, 157
Fowler, Linda L., 150
Franklin, Charles H., 148
Fraser, Donald, 162
Fraser, Janet, 111-12
Fund raising, 2-9, 16, 18-20, 27-28, 40, 63, 74-77, 80, 103, 120-32, 136-39, 177, 181, 207, 227-28, 232, 242-43, 247, 249, 266, 268. *See also* Campaign finance; Direct mail

Gallup poll, 15, 26
Garth, David, 75
Gaunt, Jeremy, 33
General Electric, 67
Germond, Jack, 71, 84
Gibson, James L., 150
Ginsberg, Benjamin, 271, 275
Goffman, Erving, 83
Goldman, Peter, 33
Goldwater, Barry, 19, 89, 92
Goodin, Robert E., 261, 275
GOPAC, 124, 126
Gramer, Rod, 184
Grassley, Charles E., 7, 172, 174-75, 192-93, 240-41
Gray, Nellie, 183, 255
Great Society program, 24
Greenstein, Fred I., 59
Gubernatorial races, 20, 68, 129, 169, 272
Guggenheim, Charles, 111
Gun Owners of America, 12, 169, 170
Gurwitt, Rob, 149
Guth, James L, 34

Hadley, Charles D., 26
Hall, Calvin S., 56
Hart, Gary, 66
Hart, Peter D., 190, 229
Haskell, Floyd, 163, 215, 219
Hatch, Orrin, 248, 252, 254-56
Hayakawa, S.I., 274
Helms, Jesse, 249, 254
Hempel, Carl G., 56
Hinckley, Barbara, 84
Hollenbeck, Harold, 184
Home styles, 106-7
Homosexual rights, 14
Horse-race reporting, 22-23, 93
House races, 7-8, 11, 20, 29, 31, 67, 123, 129-32, 138-40, 147, 162, 166-69, 173, 202. *See also* Congressional races
Human Life Amendment, 162, 165, 170, 173, 176-77, 179, 191, 193, 196-97, 200, 207, 224, 233-35, 249, 255
Human Life Statute, 212, 252, 254
Hume, Ellen, 150-51
Humphrey, Hubert, 75, 124
Hyde Amendments, 161, 167, 183, 197, 211, 264
Hyde, Henry J., 161

Idaho Pro-Life PAC, 173, 195-96
Idaho Right to Life, 173
Incumbency, 7, 10, 16, 29-31, 54, 67, 72, 74, 78, 80-81, 103-7, 110, 112, 119, 121, 135-36, 166-68, 179-80, 184, 219-20, 248, 257, 265-73
Independent spending, 2, 9-11, 155, 169, 177
Indiana Right to Life PAC, 170-71, 200-201, 203
Inflation, 11-12, 139
Innovation, 47-48, 58, 78-79, 107, 142, 144, 147, 186, 267-68, 275
Interest groups, 2-3, 8-9, 20, 39, 62, 70, 79, 90, 96, 97, 109, 137, 172, 263. *See also* Political Action Committees; Single-issue groups
Internal Revenue Service, 15
International Telephone and Telegraph, 3
Iowa Democrats for Life, 192, 245
Iowa Pro-Life Action Council, 175, 186-94, 200, 202-4, 206, 211, 232, 234, 243
Issue webs, 160
Iyengar, Shanto, 275

Jackson, John E., 148
Jackson, John S., III, 111
Jacob, Herbert, 84
Jacobson, Gary C., 32-33, 35, 58, 116, 149-51, 183, 245, 275
Jepsen, Roger, 190
John Birch Society, 170
Johnson, Lyndon, 24, 108

Index

Jones, Charles O., 149
Jordan, Hamilton, 71, 76
Justice Department, 3

Kamber, Victor, 248
Karps, Paul D., 59
Katz, Elihu, 85
Kayden, Xandra, 84, 111
Kazee, Thomas A., 150
Keene, David, 101
Keller, Bill, 33-34, 273-74
Kelley, Stanley, Jr., 275
Kennedy, Edward M., 58, 174, 251, 255
Kennedy, John F., 12, 30, 108
Kernell, Samuel, 58, 245
Kessel, John H., 32, 34, 111, 151
Key, V.O., 94
King, Anthony, 34
King, Seth S., 185
Kingdon, John W., 58, 84-85, 149, 151, 259, 274
Kirkland, Lane, 27
Kirkpatrick, Jeane J., 85
Kissinger, Henry, 101
Kneeland, Douglas E., 85
Kuklinski, James H., 59
Kulongoski, Ted, 172, 178-79, 241

Labor unions, 3, 5, 7-8, 14, 27, 42, 74, 86-87, 107, 171-72, 178, 222, 225
Ladd, Everett Carll, Jr., 26, 34, 183
Lasswell, Harold D., 56
Lawyers, 66-67, 80-81
Leafletting, 187-212, 220-21, 225-26, 233-37, 241-42, 245, 256, 259
Leahy, Patrick J., 163, 172, 175-76, 197, 211, 216, 229, 233, 236, 238, 240-41, 244-45
Lear, Norman, 249
Learning history, 39-40, 54, 60-63, 66-68, 237-38
Ledbetter, Stewart, 172, 176, 197, 211, 241

Leuthold, David A., 112
Life Amendment PAC, 13, 162-64, 167, 169-70, 177-80, 194-96, 199, 200, 206, 215, 245-46, 250-56, 265, 274
Life Amendment PAC of Oregon, 178-79, 197-98
Life-PAC, 162
Light, Larry, 32-33, 149
Lindzey, Gardner, 56
Loomis, Burdett A., 33
Lowi, Theodore J., 33, 84, 267, 275
Luttbeg, Norman R., 110

McCarthy, Eugene, 79, 81
McCormack, Ellen, 162
McCormack, Patricia, 274
McCrone, Donald J., 59
McGinniss, Joe, 257, 274
McGovern, George, 14, 19, 34, 62-64, 66, 73, 81, 83, 85, 92, 124, 163, 169, 172, 176-77, 185, 199, 200, 213, 216, 218, 221, 225-26, 228-29, 234-36, 241, 244-51, 258, 263, 267, 275
McIntyre, Thomas, 163, 215-19, 221, 225, 229, 239, 242, 244
MacNeil, Neil, 125, 149-50
Maisel, Louis Sandy, 111, 274
Manatt, Charles T., 127, 134, 249
Mandates, 87, 102
Mann, Thomas E., 58, 112
March, James G., 84-85
Marshall, Robert G., 212
Mass media, 2, 16-17, 21-23, 28-29, 39, 63, 65, 74, 80, 89, 113, 135-36, 148, 155, 160, 166, 168-69, 191, 202, 207-9, 212-13, 225-26, 230, 234, 239-40, 262, 265, 272
Mathews, Tom, 33
Matthews, Donald R., 58, 84
May, Ernest R., 111
Mayer, Allan J., 34-35
Mayhew, David, 267, 273, 275
Media events, 21-23
Medicaid, 162, 176, 183

Medicare, 24
Metzenbaum, Howard, 274
Milgram, Stanley, 58
Minimum wage laws, 24
Minnesota Human Life Alliance, 187, 208
Mischel, Walter, 57
Modeling. *See* Observational learning
Mohr, James C., 183
Mondale, Walter, 109
Moore, Jonathan, 111-12
Moral Issues Index, 16-17, 238
Moral Majority, Inc., 15-17, 162, 169-70, 174, 178, 238, 253
Moral Response, 211
Mormon church, 173
Moxley, Warden, 185
Moyers, Bill, 33-34, 151
Moynihan, Daniel Patrick, 274
Mulhauser, Karen, 228
Myers, Lisa, 34

Napolitan, Joseph, 75
National Abortion Rights Action League, 207, 228, 245, 249
National Christian Action Coalition, 16
National Committee for an Effective Congress, 74
National Conference of Catholic Bishops, 157, 224 252
National Conservative PAC (NCPAC), 9-10, 33, 146, 169-70, 173, 175, 177-79, 214, 219-20, 225, 245, 247-48, 250-51, 255
National Organization for Women (NOW), 207
National Pro-Life PAC, 162
National Republican Congressional Committee, 122, 125, 140, 143
National Republican Senatorial Committee, 122, 171, 178
National Rifle Association, 12, 204
National Right to Life Committee, 13, 162-63, 194, 200, 205-7, 250, 252

National Right to Life PAC, 164, 197, 207-8, 251
National Right to Work Committee, 175
Negative campaigns, 10-11, 169, 200, 247-50
"Negative models," 73, 180-81, 218-25, 232, 243-44
Nelson, Gaylord, 216
New Christian Right, 14-18, 169, 238. *See also* Evangelical Right
New Deal, 24, 27, 116
New England Conservative Political Action Committee, 175
New Right, 8, 14-15, 18-19, 82, 98, 126-27, 145, 166, 169, 174-77, 179, 204, 214, 217, 222, 225-26, 230, 234, 238, 246-50, 254-56
New York Times-CBS poll, 164-65
Nie, Norman H., 34, 57, 84, 111, 148, 261, 274
Nilsson, Lennart, 199, 211
Nixon, Richard M., 3, 63-65, 108, 121, 257
Novak, Robert, 98, 111
Nuclear freeze, 11, 18-19, 45, 146

Observational learning, 41-48, 50-52, 60, 69-83, 102, 118, 139-47, 180-82, 192-211, 214-38, 242-44, 261-63, 268, 270
O'Connor, Sandra Day, 253-56
O'Neill, Thomas P., Jr., 2, 77, 98-99, 113, 127, 248
Oppenheimer, Bruce I., 149
Ornstein, Norman J., 58, 112, 149

Pack journalism, 92
Packwood, Bob, 163-64, 172, 177-79, 198, 216, 227-28, 232-33, 236, 241-44, 256, 263, 265-66, 275
Paletz, David L., 34
Panama Canal, 13, 100-102, 171, 173-74, 178, 238, 264
Parliamentary system, 147

Index 303

Party decline, 114-18
Party discipline, 129, 147
Party identification, 24-25, 114-15, 264
Party organization, 2, 20, 23, 28, 61-62, 113, 115-48, 190
Party platforms, 137, 165
Party reform, 27-28, 124, 136-37
"Pastoral Plan for Pro-Life Activities," 162
Patterson, Thomas E., 34
Peabody, Robert L., 149
People for the American Way, 249
Perry, James M., 33
Personality characteristics, 37, 107-8
Person variables, 54-55, 59
Pett, Saul, 84
Phillips, Howard, 15
Pitkin, Hanna, 275
Planned Parenthood, 160, 249
Plattner, Andy, 275
Political Action Committees, 2-10, 20, 28, 33, 53, 116, 121-25, 130-31, 134-39, 145-48, 155, 162, 214
Political parties, 2, 12, 20-28, 32, 34, 67, 72, 75-76, 82-83, 113-52, 155, 182, 206, 257, 262-63, 267
Polls, 20, 22, 45-46, 58, 87-89, 92, 96-97, 103, 111, 116, 123, 132, 134, 141, 146, 148, 167-68, 174-75, 177, 190, 204, 206, 215-20, 223, 227, 229, 239-40, 248, 258-60, 271
Polsby, Nelson W., 58
Pomper Gerald, 32, 35
Pork barrel projects, 45, 166
Prayer in public schools, 11, 14-15, 47, 91, 173, 254, 255
Precinct targeting, 20, 42, 66, 133
Preminger, Otto, 84
Presentation of self, 29, 61-62, 66, 74, 77-78, 80, 107, 141, 224, 242, 267
Presidential races, 1, 4-5, 20, 22, 28, 29, 32, 63, 65, 71, 99-102, 138, 169, 177, 257
Primaries, 1, 4-5, 22, 28, 35, 63, 71, 99-102, 115, 117, 119-20, 137, 147, 162, 176-78, 189-94, 197, 199-200, 202-3, 220, 225
Pro-choice groups, 158, 160-61, 163-65, 171, 173, 177-79, 189-91, 193, 196, 204, 208-9, 220, 224, 227-28, 230, 236, 239, 249-51, 254-56, 265
Progressive movement, 115
Prohibition, 11
Pro-life groups, 9, 12, 32, 45, 152, 155, 158-67, 170-71, 173, 175-82, 186-246, 249-56, 259, 261-62, 264-67
PROPAC, 10, 248
Przeworski, Adam, 57
Psychoanalytic theories, 37, 55
Public funding of campaigns, 4, 32, 138, 271
Public housing, 24
Public opinion, 20, 87-90, 268-73

Quayle, Dan, 170-72, 201, 211, 241

Ranney, Austin, 34-35, 58, 267, 275
Rational-choice theories, 38, 55, 111
Reagan, Ronald, 4, 21-23, 27, 43-44, 49, 51, 54, 64, 67-68, 77, 84, 87-88, 91, 97-102, 108, 117, 126, 201, 222, 241, 246, 252-55, 261-62
Redistricting, 69, 77, 132
Reese, Matt, 134
Reference standard, 54
Referential symbols, 153
Regional Campaign Management Workshops, 140
Religious broadcasting networks, 2
Religious Roundtable, 16, 253
Representation, 2, 27, 31-32, 55-56, 59, 244, 246, 257, 268-73
Republican National Committee, 19-20, 113, 122, 125-26, 132-33, 140-41
Republican National Committee Local Elections Division, 124, 133

Republican National Convention, 3, 164
Response consequences, 40-42, 50, 52, 56-58, 70, 93-95, 103, 110, 118, 139, 193, 199-200, 238, 243, 247
Right to privacy, 157, 183
Right-to-work groups, 107, 175
Roberts, Steven V., 213
Rodino, Peter, 127
Roe v. Wade, 157-59, 161, 167, 187, 250, 252, 255, 264
Rogers, Everett M., 58, 85
Rohde, David W., 149
Role theory, 37
Roosevelt, Franklin D., 24, 108
Rosenthal, Ted L., 57
Rutland Herald, 176

Sabato, Larry J., 88, 110, 151
Sagebrush rebellion, 239
Samuelson, Robert J., 34, 148
Sandoz, Ellis, 149
Sarbanes, Paul, 10, 248, 274
Sarbin, Theodore R., 56
Sasser, Jim, 255
Satisficing, 56
School busing, 16-17, 27
Schumaker, Larry, 199
Sears, John, 64, 84, 101
Secular humanism, 159-60
Self-esteem, 43, 107-8
Self-regulation, 40, 52-54, 68
Senate Foreign Relations Committee, 171
Senate Intelligence Committee, 170
Senate races, 7-11, 20, 29, 32, 51, 65, 113, 123, 129-31, 136, 139, 146-47, 152, 162-63, 166-81, 186, 190-203, 213-45, 251, 262-67, 272. *See also* Congressional races
Separation of powers, 147
Sex education, 11, 16
Shoemaker, F. Floyd, 58, 85
Shriver, Sargent, 62
Simon, Herbert A., 56, 84, 85

Simulated campaigns, 20, 28, 140-41, 145
Single-issue groups, 2, 11-14, 16, 20, 28, 148, 154-55, 193, 202, 206, 216, 219, 230, 239, 242, 244, 263-64
Single issues, 11-14, 16, 152-55, 158-61, 176, 182, 187, 189, 193, 202, 205-6, 216-20, 230, 237-44, 263-65
Skinner, B.F., 56
Slavery, 11, 14, 159
Sniderman, Paul M., 35, 112
Social-learning theory, 31-32, 36-59, 67, 86, 109, 118, 152, 179, 190, 192, 210, 211, 242, 244, 257, 268
Social Security, 24
"Soft money," 138
Sorauf, Frank J., 149
Stamenkovich, Dragutin, 7
State and local races, 7, 29, 69, 88, 124, 129, 132-36, 140, 147, 169, 187, 189-90, 200, 202, 258, 260, 272
State Party Works Plan, 134
States' Rights Amendment, 173, 196, 203
Steinem, Gloria, 227-29, 243
Stewart, Richard H., 111
Stimson, James A., 58
Straight-ticket voting, 24, 26
Strategic Arms Limitation agreements, 16-17, 173
Supreme Court, 4, 9, 12, 15, 155-59, 161, 167, 183, 186, 253-55, 264
Swerdlow, Joel, 34
Symbolic models, 48, 76, 217
Symbolism, 30, 50-51, 102, 153, 165, 247-49, 254
Symms, Steve, 172-73, 196, 211, 219, 239, 241

Talmadge, Herman, 177
Target McGovern, 177
Tracking polls, 239
Traugott, Michael W., 183

Index

Tribe, Laurence H., 274

Udall, Morris, 184
Ullman, Al, 198
Uncertainty, 95, 179, 192, 202-4, 232, 239, 243, 258, 265

Verba, Sidney, 84, 111, 261, 274
Vermont Pro-Life PAC, 176, 197
Vicarious learning. *See* Observational learning
Vice-presidential selection, 73, 100
Vidal, David, 85
Vietnam War, 14, 23, 79, 153, 176
Viguerie, Richard, 19-21, 33-34, 166, 253
Vinovskis, Maris, 183
Voter identification programs, 2, 81, 134, 170, 192-93, 200-203, 206-7, 209-12, 218, 236
Voter turnout, 13, 134, 154, 188-90, 201, 211, 217, 222, 225
Voting, 1, 13, 15, 18, 23-24, 29, 61, 63, 89-104, 106, 109-10, 114-15, 118, 133, 154, 220, 221, 241-42, 247-48, 258, 260-61, 264-65, 269, 272-73

Wallace, George, 19
Watergate, 108, 121, 125, 214, 268
Watson, Tom, 84, 149
Wattenberg, Martin P., 34, 149
Weicker, Lowell, 120, 274
Weinraub, Bernard, 33, 85, 184
Weiss, Kenneth, 183
Werth, Brian, 111
West, Darrell M., 33, 150, 184-86, 213
Westlye, Mark C., 184
Weyrich, Paul, 15-17
White, Clifton, 75
White, Theodore H., 257, 274
Williams, Harrison, 274
Williams, Roger M., 184
Willke, John, 250
Wilson, Pete, 123
Wilson, Ted, 248
Wirthlin, Richard, 101
Witcover, Jules, 1, 30, 32, 71, 76, 84-85, 111
Wohl, Lisa Cronin, 211
Women's rights, 14, 27, 156, 160
Woodward, Bob, 183

Zimmerman, Barry J., 57

About the Author

MARJORIE RANDON HERSHEY grew up in Evanston, Illinois. She graduated from the University of Michigan in 1966 with a B.A. in journalism, and received a Ph.D. in political science from the University of Wisconsin in 1972.

She taught at Florida State University before joining the faculty at Indiana University, where she is an associate professor of political science.

Professor Hershey is the author of *The Making of Campaign Strategy* (1974) as well as articles in journals including the *American Journal of Political Science,* the *American Politics Quarterly, Micropolitics,* the *Public Opinion Quarterly, Sex Roles,* the *Social Science Quarterly, Youth and Society,* and several edited volumes.

She and her husband Howard are also the authors of two children, Katie and Lissa.